LLEWELLYN'S

COMPLETE BOOK OF

ASTROLOGY

ABOUT THE AUTHOR

Kris Brandt Riske, M.A., is executive director and a professional member of the American Federation of Astrologers, the oldest U.S. astrological organization, founded in 1938. She is also a member of the NCGR (National Council for Geocosmic Research) and served on its board of directors.

Kris has been a speaker at various astrological conferences and has written for several astrological publications. She currently writes for *Llewellyn's Sun Sign Book*, *Llewellyn's Moon Sign Book*, and American Media. Kris is also the author of *Mapping Your Future* and *Mapping Your Money* and co-author of *Mapping Your Travels & Relocation*. She is particularly interested in astrometeorology (astrological weather forecasting) and is the author of *Astrometeorology: Planetary Power in Weather Forecasting* and the annual weather forecast published in *Llewellyn's Moon Sign Book*.

Kris is an avid stock car (NASCAR) fan, although she'd rather be driving than watching. She also enjoys gardening, needlework, and computer gaming. An Illinois native, Kris has a master's degree in journalism and is a Chinese language student.

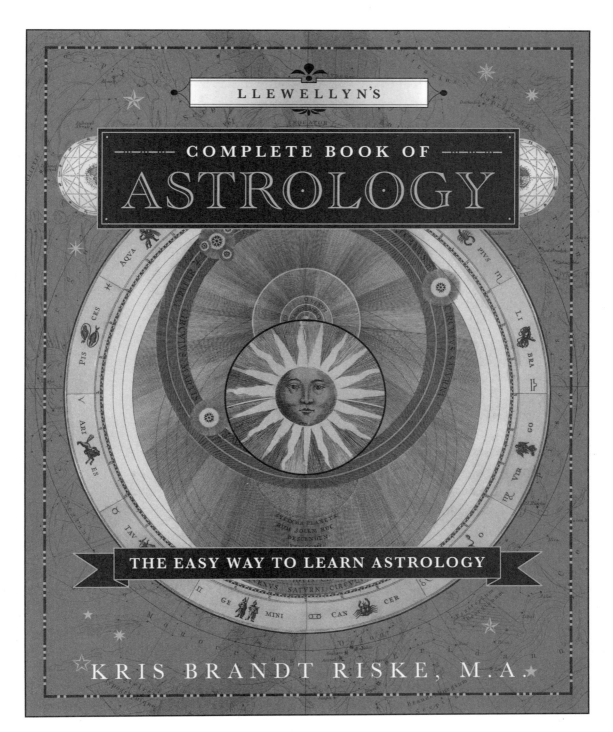

LLEWELLYN'S

COMPLETE BOOK OF

ASTROLOGY

THE EASY WAY TO LEARN ASTROLOGY

★ KRIS BRANDT RISKE, M.A. ★

Llewellyn Publications
Woodbury, Minnesota

First Edition
First Printing, 2007

Book design and format by Donna Burch
Cover celestial map images ©Visual Language/PunchStock
Cover design by Kevin R. Brown
Editing by Andrea Neff
Interior illustrations by the Llewellyn Art Department except on pages 34, 39, 44, 49, 54, 59, 64, 69, 74, 79, 84, 89 © 2007 by Rik Olson
Llewellyn is a registered trademark of Llewellyn Worldwide, Ltd.

Chart wheels were produced by the Kepler program by permission of Cosmic Patterns Software, Inc. (www.AstroSoftware.com)

Page 103 of *Astro America's Daily Ephemeris, 2000–2020 at Midnight* is reprinted with the kind permission of David R. Roell at Astrology Classics (www.astroamerica.com).

Library of Congress Cataloging-in-Publication Data
Riske, Kris Brandt.
     Llewellyn's complete book of astrology : the easy way to learn
        astrology / by Kris Brandt Riske.—1st ed.
     p. cm.
     Includes bibliographical references.
     ISBN 978-0-7387-1071-6
     1. Astrology. I. Title. II. Title: Complete book of astrology.

BF1708.1.R57 2007
133.5—dc22
2007021764

Llewellyn Publications
A Division of Llewellyn Worldwide, Ltd.
2143 Wooddale Drive, Dept. 978-0-7387-1071-6
Woodbury, Minnesota 55125-2989, U.S.A.
www.llewellyn.com

Printed in the United States of America

OTHER BOOKS AND ARTICLES BY KRIS BRANDT RISKE, M.A.

Mapping Your Travels & Relocation (co-author)
(Llewellyn Publications, 2005)

Mapping Your Money
(Llewellyn Publications, 2005)

Mapping Your Future
(Llewellyn Publications, 2004)

Astrometeorology: Planetary Power in Weather Forecasting
(American Federation of Astrologers, 1997)

Llewellyn's Moon Sign Book (contributor)
(Llewellyn Publications, 2002–2009)

Llewellyn's Sun Sign Book (contributor)
(Llewellyn Publications, 2007–2009)

Llewellyn's Starview Almanac (contributor)
(Llewellyn Publications, 2005–2006)

Civilization Under Attack (contributor)
(Llewellyn Publications, 2001)

DEDICATION

To some special friends, each of whom in some way contributed to this book:

Jack Cipolla

Vianne Higgins

Jim Holden

Sharon Leah

Linda Miller

Carol Caruso

Ed Carr

Joey Stiver

Frances Griffin

Joan Kopf

Aurora Isaac

ACKNOWLEDGMENTS

Once again I am deeply indebted to Andrea Neff for her superb and insightful editorial skills, wisdom, friendship, and humor, all of which guided this book to completion. Thanks, Andrea, for all your efforts and your objective view.

Donna Burch deserves tremendous credit for her design skills in creating a visually appealing and easy-to-read format. She also did an exceptional job with the many illustrations. Thanks, Donna.

And thanks to Kevin Brown, who once again created a beautifully eye-catching cover.

Thanks, also, to Dave Roell of Astrology Center of America for granting permission to use a page from the ephemeris published by him.

CONTENTS

Contents

Contents

Contents

CHARTS AND FIGURES

Charts

Figures

BIRTH CHARTS

INTRODUCTION

Your birth chart is all about you—your potential, talents, and life possibilities. It reflects what comes easily to you, what you can master with effort, and what probably would not be worth your time.

As you unravel your chart, you'll discover many traits you're already aware of and many you're not. Astrology can help you resolve life issues through self-understanding, identify the qualities you seek in an ideal mate, realize your career and financial potential, develop your communication skills, and discover your inner strength. Some of what you learn will amuse you, some will prompt further in-depth learning, and some will motivate and inspire you to become the very best you can be.

You can do the same for your friends, family, colleagues, children, parents, siblings, love interests, partner, and all the other people in your life.

Don't be surprised if this book triggers your thirst for more astrology. Many astrologers got their start by doing just what you're about to do. By reading this book, you can master the basics of astrology and be well on your way to learning how to read a birth chart just like professional astrologers do.

As is typical for those who share my Aquarius Sun sign, the universe has carried me in many diverse directions and always for reasons that were not initially evident. Aquarians seem to attract unusual and unexpected opportunities, almost as if the universe is carving out a new path for them to follow. And so it was with me and astrology.

Of course, my journey began when the astrological timing was right, although I didn't learn that until some years later. That undoubtedly will be the case with you, too, as you begin your astrological journey.

Many years ago I was visiting a friend, Joan Kopf, in Nebraska. By chance—or really not, if you recognize the power of the universe—she made a few comments about astrology that for some reason caught my interest. Joan then offered that her mother was the family astrologer and had been interested in the subject for years, reading the family's charts. What was this all about? I wondered. The next thing I knew, we were off to visit her mother.

Joan's mother gave me a brief introduction to astrology and showed me some books. I was hooked within an hour of our arrival.

Back home, I immediately purchased the beginner's book she had recommended to get started. I opened it at 8:00 one Saturday morning and by 10:00 that night I was still at it. Now I was really hooked! That day I managed to calculate my birth chart—by hand, using addition, subtraction, and the information in the book. (Although the do-it-yourself method wasn't terribly difficult, I soon graduated to my first astrological computer calculation program.) I read all about my Sun, Moon, and rising signs and all the other planets in my chart, as well as houses and aspects. I was intrigued. How could planets zillions of miles away in outer space say so much about me?

That's a question that has perplexed astrologers for four thousand years. Astrology works, but no one knows how. People sometimes ask me if I really believe in "that stuff." And they always seem to be shocked when I reply in the affirmative, adding that I've used it to my advantage on many occasions and have done the same for hundreds of clients. Now, really, what would they expect an astrologer to say? I sometimes follow up by asking for the person's month and date of birth and then offer a few insights into what has recently occurred or is currently going on in his or her life. The person is always amazed, and I figure I've done a little something to enlighten another individual about the power of astrology.

Back to my personal adventure. I read every astrology book and magazine I could find for the next six months or so, and then one day discovered that the headquarters of the American Federation of Astrologers is in Arizona, where I live. This organization has a library filled with books and more books—a gold mine! I spent an entire afternoon there, totally in awe of all that knowledge in one place. I went home with a hefty stack of books.

By chance (there's that Aquarius word again), Linda Miller, an employee there, asked if I would be interested in having a list of certified astrologers who were also teachers. Certified? Teachers? That, too, was an eye opener and just what I needed.

Again, by chance, I hit the jackpot with the first one I called, Aurora Isaac. She said she had a class beginning within a few weeks and asked if I would be interested. You bet! Three months later, at the end of the class, I was reading charts! Her practical experience and outstanding teaching skills helped me pull together all that I'd read and learned on my own.

Then I begged Aurora to teach me predictive astrology. She agreed, much to my delight. Secret revealed: once I discovered that astrology could be used to forecast trends and to identify the best timing for events, such as when to apply for a job, that knowledge further fueled my interest and my studies. This is more Aquarius, a sign known to live in the future and to have an insatiable curiosity about what's going to happen and when.

Aurora made an important point that I'll never forget. She emphasized the importance of learning natal astrology (birth chart astrology) before learning forecasting. And she was so right. Without that foundation, it's next to impossible to have any success with predictive astrology or any one of the many other branches, or specialties, of astrology. After all, if your birth chart doesn't indicate musical talent, for example, then the very best current astro-

logical conditions won't land you a spot on a Broadway stage.

So you've begun your astrological journey in the right place and with the right person—you! Start with your birth chart. You know yourself best, so you'll quickly be able to see how astrology works in real life. Even with a little knowledge, you'll begin to learn why you react the way you do in certain situations and enjoy the ego boost that comes from knowing that your strengths and talents are even greater than you ever imagined.

It isn't by chance that you picked up this book. Enjoy your journey just for the fun of it, to learn more about yourself and the people around you, or even to someday become an astrologer!

THE BASICS OF ASTROLOGY

You've probably read your horoscope online, in newspapers or magazines, or in publications that focus on the year ahead. These forecasts are based on your Sun sign, which is easily determined by your birth month and day. You might even know some of the characteristics associated with your Sun sign and those of family and friends. Sun sign descriptions are amazingly accurate, even though there's no rational explanation why astrology should work. After all, the Sun, Moon, and planets are millions of miles away from Earth. How can a body in outer space realistically affect a person on Earth?

A Sun sign is just a Sun sign. It's important, yes, because it's the essence of you. It's your ego at work. But from an astrological viewpoint, there's so much more that defines you—your character, talents, strengths, and challenges.

The ancient Babylonians were as perplexed by this astrological phenomenon as we are today. In the four thousand or so years since they invented astrology, no one has discovered an explanation for why it works. But work it does.

Around the sixteenth century BC, the Babylonians began to observe that events on Earth could be correlated to celestial phenomena. Their brand of astrology is what is today called *mundane astrology*, or the astrology of countries, wars, coups, economic conditions, and weather, to name a few. It eventually evolved into what is now known as *electional astrology*, the branch in which the planetary positions are used to select a favorable time to launch an event, such as a wedding, business opening, meeting, or job application. Babylonian astrologers used the 360° circle (a zodiac of twelve signs similar to what is used today) and also developed *ephemeredes* (tables of astrological data) that listed the planetary positions and eclipses. At that point in time, no connection had been made between astrology and the individual.

It wasn't until more than a thousand years later, sometime between the seventh and fourth centuries BC, that the Babylonians developed the concept of natal astrology. The natal horoscopes of the time, which probably were limited to royalty and wealthy people, were inscribed on cuneiform tablets and listed the planetary positions along with comments referring to wealth potential, longevity, family, and status. The natal horoscope was seen as a predictor of the person's life, much as it is today, the difference being that twenty-first-century astrologers—and people— recognize that everyone has free will; the Babylonians considered the chart fateful.

The Babylonian knowledge was passed to the Persians, Egyptians, and Indians. It was readily adopted in India, where today it is considered not only valid but necessary to a successful life.

Great advances in astrology were made in Alexandria, Egypt, in the second and third centuries AD, partly as a result of King Ptolemy I Soter, who ordered the construction of a great library that attracted scholars. During this period, the following concepts were developed: the Ascendant (rising sign) and Midheaven, astrological houses, planetary rulers, aspects, and predictive techniques. Astrology was considered a science and spread to western Europe, where educated people knew Greek and Latin.

Although astrology died out in western Europe with the collapse of the Western Roman Empire, it survived somewhat in the Eastern Roman Empire. A general revival of astrology began around 1000 AD and continued for the next five hundred years. Like all else, astrology benefited from the invention of the printing press, which made information more readily available to the populace. Astrology was taught in colleges and universities and was a required subject for medical students.

Astrology then experienced another decline, which began in the late seventeenth century and lasted about two hundred years. It was still popular in England, however, because the annual astrological almanacs that had been printed since the sixteenth century continued to be in demand by the public. Renewed interest in astrology developed in the eighteenth and nineteenth centuries, but it wasn't until the 1930s that first weekly and then daily horoscopes began to appear in newspapers. The first such column appeared in the London *Sunday Express*.

The twentieth century saw refinements in astrological technique and an emphasis on psychological astrology versus event-oriented astrology. But the basics remain the same today as those developed by the earliest astrologers, and there is a growing interest in older astrological literature as more of these works are translated and made available.

WHY STUDY ASTROLOGY?

Metaphysics encompasses a wide range of subjects and areas, most of which are focused solely on divination, or predicting the future. What makes astrology different from the tarot, I Ching, runes, and other forecasting methods is that it is all-encompassing. You can use astrology not only to forecast events but also to gain great insights into your personality. You may think you know yourself better than anyone else walking the planet; that's probably true. But has someone ever commented on a personality trait that you were unaware of, at least on a conscious level? Something that you only then realized was a strength—or a detriment—because it is such a natural part of your personality? Something that made you realize you'd just discovered another whole side of yourself? This is part of the natural growth process.

Have you ever asked yourself why you react the way you do in certain situations? Why you repeat negative behaviors even though you know better? Have you ever knocked yourself out trying to do something, when your energy would have been better directed elsewhere? This, too, is part of the natural growth process. It is how we evolve as humans.

Now suppose you had all this information sooner rather than later. You'd be able to use it to your advantage for many more years, to make the most of your potential and in essence speed up that growth process. After all, we don't have all that many years in a lifetime to do everything we want to do.

This is one fabulous reason to study astrology: self-knowledge is the ultimate form of personal empowerment.

You may have heard people say that astrology is difficult, that it requires "all that math." Yes and no.

The math of astrology is nothing more than simple addition and subtraction using preset formulas. But in today's world you don't ever have to pick up a pencil. There are numerous online sites where you can get a computer-calculated birth chart in seconds (see appendix III), or you can take advantage of the free birth chart offer at the back of this book. Later, when you're more advanced in your studies and want

to become a certified astrologer, you can learn the math in preparation for taking an exam. Or, if you're not at all intimidated by math or just want to challenge yourself, you might want to learn this nuts-and-bolts side of astrology now. The point is that it's no longer necessary to first learn the calculations. You can get started right now!

Now, the question about difficulty. Is astrology difficult or isn't it? Yes, it is, or can be, but no, it's not.

Have you ever done anything in your life that was difficult at first but then came easily, such as playing a musical instrument or sport, speaking in public, or learning a language? Chances are, you have. And each came with a learning curve that began with initial excitement and quickly acquired skills, followed by the middle ground that required more study or practice to jump the hurdle to a comfort zone of confidence. Learning astrology is no different than learning anything else. It requires some patience and a lot of practice.

But how difficult is it, really, to read a birth chart? To glean all the insightful information about you and your personality? Not as hard as you might think. It's a matter of learning what each factor in the birth chart symbolizes and then blending the information until you have a full picture. Although that might seem like an oversimplified answer, consider this example using astrological keywords, which is the way every future astrologer learns to interpret a chart: Sun (ego) in Capricorn (ambitious) in the personal financial sector (second house) conjunct (next to) Jupiter (expansion) adds up to an individual whose self-esteem is linked to achievement and high earnings but who also spends freely on status symbols. It's that simple!

There are a few important tips I can give you to speed up the learning process (you'll learn the terminology mentioned below as you read this book):

1. Learn, and practice writing, the glyphs (symbols) for the planets, signs, and aspects. The inside back cover of this book has a handy list of astrological glyphs for your reference.

2. Learn the essential keywords for each sign, angle, planet, house, and aspect.

3. Learn the rulership relationships of the signs, planets, and houses, and the essential keywords for each.

4. Use the charts of people you know well—friends and family. This will help you see how the various factors manifest in real life.

5. When you study the chart, focus on a single planet or angle at a time and then move on to the next and the next until you've studied them all. Make notes and sentences using the keywords (as in the previous example) as you do this.

6. Talk with the person whose chart you've studied and explain what you've learned. Ask for feedback and listen closely to what you hear in order to determine what was correct or incorrect in your assessment.

Before long, you'll be reading a chart just like an astrologer!

WHAT YOUR BIRTH CHART REVEALS

As the ancient Babylonians observed, astrology is the correlation of celestial events to life on Earth. The planets do not cause events to happen on Earth or in individual lives; rather, they reflect the events that occur on Earth and in individual lives. As above, so below.

Life may appear to be random or even fateful, but it's not. Have you ever made a decision you later regretted? Of course you have. Everyone has. But what if you could almost always make the right decision about major life events, such as finances, relationships, and career? Astrology has the potential to help you do just that.

You can glean a phenomenal amount of information from a birth chart. In fact, you will be astounded once you discover just how much you can learn. To give you an example, a friend of mine asked me to look at the chart of her daughter's fiancé. My friend had some nagging doubts about the relationship and wondered if I could discover the reason why. (She did this with her daughter's knowledge.) I looked at the fiancé's chart, mentioned several things, and then asked about the man's financial attitudes. The chart indicated that he was a high roller, a big spender who had the potential for serious financial problems. My friend said that, to her knowledge, this had never been an issue, and her daughter confirmed that, adding that her fiancé was somewhat secretive about money matters. I suggested that she ask to see the man's credit report before they proceeded with the wedding plans. It was no surprise to me that he refused, and that she broke off the relationship rather than risk her excellent credit rating.

My friend's daughter later learned that her former fiancé did indeed have a history of serious financial problems. Needless to say, they were and are extremely grateful.

Life is about making choices. In this case, my friend's daughter used the power of astrology to make an informed major life decision that undoubtedly saved her from years of regret. This is what you will be able to do in almost any situation, for yourself, your friends, your family members, and possibly even clients.

I've seen a look of amazement on the faces of countless clients. Most people who know little or nothing about astrology don't realize just how much an astrologer can learn about them from their birth chart. This is one reason that many people in the know are reluctant to give their birth information to just anyone. Inevitably, some of these clients, first through body language and then through words (or the lack thereof), clam up when they realize that their personality, attitudes, and issues are as visible to an astrologer as are their talents and skills. Those who are open to the information use this powerful tool of self-awareness to learn about (or perhaps become fully aware of) their detrimental patterns of behavior and how they can reverse them. Astrology can be used not only to identify what holds you back but also to learn how to change these things to improve every facet of your life.

Astrology is a symbolic language. Each planet and every other factor in a birth chart represents certain traits, characteristics, people, talents, and areas of life. Everything that involves your life on Earth is represented in your horoscope.

A birth chart is also a map. Your birth chart is a map of your life and your potential as represented by the planetary positions at the exact time, date, and place of your birth. In it are eight planets and the Sun and Moon, along with other factors that provide much more insight into your personality. (Astrologers refer to the Sun and Moon as planets for ease in terminology and thus use a group of ten planets, not eight.)

Your birth chart is unique to you and thus reflects you, the individual. You share certain personality traits with others born with the same Sun sign, but the Sun is only one of ten planets and the many other factors that go into a birth chart. You're a person of many facets, likes and dislikes, and strengths and weaknesses. By studying your birth chart, you can identify the areas in which you naturally excel, those that are challenging, and everything in between. Astrology has the potential to teach you more about yourself than any other field of study. And when you know yourself well, you can make the most of the map of life that is your birth chart.

It's well recognized that environment helps shape personality and that people are a complex mix of innate talents and skills, experience, and family influences. Your birth chart is a reflection of all these things. If you study the birth charts of your family members, you will see many similarities to yours. These common factors symbolize not only your similar childhood experiences but also the genetic traits you've inherited from your parents, grandparents, great grandparents, and so on. These similarities will add to your depth of understanding about your own personality because you'll immediately identify behavior patterns as well as skills and talents that you have in common with the rest of your family and be better able to make the most of them in your own life. You thus will have an advantage, a head start, in not repeating the mistakes of your elders, whether negative traits or failure to fulfill potential in a certain area. This is another good reason to study astrology.

Although your birth chart reveals everything in your life, there are certain main areas of interest for most people: relationships, career, money, family, and health. As you become more proficient at astrology, you can explore the depths of your chart for specifics such as your relationships with in-laws, bosses, and coworkers; your partner's spending habits and career potential; your life lessons; your people skills and communication style; and where you're lucky, because everyone is lucky in some way just as everyone has challenges.

With more than six billion people on Earth, relationships are a major focus. We all have relationships with romantic partners, business partners, children, parents, relatives, friends, neighbors, store clerks, colleagues, and supervisors, yet the first relationship that comes to mind is usually a romantic partnership. Some fortunate people experience complete happiness, a union in which a harsh word is never spoken. Most partnerships go through ups and downs as each person's needs and interests change. Some people are totally unsuited for each other, as they discover too late.

Relationships are a good example of how astrology works and what you can learn from your birth chart. There are, for example, some planetary configurations that indicate divorce, disappointment, or deception. Does this mean

that everyone who has one of these configurations will experience a negative outcome? Absolutely not! Awareness and learning more about how you react in various situations can go a long way toward reversing what appears (to others who don't have your knowledge of astrology) to be fated. Possibly more important is knowing how to direct the specific energy represented into constructive activities that will strengthen the relationship. That's what astrology can do for you and your relationships.

A woman I know who had a series of failed relationships, each ending with the potential partner moving on, learned through astrology that she was the common denominator, and not men in general, as she had come to believe. She discovered that she had a fear of commitment and found it difficult to express her emotions. After examining her specific reactions, which were reflected in her birth chart, she was able to trace them back to her childhood and her parental relationships. Her next serious relationship led to a successful marriage because she gained the self-knowledge she needed and learned to express herself more fully and easily.

Another woman I know, however, continues to blame every failed romantic and business relationship on men, several of whom have left her in a tight financial spot. She refuses to accept that it's her overly trusting attitude toward people in general and especially men that attracts those she should steer clear of, and this will continue to happen until she accepts that fact. We tend to attract the people and situations we need to deal with during our lifetimes in order to grow and to learn life lessons. But why invite negative influences into our lives one more time or even at all? Astrology makes it possible to escape our self-defeating behavior, as well as the potential for it in situations yet to be encountered.

If you're dissatisfied with your career choice or unable to find your niche, astrology can help you identify your major strengths and talents, a specific career field, and your ideal working conditions. People who are perpetual job hoppers or have difficulty hanging on to a job can learn the reasons for this through their birth chart and take action to change the behavior that prompts it.

I know a man who held a dozen jobs in half as many years before finally realizing, through the help of his birth chart, that he had issues with women largely as a result of his negative relationship with his mother. In every one of those jobs he had a female boss whom he considered to be incompetent, just as he viewed his mother. Once he realized this, he was able to view his next female boss more objectively and has had a successful, long-term relationship with her and the company.

Money. For many people this is the single most stressful area of life. Money represents security and freedom. Almost everyone wants more money, and many people want more just to spend more. Your chart reflects your earning power, spending and saving habits, risk tolerance, inheritance potential, and attitude about debt. By combining this information with common sense and professional advice, you can maximize your financial potential.

Consider the example of a couple who earn a six-figure income. Their debt far exceeds their income, and every time money is tight they refinance their mortgage to pay down their credit cards and other consumer debt. They've even tried credit counseling, yet each time they run up new debt, buying new vehicles and max-

ing out their credit cards. As their birth charts reveal, they're motivated by two factors: a desire for status and for material proof of their success. An astrologer explained this to them, but they chose not to change, instead putting their faith in the false belief that their habits will never catch up with them. Their birth charts say that sooner or later they will. Then, if my experience with some clients holds true, they'll consult an astrologer, not to learn where they went wrong but instead to find a magic fix for their dilemma. They will be sorely disappointed to learn—if they truly are ready to hear the information—that the only magic fix is to change their financial attitudes.

Astrology gives you information, but it's up to you to use this knowledge and put it to work to improve your life.

THE LANGUAGE OF ASTROLOGY

Like any other field of study, astrology has its own language. With a little practice, you can learn the language fairly quickly and begin to interpret your chart and those of friends and relatives. A natal chart has four essential components—the same ones astrologers have used for centuries. They are:

- twelve signs of the zodiac
- ten planets
- twelve houses
- aspects

I will explain these four elements in detail in subsequent chapters of this book. My goal here is to give you a basic overview so you can begin to understand the components of a birth chart.

Signs

There are twelve signs in the zodiac (Aries through Pisces), which are also the names of the constellations. Each sign is 30 degrees of a perfect 360° circle. Each single degree of the 30° in a sign is further divided into 60 minutes (60'), which are each again divided into 60 seconds (60"). Most astrologers use only degrees and minutes. Each sign is represented by a glyph. Once you learn these glyphs, you can use them instead of writing out the full name of the sign. Refer to the inside back cover of this book for a list of astrological glyphs.

> One sign = 30 degrees
>
> One degree = 60 minutes
>
> One minute = 60 seconds

Figure 1 is an illustration of what is called the *natural chart*. It shows the zodiac signs, along with their glyphs, in order, beginning with Aries at the left center point and continuing around counterclockwise to Pisces. This is the natural order of the zodiac.

Notice that the directions are reversed. Unlike the usual map orientation, south is above, north below, east to the left, and west to the right. There is a simple explanation for this: the Sun rises in the east and sets in the west. So the birth chart is a depiction of the path of the Sun as it appears from Earth, which is the center point of the chart.

Notice also that the clock times correspond to the Sun's position relative to Earth. The Sun rises in the east at sunrise (approximately 6:00

a.m.), reaches its highest point at noon, sets in the west (approximately 6:00 p.m.), and reaches its lowest point at midnight. So if, for example, you were born at noon, then the Sun would be at the top of your chart, when the Sun is at its highest point. If you were born at 9:00 p.m., then the Sun would be halfway between west (6:00 p.m.) and north (midnight), which is northwest by direction.

The signs and their glyphs are:

Sign	Glyph
Aries	♈
Taurus	♉
Gemini	♊
Cancer	♋
Leo	♌
Virgo	♍
Libra	♎
Scorpio	♏
Sagittarius	♐
Capricorn	♑
Aquarius	♒
Pisces	♓

The annual equinox or solstice that signals the start of each season coincides with the Sun's entrance into one of four signs: Aries (spring equinox), Cancer (summer solstice), Libra (autumnal equinox), and Capricorn (winter solstice).

The zodiac used by most Western astrologers is called the *tropical zodiac*. It is an accurate depiction of the constellations and the signs associated with them as they were viewed by the Babylonians rather than by present-day astronomers. Since ancient times, the constellations have precessed, or moved backward, in the heavens. Astrologers who equate the signs with the cur-

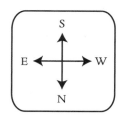

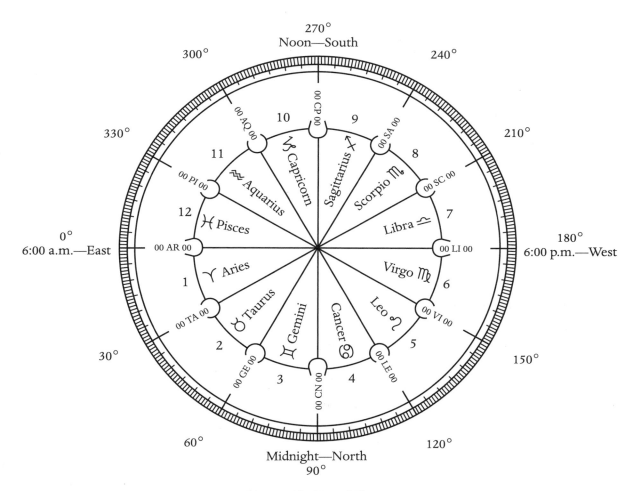

Figure 1. The Natural Chart

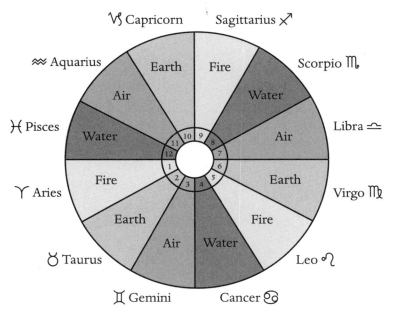

Figure 2. The Elements: Fire, Earth, Air, and Water

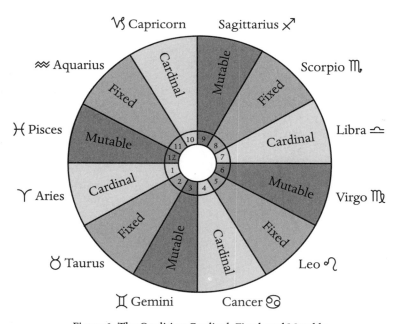

Figure 3. The Qualities: Cardinal, Fixed, and Mutable

rent positions of the constellations practice *sidereal astrology*, which is used extensively in India.

Each sign is associated with certain characteristics that describe personality traits. People born under the same Sun sign share these traits to a greater or lesser degree depending on other influences in the birth chart, but the basic nature of each sign is easily described through its *element* and *quality*.

The four elements are fire, earth, air, and water (figure 2). The three qualities are cardinal, fixed, and mutable (figure 3). Each sign falls into one element and one quality. You can learn a lot about your basic nature just by observing the dominant elements and qualities in your chart. Briefly, here are the signs and their elements/qualities and characteristics (you'll learn more about the signs in chapter 2):

Fire signs: Aries, Leo, Sagittarius—are outgoing and action-oriented.

Earth signs: Taurus, Virgo, Capricorn—are practical and realistic.

Air signs: Gemini, Libra, Aquarius—are intellectual and people-oriented.

Water signs: Cancer, Scorpio, Pisces—are emotional and intuitive.

Cardinal signs: Aries, Cancer, Libra, Capricorn—are self-starters.

Fixed signs: Taurus, Leo, Scorpio, Aquarius—are determined.

Mutable signs: Gemini, Virgo, Sagittarius, Pisces—are easygoing.

Each of these signs is represented somewhere in your chart, and you express each of them in one way or another, to a greater or lesser degree. For example, a certain sign placement in your chart might indicate that you excel when you have a high level of job autonomy or that you're happiest in a team environment; this is valuable information in a job search. The point is that you experience every sign, not just your Sun sign, and some signs more than others.

Planets

Each of the ten planets in your birth chart is in a sign, as is your Sun. So you have a Moon sign, a Venus sign, a Mercury sign, and so on. Although the Sun and Moon are commonly called planets, you'll also see them referred to as "luminaries" or the "Lights," because the Sun provides light during daylight hours and the Moon illuminates the night. These terms were first used by ancient astrologers.

A planet's characteristics and energy are modified and expressed according to its sign. For example, Mercury is associated with all forms of communication, so your communication style thus is influenced by the sign that your Mercury is in. This is one reason that one person may be a dynamic speaker (Mercury in Leo) while another has the ability to instantly put other people at ease (Mercury in Libra).

Each of the planets is associated with one or two signs. This is called *rulership*. Astrologers say, for example, that Jupiter "rules" Sagittarius, and Mars "rules" Aries. A planet and the sign it rules are very compatible, and the meanings of both are similar. Because there are twelve signs but only ten planets, Mercury and Venus each rule two signs.

Before the outer planets (Uranus, Neptune, and Pluto) were discovered, astrologers used what are now called *traditional rulers* for three of the signs: Mars for Scorpio (modern ruler,

Planet	Rules	Planetary Keywords
Sun ☉	Leo ♌	Ego, individuality, confidence
Moon ☽	Cancer ♋	Emotions, habits
Mercury ☿	Gemini ♊, Virgo ♍	Communication, thought process
Venus ♀	Taurus ♉, Libra ♎	Love, money, powers of attraction
Mars ♂	Aries ♈	Energy, initiative, temper
Jupiter ♃	Sagittarius ♐	Expansion, good fortune
Saturn ♄	Capricorn ♑	Restriction, responsibility, life lessons
Uranus ♅	Aquarius ♒	Independence, eccentricity
Neptune ♆	Pisces ♓	Vision, creativity, illusion
Pluto ♇	Scorpio ♏	Transformation, major change

Chart 1. Planetary Rulers and Keywords

Pluto), Saturn for Uranus (modern ruler, Uranus), and Jupiter for Pisces (modern ruler, Jupiter). Some astrologers use both the traditional and modern rulers when reading charts today. I've found the traditional rulers to be useful, just as ancient astrologers did, so give them a try. To simplify things, this book uses the modern rulers for Uranus, Neptune, and Pluto.

The planets (in astrological order), their glyphs, the sign(s) they rule, and their basic meanings are shown in chart 1.

Retrograde and Direct Motion

All of the planets except the Sun and Moon periodically travel in *retrograde*, or backward, motion. They don't actually back up, but appear to do so when viewed from Earth; this is an astronomical phenomenon. A planet travels forward in direct motion, appears to stop—which is called its *stationary* point or *station*—and then resumes motion, moving backward to retrace its steps. When the retrograde period is completed, the planet again stops, or stations, and then resumes forward motion.

Retrograde motion is relative motion. If you're on a slow-moving train and a faster, parallel train moves forward and passes you, you feel like you're moving backward. The same sensation can occur if you're in a stopped car and a car in the next lane suddenly moves forward; your reaction is to step on the brake.

Almost everyone is born when at least one planet is retrograde, and most people have several retrograde planets in their birth chart. Sometimes as many as half the planets in a chart are retrograde. You can identify the retrograde planets in your chart by looking for a retrograde glyph (℞) next to each planet.

Birth chart planets that are stationary are more powerful and usually have strong significance in the individual's life because the energy is highly concentrated. The energy of a retrograde planet is more internalized, lacking some of its natural outward expression. This can be helpful and productive or not, depending on

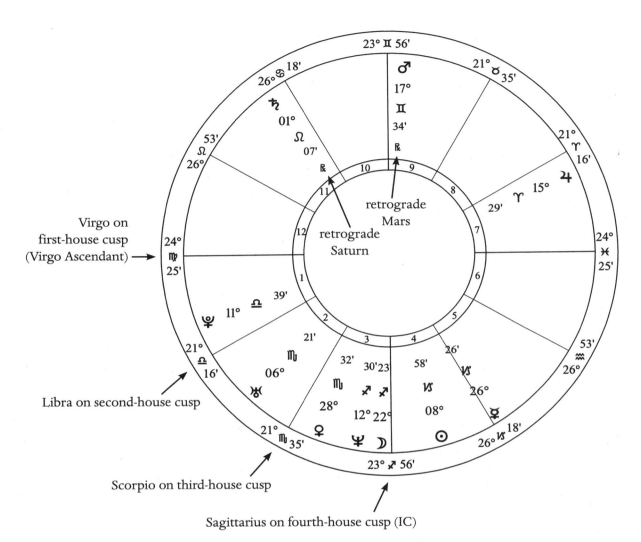

Figure 4. Retrograde Planets and House Cusps in Tiger Woods's Chart
December 30, 1975 / 10:50 p.m. PST / Long Beach, CA
Placidus Houses

how the individual handles and focuses the planetary energy.

Notice in Tiger Woods's chart (figure 4) that only two planets—Mars and Saturn—are retrograde, as indicated by the ℞ symbol near the glyphs for ♂ (Mars) and ♄ (Saturn). It is highly unusual to see only two retrograde planets in a birth chart because Uranus, Neptune, and Pluto are retrograde as much as half of each year, and Saturn for four to five months. With only two planets retrograde, Woods has well-above-average drive, determination, and initiative. But this is also a good example of the potential power of retrograde planets and why they're not necessarily weak or weaker than direct planets.

Mars is the premier action planet. So if we assume that direct planets are stronger than weaker ones, then Woods should be someone who has reduced initiative and drive. Nothing could be further from the truth. He instead uses the retrograde (internalized) Mars (action) in Gemini (thought process) for focused concentration. Any golfer will tell you that the game is far more mental than physical and that success is limited without the mental focus. Saturn, also retrograde, is associated with career and ambition. With the energy of this planet focused inward and in Leo, the sign of the ego, Woods has a strong ego investment in achieving his ambitions and career success.

So how do you know if a retrograde planet is an advantage or disadvantage? To be honest, you don't, or at least not for sure. Much depends on other factors in the birth chart (you'll learn more about these later in this book), which can increase the probability that the retrograde planet(s) will work in the individual's favor, as well as on the choices made by the person. So if you were counseling Tiger Woods and you did not already know that he is one of the all-time

House	Natural Sign	Planetary Ruler	Areas of Life Ruled by House
First	Aries ♈	Mars ♂	Self, personality
Second	Taurus ♉	Venus ♀	Personal finances, possessions
Third	Gemini ♊	Mercury ☿	Communication, learning style
Fourth	Cancer ♋	Moon ☽	Home, family
Fifth	Leo ♌	Sun ☉	Children, sports, creativity
Sixth	Virgo ♍	Mercury ☿	Work environment, health
Seventh	Libra ♎	Venus ♀	Partnerships, close relationships
Eighth	Scorpio ♏	Pluto ♇	Joint resources, other people's money
Ninth	Sagittarius ♐	Jupiter ♃	Higher education, travel
Tenth	Capricorn ♑	Saturn ♄	Career, status
Eleventh	Aquarius ♒	Uranus ♅	Friends, group associations
Twelfth	Pisces ♓	Neptune ♆	Subconscious, spirituality

Chart 2. The Houses: Signs and Rulerships

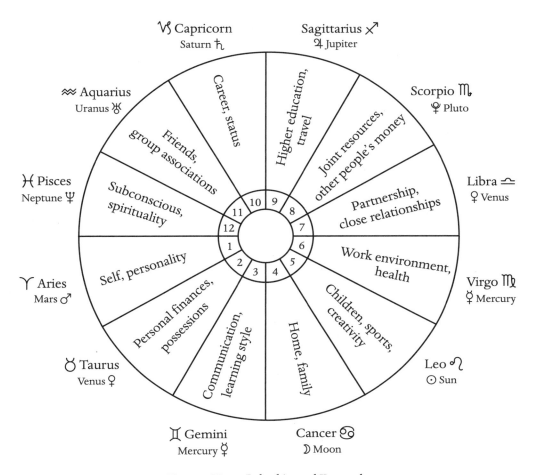

Figure 5. House Rulerships and Keywords

most successful professional golfers, you would tell him how he could use the energy of his retrograde Mars and Saturn to pursue his ambitions and succeed in the sports field.

Houses

There are twelve houses in a chart, each associated with a specific area or areas of life, such as career, money, relationships, and friendship (figure 5). They are numbered counterclockwise beginning with the left center, where Aries is located in the natural chart. Look again at Tiger

Woods's chart (page 17) and notice that Virgo (♍) is at the left center point—the Ascendant—of the chart instead of Aries, as it would be in the natural chart. This is because the chart was calculated for the exact date, time, and place of Woods's birth.

The importance of birth time accuracy cannot be overemphasized. Even a few minutes can make a big difference because the Ascendant sign changes about every two hours, or one degree every four minutes. So always use an actual birth time, preferably from a birth certificate.

Mothers' memories are often faulty, and a birth chart based on an approximate time, such as "about 6:00," isn't worth your time and effort. From my experience, these "about" times are usually hours away from the actual birth time. (For help obtaining an official U.S. birth certificate, go to http://www.cdc.gov/nchs/howto/w2w/w2welcom.htm.)

The dividing line between two houses is called a *cusp*. In Tiger Woods's chart, the second-house cusp is Libra (♎), the third-house cusp is Scorpio (♏), the fourth-house cusp is Sagittarius (♐), and so on, counterclockwise around the chart following the natural order of the zodiac.

The planet that rules the sign on the house cusp is said to be the house's ruler. In Tiger Woods's chart, for example, Saturn rules the fifth house because Capricorn (♑) is on the fifth-house cusp. Rulership is an important concept in astrology. In order to gain additional insights into the meaning of a house in a specific chart, you also look at the planetary ruler of the house (see chart 2). In Woods's chart, Saturn (♄) is in Leo (♌) in the eleventh house. You'll learn more about this concept later in this book.

The sign on the house cusp reveals a great deal of information about that area of life. But whatever the sign on a house cusp, the house also has some of the characteristics of the natural chart sign that is located there. For example, any planet in the first house somewhat exemplifies the initiative and energy, but also the impatience, of Aries. A planet in the sixth house takes on some Virgo characteristics, such as meticulousness and dependability.

Now that you're familiar with the basics of signs, planets, and houses, you can learn about another rulership concept: *universal rulership*.

This concept goes back to the natural chart (figure 1 on page 13). Each planet rules a sign, and both are associated with a house in the natural chart. For example, the Moon is the universal ruler of home and family because the Moon rules Cancer, the fourth-house sign of the natural chart; the fourth house is the house of home and family. So when reading a chart, you would study the Moon and the sign and house it's in, wherever it is in the chart, in addition to looking at the fourth house in the specific chart. You can see how doing this will give you much more information than will just looking at the fourth house of your chart.

Here's an example of what you can learn from house-cusp signs and rulerships and how astrologers read a chart. In Tiger Woods's chart (page 17), Mercury (☿) in Capricorn (♑) (the universal sign of career) in the fifth house of sports rules Woods's tenth house of career through Gemini (♊), the sign on the tenth-house cusp of Woods's chart (Mercury is the planet that rules Gemini). You thus immediately know that Woods's chart shows excellent potential for a career in sports because the energies of the fifth and tenth houses are linked through Mercury in Capricorn. To take this a step further, the fifth is the natural house of Leo (♌), and Saturn (the planet that rules Capricorn), the ruler of the fifth house in Woods's chart, is in Leo. Saturn in Leo thus reinforces the initial indication (Mercury, ruler of Woods's tenth house, in the fifth house) that the sports field is an excellent career choice for Tiger Woods.

To simplify this a bit, here is the formula: Mercury (Woods's tenth-house ruler—Gemini on the cusp) + in the fifth house (sports) + in Capricorn (tenth house of career in natural chart) + Saturn (ruler of Capricorn) + in Leo (ruler of the fifth house of sports in natural chart). Don't be concerned if this sounds confusing at first. With practice, you'll get the hang of it.

Angular House Cusps

There are four angular house cusps (figure 6), collectively referred to as *the angles*: the Ascendant (first-house cusp), the Descendant (seventh-house cusp), the Midheaven (tenth-house cusp), and the *Imum Coeli* (or the IC; the fourth-house cusp). The angles signify important areas of life that are a major focus for most people.

The Ascendant (first-house cusp) represents you as an individual, and it's usually the first impression you make on others. In fact, anyone who knows a little astrology may instantly identify someone's rising sign as his or her Sun sign.

Sometimes the traits of the Ascendant and Sun signs are so different that the latter emerges only when you really get to know the person.

The Ascendant (also called the *rising sign*) indicates much of the outward manifestation of your personality. It's the point through which planetary energy is expressed, the face you show the world, and your subjective reaction to events and situations. While the Sun represents your internal motivations, the Ascendant represents your external responses. For example, someone with a Capricorn Sun may be reserved, cautious, and career-oriented. If the rising sign is Leo, the person is probably more outgoing and fun-loving, using Leo's warmth and leadership ability to further career ambitions.

The Descendant (seventh-house cusp), the point opposite the Ascendant, represents close relationships—with a mate or business partner

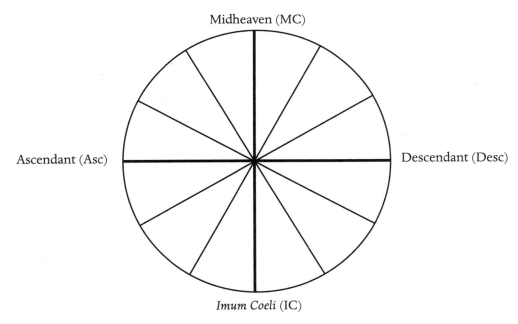

Figure 6. The Angles

Aspect	Degrees	Glyph	Keywords
Conjunction	0°	☌	Intensity, focus
Sextile	60°	✳	Opportunity
Trine	120°	△	Luck, ease
Square	90°	□	Obstacle, action
Opposition	180°	☍	Separation, polarity

Chart 3. The Major Aspects: Degrees, Glyphs, and Keywords

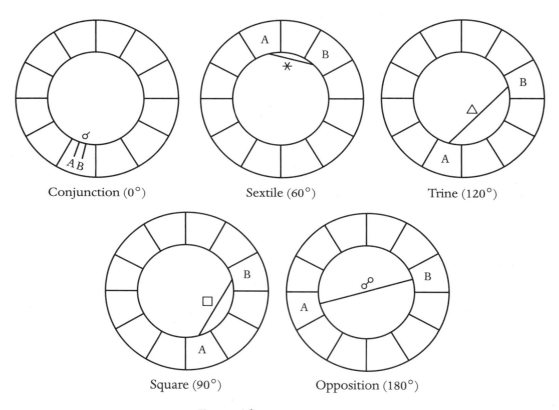

Conjunction (0°)   Sextile (60°)   Trine (120°)

Square (90°)   Opposition (180°)

Figure 7. The Five Major Aspects

and sometimes long-term friends. This point in the chart indicates how you react to and interact with other people, the qualities you look for in a partner, and the general character of your close relationships.

The Midheaven (tenth-house cusp) sign shows where you want to shine in the world and in your career. It indicates what you want to be noted for, how you perceive status, what makes you feel important, and how you can expect your career life to develop. It also can offer insight into career interests.

The IC (fourth-house cusp) is associated with home and family, parents, your roots and childhood, as well as the physical environment of your home. This is the place you call your own and share with loved ones, literally and figuratively.

The sign on each angle gives a general indication of the affairs of that house. Planets in these houses also contribute to the overall chart interpretation, as you will see later in this book.

Aspects

Aspects are geometric angles, such as 90° or 120°. They connect the energy of two or more planets, reflecting ease, obstacles, challenges, or opportunities. The major "easy" aspects are the *sextile* and *trine*, and the aspects representing challenges are the *square* and *opposition*. The *conjunction* aspect can be either easy or challenging, depending on the planets involved (see figure 7). Chart 3 shows the major aspects and their degrees, glyphs, and keywords.

Ancient astrologers described the aspects as "bad" and "good," or "malefic" and "benefic." Although these definitions are still somewhat pertinent today, the meanings have been expanded and modified through centuries of experience and knowledge. Life today is also far different from what it was even as recently as a hundred years ago. So while in the past a square was interpreted as a sign of war, battle, or conflict, it's now defined as an aspect of personal challenge, a life lesson, or what motivates an individual to take action. A Mercury-Mars square, for example, might have indicated physical battle in the past, while today it is associated more with temper, arguments, and verbal battles.

In Tiger Woods's chart (page 17), Mars is trine (120° from) Pluto. An exact trine would occur if Mars were at 11°39' Gemini or Pluto were at 17°34' Libra, but the allowable *orb of influence* for a trine is 8°, meaning the two planets would be in trine aspect if they were anywhere from 112° to 128° degrees apart. Mars and Pluto are 125°59' apart, so they are "within orb." You will learn more about orbs in chapter 5.

The Mars-Pluto trine reflects determination, ambition, willpower, and success easily achieved, and thus also reinforces the strength of the retrograde Mars energy in Woods's chart.

EPHEMERIS

Figure 8 shows a page from an *ephemeris*, the astrologer's most valuable tool. You can purchase an ephemeris in book form that covers a time frame ranging from a single year to one hundred years, or use a computer program to generate your own ephemeris for any time period. An ephemeris is an essential astrological quick reference guide that lists the position of each planet—its sign and degree—on a given day. It also indicates when planets change direction to direct (D) or retrograde (Rx) motion.

An ephemeris is a gold mine of information. It's greatest use is in predictive astrology, but

13 06:55 20♍10 ○ Solar Eclipse (mag 0.788)
28 02:49 04♈40 ✹ Total Lunar Eclipse (mag 1.282)

September 2015

Day	S. T. h m s	☉ ° ' "	☽ ° ' "	☿ ° '	♀ ° '	♂ ° '	♃ ° '	♄ ° '	♅ ° '	♆ ° '	♇ ° '	☊ True ° '
01 Tu	22 39 22	08♍ 15 31	09♈ 39 26	05♎ 05	14♌R58	14♌ 47	04♍ 27	28♏ 59	19♈R59	08♓R25	13♑R07	01♎D04
02 We	22 43 19	09 13 33	24 29 14	06 10	14 46	15 25	04 40	29 02	19 57	08 23	13 06	01 05
03 Th	22 47 15	10 11 37	09♉ 00 40	07 12	14 37	16 03	04 53	29 05	19 56	08 21	13 06	01 06
04 Fr	22 51 12	11 09 42	23 10 15	08 12	14 30	16 42	05 06	29 08	19 54	08 20	13 05	01 07
05 Sa	22 55 08	12 07 50	06♊ 56 48	09 09	14 25	17 20	05 19	29 11	19 52	08 18	13 04	01 08
06 Su	22 59 05	13 06 00	20 20 54	10 04	14 23	17 58	05 32	29 15	19 51	08 16	13 04	01R 08
07 Mo	23 03 01	14 04 12	03♋ 24 19	10 55	14D 24	18 36	05 45	29 18	19 49	08 15	13 03	01 07
08 Tu	23 06 58	15 02 25	16 09 28	11 43	14 26	19 14	05 58	29 21	19 47	08 13	13 03	01 05
09 We	23 10 55	16 00 41	28 39 04	12 28	14 31	19 52	06 11	29 25	19 45	08 11	13 02	01 04
10 Th	23 14 51	16 58 59	10♌ 55 44	13 10	14 39	20 30	06 24	29 28	19 43	08 10	13 02	01 01
11 Fr	23 18 48	17 57 19	23 02 00	13 47	14 48	21 08	06 37	29 32	19 41	08 08	13 01	01 00
12 Sa	23 22 44	18 55 40	05♍ 00 09	14 20	15 00	21 46	06 50	29 36	19 39	08 07	13 01	00 58
13 Su	23 26 41	19 54 03	16 52 19	14 49	15 13	22 24	07 03	29 39	19 37	08 05	13 01	00 57
14 Mo	23 30 37	20 52 29	28 40 38	15 13	15 29	23 02	07 16	29 43	19 35	08 03	13 00	00D 57
15 Tu	23 34 34	21 50 56	10♎ 27 20	15 32	15 46	23 39	07 29	29 47	19 33	08 02	13 00	00 57
16 We	23 38 30	22 49 24	22 14 53	15 46	16 06	24 17	07 42	29 51	19 31	08 00	13 00	00 58
17 Th	23 42 27	23 47 55	04♏ 06 00	15 53	16 27	24 55	07 54	29 55	19 29	07 59	12 59	00 59
18 Fr	23 46 23	24 46 27	16 03 49	15R 55	16 50	25 33	08 07	30 00	19 27	07 57	12 59	00 59
19 Sa	23 50 20	25 45 01	28 11 52	15 50	17 15	26 11	08 20	00♐ 04	19 25	07 55	12 59	01 00
20 Su	23 54 17	26 43 37	10♐ 33 57	15 39	17 41	26 48	08 33	00 08	19 22	07 54	12 59	01 00
21 Mo	23 58 13	27 42 15	23 14 02	15 20	18 09	27 26	08 45	00 12	19 20	07 52	12 59	01R 00
22 Tu	00 02 10	28 40 54	06♑ 15 51	14 54	18 39	28 04	08 58	00 17	19 18	07 51	12 58	01 00
23 We	00 06 06	29 39 35	19 42 27	14 22	19 10	28 41	09 11	00 22	19 16	07 49	12 58	01D 00
24 Th	00 10 03	00♎ 38 17	03♒ 35 36	13 42	19 43	29 19	09 23	00 26	19 14	07 48	12 58	01 00
25 Fr	00 13 59	01 37 01	17 55 05	12 55	20 17	29 56	09 36	00 31	19 11	07 46	12 58	01 00
26 Sa	00 17 56	02 35 47	02♓ 38 15	12 03	20 52	00♍ 34	09 48	00 36	19 09	07 45	12D 58	01 01
27 Su	00 21 52	03 34 35	17 39 38	11 04	21 28	01 11	10 01	00 40	19 07	07 43	12 58	01 01
28 Mo	00 25 49	04 33 24	02♈ 51 25	10 02	22 06	01 49	10 13	00 45	19 04	07 42	12 58	01 01
29 Tu	00 29 46	05 32 16	18 04 13	08 56	22 45	02 26	10 26	00 50	19 02	07 41	12 59	01R 01
30 We	00 33 42	06 31 09	03♉ 08 23	07 48	23 25	03 04	10 38	00 55	19 00	07 39	12 59	01 00

Data for	09-01-2015
Julian Day	2457266.50
Ayanamsa	24 04 33
SVP	05 ♓ 02 29
☽ ☊ Mean	02 ♎ 04 R

● ◐ PHASES ○ ◑

05	09:55	◑	12♊32
13	06:41	○	20♍10
21	08:59	◐	28♐04
28	02:51	✹	04♈40

LAST ASPECT Day	h m	☽ INGRESS Day	h m	
01	16:38	02	09:03	♉
04	10:21	04	11:49	♊
05	23:05	06	17:41	♋
09	01:29	09	02:37	♌
11	13:04	11	13:56	♍
14	02:08	14	02:42	♎
16	04:22	16	15:43	♏
18	19:49	19	03:32	♐
21	08:59	21	12:33	♑
22	23:13	23	17:52	♒
25	04:03	25	19:44	♓
26	16:33	27	19:30	♈
29	07:46	29	18:58	♉

DECLINATION

Day	☉	☽	☿	♀	♂	♃	♄	♅	♆	♇
01 Tu	08N28	03N06	03S46	09N01	17N29	10N42	18S07	07N12	09S10	20S56
02 We	08 07	07 32	04 20	09 11	17 18	10 37	18 08	07 11	09 11	20 56
03 Th	07 45	11 25	04 53	09 20	17 07	10 32	18 09	07 10	09 12	20 56
04 Fr	07 23	14 32	05 25	09 29	16 56	10 27	18 10	07 10	09 12	20 57
05 Sa	07 01	16 43	05 56	09 38	16 44	10 23	18 10	07 09	09 13	20 57
06 Su	06 38	17 55	06 25	09 46	16 33	10 18	18 11	07 08	09 13	20 57
07 Mo	06 16	18 07	06 53	09 54	16 22	10 13	18 12	07 08	09 14	20 57
08 Tu	05 54	17 23	07 20	10 01	16 10	10 09	18 13	07 07	09 15	20 57
09 We	05 31	15 50	07 45	10 08	15 58	10 04	18 14	07 06	09 15	20 58
10 Th	05 08	13 35	08 08	10 15	15 46	09 59	18 15	07 06	09 16	20 58
11 Fr	04 46	10 45	08 30	10 21	15 35	09 54	18 16	07 05	09 16	20 58
12 Sa	04 23	07 31	08 49	10 27	15 23	09 50	18 17	07 04	09 17	20 58
13 Su	04 00	03 59	09 07	10 32	15 11	09 45	18 18	07 03	09 18	20 58
14 Mo	03 37	00 20	09 22	10 36	14 58	09 40	18 19	07 03	09 18	20 58
15 Tu	03 14	03S 20	09 34	10 40	14 46	09 36	18 20	07 02	09 19	20 59
16 We	02 51	06 53	09 44	10 44	14 34	09 31	18 21	07 01	09 19	20 59
17 Th	02 28	10 09	09 50	10 47	14 21	09 26	18 22	07 00	09 20	20 59
18 Fr	02 05	13 02	09 54	10 49	14 09	09 21	18 23	06 59	09 21	20 59
19 Sa	01 41	15 24	09 54	10 51	13 56	09 17	18 24	06 58	09 21	20 59
20 Su	01 18	17 06	09 50	10 52	13 44	09 12	18 26	06 58	09 22	21 00
21 Mo	00 55	18 01	09 42	10 53	13 31	09 07	18 27	06 57	09 22	21 00
22 Tu	00 31	18 01	09 31	10 53	13 18	09 03	18 28	06 56	09 23	21 00
23 We	00 08	17 01	09 15	10 53	13 05	08 58	18 29	06 55	09 24	21 00
24 Th	00S 15	15 00	08 54	10 52	12 53	08 53	18 30	06 54	09 24	21 00
25 Fr	00 39	12 00	08 30	10 50	12 40	08 49	18 31	06 53	09 25	21 00
26 Sa	01 02	08 10	08 01	10 48	12 27	08 44	18 32	06 53	09 25	21 01
27 Su	01 25	03 44	07 28	10 46	12 13	08 40	18 34	06 52	09 26	21 01
28 Mo	01 49	00N59	06 52	10 42	12 00	08 35	18 35	06 51	09 26	21 01
29 Tu	02 12	05 39	06 13	10 38	11 47	08 30	.18 36	06 50	09 27	21 01
30 We	02 35	09 55	05 31	10 34	11 34	08 26	18 37	06 49	09 27	21 01

ASPECTARIAN

01 03:40 ☉ ☍ ♆
03:56 ☽ ⋕ ☿
05:04 ♀ ☌ ♂
05:33 ☽ □ ♇
08:25 ☽ △ ♀
08:37 ☽ △ ♂
16:38 ☽ ☌ ♅
22:00 ☽ ∥ ♅
23:48 ♀ ⋕ ♆
02 03:02 ☽ ∥ ☉
09:41 ☽ ⋕ ♆
10:04 ☽ ∥ ♀
17:02 ☽ △ ♃
18:14 ☽ ∥ ♃
22:54 ☽ ✱ ♆
03 02:07 ☽ △ ☉
06:51 ☽ △ ♇
09:20 ☽ □ ♀
12:25 ☽ □ ♂
04 10:21 ☽ ☍ ♄
14:27 ☉ ∥ ♅
21:06 ☽ □ ♃
05 00:17 ☽ ∥ ♂
02:23 ☽ □ ♆
04:12 ☽ △ ☿
13:16 ☽ ✱ ♀
19:28 ☽ ✱ ♂
23:05 ☽ ✱ ♅
23:09 ☉ △ ♇
06 06:15 ☿ ⋕ ☉
08:30 ♀ SD
07 04:28 ☽ ✱ ♃
09:02 ☽ △ ♆
12:32 ☿ ⋕ ♅
15:02 ☽ □ ☿
18:06 ☽ ☍ ♇
21:42 ☽ ✱ ☉
08 06:54 ☽ □ ♅
14:37 ♀ ∥ ♃
19:53 ♂ △ ♅
22:13 ☽ ∥ ♂
09 01:29 ☽ △ ♄
19:24 ☿ □ ♇
10 04:39 ☽ ✱ ☿
07:25 ☽ ☌ ♀
17:21 ☽ △ ♅
20:00 ☽ ☌ ♂
11 03:06 ☽ ∥ ♀
06:45 ☽ ∥ ♃
11:17 ☽ ⋕ ♆
13:04 ☽ □ ♄
15:26 ☽ ⋕ ☿
12 03:09 ☽ ∥ ♅
03:46 ☽ ☌ ♃
06:15 ☽ ☍ ♆
16:11 ☽ △ ♇
23:58 ☽ ∥ ☉
13 17:50 ☿ ∥ ♆
14 02:08 ☽ ✱ ♄
23:25 ☽ ⋕ ☉
15 02:14 ☿ ⋕ ♃
05:11 ☽ □ ♇
10:34 ☽ ☌ ☿
11:08 ☽ ✱ ♀
18:28 ☽ ☍ ♅
16 01:01 ☽ ⋕ ♅
04:22 ☽ ✱ ♂
17:47 ☽ ∥ ♆
18:42 ☽ ⋕ ♃
21:34 ☽ ∥ ☿
17 05:01 ☽ ⋕ ♀
06:56 ♃ ☍ ♆
07:48 ☽ △ ♆
07:49 ☽ ✱ ♃
17:51 ☽ ✱ ♇
18:11 ☿ SR
18 01:35 ☽ □ ♀
02:47 ♄ ♐
03:51 ♃ ⋕ ♆
09:44 ☽ ⋕ ♂
18:46 ☽ ✱ ☉
19:49 ☽ □ ♂
19 03:40 ☽ ☌ ♄
18:53 ☽ □ ♆
20:03 ☽ □ ♃
20 09:29 ☽ ✱ ☿
14:05 ☽ △ ♀
16:42 ☽ △ ♅
21 08:12 ☽ △ ♂
22 02:52 ☽ ✱ ♆
04:58 ☽ △ ♃
11:59 ☿ ∥ ♆
12:04 ☽ ☌ ♇
14:56 ☽ □ ☿
23:13 ☽ □ ♅
23 04:00 ♀ △ ♅
08:21 ☉ ♎
18:35 ☽ △ ☉
18:35 ☽ ✱ ♄
18:37 ☉ ✱ ♄
24 01:11 ☿ ⋕ ♃
16:09 ☽ △ ☿
18:58 ☽ ⋕ ♂
22:32 ☿ □ ♇
25 02:05 ☽ ✱ ♅
02:19 ♂ ♍
04:03 ☽ ☍ ♀
06:56 ♇ SD
07:53 ☽ ⋕ ♀
16:42 ☽ ∥ ♆
20:31 ☽ ☍ ♂
20:40 ☽ ⋕ ♃
20:41 ☽ □ ♄
26 01:03 ☽ ∥ ☿
01:13 ♂ □ ♄
07:20 ☽ ⋕ ♅
08:12 ☽ ☌ ♆
11:40 ☽ ☍ ♃
16:33 ☽ ✱ ♇
27 10:59 ☽ ∥ ☉
20:40 ☽ △ ♄
28 00:42 ☿ ⋕ ♅
04:35 ☽ ⋕ ☉
10:33 ☽ ☍ ☿
15:57 ☽ □ ♇
29 01:31 ☽ ☌ ♅
02:37 ☽ ⋕ ☿
06:22 ☽ ∥ ♅
07:46 ☽ △ ♀
15:29 ☽ ∥ ♃
21:18 ☽ ⋕ ♆
23:52 ☽ △ ♂
30 04:02 ☽ ∥ ♀
07:15 ☽ ✱ ♆
09:57 ☽ ∥ ♂
12:16 ☽ △ ♃
14:39 ☿ ☌ ☉
15:54 ☽ △ ♇

⚷ Chiron

01	Dec.	00 N 19
03		19♓38R
06		19 30
09		19 22
12		19 13
15		19 05
18		18 57
21		18 49
24		18 40
27		18 32
30		18 24

Figure 8. *Astro America's Daily Ephemeris*, Page for September 2015

it's also essential if you want to hand-calculate a chart. An ephemeris is also very important for another reason: A computer-calculated chart shows you the positions of the planets on the day you were born. What it doesn't show you is whether a planet in your chart was stationing to turn direct or retrograde on the day you were born. The best way to find this information is to look at an ephemeris and find your birth date. Then you can scan from a week to ten days before and after your birthday to see if any of the planets were stationing.

Notice at the very top of the left-hand side of the ephemeris page that both a solar eclipse and a lunar eclipse are listed for that month. (A solar eclipse is also a New Moon, and a lunar eclipse is a Full Moon.) The data for the solar eclipse is "13 06:55 20♍10," followed by the Sun symbol and "Solar Eclipse (mag 0.788)." This means that the solar eclipse occurs on September 13, 2015, at 6:55 a.m. GMT (Greenwich Mean Time) at 20° 10' Virgo, with a magnitude of 0.788.

Moving down, you can see the column headings for Day, S.T. (Sidereal Time, which is used to calculate a chart by hand), and the planets and North Node. The Sun and Moon are listed in degrees, minutes, and seconds, and the other planets are listed in degrees and minutes. Notice that the sign for each planet is listed after the degrees (the Sun is at 08°♍15'31").

Look at September 1 in the Venus column. It shows that Venus is retrograde. This is indicated by the "℞" in "14♌℞58." Uranus, Neptune, and Pluto are also retrograde as the month begins. Now look down the Venus column to September 7, and notice the "D" for "direct." This indicates that Venus is in direct motion as of that date. Look at September 1, when Venus is at 14♌℞58, and how it barely moves during the

first ten days of the month as it slows, stations direct, and then begins to move forward. You can see a similar pattern in Mercury, which is retrograde as of September 18.

In the upper left of the bottom half of the ephemeris page below the data for the day are the lunar phases for the month—third quarter (September 5), New Moon (September 13), first quarter (September 21), and Full Moon (September 28). Below that is an aspectarian showing the planetary aspects for every day of the month. (Aspects are explained in chapter 5.)

To the right of the aspectarian is a small table that lists the date and time of the Moon's last planetary aspect in each sign and the date and time when the Moon enters the next sign. The time in between is when the Moon is *void of course*. Looking at the Moon column on the upper half of the page, you can see that the Moon begins the month in Aries. Then looking at the small table that shows the Moon's last aspect, you see that the Moon's last planetary aspect in Aries is formed on September 1 at 16:38 (4:38 p.m.) GMT. The Moon enters Taurus on September 2 at 9:03 a.m. GMT. So the Moon is void of course between September 1 at 4:38 p.m. and September 2 at 9:03 a.m.

This ephemeris includes the declination of each planet (not every ephemeris has declinations). This measures the planet's place in degrees north or south of the celestial equator (Earth's equator projected into space). Although declinations are not widely used, interest is increasing and some astrologers find them to be invaluable, especially in predictive astrology.

It's also fun to track the Moon's daily transit through your chart. The Moon will visit every house in your chart every month. You'll begin to learn a little about predictive astrology just

Time Zone	Number of hours to subtract from GMT for North American locations:	
	Standard Time	*Daylight Time*
Atlantic	−4	−3
Eastern	−5	−4
Central	−6	−5
Mountain	−7	−6
Pacific	−8	−7

Chart 4. Time Zone Conversions

by doing this, and within a few months you'll see a pattern begin to emerge. On some days you'll be almost consistently upbeat, and on others you'll want companionship or be in the mood to see friends or shop. Keep a diary so you can refer to it when you later begin to study predictive astrology.

Using your chart and an ephemeris for the current month, write outside the chart wheel the dates when the Moon will be (by sign) in each house. If you're using an ephemeris from a book, then the times when the Moon enters and departs each sign will be listed as either noon or midnight GMT (look for this information on the cover of the ephemeris), so you will need to subtract the appropriate number of hours for a North American location (see chart 4). Because of this, the date when the Moon changes signs might actually be the day prior to what is listed in the ephemeris. If you're using a computer program to create an ephemeris, you can set it for your time zone.

I find a noon GMT ephemeris to be the most useful when looking at the Moon's transits because it results in a morning (a.m.) time when the time zone adjustment is made.

Take a few minutes every evening to jot notes in your astrological diary about how you

felt that day and about any activities or outstanding events that occurred. Then compare your impressions to the transiting Moon's position in your chart. You'll probably see a pattern during the approximately two and a half days that the Moon is in each house, and you'll certainly see one if you do this for several months. Take special note of the days when the Moon is at the same point as a planet in a house. They're likely to be especially eventful.

Now that you're familiar with the basics of astrology, you're ready to take an in-depth look at the signs, planets, houses, and aspects. There is a chapter on each of these. In the last chapter you'll learn how to read, or synthesize, a chart. Chart synthesis is the art of blending all the astrological symbolism to discover the many facets of your personality as well as your strengths, talents, interests, and challenges. Be sure to also look at the appendices. There you will find information about additional astrological factors, the branches of astrology, astrological organizations, and websites where you can get a free birth chart. There also is an extensive suggested reading list and glossary, plus a list of glyphs on the inside back cover.

CHAPTER TWO

THE SIGNS

SUN SIGNS

What exactly is a Sun sign? It's where the Sun was when you were born. That's it. This sign has taken on an almost larger-than-life significance in astrology because it's easy to identify. All you need is your birth month and day. This is one reason for the popularity of Sun sign horoscope columns.

Your Sun sign is very important because it represents your basic ego and identity. Some people discover that their Sun sign is a completely accurate description of their personality. Others identify with some of the traits but not others, and a few feel they're quite different from their Sun sign. Doubters, of course, cite this as proof that astrology is nothing more than amusement and call it a pseudoscience.

There's a simple explanation for why you may not reflect all the traits of your Sun sign. There are ten planets in your chart, each of which contributes to your personality. That's one reason. But there are two others that are far more important. The Ascendant, or rising sign, is the outward expression of your personality, and it is often a dominant personality component; it can be determined only by calculating your chart for the exact date, time, and place you were born. (You'll learn more about this in chapter 4.) Once you know your Ascendant, you should read the Sun sign section for that sign, as it will tell you more about your personality. The other factor, and one that's tied directly to the Sun, is that another planet may have been very close to your Sun when you were born. Your Sun thus will take on some of the characteristics of this planet and the sign it rules. (You'll learn more about this in chapter 5.) For example, if the Sun was close to Pluto when you were born, then you would have some of the traits of Scorpio, the sign that Pluto rules. But if you had two or three planets in the same sign as your Sun sign, then your personality would be much more true to your Sun sign.

There's another factor that's influential in some people's personalities. If you were born near the beginning or end of your Sun sign period, then you were born "on the cusp" of the sign, as the Sun was transitioning from one sign to the next. For example, if the Sun enters Taurus on April 20 at 6:08 a.m. in Chicago (Central Daylight Time), then anyone born at that time and in that place at 6:08 a.m. or later is a Taurus. Anyone born in that location on the same date but before that time is an Aries. Cuspal birthdays generally are considered to be those that occur within about two or three days of when the Sun changes signs.

If yours is a cuspal birthday, then you probably will have some characteristics of both signs. In this case, the only way you can determine your true Sun sign is by calculating your chart.

Elements and Qualities

Every sign has an element and a quality. These represent the basic energy of the sign, and many of the characteristics associated with each sign are derived from these. No two signs have the same element and quality. The elements are also called *triplicities*, and the qualities are also called *modes* or *quadruplicities*.

There are four elements—fire, earth, air, and water—and three qualities—cardinal, fixed, and mutable. You should become very familiar with these, as they are key components of astrology and useful in finding the connections between planets, which are called aspects.

The fire signs are Aries, Leo, and Sagittarius. They're energetic, adventuresome, outgoing, enthusiastic, and optimistic. People with a strong fire emphasis are often leaders and risk takers, with a can-do attitude. They also can be impatient, egotistical, and self-centered.

The earth signs are Taurus, Virgo, and Capricorn. These signs are steadfast, determined, realistic, and down-to-earth. A strong earth emphasis indicates common sense and is usually excellent for attaining material success. These people can be practical to a fault and so cautious that they may miss out on opportunities.

The air signs are Gemini, Libra, and Aquarius. They're the thinkers, mentally oriented and intellectual; they specialize in ideas and communication. Air signs are intuitive, detached, and at times aloof and difficult to get to know.

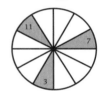

The water signs are Cancer, Scorpio, and Pisces. These sensitive, emotional signs are associated with psychic ability, compassion, and creativity. People with a strong water emphasis often are moody, reflective, and protective of their emotions.

The cardinal signs are Aries, Cancer, Libra, and Capricorn. These people have high energy and initiative and are self-starters. They like change and anything new, but they also can be impatient and impulsive and fail to complete what they start.

The fixed signs are Taurus, Leo, Scorpio, and Aquarius. People with fixed signs tend to dislike change unless it's initiated by them. They have excellent follow-through and use their determination to achieve goals and overall life success. They can be as stubborn as they are determined.

The mutable signs are Gemini, Virgo, Sagittarius, and Pisces. These are go-with-the-flow people who adapt easily and quickly to any situation. They are comfortable with change, but can spread themselves too thin and be surrounded by half-completed projects.

These are some of the characteristics of the signs when the elements and qualities are combined:

Aries, cardinal fire: courage, initiative, impatient, impulsive, competitive, high energy

Taurus, fixed earth: stable, stubborn, determined, lazy, conservative, devoted

Gemini, mutable air: sociable, flirtatious, scattered, restless, alert, adaptable

Cancer, cardinal water: emotional, domestic, nurturing, protective, intuitive, receptive

Leo, fixed fire: confident, loyal, stubborn, snobbish, selfish, generous, affectionate

Virgo, mutable earth: practical, critical, reserved, discriminating, dependable, intuitive

Libra, cardinal air: people person, cooperative, impatient, fair, vain, dependent

Scorpio, fixed water: stubborn, relentless, emotional, distrustful, resilient

Sagittarius, mutable fire: freedom-loving, optimistic, honest, spendthrift, indulgent

Capricorn, cardinal earth: ambitious, conservative, responsible, pessimistic, patient

Aquarius, fixed air: independent, rebellious, aloof, inventive, intellectual

Pisces, mutable water: compassionate, sensitive, impressionable, impractical, self-absorbed

Masculine and Feminine Signs

The signs are classified as masculine or feminine (figure 9). This has no relationship to gender. A man can have a feminine Sun sign and be just as masculine as any other man, and a woman can have a masculine Sun sign and be very feminine. Some astrologers refer to these as positive (masculine) and negative (feminine), but these descriptors are also misleading.

Basically, the masculine signs are more extroverted and the feminine signs are more introverted. This is astrological tradition, even though some of them, such as Venus-ruled Libra, which is a masculine sign, hardly seem to fit

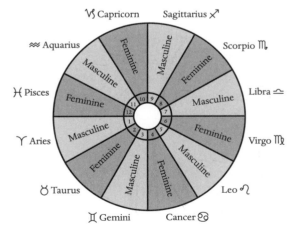

Figure 9. Masculine and Feminine Signs

the category. The masculine and feminine signs alternate, beginning with Aries.

The masculine signs are Aries, Gemini, Leo, Libra, Sagittarius, and Aquarius.

The feminine signs are Taurus, Cancer, Virgo, Scorpio, Capricorn, and Pisces.

Polarities

The polarities are signs that are opposite each other (figure 10). For example, Aries is opposite Libra, and Taurus is opposite Scorpio. Although these signs in some respects are opposite in their characteristics, the real significance is that they complement each other. What one sign has, its polar opposite lacks, and vice versa. Yet they also share some of the same characteristics and thus are able to relate to one another. They also can learn a lot about life from each other. Most people attract people whose sign is the polar opposite of their Sun or rising (Ascendant) sign. There's a lot of truth to the adage that opposites attract. The polarities are:

Aries/Libra
Taurus/Scorpio
Gemini/Sagittarius
Cancer/Capricorn
Leo/Aquarius
Virgo/Pisces

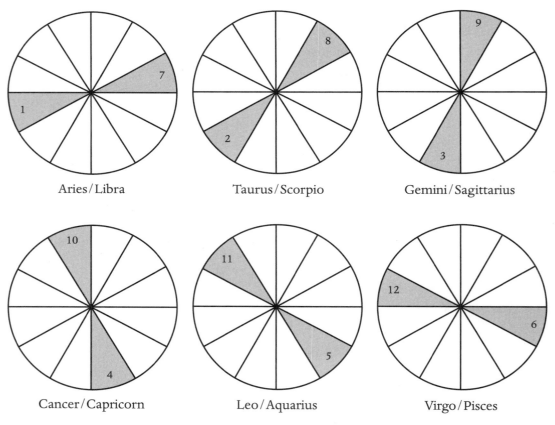

Aries/Libra   Taurus/Scorpio   Gemini/Sagittarius

Cancer/Capricorn   Leo/Aquarius   Virgo/Pisces

Figure 10. Sign Polarities

Decanates

Each 30° sign is divided into three 10° sections called *decanates* (figure 11 and chart 5). These are used extensively in Vedic, or Indian, astrology, and by some Western astrologers. Decanates add another interesting dimension to sign interpretation, primarily with the Sun and Ascendant, that seems to be valid from my experience.

The first ten degrees of a sign are ruled by that sign, the second ten degrees are ruled by the next sign of the same element, and the third ten degrees are ruled by the third sign of the same element. For example, the first decanate of Taurus is Taurus, the second decanate is Virgo, and the third decanate is Capricorn, representing the three earth signs. For Virgo, the first decanate is Virgo, the second is Capricorn, and the third is Taurus.

A first-decanate Virgo (a person born with his or her Sun between 0° and 10° Virgo) is thus a "true" Virgo, displaying all the Virgo characteristics in their purest form. A second-decanate Virgo (Sun between 11° and 20° Virgo) has a Capricorn influence and is thus more ambitious and concerned about status than a traditional Virgo. A third-decanate Virgo (Sun between 21° and 30° Virgo), with a Taurus influence, is more determined and stubborn than a traditional Virgo.

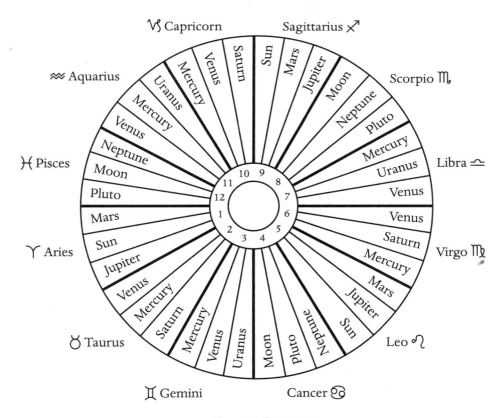

Figure 11. Decanates

Sign	First Decanate 0°–10°	Second Decanate 11°–20°	Third Decanate 21°–30°
Aries ♈	Mars ♂	Sun ☉	Jupiter ♃
Taurus ♉	Venus ♀	Mercury ☿	Saturn ♄
Gemini ♊	Mercury ☿	Venus ♀	Uranus ♅
Cancer ♋	Moon ☽	Pluto ♇	Neptune ♆
Leo ♌	Sun ☉	Jupiter ♃	Mars ♂
Virgo ♍	Mercury ☿	Saturn ♄	Venus ♀
Libra ♎	Venus ♀	Uranus ♅	Mercury ☿
Scorpio ♏	Pluto ♇	Neptune ♆	Moon ☽
Sagittarius ♐	Jupiter ♃	Mars ♂	Sun ☉
Capricorn ♑	Saturn ♄	Venus ♀	Mercury ☿
Aquarius ♒	Uranus ♅	Mercury ☿	Venus ♀
Pisces ♓	Neptune ♆	Moon ☽	Pluto ♇

Chart 5. The Decanates

You've already learned a lot about astrology and the basic traits of the signs as revealed through the elements, qualities, polarities, decanates, and masculine / feminine nature. This background is an excellent foundation for the next step—learning about the signs in more detail.

Take the time to study the first page for each Sun sign in this chapter. Each is a synopsis of the qualities of that sign that you can refer to over and over as you continue on your astrological journey. You'll also find listed some famous people born under that sign. By observing them during media events, you'll soon be able to spot characteristics associated with their Sun signs.

You can do something similar with the common things ruled by each sign. Think astrology as you go about your daily life, and begin to associate objects and events with the signs. For example, the next time you chop garlic, think of Aries, which rules knives and garlic. Libra rules jewelry, Capricorn rules watches, and Gemini rules mail. You can do the same with colors, flowers, and gemstones.

In addition to listing general personality traits, each Sun sign section includes information on relationships, career, and money.

Once you know your Ascendant sign (from a chart calculated for your exact birth date, time, and place), study that Sun sign section for additional insights into your personality. You might find the description of your Ascendant sign to be truer of you than that of your Sun sign on an outward, everyday level as you interact with people and your environment.

HOW TO SPOT AN ARIES

Scar on head or face
Head and/or body lean forward
Impatience

Glyph: ♈

Symbol: the Ram

Ruling planet: Mars

Natural house: first house

Element: fire

Quality: cardinal

Body areas: head, eyes, face

Gemstone: diamond

Color: red

Flower: geranium

Key phrase: I am

Keyword: initiative

Personality traits: assertive, aggressive, leader, dynamic, pioneering, confident, risk taker, impatient, energetic, adventurous, daredevil, selfish, action-oriented

Countries/regions: Denmark, England, Israel, Palestine, Germany

Cities: Leicester and Birmingham, England; Berlin, Germany; Florence and Naples, Italy; Krakow, Poland; Marseilles, France

Common things ruled by Aries: furnace, fireplace, chimney, hat, stove/oven, garlic, knife, mustard, onion, surgery, pepper, acne, rhubarb, insomnia, thistle, tool, cactus, sheep

Famous people: Thomas Jefferson, Sarah Jessica Parker, Reese Witherspoon, Harry Houdini, Bob Woodward, Nancy Pelosi, Warren Beatty, David Letterman, Quentin Tarantino, Al Gore, Kate Hudson, Norah Jones, Rosie O'Donnell, Keira Knightley, Jennifer Garner

Major strengths: leadership, confidence, courage

Major challenges: impulsive, impatient, limited follow-through

Think spring. Ice melts, rivers flow, plants emerge, everything is fresh and new. That's Aries, the first sign of the zodiac. Spring begins when the Sun enters Aries on the spring equinox.

Aries is refreshing, with a naiveté that's both charming and invigorating. The Aries motto, "I can," sums up the essence of this sign, which embodies its adventuresome, risk-taking, impulsive qualities. "Why waste time thinking about it?" Aries asks. "Just do it!" As the first sign of the zodiac, Aries might lack wisdom, but it makes up for it with initiative. That's evident in the Aries glyph, Υ, which is the horns of the Ram, the Aries symbol. Aries rams ahead with zesty enthusiasm.

As the first of the fire signs, Aries is the leader of the leadership pack, and the same can be said of its quality, cardinal. Together, the fire element and the cardinal quality add up to the ultimate live wire, with high energy, drive, instant action, and motivation. And Mars, Aries' ruling planet, adds more fuel to the fiery nature of this sign.

Want to conquer new territory? Start a new project or jump-start an old one? Call an Aries to get things moving. Just don't expect an Aries to hang around to see how it all turns out. If you need a lift or a fresh perspective, do lunch with an Aries. Just being in the presence of one will change your attitude to "can-do."

Aries is all about Aries. It's about I rather than we, about self rather than a duo, trio, group, or the world. Aries views everything from a personal perspective. Although Aries can be self-centered, that's really not what this sign is all about. It's more that Aries sees everything in terms of self: will it help me, will I profit from it, can I have it and can I have it now?

The Aries people I know are true go-getters and leaders. They're also fearless, or at least that's what those who don't know them believe. Like everyone else, they have real fears, but they're outweighed by a stronger urge: risk taking that's sort of an I-dare-myself-to-do-it energy. And every one of them expects to succeed and does, more often than not.

Look to the house in your chart that has Aries on the cusp. That's where you experience this sign's energy. Whether it's money, romance, friendship, or something else, you're direct about it, willing to take risks, confident, and impulsive. You also take action based on what's best for you.

Aries Sun Sign

As an Aries, you're first in line—literally, figuratively, and zodiacally. Chances are, you were among the first to walk and the first to boldly explore your ever-widening environment, from home to neighborhood to city and the world. Where other people hesitate, you charge, embracing every new experience with the freshness of your springtime sign, the first in the zodiac. You're a pioneer and a natural leader.

The original self-starter, you're highly motivated and competitive, and often accept a challenge—or a dare—just to rack up another success. That's great within reason, but bravery and boldness aren't all it takes to succeed. Any accomplished general, athlete, or entrepreneur (many of whom share your Sun sign) knows that true success has its roots in planning, training/education, and experience, which anyone can do. What makes you unique and successful

is a willingness to take the *calculated* risk that less courageous people shy away from.

A calculated risk, however, is far different from the impulsive (and sometimes reckless) actions associated with Aries. Seize every one of the many genuine opportunities that come your way—after you've thoroughly considered the potential downsides. Make the odds work in your favor, rather than take the 50–50 chance that could trigger a firestorm and consequences best avoided. Limit the number of lessons learned the hard way.

Quick thinking can get you out of a jam in a flash. Making snap decisions about life's most important matters, however, can backfire just as quickly. There's also a fine line between competition and combativeness, assertion and aggression, and you can be as tactless as you are charming, loyal, and generous. You'll get further by wisely choosing your battles—not all are worth fighting.

You move through life with high energy and enthusiasm, and your self-confidence instantly puts others at ease. That's the ideal, but because you hate to wait for anybody or anything, it can be tempting to push others to meet your timeline. Learn to be patient with people and to respect their individuality. Not everyone is as perfect a match for today's fast-paced, instantaneous world as you are.

Your lack of follow-through is both your greatest strength and greatest weakness. You love whatever is fresh and new and exciting, and want to be on top of the latest news, trends, and happenings, at the center of the action. Start-ups are your specialty, and you're content to leave the rest to those better suited to follow-through and completion. Leadership is a real asset in the right situation, but good leaders are also good followers.

Relationships

Loyal and warmhearted, you're devoted to your family, friends, and partner. You delight in helping others with advice and good works, yet it's equally vital to you to maintain your independence. Doing both can be quite a juggling act, but because you want it all, you're more than up to the task.

You know instinctively how to romance a date or your partner of many years. Only the royal treatment is good enough for someone you care about, and doing that pleases you more than receiving the same in return. As much as you enjoy welcoming new love into your life, you focus on one relationship at a time and are faithful to your date du jour. At times, it can be tough to let go and move on, but your adventuresome spirit—and the thrill of someone new—eventually prevails.

Long-lasting love, however, is entirely different. What you seek is a true partner, someone who's supportive yet also understands your need to follow your own path. A meeting of the minds is as important as one of the heart.

You're also devoted to loved ones—parents, siblings, and extended family—and the desire for a family of your own could motivate you to trade in your free-spirited lifestyle for a more stable one. For most born under your sign, family life is ultimately a stronger draw than going it alone.

Career

You might leave the impression that you're here today, gone tomorrow, concerned only with the immediate future. Nothing could be further from the truth. Aries is ambitious. Within you is a driving force to reach the top, where your sterling qualities shine brightly.

Getting there, however, could be a challenge. It all depends on you—your day-to-day decisions and keeping the end goal in sight. If promotion or perceived progress lags, your first thought might be to chase a new opportunity. That's okay if it's the right one and a step up, or will lead to one. Like a mountain climber, your surest route to the top is a series of well-planned moves, step by step.

Remember, too, that you can showcase your leadership ability at the lowest levels of your career. Lead by example—show others the way, motivate them, and be everyone's favorite team player. That, combined with knowledge and experience, is a formula for success.

Aries can excel in a wide variety of careers. You could be an exceptional business executive, entrepreneur, firefighter, athlete, surgeon, dentist or dental hygienist, machinist, or sculptor. Or you might find success in the military or construction trades.

Money

Although you have the occasional urge to splurge, it's not your norm except when in the company of close friends, loved ones, or a date you want to impress. It's your generous nature at its best and an expression of genuine caring.

You have a talent for making, managing, saving, and investing money, and tend to be more conservative than not. Generally thrifty, you willingly pay the price for what you want, but only if it's fair value.

Finances are one area in which you should definitely avoid the tendency to make snap decisions, especially with investments. Here, too, planning and long-term goals can net the highest yield.

You also have a knack for making money work for you. Research the market for the best terms and interest rates and then bargain for more. Real estate—or just owning your own home—could net you a handsome profit.

Bottom line: you have the potential to amass a fortune. Your net worth also could increase through a family legacy, and possibly a far larger one than you ever imagined.

HOW TO SPOT A TAURUS

Stocky

Moves slowly

Dimple

Glyph: ♉

Symbol: the Bull

Ruling planet: Venus

Natural house: second house

Element: earth

Quality: fixed

Body areas: throat, neck, vocal cords

Gemstone: emerald

Color: green

Flower: violet

Key phrase: I have

Keyword: possessive

Personality traits: patient, jealous, comfort- and pleasure-loving, stable, reliable, thrifty, practical, materialistic, thorough, steady, endurance, lazy, greedy, hard worker, planner, determined, common sense, logical

Countries/regions: Australia, Iran, the Netherlands, Ireland, Tasmania

Cities: Dublin, Ireland; Parma and Palermo, Italy; Rhodes, Greece; St. Louis, Missouri

Common things ruled by Taurus: money, copper, culture, artwork, purse, bank, storeroom, cattle, lily, pig, spinach, stock, wallet, wheat

Famous people: George Clooney, Bono, Cate Blanchett, Cher, Shirley MacLaine, Michelle Pfeiffer, Leonardo da Vinci, Tony Blair, Jack Nicholson, Sue Grafton, Barbra Streisand, David Beckham, Uma Thurman, Jessica Alba, Tim McGraw, Carmen Electra, Stephen Colbert, Mike Wallace

TAURUS

APRIL 19 TO MAY 20

Major strengths: determination, common sense, thoroughness

Major challenges: stubbornness, possessiveness, inflexibility

Where Aries gets things moving, Taurus says, "Okay, we need to get organized and develop an action plan." And where Taurus is involved, nothing goes unfinished. This fixed sign is the be-all and end-all of determination and more than a little stubborn. "Giving in" and "going with the flow" are not part of the Taurus vocabulary, unless of course Taurus makes that choice.

If you want a project completed, ask a Taurus, whose glyph (☐) is the head and horns of the Bull, the Taurus symbol. But be prepared to wait. Taurus represents the ultimate in patience and is steady and reliable. This sign plods along at an even pace, reaching the finish line in its own time, with everything in order. Taurus will not be rushed.

There's something very calming about Taurus energy. It can relax the most uptight, high-strung people just by being in the same space. And it's even better when a Taurus also talks because most have soothing voices. (Some of the most outstanding singers and broadcast media personalities have a strong Taurus influence.)

The Taurus motto is "I have"—life is about me and my resources. Taurus is thrifty, being a practical earth sign, but this sign's influence encompasses much more than money. Money is a security factor for Taurus, but so are possessions. Visit a Taurus and you'll see a home that's beautifully decorated with lovely furnishings. What you'll notice most, however, is all the "stuff"—collectibles, dishes, knickknacks, plants (Taurus is the sign of the green thumb), artwork, anything in silver, and more. The other thing you'll notice about a Taurus home is that it's designed for comfort. This is a comfort-loving sign, with a preference for comfort food and a set daily routine.

Every Taurus I know is a master shopper. They all find the most incredible deals on absolutely anything they want. And they never hesitate to bargain for an even better deal. They're the ones who say "take it or leave it" and never hesitate to walk away if the price isn't right. Shop with a Taurus next time and cash in on this energy.

Artwork and anything beautiful appeals to this Venus-ruled sign, which also is happiest when in a relationship. Venus is, after all, the love planet. The Taurus eye for quality and beauty extends to people as well as possessions.

The house in your chart with Taurus on the cusp is where you're practical and thorough but also slow, moving at your own pace. This is where your determination is strong and where you aim for completion. The areas associated with this house are fortunate overall, although you also can get too comfortable and resist change.

Taurus Sun Sign

You're something of an enigma in this fast-paced world, preferring the slow, steady approach. And why not? After all, you usually reach the finish line right on schedule and sometimes ahead of time. Whatever you do, you do thoroughly and completely, to the best of your ability.

You rarely, if ever, jump into anything. You first think things through, examining all the pros and cons, the potential benefits and pitfalls. Although you savor the planning process and the anticipation of a new challenge, this thoroughness has much to do with another of your strong traits: determination. Once committed to a goal, you persevere, surmounting obstacles

and difficulties that would deter even the bravest souls. Setting goals is thus not something you take lightly. Each goal is carefully considered for its success potential because you are reluctant to pursue any avenue that lacks a high probability of success. Patient to the max, you think nothing of working for years to get where you want to be.

You also know you're stubborn—the flip side of determination—and there are times when your mind is set and you absolutely refuse to budge. This is especially evident when anyone asks, pleads, or insists that you change your habits. Very set in your ways, you cherish routine and dislike circumstances that threaten your material or personal security and stability. Even when you know deep down that change is positive, you tend to cling to the familiar, to stay in a rut, rather than take a chance on something new. Adaptability is a trait to strive for.

Possessions and money in the bank (plus investment and retirement funds) boost your comfort level. Beautiful objects appeal to your artistic nature, and the homes of some Taureans are filled with collectibles, memorabilia, and knickknacks. "Packrat" is an apt description for many born under your sign. If you're among them, and clutter best describes your home décor, ask yourself why you feel compelled to save it all—even things that are no longer useful or usable. A cluttered environment often signals a cluttered mind and lifestyle. Simplify!

There's no sign quite so sensual as Taurus, which is the first of the earth signs (the others are Virgo and Capricorn). You're particularly attuned to the sense of touch and enjoy working with your hands. When shopping, you often judge the merits of a purchase partly by touch, and you won't sacrifice comfort for the latest fashion. You also have excellent visual senses, especially for color and art. Many Taureans have distinctive voices and musical talent.

Relationships

You're a devoted friend, partner, and family member and place high value on these relationships. Your concern for those you love is evident, and they appreciate your gentle, warmhearted people skills.

Your idealistic, compassionate side emerges with friends, and at times you put your own needs on hold in favor of theirs, doing all you can to make their lives easier. That's a wonderful quality, but also one that makes you vulnerable to less ethical people. Place your trust only in those who have earned it.

Venus, your ruler, is also the universal planet of love. You place a high premium on romance and commitment, both of which are vital to your well-being. But strong emotions can trigger possessiveness and even jealousy when you feel insecure in a close relationship. You attract and are attracted to potential partners who share these traits, so it's important to establish ground rules that foster independent lives within the union and a strong foundation of trust. Your relationship will be stronger for it.

Taureans cherish their families, and family life takes priority over all else for many born under this sign. Loyalty and pride run deep, and you go out of your way to give your loved ones only the best. If you're a parent, you aim to give your children every advantage. But in that role you're a worrier and can be critical and encourage an unrealistic level of perfection. Find the middle ground and let them explore and develop their strengths and talents, and allow them to make a few mistakes along the way.

Career

You strive for the same stability in your career as you do in every other area of life. That's reality for some Taureans but not for others. Career changes can be sudden and unexpected, which is unsettling at best, unless you're the initiator. You also have a knack for attracting opportunities. By following through with the most promising opportunities, you actually increase the odds for career stability and success—because then you're in control of your future. So you might want to skip the thought of a lifetime married to one specific career and job and instead pursue new avenues that pop up where you can maximize your skills and talents.

Harmony and a pleasant, congenial working environment are essential to job happiness. You also need mental stimulation, people contact, and the freedom to work at your own pace and be creative. A never-ending chain of pressure-filled deadlines is not for you. You're by far the best with follow-through and will see every task through to completion if it's humanly possible.

When conditions are optimal, you're a hard worker and you feel valued and appreciated. Otherwise, you become discouraged. Even so, you resist necessary job changes because of strong ties with coworkers. Putting yourself and your best interests first, however, is seldom a bad idea; move on when the time is right for you.

Because you enjoy working with your hands, you could find success as a massage therapist, florist, or hair stylist. If you have artistic talent or are interested in the arts, you might excel as an artist, singer, interior decorator, or art dealer, or in any number of fields in the theater or art or history museums. Financial careers interest many Taureans, who use their skills as mortgage or loan officers, tellers, and investment bankers. Others find their niche in the retail field.

Money

You're naturally in tune with money matters. Common sense and a powerful drive for material and emotional security govern everything from your financial decisions to investments to your work life and even purchases.

Thrifty to the max, you have a sixth sense for finding bargains. Value is the determining factor, and even with millions in the bank you won't buy unless the price is right. You also buy only the best and would rather own one expensive item—purchased on sale—than several of lesser quality.

But if you're among the packrat set, your budget can get lost in the desire to snap up every good deal you find. If that's true of you, set a monthly limit for must-have bargains and stick to it. Otherwise, one day you'll awaken to discover every closet, drawer, and storage space filled with what have become useless purchases, some with the price tags still attached. A bargain unused isn't a bargain—it's only clutter.

Luck is part of your financial equation. You're often at the right place at the right time to cash in on potentially lucrative investments, and can successfully negotiate a higher salary, incentives, and benefits. You also usually latch on to favorable interest rates more often than not.

Many Taureans accumulate sizable assets in their lifetimes, and gain through an inheritance from a family member or friend.

HOW TO SPOT A GEMINI

Long fingers and/or legs and arms
Talkative
Hand gestures

Glyph: ♊

Symbol: the Twins

Ruling planet: Mercury

Natural house: third house

Element: air

Quality: mutable

Body areas: lungs, arms, hands

Gemstone: tourmaline

Colors: bright colors

Flower: lily of the valley

Key phrase: I think

Keyword: versatility

Personality traits: witty, lively, curious, restless, intelligent, multitasker, fickle, flirtatious, inquisitive, nervous, superficial, short attention span, scattered, communicator, curious, high-strung, fun-loving, quick thinker

Countries/regions: Belgium, northeast coast of Africa, Egypt, Wales, Sardinia

Cities: London, England; Nuremberg, Germany; Metz, France; San Francisco, California

Common things ruled by Gemini: errand, vehicle, mercury, mail, butterfly, book, bicycle, commute, neighbor, contract, sibling, desk, escalator, mechanic, monkey, paper, road, train, twins, walking, writing, speaking, puzzle

Famous people: John F. Kennedy, Nicole Kidman, Clint Eastwood, Mark Wahlberg, Angelina Jolie, Natalie Portman, Marilyn Monroe, Drew Carey, Donald Trump, George H. W. Bush, Paul McCartney, Barbara Bush, Steffi Graf, Johnny Depp, Heidi Klum, Prince

GEMINI

MAY 20 TO JUNE 21

Major strengths: versatility, curiosity, communication

Major challenges: high-strung, inconsistent, restless

Need to know something? Ask a Gemini. Communication is the essence of this air sign, which specializes in information, writing, and speaking. Gemini is also about learning and the thought process, just like Mercury, its ruling planet. This sign's motto is, appropriately, "I think," and this is what Gemini does best. The Gemini brain is highly active, with synapses firing at a rapid pace, processing an astounding amount of information. And a Gemini brain usually can think about two (or more) things at once.

Every time you read a book, newspaper, magazine, or web page, run errands, talk with someone, send an e-mail, or play a game, you're doing a Gemini activity. And a true Gemini can do several of these things at once, just like its symbol, the Twins. All this activity also represents the mutable quality of this sign, which takes most everything in stride and is highly adaptable to changing conditions.

Gemini is the sign that appears to be, and attempts to be, everywhere at once in order to satisfy an insatiable curiosity, be in the middle of everything, and know everything that's going on. The more variety, the better, is how Gemini views life. So it's easy for people with a strong Gemini influence to spread themselves too thin. Gemini also is known for scattered energy, nervous tension, and a short attention span.

People with a strong Gemini influence don't like to take life too seriously. They prefer the lighter side, with plenty of socializing, where their wit, charm, and people skills make an impact. And Gemini is the consummate flirt.

It's tough to keep up with a restless, inquisitive Gemini. They're constantly on the go, in motion, walking, thinking, gesturing with their hands, tapping their feet, and talking—all with marvelous physical and hand-eye coordination.

One Gemini I know is a fabulous joke teller and an excellent public speaker, which are two talents associated with this sign. Two other Gemini friends, however, are nonstop talkers who rarely listen; they have no idea how to have a give-and-take conversation, which is one of the less-favorable traits of this sign.

The house in your chart with Gemini on the cusp is where your curiosity comes alive. This is also the area of life that you think and talk about a lot, and where you can quickly become overprogrammed and overcommitted. There are also many changes associated with this house and its affairs.

Gemini Sun Sign

Multitasking is one of Gemini's greatest talents. In fact, boredom sets in when life requires anything else. You prefer to be here, there, and everywhere all at the same time, and Gemini is the only sign that comes close to literally being in two places at once. Actually, your mind is often in one location, and your physical presence in another, giving you the best of both. Yet you can focus intensely for short periods of time, and grasp as much or more than others do in twice as much time.

Curiosity is another of your strengths, which makes you a perfect fit for the information age. Information fuels your mind and body, and you're forever in search of the latest news in your immediate environment and the world at large. Geminis are usually avid readers and conversationalists, and many are excellent public speakers or writers. But some slip into a negative pattern in which they talk far more than they listen, and prefer gossip to facts.

People often perceive you as an expert in many subjects and fields of study. What they don't know is that your vast data bank includes bits and pieces of this and that, as well as a wider spectrum of information about any area that interests you. Although you might view this as a lack of depth and even envy those who possess true expertise, you're actually way ahead of the crowd. It's your true nature to be able to do many things well, rather than just one or a few.

You're also clever and a quick study. You remember what you learn and can easily apply knowledge gained in one area to another, unrelated task.

As with everyone, however, there are times when your greatest strengths also can be your greatest challenges. For you, this involves blending your many talents and interests into a unified effort in order to reach your full potential. For example, you could combine computer knowledge with verbal skills for a career in tech support.

Geminis are noted for their youthful appearance, wit, and charm, as well as their adaptability. Sidestepping obstacles comes naturally to you, and you're stimulated by change, action, and opportunity. Novelties catch your interest, and you're often among the first to acquire the latest techno-gadget.

A true free spirit, you resist conformity unless it suits your purposes, and you excel at finding an alternate path around rules and regulations that might limit your individuality. Freedom of movement, both physical and mental, is extremely important to your well-being.

Relationships

Geminis are fun and flirtatious, carefree and lighthearted, popular and clever. That's an ideal formula for an active social life that includes many friends. People tend to pop in and out of your life, creating a nonstop supply of fresh faces to satisfy your curiosity about human nature.

You seek mental stimulation in a partnership, as well as someone who shares your free-spirited, impromptu approach to life. Action and adventure are your secrets to romantic success and keeping the love alive. You might choose instead to remain single (at least until later in life) so you can delight in each new love interest who comes your way. One thing is sure: when a relationship ends, you're quick to move on in search of someone new.

Gemini's mental focus and tendency to intellectualize feelings may also contribute to a reluctance to commit to a partnership. You're far more comfortable with ideas than feelings, which can interfere with experiencing love at its fullest depth. That's not right nor wrong—it's the way you are. With the right partner, though, someone whose approach is the same, you can have a world-class romance.

Gemini parents are closely aligned with their children and see them more as peers than as the next generation. That's partly because you're the kid who never totally grows up, welcoming each day with the curiosity and optimism of youth. Your connection with your children is more intellectual than emotional, and you do all you can to provide them with a stress-free and opportunity-filled childhood.

Career

Your toughest career challenge is deciding what you want to do and where to direct your many talents. Where others are content to focus on a single area and develop depth of expertise, you're attracted by new interests and opportunities that seem to materialize out of thin air. Job- and career-hopping might keep boredom at bay but are essentially nonproductive for the long term.

So what's a Gemini to do? Even you have identifiable strengths and weaknesses, likes and dislikes, and outstanding skills—in not just a few but several areas. Zero in on and differentiate them from the hundreds of topics, interests, and leisure-time activities, and find the career that maximizes all you have to offer. If another (or a related) career choice is a close second, develop it on a freelance or weekend basis, as many Geminis do. Look also for areas that you can blend into a single rewarding career, such as writing and construction, or the computer field and public speaking.

Your versatility and restless mind require a job and work environment with plenty of activity, communication, and a fast pace, where you can multitask your way to success. You need the freedom to establish your own work priorities without constant supervision. Boring tasks and micromanagement will quickly send you in search of something new. What interests you, though, brings out your powers of concentration.

The communication field is a natural career choice for Geminis, but any field that requires strong communication skills is one in which you can excel. You might want to consider a career in computer or communication technology, news, acting, sales, or publishing. The transportation field appeals to many Geminis, and others find success working with their hands as nail technicians or in the construction trades.

Money

You have more financial sense than many people give you credit for. Putting it into practice, however, can be a challenge at times. You're prone to spending sprees, particularly when you need a mental or emotional boost. Think before you splurge, especially on credit, which can quickly get out of hand. Your financial security needs are better satisfied through savings and investments for the long term, not through monthly payments on high-interest credit cards.

You have above-average income potential if you successfully manage your career life, and earnings are likely to rise later in life. Until then, you could be underpaid unless you plan for steady and continuing advancement with increasing responsibilities.

Real estate could be an income source, especially if you have do-it-yourself skills. You also could turn a hobby or another home-based business into a lucrative side income. But you should start slowly and keep your investment low. Slow but steady growth is your best avenue to financial security.

HOW TO SPOT A CANCER

Solicitous
Talks about family
Moody

Glyph: ♋

Symbol: the Crab

Ruling planet: Moon

Natural house: fourth house

Element: water

Quality: cardinal

Body areas: chest, breasts, stomach

Gemstone: pearl

Colors: white, silver

Flower: larkspur

Key phrase: I feel

Keyword: receptive

Personality traits: protective, nurturing, security-conscious, family-oriented, moody, psychic, sympathetic, tenacious, clingy, cautious, emotional, loving, shy, caring, overly sensitive

Countries/regions: West Africa, Algeria, Scotland, New Zealand, Paraguay

Cities: Berne, Switzerland; Cadiz, Spain; Manchester, England; New York City; Milan; Amsterdam; Tokyo; Stockholm

Common things ruled by Cancer: silver, chalk, cooking, crab, black onyx, boat, water, river, lake, bathing, cabbage, melon, family, sink, bathtub, shrimp, female, laundry, nutrition, motherhood, plumbing

Famous people: Ross Perot, Meryl Streep, Tom Cruise, Tom Hanks, Pamela Anderson, George W. Bush, Ringo Starr, Princess Diana, John Quincy Adams, John Jacob Astor, Bill Cosby, Nelson Rockefeller, Lindsay Lohan, Jessica Simpson

Major strengths: nurturing, persistent, intuitive

Major challenges: sensitive, moody, changeable

Cancer is the "mom" sign. It's also the home and family sign. Cancer is all about nurturing, caring, and empathy. It's also about hugs and feeling that someone cares. It's that warm and cozy feeling that comes from being in our own space, enjoying the comforts and safety of home.

Cancer's motto, "I feel," sums up the emotional qualities associated with this sign and its ruling planet, the Moon. Emotions fluctuate with daily experiences, events, situations, and the people you encounter; you feel differently about each—up, down, and in between. So it goes with the territory that Cancer is a moody sign. It's also an intuitive and receptive one, easily picking up on current vibrations, a trait of this sign's water element. At times, Cancer can be overly sensitive to small slights and upsets.

Because of this emphasis on feelings, people sometimes think Cancer is a weak sign. Not so! The essence of Cancer is in its symbol, the Crab. A crab moves sideways, steering clear of any potential difficulties, and when it feels threatened, it retreats into its hard, protective shell. Cancer, the person, does the same. But when riled, out come the claws, especially when someone targets a loved one.

Cancer and the Moon also represent security. Anyone with a strong Cancer influence needs financial as well as emotional security. This is a money sign, and every Cancer I've encountered strives for a sizable bank balance as well as an impressive portfolio of investments. Some of them, however, never seem to know when to stop. They can have assets totaling six figures, seven figures, even ten figures, and they still feel financially insecure on some level.

I also know Cancers who are wonderful family people, who go out of their way to provide a loving home, and who are fabulous cooks. One client enrolled in a culinary school just because she liked to cook and wanted to learn more. Today, she is a chef at an upscale resort, doing what she loves and being paid well for it—definitely a happy Cancer.

The house in your chart that has Cancer on the cusp represents the people or things that touch your heart and your emotions and of which you're very protective. You have an emotional investment there, as well as strong instincts. Change is a given in matters related to this house, although you're usually quick to take action to resolve challenges because this is where you need to feel secure.

Cancer Sun Sign

With your Sun in Cancer, the quest for security is one of your main life motivations and the underlying principle that guides your actions and decisions. Physical and financial security are the outward manifestations of your basic inner drive: emotional security. Protecting that side of yourself is paramount. You are reluctant to reveal much of yourself partly because you're somewhat secretive and partly because you're particularly sensitive to disapproval and negative energy.

Yet for all your sensitivity, few outsiders are aware of your internal vulnerability. With it comes an incredible inner strength that sees you through difficult situations, all with the outward appearance of supreme confidence. Usually one of the last to argue or jump into a confrontation, you rarely hesitate when it's necessary to protect your interests or those in your inner circle. You prefer a passive yet persistent approach, and can outlast even the stiffest competition in time.

Cancer is the universal sign of home and family, which you strive for both literally and figuratively. In the context of the outer world—friendship and business—you create a family group that emulates your personal one, ever conscious of the needs of others. You remember favors and kindnesses, sometimes for years, until you have the opportunity to do the same in return. But you also almost never give anyone who has crossed you a second chance.

Your reactions in any given situation depend on your changeable moods, which vary from upbeat and cheerful to feeling low and everything in between. When you're at your best, you're friendly, caring, and affectionate, and go out of your way to make others feel at ease. Essentially a people person, you periodically need time alone to recenter and think about your feelings.

Because you're so receptive and impressionable, you easily pick up vibrations from other people and your immediate environment. These nearly tangible feelings can color your mood and outlook and bring you down as quickly as they can uplift you. Your intuition is strong, and you often sense what people are thinking and whether their intentions are honorable.

You're imaginative and creative in every facet of your life, and particularly enjoy using your talents to create a warm, comfortable home. If your work life is office-centered, or even if it's not, you create the same comfortable environment there that makes others feel at ease.

People can underestimate you at times, especially those who perceive you as modest and unassuming. Nothing could be further from the truth once you set your sights on a goal. Then little can deter you from your objective. You can be tenacious and action-oriented when you want to be—a dynamic leader who takes charge.

Relationships

Family ties are the most important relationships in your life. You tend your "flock"—partner and immediate and extended family—with loving care and concern. Time with loved ones is a priority, and you go out of your way to create a warm and welcoming home for family and friends.

Your nurturing instinct is strong, and most Cancers feel incomplete without children of their own. As a parent, you're fully involved in your children's lives from newborn through adulthood. When necessary (and even at times when it's not), you put your own needs on hold to give your children every opportunity possible and to ensure they experience all the benefits of a wholesome family life.

However, some Cancers overdo it. Too much involvement can negate the positives when nurturing becomes "smothering." Even the best parents can't shield a child from all of life's disappointments and lessons. Nor should they. Knowledge gained through experience is invaluable, so steel yourself and let your children live the challenges as well as the successes. And when the time comes, let them fly on their own.

Some Cancers delay commitment or having a family until they've established their career and/or financial stability. For others, it simply takes a while to meet a soul mate, which is probably how you would describe your partner.

Your ideal mate shares your need for financial and material security, and is likely to be practical and ambitious. But compromise and understanding are necessary to achieve a workable balance. Where you're emotional, your partner is likely to be reserved, and his or her career life can limit family time. View it as a trade-off for the security you desire.

A few close friends are also part of your family circle, and you share your love and loyalty with them as you do with your family. They're a joy in your life, contributing to your overall well-being and security. Once friends arrive in your inner circle, you never let them go, and do all you can to maintain close ties. You remember kindnesses and repay them whenever and however possible, sometimes years later.

Career

In the right career and the right environment, you excel as a leader and in supervisory positions. But you're also quick to move on if compensation and advancement fall short of expectations. Approval and a paycheck to match are necessities.

Although self-protection is a strong theme in your life, you're more willing to take risks in your career. Some Cancers are successful entrepreneurs, where their people and financial skills net positive results.

With the Moon as your ruling planet (the Moon is the planet associated with Cancer), you excel in any career that has you in touch with the public. Government service appeals to some Cancers, and others find success in the food or hotel industry, real estate, the military, teaching, child care, or pediatrics. You might use your creativity and money sense to establish a home-based business as an artisan or caterer.

A positive, upbeat atmosphere is a must for job happiness. You also need an environment that encourages learning and in which you have the freedom to structure your day and tasks mostly as you wish. You have a tendency to take on more than your fair share of the workload. It's fine and admirable to help others, but don't let them take advantage of you and your protective nature.

Lucky breaks expand job opportunities, and you easily spot trends in the making. That's partly because of your strong sixth sense. You also have a knack for expanding job responsibilities and, in essence, can create your own position with a job description that incorporates all your skills and talents.

Money

You're more of a saver than a spender, thrifty but not miserly. Because only the best will do, you frequent stores that offer deep discounts and upscale labels at greatly reduced prices. It's a matter of pride to you to get the most for every dollar, and you delight in bargaining for more.

Some of the wealthiest people born under your sign never feel a hundred percent financially secure, so you're in good company. It's not too much of an exaggeration to say that even a bank

account that stretches from here to infinity isn't quite enough to ease your mind. Money is safety, and your confidence level rises in proportion to your assets.

Not one to use credit unless it's to your advantage, you have a natural aversion to debt. You will, however, make it work for you at times, such as when a low interest rate is a wiser choice than reducing a bank balance, or when you can "use" the bank's money by buying on credit and paying the monthly bill in full. The major exception is home ownership, which is high on your priority list. There you see the value in a mortgage, although you'll pay it off sooner rather than later if you can.

You also can do well with investments, and long-term holdings appeal more to you than short-term ones. Although "risk-averse" aptly describes you, from time to time you can be tempted to be a little less cautious. Do so only after conducting your own research and weighing all the pros and cons.

In general, you're lucky in money matters, and realize unexpected gains throughout your life. Inheritance and winnings are possible.

HOW TO SPOT A LEO

Thick hair
Dramatic
Wears gold jewelry and clothing

Glyph: ♌

Symbol: the Lion

Ruling planet: Sun

Natural house: fifth house

Element: fire

Quality: fixed

Body area: heart

Gemstone: ruby

Colors: orange, gold, scarlet

Flower: marigold

Key phrase: I will

Keyword: illumination

Personality traits: affectionate, enthusiastic, leader, romantic, temperamental, dramatic, warmhearted, creative, pompous, loyal, show-off, outgoing, generous, egocentric, bossy, stubborn, self-centered

Countries/regions: Italy, France, Sicily, Romania

Cities: Bath and Bristol, England; Philadelphia, Pennsylvania; Rome; Chicago; Bombay, India; Madrid, Spain; Prague

Common things ruled by Leo: theater, gambling, citrus tree, dill, lion, stage, royalty, poppy, children, palace, party, sun porch, throne

Famous people: Martha Stewart, Bill Clinton, Halle Berry, Amelia Earhart, Ben Affleck, Louis Vuitton, Llewellyn George, Dorothy Hamill, Whitney Houston, Robert DeNiro, Jennifer Lopez, Antonio Banderas, Charlize Theron, Sandra Bullock

LEO

JULY 21 TO AUGUST 22

Major strengths: generous, warmhearted, creative

Major challenges: stubborn, bossy, self-centered

Leo represents the ego, and also a person's identity. People define themselves, in part, through their place in the world, whether in terms of a career, hobby, children, family, or their most recent fifteen minutes of fame. Some people have mega-sized, insatiable egos, while others are content with occasional praise. The point is that everyone has an identity and an ego that needs to be stroked. It's just that anyone with a strong Leo influence needs more strokes than most.

Leo does almost everything on a grand scale, with much drama. The showy, self-centered Leo is the stereotype of this sign, but there is much more to Leo than a starring role on a Broadway stage.

I know a couple of Leos who embody this sign's wonderful trait of generosity. Both share their time, talents, and resources with family and friends, albeit sometimes more than they should, and they always visit with a gift in hand. They're warm and loving people.

This sunshiny sign is ruled by the Sun. Without these solar rays, there would be no life on Earth as we know it. So it's fitting that people with a strong Leo influence would feel they're as essential as life itself and naturally want to be at the center of the universe, some way, somehow.

Leo's element is fire, and its quality is fixed. Together, the fixed-fire nature of Leo is one of action and follow-through, which makes this a sign of leadership. The downside is not so much that Leo likes to be in charge as that Leo takes charge even when it would be better to be a team player. Being center stage and stealing the show is great as long as the limelight is shared with the supporting cast and crew.

Another outstanding trait associated with Leo is creativity, which can take myriad forms—from acting, to artistic talent, to bright ideas, to leisure-time activities and children. Some people automatically assume that everyone with a strong Leo influence has or wants children. Not so. Some have children of the mind—projects that are the offspring of Leo's creative, fun-loving energy.

Leo's influence in your chart will manifest through the house with Leo on the cusp. That's where you'll find your creativity or the best environment or situation to spark your creativity. This house will tell you where and how you want to stand out from the crowd, what you're passionate about, and where you have a strong ego investment. Because Leo is the sign of pleasure, leisure, fun, and romance, you also can gain insights into these areas of your life.

Leo Sun Sign

As a Leo, you're the star of the zodiac, an attention-getter wherever you go, whatever you do. When in your presence, people sense a subtle shift, an indefinable glow that's your aura of confidence and vitality and your flair for the dramatic. With the Sun as your ruling planet, it's easy for you to step into the role as the center of the solar system.

Underlying your at times flamboyant style is a powerful drive to rise to the top. Those who accurately perceive you as fun-loving and fond of center stage often miss the innate ambition of Leo—much to their regret.

You're popular, outgoing, and creative, and people look to you for advice and guidance. They also want and expect you to take charge.

That's your natural leadership ability, which emerges at work and at play.

Ethics are serious business to you, and you take pride in your reliability, honesty, and integrity. Although these are your core beliefs, your secondary motivation is to achieve and maintain the highest reputation. Likewise, you consciously avoid actions and words that would dent your self-esteem.

For one with such high self-esteem—or maybe because of it—your ego is more fragile than most suspect. An unkind comment, someone who wounds your pride, or a lack of recognition for your efforts throws you off balance. Where other people can toss off such life events, you take them to heart. You benefit when you learn to put things in perspective and consider the source, thereby taming your ego somewhat.

Leo is a fixed sign, so you have all the determination necessary to accomplish everything from daily tasks to major life achievements. This inner strength helps you navigate obstacles and outlast the competition. But there is a fine line between determination and stubbornness. You can dig in your heels and refuse to listen to reason, good advice, and alternative opinions. That's not in your best interests even when your firmly entrenched beliefs and thoughts are questioned. You might be surprised if you listen and open the door to change. New ideas, opinions, and techniques are worth consideration. And you never know—they might become your own.

No one has to convince you that a balanced lifestyle is important. Fun-loving Leos value leisure time and fill evenings and weekends with socializing, sports, hobbies, and creative endeavors. Most also enjoy travel and think nothing of dashing off on the spur of the moment.

Relationships

Your cheerfulness, optimism, and charm ensure a wide circle of friends, and you're usually among the first to be invited to social events. Any gathering that includes you takes on a festive air, and the room comes alive upon your arrival.

You enjoy stimulating conversation with your many acquaintances and few close friends, and people drift in and out of your life as your interests shift. You excel at socializing and seamlessly circulate to meet and greet.

In love, you're ardent and affectionate, and need a partner (and other close friends) who will shower you with attention and admiration. You're happiest with someone who's comfortable with letting you play the leading role and who is, above all, your best friend. The love of your life is likely to be more independent than you are, with more of a humanitarian philosophy, and to encourage you to explore the wider world outside of your orbit. Remember to give at least as much as you get. Everyone likes TLC.

Playful Leo is the universal sign of children, and most Leos make excellent parents. They shower their children with love and affection and are actively involved in their lives. High ethical standards are as important to Leo parents as education, and you'll want to give your children every opportunity to get ahead in the world. You also expect them to be respectful, and at times you can be overly demanding.

Career

Being a creative, take-charge leader, you're ideally suited for supervisory and other leadership positions. Your talent in this area is based in your "stage presence" and your enthusiastic ability to motivate others to be the best they can be. The more you share the load and the credit, the further you'll go.

Once committed, it's unusual for a Leo to change careers. That's because you have your sights set on an elevated position and are determined to get there. You will, however, shift your direction within the same field if you believe another avenue offers more opportunities to excel.

You prefer to work in a structured environment, and many Leos adapt well to the corporate world. But you also need the freedom to establish your own work routine without constant supervision. Jobs without the chance for advancement hold no interest for you, and before accepting a new position you're careful to check all the details and ask pointed questions. You accept a job only after much thought, and only if it's is a step up or a lateral move with a salary increase that will further your goals.

You might enjoy a career in the financial arena, such as the stock market or investment banking. Leos love gold and gems, so the jewelry business might be the right choice for you. Others do well in the entertainment or gambling industry, and some Leos find success in professional sports as players, coaches, or commentators.

Money

You're meticulous about money matters, financial records, and budgeting. But your generous nature and love of quality can encourage you to pick up the tab and splurge on high-priced luxuries. It's okay to treat yourself and others once in a while, although constant spending can leave you deep in debt.

Instead, use your practical money-management skills to shop sales and outlets for the best items at bargain prices. After all, only you and your bank account will know what you paid for that designer label.

Take care to always read the fine print in loan papers and contracts, rather than take someone else's word for it. The same applies to investments, where you should only listen to the advice of credentialed pros who have proven themselves—and then only when the decision is backed up by your own research.

You have a sixth sense about money matters and often know when the time is right to get the best deal.

Financial luck is with you more often than not. Take an occasional chance on the lottery, but beware of gambling. Set limits and stick to them.

Many Leos benefit from a family legacy.

HOW TO SPOT A VIRGO

Does things precisely
Likes and collects boxes
Puts things in piles

Glyph: ♍

Symbol: the Virgin

Ruling planet: Mercury

Natural house: sixth house

Element: earth

Quality: mutable

Body area: intestines

Gemstone: sapphire

Colors: navy blue, dark brown, gray

Flower: pansy

Key phrase: I analyze

Keyword: service

Personality traits: worrier, meticulous, modest, diligent, reliable, critical, practical, cautious, sensible, perfectionist, methodical, discriminating, shy, analytical, organized, efficient, detail-oriented

Countries/regions: Brazil, Greece, Crete, Turkey, Switzerland

Cities: Boston, Massachusetts; Cheltenham, England; Los Angeles; Jerusalem; Brindisi and Padua, Italy; Basel, Switzerland; Baghdad, Iraq; Lyons, France

Common things ruled by Virgo: mercury, list, grain, harvest, bookcase, butler, pet, humane society, medical facility, poultry, endive, first aid, closet, oats, menu, desk, workplace, textiles, sewing, needlework, nutrition, pantry, refrigerator, valerian

Famous people: Lauren Bacall, John McCain, Cameron Diaz, Brian De Palma, Sean Connery, Agatha Christie, Lyndon B. Johnson, Hugh Grant, Adam Sandler, Lance Armstrong, Beyoncé, Faith Hill, Salma Hayek, Tommy Lee Jones, Sophia Loren

VIRGO

AUGUST 22 TO SEPTEMBER 22

Major strengths: organized, efficient, practical

Major challenges: reserved, worrisome, critical

The world and everyone in it would go almost nowhere without Virgo, the earth sign that's practical, organized, and efficient. Virgo excels in the details, which is a terrific asset for anything that has to be planned and executed with precision. This is Virgo's real strength.

Virgo is an analytical sign, and you can watch people with a strong Virgo emphasis check and recheck every option. These are the list makers and the ones who write out the pros and cons before making a decision. But when taken too far, Virgo can get caught in the trap of paralysis by analysis.

Indecision and restlessness are the outward manifestations of Virgo's mutable energy, which is adaptable and versatile. Sometimes, however, Virgo is too flexible, when taking a stand would be better than going with the flow.

Mercury, Virgo's ruling planet, reflects Virgo's emphasis on communication, but it also makes this sign prone to nervous tension and worry. A Virgo friend of mine admitted to me that he's such a worrier that when life is humming along, he worries that something is wrong! Yet this same man has marvelous speaking and writing abilities and a real talent for explaining the most complex concepts in simple terms that anyone can understand. He's also a workaholic, a tendency that this sign is noted for. Virgos get great pleasure from work, but only if they feel they're performing a valuable service and contributing to the betterment of their community, company, family, or the world.

Virgo is discriminating and particular about everything, which is where this sign gets its reputation for being meticulous and critical. It's just that Virgo has the highest of standards and sees no point in doing anything halfway.

Virgo's symbol is the Virgin, a woman holding a recently harvested shaft of wheat. This is the essence of Virgo, the sign of a strong work ethic that reaps the rewards of its efforts. The same symbol also might be the reason for Virgo's stereotype of being prim and proper. From my experience in talking with many Virgos, they only appear to be that way. That's just their identity in the eyes of those who don't really know them. It's also because Virgo tends to be reserved and cautious, especially in unfamiliar situations, and many people with this emphasis are shy or lack confidence in their outstanding abilities.

The house in your chart with Virgo on the cusp is where you focus on the details and go out of your way to be sure all is as perfect as is humanly possible. You're somewhat cautious about the affairs of this house, testing yourself, planning and analyzing the various factors before going into any endeavor. It's also where you're exceptionally organized, and can indicate the work methods and environment you prefer.

Virgo Sun Sign

Virgo's stereotype is "the perfectionist." Some Virgos are, and some aren't. Many embrace that principle through their young adult years or even middle age, often because of parental or environmental influence, and eventually realize and accept that the world is an imperfect place.

What you are is meticulous, but not necessarily neat, another Virgo stereotype. Some Virgos are downright messy and fond of their "organized messes." Either way, you can reach into a pile of paper and pull out exactly what you're looking for with an uncanny and unfailing accuracy. That's part of your overall efficiency, which includes always taking the shortest route between two points, whether on the road, behind a desk, or immersed in a domestic, mechanical, or hobby project.

Virgo's element is earth, so you have the corner on practicality and are literally down-to-earth, sensible, and dependable. You're also somewhat reserved and modest—at least in outward appearances. Earth signs are the most sensual, both from a sexual and sensory perspective.

Discriminating in all things, you have a knack for detail and analysis. But as a result, you miss the big picture at times. It's easy to get bogged down in the little things. Take a periodic step back and put the issue or task at hand in perspective. That's also a helpful technique when worries dominate your thoughts, which they often do. It's far more productive to put indecision aside, meet a problem head-on, and take action rather than let it control your thoughts.

Virgo is the sign of work and service. What others view as work, you see as fun, and even your leisure hours are filled with what others perceive as just another item for the to-do list. That's partly because of your work ethic and the fulfillment and pride you feel with each task completed, both personally and professionally. Many Virgos are devoted volunteers, sharing their skills and talents with a wide variety of nonprofit organizations and groups.

Mercury, the planet associated with Virgo, makes intellectual stimulation a must in your life. Most Virgos are intelligent, avid readers and enthusiastic conversationalists with people they know well and who appreciate hearing all the fine points of a subject.

Because Virgo is a mutable sign, you're adaptable and easygoing in most situations. The exception is when your exacting standards and high principles come into question. You rarely, if ever, compromise your beliefs for anyone or anything. In other situations, however, there are times when you can be too accommodating to the wishes of others. Take a stand now and then; state your preference and don't bend.

Relationships

Friends are like family to you, and you form lasting associations that span decades. Loyal and devoted to those in your inner circle, you go out of your way to maintain close ties with your friends and help them however you can.

The meet-and-greet party scene is low on your social list, which is part of the reason Virgos have a reputation for being reserved or shy. It's really all about your comfort zone. You're at ease with people you know well and small groups that encourage deeper discussion. Then you come alive and let your sparkling personality emerge.

You're idealistic in matters of the heart, and your search for a partner revolves around your idea of perfection. The chances are slim to none of meeting anyone who can live up to that expectation, so some Virgos choose to remain single, content with their own company and that of friends and family.

Even Virgos who commit often go through a period of disillusionment when they see their partner as he or she really is—and always has been. But you also can fall in love and stay in

love, enveloped in a lifetime of romance. Much depends on you and your mate and your individual personalities and life goals.

Virgos who choose to be parents usually have small families and often later in life. Because rules and practicalities are important to you, you encourage these values in your children and establish clear expectations. You also push them to succeed (and can be the ultimate stage mother or father), encouraging ambition and high achievement. Be careful not to overprogram their lives. Let them explore their own talents and follow their own interests. Also let them express their independence and learn the hard way when appropriate.

Career

It's simple: you love to work. Your career and job are a major life focus and essential to your well-being. Difficult work periods (which are inevitable from time to time) leave you feeling incomplete and unfulfilled because you gain ultimate satisfaction from performing a useful service. You move on when you feel your contributions no longer meet that criterion.

No task is too large or too small for you, and you approach each one with enthusiasm and a discriminating eye for detail. This contributes to your success and self-esteem, as does your willingness to take on extra responsibilities.

Your strong work ethic is matched by an equally strong need for a job that allows a high degree of independence. You find hovering supervisors stifling and resent the implication that you're even remotely incapable of managing your work flow. Clarify the level of autonomy before you accept any position.

Friendly with coworkers and a team player, you nevertheless share little of your personal life at work.

Your career is, to some extent, a work in progress, where change is more the norm than the exception. Versatility promotes success and is necessary for advancement, which you may or may not be interested in. Many Virgos are content with simply doing the job to the best of their ability.

The need for freedom extends in some way to your work environment. You might choose a career "without walls," such as being a driver or delivery person, or one in retail or health care that allows freedom of movement and variety.

Other careers that attract Virgos are alternative healing, massage therapy, accounting and bookkeeping, and veterinary medicine. Some excel in the communications field as editors, writers, and librarians. Virgos also are excellent analysts, engineers, mechanics, and computer programmers and technicians.

Money

Money flows your way, and you're excellent with the daily details of budgeting, record keeping, and bill paying. You're practical and somewhat cautious, and your spending weakness is for those you love. You enjoy gift giving and fulfilling every possible material wish of those closest to you.

But what about you? Learn to treat yourself as benevolently as you treat others, and elevate your needs and desires to a higher place on the priority list. Start with savings; pay yourself first.

For all your money sense, there are times when you can be impulsive and fall into the trap of easy credit. Yet you're also quick to spot moneymaking opportunities and to take action to increase earnings.

Sound finances also require a big-picture, long-term view. Incorporate that perspective into your planning, and expand the details to include annual, five-year, ten-year, and lifetime goals. You'll feel more secure knowing you have funds for unexpected expenses, major purchases, and, ultimately, your retirement years. A family inheritance could boost your net worth, but there might be challenges associated with it, such as conflict with siblings or other relatives.

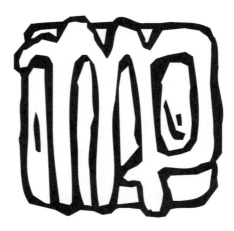

HOW TO SPOT A LIBRA

Diplomatic
Seldom goes anywhere alone
Likes pastels and beautiful objects

Glyph: ♎

Symbol: the Scales

Ruling planet: Venus

Natural house: seventh house

Element: air

Quality: cardinal

Body areas: kidneys, lower back, appendix

Gemstone: opal

Colors: blue, pink, pastels

Flower: rose

Key phrase: I balance

Keyword: harmony

Personality traits: tactful, cooperative, romantic, fickle, lazy, extravagant, gracious, gullible, dependent, charming, sympathetic, partnership-oriented, people person, self-indulgent, social, idealistic, easily influenced, fair, indecisive

Countries/regions: China, Burma, Tibet, Japan, Austria, Canada, Argentina

Cities: Copenhagen, Denmark; Vienna, Austria; Leeds, England; Lisbon, Portugal; Antwerp, Belgium; Frankfurt-am-Main, Germany

Common things ruled by Libra: bedroom, candy, love, partner, copper, mint, asparagus, artwork, fashion, hair salon, cosmetics, clothing, contract, piano, jewelry, litigation, décor, furniture, coral, strawberry, wedding

Famous people: Jimmy Carter, Gwyneth Paltrow, Gwen Stefani, Hugh Jackman, Dwight D. Eisenhower, Dale Earnhardt Jr., Chuck Berry, Emeril Lagasse, John Lennon, Matt Damon, Sylvia Browne, Bruce Springsteen, John Mayer, Will Smith

Major strengths: tactful, fair, cooperative

Major challenges: indecisive, idealistic, self-indulgent

Libra's glyph (♎) represents its symbol, the Scales, which sums up a lot of what this sign is about: balance and justice, or fairness.

In a perfect Libra world, everyone would get along, everyone would be treated fairly, and there would be no disputes or disagreements—definitely a lofty aim, but also an idealistic one, which this sign is noted for. Nevertheless, Libra strives to create this balanced world and is thus the sign of the diplomat and consensus builder, the promoter of peace and harmony. But when this tendency is taken too far, Libra is more of a people pleaser than a people person who benefits from all of this air sign's communication skills.

Yet Libra also can be a fighting sign, the knight in shining armor charging to the defense of the underdog. That's Libra's strong sense of justice and fairness in action, which sometimes extends to the legal system. As the sign of the strategist, Libra has a knack for outwitting adversaries at their own game and for outthinking the competition, or the enemy, all with the innate charm that this sign possesses.

Libra's ruling planet, Venus, and its natural house, the seventh, make it the universal relationship sign. The lives of most people with a Libra emphasis are intertwined with other people—friends, family, colleagues, and, most of all, a romantic partner. They don't like to go it alone, and often choose careers, activities, and interests that involve contact with other people. In a sense, this people contact gives them the confidence to pursue their own interests and individuality in the outer world. But some Libras focus all their energy on others and thus become dependent rather than independent.

The indecisiveness of Libra, which in reality is the ability to see both sides of any question, can drive others to distraction. Several Libras I know almost never make a decision unless someone without this influence makes it for them, which is exactly what they want. When the decision is made for them, it's much easier to avoid conflict because they don't have to disappoint anyone. But how productive is that? Well, it depends on your perspective.

With Venus as its ruler, Libra is also the sign of beauty, both physical attractiveness and an attraction to all things pleasing to the eye. This influence gives most people with a Libra emphasis an interest in art, either with the talent to produce works of art, a design instinct, or an appreciation for the arts. You'll rarely see a Libra in anything but the most flattering clothing.

Because Venus is also a money planet, the house in your chart with Libra on the cusp is where you have the potential to increase your resources. This house is where you go out of your way to maintain harmony, develop the most congenial of relationships, and find it easiest to use your people skills. It's also where you can be lazy and self-indulgent, because Venus is a comfort-loving planet.

Libra Sun Sign

Libra's life mission is twofold: balance and relationships. Both encompass all facets of your life, from business to friendship to family.

Balance signifies compromise, mediation, equality, diplomacy, and negotiation. Relationships encompass the same qualities because every interaction between two (or more) people requires give and take. Libra excels at both.

Your people skills are among the best, and your sociable, gracious, genteel nature boosts your popularity. This can encourage others to perceive you as a soft touch, but nothing could be further from the truth. Although you dislike confrontation, when pushed you will fight back. But because Libra is an air sign, you prefer to use brains rather than brawn.

An excellent strategist, you can outwit the competition at every turn. That's part of your skill as a mediator, as is your ability to persuade others to see things your way. This subtle approach is also an asset that allows you to plant ideas through casual suggestion and thus maneuver others into thinking your ideas are their own.

Other people often see you as indecisive, a trait that's associated with Libra. You are and you aren't. This aspect of your personality is nothing more or less than your sense of fair play in action. The dilemma is that you can see both sides of any issue—positive and negative, pro and con, black and white. You're an excellent debater. Your decision-making process involves weighing all factors involved, back and forth, until you reach a conclusion. But in the process you also can get stuck on finding a 50–50 solution, which is nonproductive. Remember that choosing to make no decision really is a decision.

Everything you say and do has a touch of grace and elegance. You find off-color jokes and crude behavior particularly offensive and are a meticulous dresser, always presenting yourself in the best possible light. Your home reflects the same good taste you bring to the outer world.

Your artistic eye helps you create a showplace that's warm, welcoming, comfortable, and uniquely yours, whether it's a small apartment, a mansion, or something in between.

Relationships

You were born with more innate knowledge of relationships than many people acquire after years of life. Your people skills are thus a cut above the rest, plus you are a quick study, genuinely like people, and have a sixth sense about human nature. Managing people is your specialty.

You go out of your way in any relationship to maintain harmony. Negotiation and compromise are your talents, but sometimes it's worth taking a stand on important issues—even if others are opposed.

Solo activities aren't your style. When you're not with your mate, you're with a pal. You're loyal and devoted to your friends, and those closest to you are friends for a lifetime. You also have many acquaintances. Important, powerful people fill both categories, and you treat everyone with the same grace and charm. You're a popular guest, and many Libras have a wide circle of friends through their involvement in the arts and other nonprofit organizations.

Libras feel incomplete without a life partner. Love and romance are second nature to you, with universal love planet Venus as your ruler. Single Libras can be found with friends, and some link hearts with someone who initially is in that category.

You're also somewhat idealistic about love, so it's easy for you to confuse infatuation with the real thing. Take your time rather than make an impulsive leap into commitment. True love will wait.

As part of a couple, you're attuned to your partner's every need. Try to put yourself and your needs first at least half the time. It will actually strengthen your bond.

As parents, Libras can be somewhat detached. Surprisingly, they also foster independence in their children from a young age and encourage them to explore their unique talents and interests. Libras have strong ties with their adult children, when their parent-child relationship evolves into one that's more of a friendship.

Career

A pleasant, congenial work environment is almost as important as your job duties. Only in the most unusual circumstances would you consider, much less accept, a position that offered anything less. Cooperative people and a mutually supportive, calm atmosphere are equally vital to job happiness. Workplace politics and dissension have no place in your life.

You can excel in a career field that involves working with the public, such as real estate or the retail or food industry. Some Libras find success in government service and other positions of public trust. If you find the arts appealing, you might want to consider a theater or museum career, or one in jewelry or art sales. A career as a florist, wedding planner, interior decorator, or psychologist might interest you, and many Libras are outstanding attorneys, hair stylists, or makeup artists.

Your career is prone to ups and downs and changing conditions. The greatest opportunities may come during times of flux, when your superb people skills help you land on your feet. You always should take advantage of any chance to network, because knowing the right people can be your magic door opener.

Money

Your wealth potential is above average. At the least, with planning and astute money management, you can achieve a comfortable lifestyle and ensure financial security through your retirement years. However, some Libras choose to live close to the edge without going into debt, spending most of what they earn. That's because you enjoy the finer things in life and willingly spend what you can afford on clothing, home décor, and socializing. Only occasionally impulsive and extravagant, you're also interested in good value for your money.

Saving is easy if you make it a priority, and you'll quickly get into the habit as you see your bank account rise. You also can do well with conservative investments and real estate, although long-term gains are your best choice. Avoid promises of high returns and financial risk, which can backfire. You are often lucky, so games of chance can net unexpected gains; set limits.

Most Libras are averse to debt, mostly because they consider paying interest to be a waste of money. When necessary, you thoroughly research options until you find the very best deal. You also know how to make money work for you by renegotiating loans and mortgages at the right time and shifting debt to venues with lower interest rates.

An inheritance is favored for many Libras, who also aim to provide the same for their children. Leaving a legacy is important to you.

HOW TO SPOT A SCORPIO

Piercing eyes
Secretive
Physical stamina

Glyph: ♏

Symbol: the Scorpion

Ruling planet: Pluto (Mars, ancient ruler)

Natural house: eighth house

Element: water

Quality: fixed

Body areas: reproductive system, colon

Gemstone: topaz

Colors: black, burgundy

Flower: chrysanthemum

Key phrase: I desire

Keyword: intensity

Personality traits: secretive, sarcastic, heroic, ruthless, jealous, vengeful, loyal, possessive, suspicious, obsessive, forceful, emotional, willpower, magnetic, stubborn, passionate, psychic, investigative, determined

Countries/regions: Algeria, Korea, Norway, Paraguay, Morocco, Bavaria

Cities: Dover and Liverpool, England; Milwaukee, Wisconsin; St. John's, Newfoundland; Halifax, Nova Scotia; Baltimore, Maryland; Messina, Sicily; New Orleans, Louisiana; Washington D.C.

Common things ruled by Scorpio: psychiatry, legacy, magic, coroner, sewer, reptile, recycling, restroom, toilet, undertaker, death, detective, espionage, hernia, butcher, money

Famous people: Leonardo DiCaprio, Julia Roberts, Hillary Clinton, Laura Bush, Dan Rather, Larry King, Michael Landon, Jodie Foster, Michael Crichton, Goldie Hawn, Maria Shriver, Matthew McConaughey, Martin Scorsese

SCORPIO

OCTOBER 22 TO NOVEMBER 22

Major strengths: determination, endurance, willpower

Major challenges: stubbornness, jealousy, vengeance

Scorpio's symbol is, appropriately, the Scorpion, an arachnid with a tail that functions as a stinger. Anyone who has ever encountered Scorpio's stinger knows that this sign can act with a vengeance. Although the revenge motive is one of the less-attractive traits of this sign, Scorpio's stinger can be overwhelmingly positive when used for honorable purposes.

Scorpio is a master at digging beneath the surface to unearth information. This is the sign of the detective, the researcher, the investigator. If you've exhausted all resources in your search for information, ask a Scorpio to take on the job. Their minds work in ways that escape other people. They approach problems from a different perspective, a different angle, and they're relentless in their pursuit of a goal. Scorpio is not easily, and only rarely, defeated in its quest. Determination is one of this sign's major strengths.

As a fixed sign, Scorpio excels at follow-through and completion. But Scorpio also can be stubborn and refuse to move on when that would be a better choice. Quitting is not an option for the Scorpio, and people with this emphasis can push themselves to the point of exhaustion.

Like the other water signs (Cancer and Pisces), Scorpio has an strong sixth sense and often is not just intuitive but psychic. This can be a powerful tool, especially when combined with Scorpio's research ability. With it, however, comes the emotional sensitivity associated with water—steely on the outside and a soft touch on the inside.

Scorpio is the sexiest sign of the zodiac, and people with the Sun here have a sexy, magnetic energy few can resist. It seems to draw people in, to mesmerize them, almost as a sort of low-level hypnotism. This is also the sign most often associated with metaphysics.

Scorpios are fascinating people. Those I know almost always have some sort of hidden agenda, something held in reserve. Some use this in manipulative ways, while others consider it to be an ace in the hole. What you see or hear with a secretive Scorpio is almost never the entire story. Many of them are thus outstanding strategists.

The house in your chart with Scorpio on the cusp is where your willpower and determination are evident, and where you are intuitive and secretive. You strive for an in-depth understanding of the matters associated with this house, but this is also where any control issues will be most evident and where you can lose perspective.

Scorpio Sun Sign

Scorpio is mysterious and intense. You do nothing halfway, and a promise or decision made is one kept. With this passionate drive comes the determination to achieve goals and objectives, personally and professionally. The word *failure* is absent from your vocabulary.

Your powerful inner strength sees you through seemingly insurmountable obstacles. Opposition rarely deters you, and you move forward, clearing the path as you go. The negative side of your strong willpower is, of course, ruthlessness. Guard against it by examining your motives before you act, and do the same if your thoughts become vengeful. Remember: living well is the best revenge.

Scorpio and its ruling planet, Pluto, signify transformation—the power and potential for change. You can transform yourself on a per-

sonal level, where unswerving commitment is your ally if, for example, you want to lose weight or change a habit. On a practical level, you might envision new décor and create exactly the look you want using odds and ends, recycled and revamped objects picked up here and there. In your career life, you have a knack for expanding your position to the point where you're almost irreplaceable (because no one really is)—creating your own job description by taking on extra tasks and new areas of responsibility.

Reserved from all outward appearances, you're anything but on the inside. Your mental wheels are always turning, sizing up people, places, and things, and storing the information for current and future use. With such strong powers of observation, intuition, and analytical ability, many of your opponents lose the match before they get started.

Along the same lines, you're a person of few words, and convey your thoughts with succinct comments. And everyone listens and gets the point.

Some call you suspicious; others say you're curious. You're both, and once on a mission to learn the truth or the facts, you stay on course until you're satisfied with the results. Shrewd and intuitive, you're rarely deceived by anyone or anything.

Relationships

You have the power to mesmerize almost anyone—except maybe another Scorpio!—with a single look. People instantly sense the depth of feeling and emotion that's wrapped in your mysterious, magnetic aura. Yet only those who know you very well realize there's an ultrasensitive, caring heart behind your steely eyes.

You take relationships seriously and are quick to right wrongs when anyone crosses a loved one or friend. Intensely loyal to those in your inner circle, you reveal your inner self to only a few—after you deem them to be ultimately trustworthy. You accept or reject people, like or dislike them. There is no middle ground.

You view commitment as for a lifetime and will let go only as a last resort. In love, you're extremely possessive and protective of your partner. But when your confidence slips, jealousy can be your first reaction. This, of course, can destroy a relationship, where trust would strengthen it.

Ardent and passionate, you shower your mate with attention and TLC. You find it easier to express your feelings through kind deeds and thoughtful tokens of love, and willingly share your time, skills, and talents. These demonstrations of love are important, but they're no substitute for communication. Learn to open up in the safety and security of love and share your innermost thoughts, desires, and frustrations.

You're highly selective about your friends, and despite how much you genuinely like and love them, each fulfills a practical need in your life. Your closest friends may be those you meet through work or as a volunteer for a charitable organization.

As a parent, you can be a total pushover at times, indulging your children in every whim. But you also expect and teach them respect for others, high ideals, etiquette, and responsibility. Nurturing their imagination and creativity is one of the best things you can do, as well as getting involved in their activities and meeting their friends.

Career

You're a go-getter, with all the determination to get to the top of your career. Although personal privacy prevails, you easily step into a starring role as a leader in your professional life. Those who don't know you well believe it begins and ends there—but they're mistaken. In reality, you're usually a step ahead of the competition, planning your next coup and turning events in your favor, all with what appears to be open and straightforward communication.

You prefer an active, vital, fast-paced work environment, where your initiative is valued. Jobs with physical activity appeal to many Scorpios, and few are content to sit behind a desk from 8 to 5. Whatever your job, you're probably the one who motivates others and sparks a fire to get things moving. Thorough and hardworking, you're also an idea person, the first to find a quicker, easier way to complete a task, whether your own or someone else's.

Workplace initiative is positive, but supporters will be few if you push others as hard as you push yourself. You prefer to work solo, where you can be in charge. Find a balance between that and teamwork to keep the boss and coworkers happy.

Scorpios are found in a wide variety of careers, including finance, recycling, mortuary science, insurance, and salvage work. Those with an interest in medicine can excel in the fields of surgery, pharmaceuticals, forensics, or hospice work. Research and investigation are natural career fields for Scorpios; some find success as detectives, medical researchers, strategists, or covert operatives.

Money

Scorpios think about money about as often as they think about passion and power. You know instinctively that money opens doors and strengthens your position. Along with this comes the ability to manage money and to amass considerable resources.

Conservative when necessary and a risk taker when it's to your advantage, you understand the financial ebb and flow. Lucky more often than not, you probably have a secret stash of funds available for emergencies and occasional splurges. That's in addition to savings, long-term investments, and retirement accounts, which can increase your net worth over the years.

You check out every potential financial move that could save or earn dollars in interest. To you, money is fluid, to be used to advance your position and security level.

Most Scorpios maintain excellent credit and easily acquire more simply by asking for it. But this financial area is also prone to change, so it's important to regularly check your credit and to avoid moves that could lower your score.

Although you're moderately conservative in money matters, you can be a free spender at times. Reconsider when thoughts of extravagance take hold, unless of course money is no object. Otherwise, enthusiastic optimism can result in big bills.

As a Scorpio, your earnings are likely to be high or at least at a level that provides a comfortable lifestyle. You seem to luck into higher-paying jobs and to earn bonuses and upper-end raises.

Many Scorpios benefit from an unexpectedly large family inheritance, but siblings can cause difficulties with any family legacy.

HOW TO SPOT A SAGITTARIUS

Long hair
Prominent hips
Blunt talk

Glyph: ↗

Symbol: the Archer

Ruling planet: Jupiter

Natural house: ninth house

Element: fire

Quality: mutable

Body areas: hips, thighs, sciatic nerve

Gemstone: turquoise

Colors: royal blue, purple

Flower: narcissus

Key phrase: I see

Keyword: optimism

Personality traits: friendly, adventuresome, leadership ability, spiritual, easygoing, fortunate, humorous, joke teller, freedom-loving, honest, restless, irresponsible, knowledgeable, tactless, enthusiastic, overly optimistic, careless

Countries/regions: Tuscany, Australia, Chile, Czech Republic, Hungary, Provence, Spain, Singapore

Cities: Toledo, Ohio; Stuttgart, Germany; Sheffield and Nottingham, England; Naples, Italy; Avignon, France

Common things ruled by Sagittarius: travel, tin, horse, sage, cinnamon, clergy, university, house of worship, college, trade school, attorney, law, publishing, religion, professor, prayer, stable, abundance, court, foreign affairs, ethics, archery, advertising, judge

Famous people: Brad Pitt, Jon Stewart, Scarlett Johansson, Lucy Liu, Jeff Bridges, Britney Spears, Bette Midler, Margaret Mead, Jane Fonda, Dick Clark, Walt Disney, Tyra Banks, Anna Nicole Smith, Ben Stiller, Tom Waits, Jimi Hendrix, Jane Austen

SAGITTARIUS

NOVEMBER 22 TO DECEMBER 21

Major strengths: enthusiastic, adventuresome, honest

Major challenges: outspoken, overly optimistic, irresponsible

Other signs are described as independent and free-spirited, and they are. But none can come close to expressing that type of energy as fully as does Sagittarius. This sign's symbol, the Archer, aptly describes what Sagittarius is all about: flying free and high, with no limits, destination unknown.

Jupiter is as expansive and adventuresome as Sagittarius, the sign it rules. Jupiter encourages excess, but it's also the luckiest planet in the zodiac, the one that can save the day at the eleventh hour. But even Sagittarius soon learns that Jupiter is free with promises but doesn't always deliver. Even so, Sagittarius usually comes out on top, often pushing the envelope and getting away with much more than any other sign.

No one ever wonders where they stand with a Sagittarius or what a Sagittarius thinks. This sign is noted for its plain talk, blunt and to the point, and usually can't understand why anyone would take offense. That's a reflection of the limited boundaries that also make Sagittarius the sign of the explorer and seeker of truth. Sagittarius places a high value on knowledge and is the seeker of truth.

Because Sagittarius is a fire sign, it shares some of the traits of Aries and Leo—leadership, enthusiasm, optimism, and high energy. But it can be a challenge for Sagittarius to channel the fiery zest in a productive direction because it's also a mutable sign. With the mutable quality comes restlessness and scattered rather than focused interests. The solution is to find and zero in on a pas-

Sun: Sagittarius
moon: ~~leo~~ Virgo
rising: leo

positive impact on the lives of countless young people.

The house in your chart with Sagittarius on the cusp is where you seek knowledge and do most everything in a big way. It's also where you're lucky and adventuresome and feel more comfortable taking risks. People you encounter through this house encourage you to excel, and you're generally friendly and outgoing with them. The matters of this house are often in a state of flux.

Sagittarius Sun Sign

As a Sagittarius, you're an adventurer, moving through life to fulfill your quest for knowledge and new experiences. You see opportunities where others see boundaries and step into each day with confidence and optimism. That's the influence of fire, the element associated with your sign.

At times, you're impulsive and overly optimistic and plow ahead without thought of potential consequences. Yet you often land on your feet. When you don't, you're quick to put the past behind you for a fresh start.

Like expansive Jupiter, your ruling planet, you see life from a big-picture perspective. With so much to explore, so many fascinating things to do, and so much knowledge to gain, you have no time for details or fences. You're a freedom-loving free spirit who's always on the go, physically or mentally.

Learning is a major life theme for Sagittarius. Almost everything piques your interest, at least for a short time. In a matter of minutes you can flip from how-to skills, to world and local news, to deep philosophical concepts. You're a seeker of truth and knowledge.

Higher education is your path to success and fulfillment of all the potential of your Sun sign. Even if you see it only as a means to an end, it's important to follow through so you can be competitive in today's world. Identify and focus on your major interest and develop it to advance in your career; set aside evenings and weekends to explore all the other intriguing ideas, places, and activities that catch your attention.

Although you'd like to be free to come and go as you wish and when you please, that's hardly realistic (unless, of course, your fabulous luck makes you independently wealthy), so the solution is to design your lifestyle to meet both needs. Because Sagittarius is a mutable sign, you have the versatility and flexibility to do just that. Use your imagination to get the best of both: freedom and stability.

Fun-loving and upbeat Sagittarians usually have a string of jokes and funny stories to tell, and many are practical jokers. You also have a way of motivating people, inciting them to take action and pursue their dreams. This, in turn, inspires you to slip into fast-forward, with a clear vision of the future and endless possibilities.

Relationships

You're friendly and outgoing, full of life and good cheer, which endears you to your many friends and acquaintances. Sagittarians are popular, and your mere presence enlivens the group. You're also generous with your time, talents, and knowledge, and people appreciate your good intentions.

Always honest, you can be too much so at times, when the truth would be better softened with kindness. Tact will get you further in life, so train yourself to think before you speak. Change the presentation, not the facts, and your message will be welcomed.

Flirtatious and charming, you enjoy the chase and the thrill of new love. But only the most unusual man or woman—and one who mirrors your free-spirited ways—can tempt you to commit. Independence and the single life often win out with your sign, or at least until later in life when partnership becomes more important.

As a parent, you're actively involved in your children's lives, although quality time usually prevails over quantity. Sports are one area where your interests can merge, and you encourage spontaneity and a high level of activity in your children. Take care, though, not to overprogram them or push them into areas where they have little interest or talent. Patience and understanding are your lessons here.

Career

Always on the go, you want and expect the same high level of activity in your career and job, which is one area where your more practical side emerges. You're industrious and hardwork-ing and follow through, leaving no task incomplete. Here, determination is your strength.

You strive for job stability and expect to be well and fairly paid for your efforts. Congenial relationships are important to job success, but you dislike interruptions when you're focused on the task at hand. You also expect your work space to be comfortable, efficient, and utilitarian, but you're unconcerned about clutter. Functionality is what matters to you.

Your career evolves and changes, and you can shift easily from one area to a related field. That's a plus if it's for the right reason, but not if your sole purpose is to add some excitement to your life. Boredom can make you leap when practical realities should prevail. Look at the big picture, the long term, rather than today's details and petty irritations.

Career fields suited to Sagittarius include teaching, the travel industry, law, and religion. Advertising and publishing draw the interest of some, while others are attracted by environmental concerns and enjoy careers in the outdoors. You also might find success in engineering, landscaping, or construction or mechanical trades. Many Sagittarians enjoy working with their hands. If the medical field interests you, you could succeed as a massage therapist, acupuncturist, or herbalist.

Money

You alternate between free spending and thrift, and your income follows a similar path. Overall financial status is much the same, with periods that range from boom to bust. You can achieve more stability—and even wealth—with careful planning, budgeting, saving, and spending. Getting there, however, requires knowledge, trial and error, and learning experiences. Then finances become more stable and income rises. Think of it as proving your good intentions to the universe.

Credit requires caution. With your expansive, optimistic outlook, it's easy to run up debt, thinking you'll have the money when the bills arrive. Sometimes you do, and sometimes you don't. Why waste hard-earned funds on interest?

Emotional satisfaction is your major hurdle when easy credit beckons. What you want, you want now—not next week, next month, or next year. As long as you give in to instant gratification, the monthly bills will keep coming.

You're a pushover when it comes to loved ones, and you indulge them whenever possible with gifts, small and large. But your bank account will thank you if you replace material largesse with kindnesses and time; they're the best gifts you can give.

Astute Sagittarians are thrifty and know how to meet expenses with ease while saving for the future. Once you get in the habit, you might even discover you like the feeling of security that comes with money in the bank.

Many Sagittarians inherit a sizable legacy from a family member, far more than they ever expected.

HOW TO SPOT A CAPRICORN

Likes clocks and watches
Bony knees
Ambitious

Glyph: ♑

Symbol: the Goat

Ruling planet: Saturn

Natural house: tenth house

Element: earth

Quality: cardinal

Body areas: skeleton, knees, teeth, skin

Gemstone: garnet

Colors: black, navy blue, gray, forest green

Flower: carnation

Key phrase: I use

Keyword: ambition

Personality traits: hard worker, frugal, cheap, practical, reliable, status-oriented, methodical, realistic, worrier, cautious, self-disciplined, reserved, patient, pessimistic, conservative

Countries/regions: Afghanistan, Lithuania, Greece, Bosnia, Mexico, India, Tibet, Bulgaria

Cities: Brandenburg, Germany; Brussels, Belgium; Port Said, Egypt; Mexico City

Common things ruled by Capricorn: stone, leather, mining, granite, gravel, construction, farming, brick, time, business, cement, watch, garden, chiropractic, quarry, ore, clock, pottery, real estate, salt, land

Famous people: Richard Nixon, A. J. Foyt, Rush Limbaugh, Kate Moss, Elvis Presley, Diane Sawyer, Nicolas Cage, Muhammad Ali, Laila Ali, Ted Danson, Jim Carrey, Jude Law, Sienna Miller, Umberto Eco, Cary Grant, Orlando Bloom, Ava Gardner

CAPRICORN

DECEMBER 21 TO JANUARY 20

Major strengths: ambitious, practical, responsible

Major challenges: rigid, unapproachable, stingy

Like all earth signs, Capricorn is practical and conservative, an excellent planner and organizer. What makes Capricorn different from Taurus and Virgo, however, is a desire for status and position. Reputation and image are very important, and part of Capricorn's success barometer is all the material goodies that come with and signal rising prominence and prestige.

Capricorn is also a cardinal sign, which gives it the initiative to put concrete plans into action. That's a key factor in satisfying this sign's ambitious nature. Above all, anyone with a strong Capricorn influence is ambitious, aimed for the top spots in life. That might be, and often is, in a career position; other Capricorns achieve the same through community or volunteer activities, or in politics. Like this sign's symbol, the (Mountain) Goat, Capricorn climbs slowly but steadily, encountering rocky patches yet learning and profiting from each obstacle encountered on the way.

Capricorn is the sign of the late bloomer, and many of these people build momentum slowly until life starts to come together as their drive and determination begin to emerge. For this reason and because Capricorn is reserved, people often underestimate the competitive nature of this sign—and soon regret their mistake.

One particular Capricorn client of mine comes to mind. It took him about ten years after graduating from college to find himself and his life direction. He gave the family retail business a try for a few years, and when that didn't work, he set out on his own and returned to school for an advanced degree to pursue a career in the financial sector. What was fascinating to me as an astrologer was that I could see (and told him) that he would be a good fit for a financial career in the corporate sector. Yet other factors in his chart reflected the strong sense of duty to family. Once established on his true career path, he told me he wished he'd taken the information I had provided more seriously, much earlier. (Astrologers frequently hear comments like this.) Would it have made a difference in his life? Maybe. But with Capricorn, it's always important to keep in mind that this is a learn-by-doing (and often the hard way) sign. This approach seems to provide the practical experience that this sign builds on.

The house in your chart with Capricorn on the cusp is where you're ambitious and willing to invest long hours to achieve success, although the matters associated with this house may not begin to fully develop until your thirties or forties. Here is where you take a practical, organized approach, as well as where you're thrifty.

Capricorn Sun Sign

Capricorn is the sign of pure ambition. Motivated by a status-seeking drive to rise to the top, you also understand and appreciate that true success and recognition—in any area of life—requires long-term effort.

Impulsive moves are a rarity for you. You think and plan before you act and approach each task and decision with organized action. Ever practical and sensible, you also embody other qualities associated with the earth element: dependability, reliability, and caution. Most Capricorns tend to be more conservative and traditional than not, and shun frivolous activities in favor of career interests. Even social events and friendships are geared toward networking and prestige.

With serious Saturn as your ruling planet, your climb to the top is not necessarily an easy one. But even obstacles and setbacks serve a purpose. Each is a learning experience to be used in the future. Some of your best lessons are learned the hard way, and your excellent memory serves you well.

Most Capricorns begin to bloom after age forty. Everything prior to that is just a warm-up. When your peers are settling in, you're just getting started. And you quickly make up for lost time and zoom ahead, thanks to what seems like several lifetimes of knowledge and experience. That's also when you begin to experience the full effect of the cardinal (action-oriented) nature of your sign.

Other people no doubt believe rules are made by Capricorns. Rules are part of your life foundation, and you also sometimes feel as though they're made just for you. When you break one, such as driving a few miles over the speed limit, you experience the delight of getting away with something while also worrying you might get caught. What is a bold step against the rules of life for a Capricorn is insignificant to most.

Many Capricorns experience "instant karma." Where others seem to get away with everything and never pay the consequences, you sometimes experience repercussions within seconds or minutes. That's the effect of Saturn, your ruling planet, which has a knack for keeping Capricorns on the straight and narrow.

Relationships

You're somewhat reserved, and at times others see you as unapproachable. That has more to do with your serious, purposeful life and lifestyle than it does a lack of people skills. Frivolous chitchat doesn't interest you, but your dry sense of humor and genuine concern for people make you a solid and popular friend.

You have many acquaintances (to further your career networking goals) and a handful of close pals. Some Capricorns have "categories" of friends with whom they share particular activities. The groups rarely overlap or mix, mostly because each has different interests, all of which are yours.

You surround yourself with like-minded people who are conservative, ambitious, practical, and refined. Planned get-togethers, not spontaneous ones, are your style, and you especially enjoy dining out to indulge your love of fine food and upscale surroundings.

You're also thoughtful and highly selective in romance. A long courtship precedes commitment for most Capricorns, who often link hearts later in life or unite with someone much older or younger. It's tough for you to commit until you (or your prospective mate) are firmly established in your career and on the way up.

Capricorns are gentle but firm and loving parents. You set high standards for your children and encourage them to develop their own talents. Committed to helping them build a solid foundation for life, you willingly fund sports and other activities. You're also generous with them, though Capricorns rarely spoil their children.

Career

Career is your single most defining life factor. It embodies you and your quest for success. When someone asks you what's new, 90 percent of the time your response is a rundown of recent career-related activities and achievements.

Despite your overall conservative attitude, you're very independent—not in a free-spirited, adventuresome way, but in one that makes it almost imperative for you to structure your own job pace and work environment. To you, anything else is unneeded and unnecessary interference, because you always deliver as promised and believe you know the best way to tackle any task. Usually you do, and therein lies the frustration.

Although you might work best this way, supervisors often have a different idea and company policy may dictate what you do when and how you do it. Rather than let this get to you (and ultimately result in a career setback), use it as an incentive to climb the ladder of success until you're the policymaker. Until then, work within the system, present your ideas to the right people, and promote positive change.

Capricorns always have their eye on the next step up and continually lay the groundwork for promotions and lucrative new jobs. You may look as though you're maintaining the status quo, but the wheels are always turning in search of an opportunity. When a hoped-for job doesn't come through, you take it in stride and await another one with patience, knowing that when the time is right, all will come together seamlessly.

Conscientious and hardworking, you expect to be recognized for your efforts, each of which you consider to be a building block of success. You're also motivated by the desire to earn a prominent place within your community, career, and circle of friends and family. Reputation is very important to you.

Many Capricorns excel in the corporate world, which is a natural fit for your strong ambition. Others do well in architecture, engineering, or masonry and other construction trades, or as contractors, orthopaedic surgeons, or chiropractors. You also might find success in government or politics.

Money

You think about money with the same practical mindset that guides your life. Money represents both security and freedom. Nearly always thrifty, you're a saver, and your confidence level rises along with your bank account, investments, and retirement funds.

Income can fluctuate, especially in your younger years, and you go through periods where unexpected expenses seem to pop up one after another. Friends and networking, however, bring you luck and are often your link to a bigger paycheck.

You can do well with investments. Some Capricorns enjoy managing their own portfolio as a hobby, or they get involved in an investment club that nets a sizable return.

Debt is seldom an issue for Capricorns once they've mastered money-management skills. Even then, ego can occasionally get in the way of common sense when the latest material status symbol catches your eye. Appearances are important to you, but you also know how to use money to advantage, negotiate better rates, find bargains, and save and invest a percentage of what you earn.

Many Capricorns receive an inheritance from a family member or friend.

HOW TO SPOT AN AQUARIUS

Strong legs
Likes gadgets and electronics
Future-oriented

Glyph: ≈

Symbol: the Water Bearer

Ruling planet: Uranus (Saturn, ancient ruler)

Natural house: eleventh house

Element: air

Quality: fixed

Body areas: circulatory system, ankles, shins, calves

Gemstone: amethyst

Colors: iridescent blue, turquoise

Flower: orchid

Key phrase: I know

Keyword: unconventional

Personality traits: Loyal, humanitarian, high-strung, individualistic, rebellious, impersonal, group-oriented, friendly, original, inventive, intellectual, aloof, detached, unpredictable, honest, logical, future-oriented, independent, stubborn, determined

Countries/regions: Sweden, Poland, Russia, Iran, Cyprus, Finland

Cities: Salzburg, Austria; Brighton, England; Bremen and Hamburg, Germany; Moscow, Russia; Helsinki, Finland

Common things ruled by Aquarius: electricity, technology, radiology, television, radio, club, organization, fraternal group, friendship, social event, airplane hangar, invention, wireless communication, aerospace, astrology, computer

Famous people: Abraham Lincoln, Oprah Winfrey, Ellen DeGeneres, Justin Timberlake, Hank Aaron, Dick Cheney, Lewis Carroll, Christian Dior, Tom Selleck, Paul Newman, Alan Alda, Jennifer Aniston, Mark Spitz, John Travolta, Sheryl Crow, Paris Hilton

Major strengths: loyal, inventive, independent

Major challenges: detached, high-strung, rebellious

Aquarius is as stable and determined—and stubborn—as the other fixed signs, but it also embraces change. This dichotomy is only one example of the unpredictability of this sign, which tends to live in the future. Aquarius is an unusual mix of old-fashioned and progressive, rebellious and conventional, friendly and aloof. All this makes it tough, if not impossible, to predict what this sign will do next. And any Aquarius will tell you this is part of their charm, because most take great pride in their individuality, in being different from others they see as "normal." This, too, adds to their eclectic magnetism that many find fascinating.

An Aquarius without friends is like an Aquarius without water. And that's another dichotomy. Aquarius is an air sign, but its symbol is the Water Bearer, a woman pouring life-giving water on humanity—the symbol of the humanitarian, which Aquarius is to its soul. Every Aquarius comes alive when near a body of water, especially the ocean, which is particularly recentering for this sign.

Friendship is one of Aquarius's strengths, as is networking. Most have a phone book full of names and numbers of acquaintances, but only a select few are true lifelong friends. Nevertheless, Aquarius sees them all as friends, and enjoys group activities and teamwork. Many also get involved in charitable organizations, where they can fulfill their need for friendship and helping others.

As an air sign, Aquarius is a communicator, interested in ideas, concepts, people, and a wide variety of information. This is also the sign of the inventive mind that sees obstacles as both a challenge and an opportunity. Aquarius sees things from a different angle and has a future-oriented perspective. The solutions are usually so simple that others not only marvel but wonder why they didn't think of that. Like the other air signs, Aquarius maintains an emotional distance, but unlike Gemini and Libra, Aquarius is detached. Although this can interfere with some relationships, it's also an advantage for this sign's objective perspective.

Yet for all their detachment, every Aquarius I know is friendly and expresses a genuine interest in other people. Most people realize only later that they learned little about the Aquarius, who learned a great deal about them. One Aquarius client in particular has excelled as an entrepreneur because of his ability to maintain an objective distance while fulfilling the client's needs. Another client is heavily involved in her community, a leader in many organizations whose networking talent has benefited many. She knows exactly whom to call for whatever she needs.

The fixed quality of Aquarius adds determination, and this sign can be relentless when in pursuit of a goal. The air element gives Aquarius the ability to shift gears when necessary and try another tactic. This sign can effectively use self-talk, but the fixed quality also promotes stubbornness. Once an Aquarius makes up his or her mind, that's it. Aquarius is open-minded prior to making a decision, but rarely after, and often asks for opinions as a final step even though the decision has been made, just not finalized. It's sort of a confirmation process that only Aquarius fully understands.

The house in your chart with Aquarius on the cusp is where you're determined yet stubborn, detached yet in touch with many people. This is also where you need the freedom to express your individuality and your innovative ideas and problem-solving skills. Here you think

in terms of the future rather than the past or present.

Aquarius Sun Sign

You're an independent soul who values privacy and freedom, yet you also welcome many people into your life. They're necessary to your well-being, especially friends.

Aquarius is the universal sign of friendship, and many Aquarians are involved in clubs, organizations, and other group endeavors. This fits well with your altruistic concern for humanity. You have friends, both male and female, from all walks of life and are attracted to people who are unusual in some way, because they're interesting. Status, education, profession, and background are unimportant to you in friendship, and rapport is based on a strong intellectual connection.

Aquarians have a reputation for being different, inconsistent, and unpredictable. You embody all these traits in some way, even if it's not immediately apparent to others. Some Aquarians express their uniqueness through unconventional clothing or home décor, while others have unusual interests, careers, or hobbies. That's a reflection of your innovative and intelligent mind, which finds realistic solutions that are also outside the norm.

People might remark that you live in the future. That's true, but not exactly as others perceive this trait. Although you're uncomfortable without an event to look forward to and regularly plan your life hours, days, weeks, months, and years in advance, what others fail to understand is that this provides a level of security and stability in your personal world of change. With this future orientation comes the ability to spot emerging trends, a talent that makes some Aquarians exceptional inventors.

Aquarius is a fixed sign, so you're determined but also stubborn, as well as persistent and self-reliant. You dislike change except when you initiate it, and at times promote change for the sake of change. To you, that's the first step toward progress and the future, and it satisfies your need to rebel against the status quo. You're fascinated by the latest gadgets and technology.

You pride yourself on your individuality, and need freedom of thought and action. Yet there's a conservative side to you as well. You learn from experience and incorporate the past into the future. Calculated risks are more your style than impulsive moves. You also have a personal code of ethics that might seem old-fashioned to some.

At times, you can be as distant and cold as your wintry sign, primarily when someone has violated what was a trusted friendship. But with nearly everyone you maintain an emotional distance that makes you feel less vulnerable. You intellectualize your feelings, as do all the air signs. Even when you're at your most charming, your approach is impersonal and somewhat detached. You learn a lot about other people through conversation, but reveal little about yourself except in the most secure relationships.

Relationships

Relationships perplex and stimulate you, but all provide new insights into human nature, which intrigues you. You accept most people at face value, and are alternately attracted and put off by those whose lives are based on self and ego rather than your worldly humanitarian view. With persistence—which you have—you can win others over to your way of thinking.

You're reluctant to get involved with most people on a deeply emotional level. You think about and analyze your feelings and are far more comfortable with ideas and conversation.

You want a partner who's also your best friend and confidant. Mutual support is vital to partnership success, and lack of it can be a deal breaker. Just as important to you is the ability to maintain your individuality and independence to pursue your own interests. Too much togetherness can stifle a relationship, from your perspective.

Aquarians make lively parents who encourage their children to learn, read, play, have an active lifestyle, and develop a diverse group of friends. You want the same for yourself. Friendship is vital to your well-being, and you set that example for your children.

Most Aquarians have an address book packed with names and numbers, and your many friends and acquaintances are also networking contacts for everything from home repairs to career matters. Likewise, you enjoy networking to benefit other people, including loved ones, and bringing them together. As the "joiner" of the zodiac, you're drawn to clubs, organizations, and other group endeavors that have a purpose beyond socializing.

Career

You view your workplace as something of a second home—not as the focus of a work-dominated life, but for the relationships you form with coworkers. That can make it tough to move on when you've outgrown your position. But it's an advantage if you move up in the company or into another department, because you simultaneously widen your network.

Aquarians like to personalize some part of their workspace with photos of family and friends and other mementos. You're also the ultimate team player and thus can do well in any position that involves group projects.

Once you settle on a career path, you're likely to stick with it throughout your work life, adding and honing skills that qualify you for expanded job opportunities. You easily transfer knowledge gained in one position to the next.

Many Aquarians seek positions of power, in part so they can maintain their independence while remaining committed to a career. If that's your choice, then your determination to reach your goal is unwavering, and you can outlast the competition through sheer willpower.

You could find success in any technology field, perhaps as an electrician or a computer programmer or technician. Some Aquarians pursue careers in radiology, neurology, or physical therapy, and others excel in the media or nonprofit sector, or as investigators or researchers.

Money

You flip from thrift to extravagance, from organization to misplaced bills, from wishful thinking to reality. As in much of your life, consistency comes and goes depending on your mood and mindset. Yet you also have the ability to achieve financial stability if that's your choice.

With rare exceptions, money seems to come when you need it. It also can slip through your fingers as if into thin air. The net result is that you just stay even unless you take charge, plan ahead, budget, and save.

Your financial strength is in the area of joint resources, including family funds, loans and mortgages, investments, and real estate. In this area you're practical, meticulous, and somewhat cautious. You gather information, analyze it, and then make a decision. Debt is something you never take lightly, and you're always careful to read the fine print. But at times you can get bogged down in the details; keep the big picture in mind.

Although you can do well with investments, the ups and downs can worry you. There's an easy solution: invest for the long term and resist the urge to buy and sell as prices fluctuate—as long as all factors indicate that's a positive and potentially profitable decision.

You can realize sizable gains from home ownership, and, if you're handy, you might do well with rental property.

HOW TO SPOT A PISCES

Small feet
Self-absorbed
Compassionate

Glyph: ♓

Symbol: the Fish

Ruling planet: Neptune (Jupiter, ancient ruler)

Natural house: twelfth house

Element: water

Quality: mutable

Body areas: feet, lymphatic system

Gemstone: aquamarine

Colors: sea green, violet

Flower: water lily

Key phrase: I believe

Keyword: compassion

Personality traits: Sensitive, impressionable, psychic, martyrdom, irresponsible, visionary, dreamy, creative, imaginative, kind, escapist, vague, deceptive, friendly, self-sacrificing, charitable, unrealistic

Countries/regions: Samoa, Normandy, Sahara Desert

Cities: Seville, Spain; Regensburg, Germany; Lancaster, England; Warsaw, Poland

Common things ruled by Pisces: photography, ocean, aquarium, drugs, alcohol, chemical, motion picture, prison, boot, gasoline, hospital, pump, institution, well, dream, sleep, water, charity, retreat, self-undoing, hidden factors and enemies, ship, pipe, submarine, swimming, swindler, lime, platinum, tin, sock, shoe

Famous people: Albert Einstein, Drew Barrymore, Nat King Cole, Clark Gable, Ralph Nader, George Washington, Patty Hearst, Al Jareau, Ansel Adams, Erma Bombeck, Richard Burton, Bruce Willis, Quincy Jones, Ron Howard, Kurt Cobain, Jessica Biel

Major strengths: compassion, creativity, intuition/psychic ability

Major challenges: escapist, impressionable, unrealistic

Some astrologers believe Pisces is the sum of all parts, that it embodies all twelve signs of the zodiac. There's some merit to that opinion, as this sign almost seems to operate on a different level, being highly spiritual and in touch with the universe. Pisces is by far the most compassionate sign and is very concerned about doing the right thing. Nearly every Pisces I know, even those who have "tougher" influences in their chart, gives to those in need in some way—money, time, energy. They rarely say no to a request for help.

As a water sign, Pisces is creative, usually through a visual medium rather than words, where their strong intuition (and often psychic ability) is an asset. Sometimes their creations seem to be almost channeled, and most people with a strong Pisces influence have vivid dreams. This sign is also highly impressionable and receptive, absorbing the surrounding energy, and can be gullible, with a tendency to believe nearly everything without question. Pisces is trusting, sometimes too much so. Highly sensitive, they go out of their way to avoid conflict and even physically retreat when faced with controversy. Pisces also takes the indirect approach whenever possible, hinting rather than clearly stating their thoughts and opinions.

Pisces is the last of the mutable signs and thus is adaptable and easygoing, like its symbol, the Fishes, swimming aimlessly through life. That can make it difficult to direct and focus the many talents of this sign. As a result, some people adopt negative escapist behavior, such as drug and alcohol abuse. Most choose a harmless escape outlet, such as television, movie viewing, computer games, or a visual hobby, as a way of recentering their energy, which is vital to the Pisces wellbeing.

Possibly the biggest challenge for Pisces is facing reality. Many are unrealistic. They prefer to see the bright side and can fall in the trap of wishing away reality simply by ignoring it, only to be disillusioned when the situation doesn't disappear.

One very talented and creative Pisces consulted me because he was having difficulty finding his career niche. He had considered and rejected fine art for several reasons, and was searching for another option. Because of other factors in his chart (including a strong Aquarius influence), it was obvious he had an aptitude for computers, which he had never explored. This was in the early days of the Internet, so I suggested he investigate website design as a career option. He did and is enjoying a tremendously successful, satisfying, and lucrative career, in part because he entered the field well ahead of many people.

The house in your chart with Pisces on the cusp is where you are compassionate and caring but also idealistic and at times unrealistic. Here is where you'll find an excellent creative outlet and the setting or situations in which your sixth sense is strongest.

Pisces Sun Sign

As a Pisces, you are caring and compassionate. You reach out to others, ever sensitive to their feelings. You're among the first to lend a helping hand, and willingly do all you can to fulfill others' needs. Many times you put their desires ahead of your own. That's admirable, but being

a perpetual soft touch isn't necessarily in your best interests. Receiving is as important as giving, and despite how you may feel, it's wise to put you and yours first. No one else will.

As is the case with all the water signs (of which Pisces is one), your moods fluctuate. Your feelings are easily hurt, but you tend to internalize your emotions as a means of self-protection. Highly sensitive to other people and your surroundings, you have a strong sixth sense. Many Pisceans are psychic. This trait has its pluses and minuses, and with awareness and practice you can maximize the positive.

You're very impressionable and absorb the subtle—or not so subtle—vibrations of people, places, and things. Next time you sense a sudden shift in your frame of mind or emotions, think about the people, events, or location that preceded it. Chances are, you picked up what was in the "air." Learn to use metaphysical techniques to protect yourself from unwanted intrusions and to maintain a more even temperament.

Used to advantage, your intuition and the flexibility associated with your mutable sign give you the edge in many situations. You're like a chameleon in that you can adapt to changing circumstances and fit in almost anywhere with anyone. Your charm is no small part of the equation, and you quickly win supporters. Be cautious, though, about becoming a "yes" person. Form your own opinions and present them with assurance, charisma, and the persuasive ability that's one of your strengths.

Trusting and idealistic, you want to see only the best in people. That's fine—to a point. But not when reality would serve you better. Practical responsibilities, the nuts and bolts of everyday life, are part of being human, and all the wishes in the world won't make them go away. Be smart and proactive. Research the facts or seek the advice of professionals (after carefully checking credentials) in financial, real estate, career, and other matters outside your area of interest or expertise.

Pisces people are exceptionally creative, and many express their strong visual orientation through art, photography, or crafts. Others excel at writing, acting, dancing, yoga, or creative ideas. Whatever avenue you choose, it's important—even vital—to your well-being to find your creative niche in leisure-time activities, professional pursuits, or both. When this urge is regularly nurtured and satisfied, you experience a sense of wholeness and are more confident and able to deal with the mundane realities of life.

Relationships

You're a charmer, a true people person who has a way with words and a smile that instantly puts others at ease. Friendly to most everyone—largely because you avoid making waves except as a last resort—only select people are part of your inner circle.

Your close friends are few, by choice, and you consider them to be soul mates. These deep and lasting associations usually span decades even if you live far apart and rarely see each other. There may be a significant age difference between you and these people, either older or younger. You also enjoy casual friendships with coworkers and others you meet through your career.

Few Pisceans do well without a mate. Commitment is a natural state for you. You dislike being alone and are content just to have someone, preferably your partner, in the same room.

Idealistic in matters of the heart, you're a romantic who can fall in love with love. That makes it wise to delay commitment until you've seen all sides of your prospective partner. He or she is likely to be realistic and discriminating, as meticulous as you are creative, and in tune with the many practicalities of daily life to which you're oblivious.

If you're a parent, you're a nurturing one whose aim is to provide a safe, secure, and loving environment that gives your children the best possible start in life. But you also can overdo it in an attempt to protect your children from all of life's challenges. That's unrealistic and also not in their best interests. They're far better off learning some life lessons on their own and asserting their independence, within reason, when they're ready for it.

Career

Although you tend to be laid-back and let others take the lead in much of your life, you have both the desire and the initiative to stand out in the workplace. You take great pride in your work and expect to be recognized and financially rewarded for your efforts. Here also you can be a leader, inspire others, and generate enthusiasm.

You want more of an upscale working environment, including all the latest tools and technology to do your job well. This is something to look for and ask about before you accept a position. Also be sure you click with your immediate supervisor.

Most Pisceans are not especially ambitious, as this factor is secondary to job and career happiness and contentment. Yet you can spot trends that others miss and guide your career in new, expanded directions. It's to your advantage, though, to remain in the same or a related field in order to progress and make the most of your skills and talents, rather than jump at every opportunity just because it's there. Many Pisceans return to school later in life to advance in their careers or, more likely, to prepare for a new direction.

If you're interested in health care, you could succeed as a physician, nurse, physical or massage therapist, herbalist, or podiatrist, or in another position that involves patient contact. You could excel in sales, the beverage or oil and gas industry, or the corrections field. Some Pisceans find success as oceanographers or in the fishing industry, and others are outstanding photographers and dancers.

Money

Finances can be a challenge for you, but they don't have to be. It's a matter of commitment, planning, knowledge, and budgeting. That's the way to control your tendency to buy on impulse with only a little thought given to the impact on monthly and long-term security. Get in the habit of giving yourself a weekly allowance and saving through a payroll deduction.

You also should avoid credit as much as possible, except for home ownership and a mortgage. It's too easy to run up debt without fully realizing it, resulting in hefty interest charges. Always read all the fine print before you sign.

You're loaded with moneymaking initiative and set high yet realistic and attainable earnings goals, which you usually achieve. Partnership funds also increase your net worth, and you're supportive of your mate's efforts to contribute to family funds. His or her income may exceed your own, which is fine with you.

Investments can be profitable, and you also value the security provided by investment funds that are earmarked for your retirement years. But think long term and ignore the short-term ups and downs, which can trigger an emotional roller coaster. Home ownership can be advantageous if you stay in one place long enough to realize a sizable gain through equity. You could inherit money from a sibling, aunt, or uncle.

THE PLANETS

Each of the ten planets plays a role in your life. Some are more prominent or influential than others. You might have a powerful Mercury (communication) in your birth chart and thus excel at communication. If your Sun is in Gemini (the sign ruled by Mercury), you could have considerable writing or speaking talent. If Neptune (creativity) is strong in your chart and your Sun is in Cancer (a domestic sign), you could work from home as an artist, artisan, or interior decorator.

The prominence of a planet in your horoscope is determined by its sign, house position, and the aspects it makes to other planets. There is no set formula to determine this. It's part of the art of astrology. With only a little experience and by studying the examples in this book, you'll quickly be able to identify the more prominent planets in your chart.

Each planet has its own characteristics and represents certain personality factors, such as independence, responsibility, love, money, or luck. All of these qualities, and many more, are a part of your life. Your life focus may be on two or three or five or six of them and what they represent. Relationships, for example, might be a dominant theme in your life, while your best friend might be career-focused. Just as it's impossible to be and do all things in one lifetime, it's also impossible to have ten strong planets and do each to the max. You'd never sleep!

You're probably aware of your personal dominant themes, but there may be others as yet unrealized or developed. Astrology can help you identify them so you can make the most of your personal planetary energy.

You know your Sun sign. You also have a Moon sign, Mars sign, Jupiter sign, and a sign for each of the other planets. Each planet is colored, or modified, by its sign. Someone with the Moon in Aries, for example, is likely to be up-front and open in his or her emotional expression, while someone with the Moon in Scorpio probably has deep feelings but expresses them only when confident of the response. The Moon and what it represents is still the Moon and what it represents; it simply manifests in many different ways.

The Sun, Moon, Mercury, Venus, and Mars, which move more quickly than the other planets through the zodiac, are called *personal planets* (chart 6). Jupiter, Saturn, Uranus, Neptune, and Pluto are the *outer planets*. Uranus, Neptune, and Pluto are also described as *generational*

planets; they move so slowly that everyone born within several or many years has these planets in the same sign. Sometimes Jupiter and Saturn are described as *transitional planets* because they move slower than the personal planets and faster than the generational planets.

The descriptions of the planets in the following section highlight the major characteristics of each, many of which you will recognize as being active in your life. The descriptions of the planets in the signs represent the same. Some will ring true for you, and others will be only somewhat familiar. Once you have a complete picture of your chart, which includes the house positions and aspects, you'll more clearly understand why some planets are strong and others are less active in your life.

Type of Planet		Planet	Orbital Cycle
Personal planets	Personal planets	Sun ☉	1 year
		Moon ☽	27.33 days
		Mercury ☿	88 days
		Venus ♀	225 days
		Mars ♂	1 year, 11 months (688 days)
Outer planets	Transitional planets	Jupiter ♃	12 years
		Saturn ♄	29½ years
	Generational planets	Uranus ♅	84 years
		Neptune ♆	165 years
		Pluto ♇	248 years

Chart 6. Orbital Cycles of the Planets

┌───┐

EASY INTERPRETATION

Keywords make chart interpretation easy. Here are a few examples of planets in signs to get you started.

Mercury + Cancer =
Thought process + emotional = emotionally based thinking

Mars + Leo =
Drive + ego = leadership

Jupiter + Taurus
Abundance + money = security

Saturn + Aquarius =
Restriction + independence = self-reliance

└───┘

SUN

Glyph: ☉

Sign rulership: Leo

Natural house: Fifth house of fun, leisure, creativity, children, romance

Significance: Your strongest ego investment and self-esteem, creative expression, basic urges, your identity

Rules: Children, gold, heart, glandular system, spinal cord, government, honors, royalty, gambling, supervisors, fame, males, playground, gym, stock market

Mythology: Apollo, the Sun god and son of Zeus, is depicted as a vibrant young man and is associated with prophecy, the arts, healing, light, and music.

Like our solar system, with the Sun at its center and the source of heat, light, and energy, you and your Sun sign are the center of your personal solar system. You express your life force through the traits of your Sun sign as well as those of the other planets in your horoscope.

Because there are ten planets in a horoscope—each of which is a personality component—no one is 100 percent true to his or her Sun sign. Some factors are always present, some occasionally, and some not at all. Yet your overall life force, the essence and foundation of you as an individual, is expressed through your Sun sign.

Just as the Sun is visibly bright on cloudless days, some traits associated with your Sun sign are true to the final detail. Some traits are apparent part of the time or in specific situations, like a partly cloudy day with intermittent sunshine. Other characteristics are hidden and yet to be revealed, just as an overcast day masks the sun.

The Sun is the most important planet in your chart. It represents your individuality and ego, your drive to achieve and self-expression, your internal motivation, and your basic likes and dislikes and interests.

(See chapter 2 for information on the Sun in the signs.)

MOON

Glyph: ☽

Sign rulership: Cancer

Natural house: Fourth house of home, family, parents

Significance: Your strongest emotional attachments, area of life with the most fluctuation, need for security, emotional expression, instincts, nurturing, intuition

Rules: Emotions, habits, instincts, moods, domestic urge, females, mother, physical home, family, breasts, stomach, body fluids, subconscious, memory, the public, changing conditions, sixth sense

Mythology: The goddess Diana was the twin sister of Apollo, the god of the Sun. Diana was the goddess of the hunt.

The Moon represents your emotional energy, conscious mind, and habits. It's your comfort zone—what makes you feel content and secure—and how you react emotionally and share yourself with others in various situations and relationships. The Moon also is associated with home and family, the domestic urge, your mother, and childhood.

Lunar energy is changeable and diverse, ranging from impulsive, to nurturing, to creative, outgoing, or reserved, depending on the Moon's sign. This is why some people need continual reassurance and others are bold and confident, freely expressing their emotions.

You can observe this on a daily basis. No two days are exactly alike, just like no two people or signs are exactly alike. On some days, people are smiley and upbeat; on others, they're testy, quiet, tense, talkative, or industrious. Much of this is related to the day's Moon sign, so it's easy to see astrology in action if you're observant.

The Moon changes signs approximately every two and a half days, traveling through the entire zodiac about every twenty-eight days. You can easily track these lunar shifts by using an astrological calendar or ephemeris (see pages 23–26). After a while, you'll begin to see patterns repeat over and over each month as the Moon visits each sign. Once you know a little more about astrology, you can use your own chart to determine which Moon sign days are best for you for certain activities.

On a practical level, the Moon reflects your physical home and the décor and furnishings that make you feel comfortable and secure.

Moon in the Signs
Moon in Aries
Courageous and confident, you're energetic, independent, and ambitious. You openly express your emotions, respond impulsively, and have a quick temper. These outbursts, although sudden, are not long-lasting, and you often regret them afterward and wonder why you reacted so strongly. The root cause might be your dislike of interference and rules that you feel shouldn't apply to you, as well as your highly competitive nature. The solution is to develop patience and a cooperative attitude; you can get further in life when you include others in plans and projects

and set an example as the outstanding leader you can be. Home life is lively, with activities, projects, and people coming and going.

Moon in Taurus

Your emotions are steady, on an even keel, which has a calming influence on those around you. Motivated by a need for financial and domestic security (both of which you're likely to achieve), you surround yourself with creature comforts and mementos, and might have artwork and cherished family heirlooms. Beware of clutter and saving outdated and unusable items just for emotional security; part with anything that fits in that category on a regular basis. Food is part of your comfort zone and can lead to weight gain. A congenial home life is necessary to your well-being, and you're protective of those you love. Remember, though, that people are not possessions. You also enjoy routine and dislike change.

Moon in Gemini

Change is the only constant in your emotional life, and thus you keep people guessing. They never know how you'll react or what your mood will be at any given moment. This fluctuation is accompanied by restlessness, adaptability, and a quick mind that has wide-ranging interests. You may become even more talkative when tension rises, yet part of this is your comfort zone. Talking out and through your feelings helps you discover how you truly feel about a person, place, thing, or event. Where others experience emotions to the depths of their souls, you think about and rationalize them. Home life is active, and it's clear to any visitor that you're involved in multiple hobbies and diversions. That's how you prevent boredom.

Moon in Cancer

The Moon is at home in Cancer, and you have deep emotional ties to loved ones. Warm and loving, you're a natural nurturer, but doing too much for the precious people in your life also can have a "smothering" effect. As much as you'd like to, you can't protect them from every potential hurt, some of which are necessary for growth. Your moods are changeable, and you withdraw when upset. Domestic and financial security are necessary to your well-being, and you go out of your way to achieve both. Be careful, though, about sliding into a hoarding mentality. Security is a state of mind as much as it is money in the bank. Many people with a Cancer Moon are excellent cooks, and all strive for domestic tranquility and a warm, welcoming home.

Moon in Leo

You need recognition and attention and want to be admired by everyone, especially those you love. Loyalty and devotion are two of your lunar strengths, but you also have a big ego that's unhappy if your affections aren't appreciated and returned. Then your emotional response can be self-centered, your only consideration being what's best for you. And you can slip into dogmatic speech as a way to assert your desire to be in charge. Overall, though, you're generous and warmhearted, freely express your emotions, and have a romantic soul that's as dramatic as a grand Hollywood passion. Your love of luxury and only the finest money can buy (or you can afford) extends to your home, which you want to be a showcase for your success. You take great pride in both home and family.

Moon in Virgo

Quiet and reserved, work and helping others bring you great emotional satisfaction. You enjoy planning and organization and have an unerring eye for detail, which at times can spark criticism if others fail to meet your definition of perfection. Routine is your comfort zone, although you can be versatile when necessary, and you pride yourself on cleanliness. Your home may be messy or neat, but either way, there's a sense of order that suits your needs. Anyone with a Virgo Moon can find anything even in a cluttered home. You're practical and analytical and thus think through your feelings by examining them from every angle to determine how you feel. Doing so makes you feel secure in decision making. Not one to openly express your emotions, you do open up with those you know well and love.

Moon in Libra

Your emotional well-being is directly linked to close, loving, affectionate relationships, and a supportive partnership is vital to happiness for most people with Moon in Libra. You also can do well in a business partnership, provided you each have an equal share in decision making, responsibilities, and earnings. Intuition adds to your exceptional people skills, which include charm, tact, fairness, and grace; you dislike anything crude. Although you avoid conflict and confrontation and go out of your way to ensure harmony, your temper emerges when you're pushed too far, much to the surprise of others.

You also have a strong need for approval and recognition and can be indecisive about feelings, seeing and weighing both sides with an intellectual approach.

Moon in Scorpio

Deeply passionate, your emotions are intense and unwavering. People might sense this, but only those closest to you know the depth of feeling behind your stoic face. Always private, you can be secretive and suspicious, questioning the motives of others, partly to protect your sensitive inner core. Extremely close to family and loved ones, you can become stubborn, possessive, and even jealous. Develop tolerance and foster independence in those you love deeply; it will result in stronger ties. Most people with a Scorpio Moon have their own space within the home, even if it's just a comfortable chair that's off-limits to everyone else. This adds to your sense of security, as do financial and material resources, which you strive to achieve.

Moon in Sagittarius

You avoid emotional ties that limit your independence. This doesn't mean all people with a Sagittarius Moon are loners. Far from it! Enthusiastic, outgoing, and popular, you're the life of the party, always ready for the next social adventure. However, anyone who attempts to restrict your freedom-loving lifestyle is soon a person of the past, and you thus might choose to remain single. Idealistic and highly principled, you speak the truth as you see it and can be tactless; add a little fluff to soften your message. Unconcerned with domestic neatness, you're content most anywhere and see your home as a haven, a place to relax and unwind from your travels.

Some people with this lunar influence are reckless risk takers.

Moon in Capricorn

You're an ambitious, hard worker who invests much of your emotional energy in getting ahead in the world. Career advancement and status are vital to your well-being, on the same level with financial security. Reserved and aloof at times, this is the outward reflection of your discomfort with freely expressed emotions, yours or almost anyone else's. Warmth emerges in close relationships when you're sure you're on solid footing. Home ownership is important, and yours might be plain and simple or a showcase of your worldly success. It's also the place where you retreat for time alone, which you need regularly to recharge yourself, body and soul. Rules and structure are important to you.

Moon in Aquarius

You're passionate about humanitarian issues, but less so about personal relationships. Friendly and independent, you're detached and keep most people somewhat at a distance. You intellectualize your emotions. You think about how you feel, taking all factors into consideration as you self-talk your way through your feelings. Intuition is part of the equation, and your hunches about people are often on target. Friendships may be the single most important relationships in your life; if not, they run a very close second, followed by your many acquaintances. You especially enjoy entertaining friends in your home, where the décor may in some way reveal your unconventional side. You also welcome people from all walks of life; Aquarius is the sign of equality.

Moon in Pisces

Sensitive and caring, you're a sympathetic, compassionate soul whose heart wants to save the world. You're thus prone to emotional hurts that others toss off and walk away from, so it's to your advantage to consider the source and rise above it. Most people with a Pisces Moon are exceptionally creative in some way, and many have psychic ability. Because you easily absorb vibrations from people and places, it's important to protect yourself from negative energy. (Metaphysical techniques, such as visualizing yourself surrounded by protective white light, can be helpful.) A romantic, you love deeply and have close family ties. You experience a sense of freedom at home, where you fill your leisure hours with a wide variety of activities.

MERCURY

Glyph: ☿

Sign rulerships: Gemini and Virgo

Natural houses: Third house of communication, sixth house of work and service

Significance: Conscious mind, thinking process, how the mind processes and directs thoughts, communication style

Rules: Communication, messages, books, letters, magazines, blogs, contracts, commuting, neighbors and neighborhood, siblings, paper, vehicles, relatives in general, mail, phones, writing, speaking, intelligence, arms, lungs, hands, shoulders, intestines, nervous system, physical coordination, decision making

Mythology: Mercury, the son of Jupiter, was the messenger god, an outstanding athlete who wore winged sandals. He was also the god of commerce and travel.

Mercury governs the mind, your thought processes, and how you problem-solve and make decisions. It also represents learning and information and thus some of your general interests and what triggers your curiosity.

Mercury also is associated with communication, quick trips and errands, mail, calls, and messages.

Some people communicate with ease and like to talk or write. Some make quick decisions, and others ponder every question. Some love details, and others see only the big picture.

There is no right or wrong communication style. Your style is your own, as reflected by the sign and house placement of your Mercury, and the planets it contacts.

Mercury moves through the entire zodiac in about year. Because it's always near the Sun (never more than 28° away), it's either in the same sign as the Sun, the sign before, or the sign after. For example, if your Sun is in Virgo, then your Mercury is in Leo (sign before), Virgo, or Libra (sign after), depending on how fast Mercury was moving when you were born. At times, Mercury's pace is quick, zipping through a sign in two weeks. At others, it moves very slowly. This is the result of retrograde motion, when a planet appears to move backward (see "Retrograde and Direct Motion" on page 16 and "Mercury Retrograde" on page 127).

People born when Mercury is retrograde are introspective, subjective, and intuitive. They often think more than they speak, and hesitate to express their ideas until they know what others think. If you were born on a day when Mercury was stationary, then your thought processes are especially active and you're an avid communicator (speaking or writing) who also tunes in to news, reads, and stays in touch with people through the latest technology. (See "Retrograde and Direct Motion" on page 16 for more information on the influence of stationary planets.)

Mercury in the Signs
Mercury in Aries

Snap decisions and quick responses are your specialties. That's an advantage much of the time, but not always. Take a moment to think before you speak, especially if you've ever wished you could retract words spoken. Competitive, impulsive and at times argumentative, you're an outstanding debater who has strong opinions. A tactful approach gains more supporters when you step into your natural leadership role, as does patience with those who aren't as quick on the uptake as you are. Your hand-eye coordination is excellent. Even so, put risk taking on hold when you're on the road, and generally err on the side of caution to help prevent accidents.

Mercury in Taurus

Your practical mind thoroughly ponders every decision. That's your nature, but it's also because once you commit, you follow through with determination. Those who attempt to push you into a decision or action soon wish they hadn't, especially if it's enough to trigger your rare but intense temper. Thoughts and decisions are often centered on material and financial security, which is of primary importance to you, and sound judgment and common sense contribute to your financial and business acumen. You can be a shrewd bargainer and nego-tiator. Your powers of concentration are among the best in the zodiac, and you're noted for your realistic solutions.

Mercury in Gemini

Information fuels your bright, curious brain, which is a storehouse of bits and pieces of data, some trivial, some useful. It's all stored in men-tal file folders, ready to use whenever you need it. People are amazed by how much you know and often view you as an expert in many sub-jects. What they don't know is that you're a quick study who amasses just enough depth to sound like an expert. Your thinking is quick, ver-satile, logical, and objective, and you may be an excellent speaker and/or writer. Staying focused is your biggest mental challenge. You're easily bored and thus can be scattered, drifting from one interest to the next. That's also why you know a little about a lot of things. Many people with the Moon in Gemini are avid readers and puzzlers.

Mercury in Cancer

Much of your thinking is in some way related to home, family, and material and financial secu-rity. Decisions are influenced by emotions and your strong sixth sense rather than purely objec-tive information. Most people with Mercury in Cancer are in regular touch with close friends and family. You also think a lot about the past and have an excellent memory. Nervous tension can build due to a tendency to internalize wor-ries; get in the habit of talking them out with a family member or someone else you trust. Though you are kind and caring, your temper

nevertheless emerges when you're provoked, especially when family or security issues arise.

Mercury in Leo

A commanding presence and a flair for the dra-matic enhance your leadership and presenta-tion skills, and you have a talent for motivating others to do and be their best. People respond to your infectious enthusiasm, but you also can be opinionated and believe you have all the answers. Sometimes you do; sometimes you don't. So keep an open mind and listen to other viewpoints. This approach also sparks your creative thinking and winning ideas. Your determination and willpower are unwavering once a goal is set, and your sharp focus sees you through to success. Painstaking in decision mak-ing, you're equally slow to change your mind.

Mercury in Virgo

You're an excellent planner and organizer who covers all the details. Thinking and analysis pre-cede any undertaking, and you proceed only when you feel mentally prepared to succeed. Decision making follows a similar pattern; you think about every factor and possible outcome and use your excellent research skills to gather information. Observant and intuitive, you quickly connect the dots, usually well ahead of anyone else. Your reasoning ability is superb, and you aim for precision and perfection. But you're also a worrier. Replace those thoughts with upbeat ones, and do the same whenever critical self-talk begins to creep into your thinking.

Mercury in Libra

You're the master of subtle persuasion, charm-ing and diplomatic. An idea person with vision, you let others think your ideas are their own. This builds instant rapport and support to achieve your own ends. As much as possible, you avoid conflict and confrontation, which upset you, preferring instead to take the initiative to promote cooperation and compromise. Decision making can challenge your sense of fairness and impartiality because you see and value both sides of any question. What others view as indecisiveness is really your 50–50 viewpoint. Though you generally are tolerant and congenial, the rare temper flare-up is nevertheless unmistakable and brief.

Mercury in Scorpio

You're an exceptional researcher and investigator, with an inquiring and intuitive mind that digs deep for information. Trivia and surface information hold no interest for you. You enjoy taking things apart to see how they work, and your cleverness and creativity are key components in your ability to transform what others see as junk into something useful. Secretive and shrewd, you speak with most people only when you have something important to say and then in as few words as possible. Decisions made are usually final, and determination (and stubbornness) keeps you focused on your goal. Some people with Mercury in Scorpio can be vengeful and jealous.

Mercury in Sagittarius

The pursuit of knowledge and understanding—not just information—is a guiding force in your life. You're highly principled, and ethics are a vital part of decision making. You see things as black or white, right or wrong. You also speak the truth, plain and simple, as you see it. Try

a little tact to soften your message and build support for your expansive ideas. Optimism is a strength, but you don't always consider the details, the finer points, which are often important. The same applies to potential consequences. Luck and positive thinking work wonders—if they're balanced with reality. Higher education leads to career advancement.

Mercury in Capricorn

Realistic thinking is your specialty, along with a high level of common sense and logical, methodical reasoning ability. You work through questions and problems step by step until an appropriate answer or solution emerges. These qualities make you an expert at planning and organization, both of which you do before beginning a project or task. In addition to your focus on practical solutions, most decisions are linked in some way to status and career as a way to further your very ambitious aims. You're a traditionalist who lives life according to rules—either society's, your own, or a little of both. Short- and long-term goals are a way of life, and you fully commit yourself to achieving them.

Mercury in Aquarius

Your unique yet practical ideas prompt people to say, "Why didn't I think of that?" That's the result of your clever, imaginative mind at its innovative best. You're also intuitive, sensing what people really think versus what they say. Open-minded, you listen to other viewpoints out of curiosity but rarely change your mind. You also have your own—albeit unusual in some way—code of ethics that guides your thinking process and decisions. Emotions rarely influence decisions, which benefit from your objective thinking. Friends are an important part of your life, and those who know you well understand that you're more comfortable expressing thoughts than feelings.

Mercury in Pisces

Your mental strengths are creativity and imagination, both of which are beneficial in your career and leisure-time activities. But this influence also diminishes practicality, so you can be unrealistic and prone to wishful thinking. Charming words and a caring, compassionate interest in others endear you to people, although you should be cautious about believing everything you hear. Form your own opinions. Your sixth sense is an asset, but it's important to protect yourself from the negative energy generated by some people and places; your receptivity makes it easy to absorb the thoughts, moods, and feelings that surround you.

VENUS

Glyph: ♀

Sign rulerships: Taurus and Libra

Natural houses: Second house of income and spending, seventh house of close relationships

Significance: What you attract, how you interact with others, partnership

Rules: Partner, cooperation, candy and sweets, perfume, social skills, vanity, grace, affection, spending habits, earning potential, cosmetics, artwork, clothing, jewelry, neck, throat, kidneys, venous circulation, compromise, love, beauty, harmony

Mythology: Venus was the goddess of love, fertility, gardens, vineyards, and beauty. She was the daughter of Jupiter.

Venus is the planet of love, close relationships, and personal resources—possessions, money, and earning power. This planet is known as the "lesser benefic," which means it's a planet of good fortune, although not as much so as Jupiter, the "greater benefic." Venus represents relationships and resources in every chart and, like the other planets, manifests according to its sign, house position, and aspects. It also represents your social skills and social life, the ways in which you're self-indulgent, how you express affection, and how you define beauty. Venus provides insights into the characteristics you seek in a partner.

Those are some of the specifics of Venus. Its influence, however, can be summarized thusly: Venus is what you attract and how you interact with others. Keep these two factors in mind as you study charts, and you will be on target every time.

Venus is a planet of refinement and in its purest form indicates grace, charm, cooperative efforts, finesse, consideration, and kindness. It also represents vanity. Venus indicates much about your spending and saving habits, whether you're extravagant, impulsive, thrifty, or generous. Possessions are very important to anyone with a prominent Venus: "Don't touch my stuff!"

Venus is never more than 48° away from the Sun. This means it can only be in the same sign as your Sun or either of the two signs that precede or follow your Sun. For example, if your Sun is in Sagittarius, then your Venus is in Libra or Scorpio (two signs before), Sagittarius, or Capricorn or Aquarius (two signs after), depending on how fast Venus was moving when you were born. At its speediest, Venus moves through a sign in about three to four weeks. Because of retrograde motion, it can spend up to four months in a sign. Venus is retrograde approximately every eighteen months.

If you were born when Venus was retrograde, you are less social and feel most comfortable with people you know well. Earnings may be limited initially, but that will change as you mature. The same time frame may apply to romantic opportunities. They might be limited or you could have difficulty finding someone who fits your partnership needs. If Venus was stationary when you were born, you have an abundant social life and excellent financial potential, and partnership is a priority. (See "Retrograde and Direct Motion" on page 16 for more information on the influence of stationary planets.)

Venus in the Signs
Venus in Aries

The thrill of new love excites you, and once committed, you keep the passion alive with spontaneity. However, you can be self-centered at times, more interested in your own desires than those of your mate. Cooperation and compromise are the solution. Generous with loved ones, you also occasionally splurge on yourself. High initiative can yield high income, but you spend almost as fast as you earn. Save and move beyond the "expenses meet income" mindset. Be wary of financial risks; do a thorough research job before you plunge.

Venus in Taurus

Warm and loving, you're an affectionate partner who's a true romantic. Love and commitment are high on your life priority list, and faith and trust contribute to a lasting partnership. Creature comforts, including gourmet food and a beautiful home, are vital to your well-being, as are financial and material security. You're a hard worker with high earning potential. You're also thrifty and expect good value for dollars spent. If the price is too high, you bargain or walk away. Some people with Venus in Taurus are hoarders.

Venus in Gemini

Variety excites you and keeps boredom at bay. This can lead to multiple partners as the desire for someone new takes hold. But many people with Venus in Gemini remain with a single mate who's a best friend and intellectually stimulating, both of which you need for lasting love. You enjoy an active social life, and your charming, witty, flirtatious nature adds to your popularity. Free spending can deplete resources at times, although you have above-average earning potential and may have two income sources. Financial luck manifests as bargains.

Venus in Cancer

Ultrasensitive in love, your feelings run deep and are easily hurt. Relationships can be affected by your periodic moodiness. You love with all your heart, and if a relationship feels right, you move ahead; if not, you don't. A desire for security motivates you, and you want a comfortable home and loving partner and family. But a tendency to "mother" everyone close to you can undermine the very security you want to achieve, because you end up smothering people and thus push them away Generally lucky in money matters, people with Venus in Cancer often amass sizable resources through savings, investments, and home ownership.

Venus in Leo

Warm, outgoing, and affectionate, you have a star-studded presence that makes you the center of attention more often than not. The social scene excites you, and you like to entertain friends in grand, dramatic style. In love, you're passionate and loyal, a true romantic who spares no expense. You have the desire and determination to earn a high salary that can fund your taste for luxury. Money matters usually go your way, although caution and common sense are advisable when other people and debt are involved. Put your ego on hold; live within a budget.

Venus in Virgo

You're choosy and idealistic in love and romance and expect a partner to live up to your high ideals and expectations. That's unrealistic and one reason why some people with Venus in Virgo remain single. With the right mate, however, you're sensual, caring, and supportive. But you can overdo it and become an enabler in the process. Focus on 50–50, and let your partner share the responsibilities of commitment. Emotionally, you think how you feel and feel how you think. Usually thrifty and practical, you occasionally will splurge, especially on loved ones. Your earning potential is above average, although credit encourages impulsive buys.

Venus in Libra

You feel incomplete without a mate. As a partner, you're loving and romantic, yet the strong urge for commitment can cause you to mistake infatuation for love. Go slowly and be sure before you commit. You also have an instinctive understanding of people, a sixth sense that gives you profound insight into human nature. That's a talent that fits well with your emphasis on tact and cooperation; you dislike controversy. A comfortable lifestyle is important to you, and you'll spend to satisfy your taste for quality and the finer things in life. You also have good financial sense and an eye for bargains.

Venus in Scorpio

Only someone with Venus in Scorpio can fully appreciate and understand your emotional depth and sensitivity. They are hidden behind a deceptively calm mask of mystery that reveals little of your true feelings, which are never ambivalent. You're protective of those you love, and insecurity (real or imagined) can spark possessiveness and jealousy that undermine the foundation of a relationship. As a result, your relationships range from stormy to serene, and you have a long memory. You're financially shrewd and know how to make and manage money. Earnings expectations are high, and you usually meet or exceed your goals.

Venus in Sagittarius

You're sociable, friendly, and outgoing, and you approach love and romance with the same easy-come, easy-go attitude that may govern much of your life. Any relationship that might limit your freedom is one you quickly walk away from. Strongly independent people with Venus in Sagittarius often choose to remain single or delay commitment until later in life. Then, mental rapport is a must. Generally unconcerned about money matters, you feel you'll always have what you need. That's true to some extent, but even your innate luck can be fickle at times. Save for lean periods; be cautious of debt.

Venus in Capricorn

You're cautious in matters of the heart, not only because that's your nature but also as a result of experience. Only when you feel totally secure do you risk making your affections known. Always the epitome of decorum in public, you express your highly sensual nature in private. Some people with Venus in Capricorn form a partnership for status or financial reasons, or choose a mate who is much younger or older. You're financially conservative, thrifty, and conscientious. (Security issues prompt some to be stingy and cheap.) You're a hard worker, and your ambitions can yield significant monetary rewards, but you sometimes spend to "prove" your success.

Venus in Aquarius

You're friendly but aloof, distant but interested in people and human nature, and your intriguing aura attracts much interest. Friendship is a constant in your life, and your ideal mate is also your best friend. Your attitude about relationships is undoubtedly unconventional in some way. Even a mildly possessive mate is not for you; you need to be free to explore your own interests. You have a good understanding of finances but are erratic in spending and saving,

flipping from the urge to splurge to stingy. Strive for more stability in this area.

Venus in Pisces

You're sensitive and romantic, in touch with your emotions. Lonely without a partner, you want and need love and affection from other people. Caring and compassionate, you're also a sentimental soul who remembers every first—first date, first kiss, first romantic moment. You need regular reassurance to feel secure. If you're less than practical in money matters, which many with this placement are, then seek advice or rely on your more realistic mate to handle finances. Otherwise, you could find yourself with significant debt. Share time, rather than what money can buy, with loved ones.

MARS

Glyph: ♂

Sign rulership: Aries

Natural house: First house of self

Significance: Where you direct your energy and strive to achieve, physical strength and stamina, what motivates you, where you show initiative

Rules: Physical activity and exercise, conflict, head, risk taking, anger, competition, weapons, tools, surgery, fever, red blood cells, cuts, accidents, knives, males, sex, action, initiative, energy, drive

Mythology: Mars initially was the god of farming and agriculture and then became the god of war. His father was Jupiter, his sons were Romulus and Remus, and his lover was Venus.

Mars represents action, energy, and drive. It's the reason you get out of bed and charge into the world every morning. Without Mars, we all might take a back seat. Of course, no one would be in the driver's seat, so we'd go nowhere except back to bed!

The red planet, according to its sign and house placement and aspects, reflects varying levels of aggression/assertiveness, risk taking, physical stamina, persistence, confidence, and self-reliance. Everyone experiences Mars as anger, as this is the planet associated with temper. Yours might be of the hair-trigger variety or the seething, contained (for a while) power of a volcano. Mars also indicates your sex drive and what you want in and give to a sexual relationship. Martian energy can be constructive or destructive; it's never in between.

Above all, Mars shows where physical activity, action, and drive are centered, where your full energy is directed, and where you strive to succeed. Its sign placement shows how you implement the highly energetic Martian get-up-and-go—directly, indirectly, toward others, in communication, or to achieve practical results.

Mars travels through the entire zodiac (all twelve signs) approximately every two years. It spends about six weeks in a sign. Its retrograde period lasts about two and a half months every two years, during which it can remain in a single sign for up to six months.

If Mars was retrograde when you were born, much of its energy is directed inward. You may have difficulty channeling its drive and may avoid conflict and confrontation. Over time, though, and with experience, most people with a retrograde Mars develop confidence and learn to use this planet effectively. People born with

a stationary Mars exhibit many of the traits of Aries—pure action and drive and a "me first" attitude. (See "Retrograde and Direct Motion" on page 16 for more information on the influence of stationary planets.)

Mars in the Signs

Mars in Aries

Mars in Aries is pure, high-powered energy. Bold and courageous, you're an independent overachiever who always wants to be first and loves a challenge—the more competitive the better. High initiative and drive can keep you on track, focused on goals, but you're far more of a starter than a finisher. You pursue tasks with enthusiasm, sometimes in an overly aggressive or persistent manner that can deter potential supporters. Try a less headstrong and more tactful approach; it will yield better results and enhance your natural leadership ability. Mars in Aries also promotes recklessness and risk taking. Be smart. Slow the pace just a little, especially on the road. Think before you act.

Mars in Taurus

Your determination is unparalleled, and perseverance and patience are your strengths. The thought of giving up rarely enters your mind. Slow but steady is your approach, along with a thoughtful, methodical, and thorough mindset that results in quality output, whatever your endeavor. But you also can be extremely stubborn and refuse to budge once you've formed an opinion. That can undermine all your hard work because others prefer those who are easygoing and cooperative. The same applies to habits and routines. Just because you've always done things a certain way doesn't mean you always should. Step out of your rut. Change is good for the soul.

Mars in Gemini

You have a quick, agile mind that grasps information in a flash. High energy is an asset, but boredom and restlessness can result in scattered interests and a lack of focus. Turn it to advantage by multitasking on a select few projects at a time to boost your interest level. Versatility keeps your thinking one step ahead, but it's also important to listen more than you talk. Always on the go, at least mentally, you can be an excellent communicator who enjoys initiating change just to keep things interesting. But you should guard against a tendency to become argumentative. Most people with Mars in Gemini enjoy challenging games and puzzles and working with their hands.

Mars in Cancer

Feelings are your main motivator, and much of what you do has an emotional undertone. You thus can get so wrapped up in a project, idea, or relationship that it's tough to keep your objectivity. That results in frustration when things don't go according to plan. Try to distance yourself a little and aim for periodic reality checks to be sure your perspective is on target. Then you can make the most of your persistence to finish what you start. Family relationships are influential in your life, although there could be conflict and difficulties with parents. If you're handy, Mars in Cancer can be an asset for do-it-yourself home improvements if you take safety precautions when working with tools or in the kitchen.

Mars in Leo

You have all the initiative, confidence, motivation, and determination to achieve your goals and the powerful career and life positions you desire. Once focused, enthusiasm and willpower fuel your drive. But be aware of a tendency to push others to meet your own ends. Choose instead to let your natural leadership ability shine through. Take charge in your innate grand style and be a motivational team player who's considerate of others. That's the way to grab your share of the limelight. You're generous with your money, time, and talents, especially with loved ones. You may or may not define yourself as creative, but you are in some way—with ideas, art, acting, speaking, or a weekend hobby.

Mars in Virgo

You are, above all, precise and efficient, something of a perfectionist who believes anything worth doing is worth doing well. You're a hard worker, and your strength is in the details. But that can become a disadvantage if you lose sight of the big picture. Both are necessary ingredients for success. You systematically plan and organize before taking action and thus can simultaneously manage several major projects. Some people with Mars in Virgo are restless and high-strung. If you're among them, set aside time each day (even if only thirty minutes) to relax and unwind. You also may have exceptional mechanical ability.

Mars in Libra

An active social life is important to you, but even more so is the desire to be with and work with other people. Cooperative efforts please you, while conflict is difficult and to be avoided, in your opinion. Your desire for harmony, however, can stop you from airing dislikes that merit discussion. You also appear indecisive at times because of your tendency to weigh the pros and cons before taking action. A common statement is, "I'll have to think about that." Physical activity isn't your favorite, and lazy periods are likely. But mentally stimulating activities excite you, as does debate, even in a casual, informal setting. Though you're generally easygoing, your anger flares at the first sign of injustice.

Mars in Scorpio

You're relentless. Like a bulldozer, you plow through obstacles, letting nothing stand in your way. Yet this strong drive can at times turn to stubbornness, when the wisest choice might be to cut your losses and move on. That's tough for you because you seldom know when to stop. But you will make an exception for something new—a project or idea—that stirs your passions even more deeply. Your physical energy is equally strong, and you can drive yourself to exhaustion without realizing it. Anyone who underestimates your strength of will sooner or later learns you're a formidable adversary. However, grudges, vengeance, and jealousy are ultimately nonproductive. Use your powerful energy instead to achieve your goals.

Mars in Sagittarius

You're ethical and highly principled, with strong beliefs about life, people, and the human condition. Together, they guide your every action, and you won't bend or lower your standards in any way, no matter the consequences. While admirable, that attitude is idealistic but not always realistic. Yet you're a risk taker and a lucky one, so events and situations generally evolve in your favor. Versatile and easygoing about most things, you're a leader who's adventuresome, daring, and courageous. You enjoy physical and mental challenges and can be highly competitive. You're also a terrific idea person, but follow-through is tough; you're a starter, not a finisher. Enthusiastic optimism is your hallmark.

Mars in Capricorn

Materialistically motivated and ambitious, you direct considerable energy into career achievement. Status, financial security, and power are your goals, and you have the incentive and determination to realize all three, step by step. Cautious and conservative, you take calculated risks to strengthen and advance your position. You're an ambitious hard worker who's also practical, disciplined, and responsible. Rules hold meaning for you, and you'll bend rather than break them to achieve your goals. Mars in Capricorn is excellent for business endeavors, the corporate world, and entrepreneurship, although persistence can net success in any career field. You excel as both employee and employer, but will strive for the top spot.

Mars in Aquarius

Independence and determination (which at times is better characterized as stubbornness) encourage you to adopt an "I'll do it myself" attitude. But you're also drawn to people and can be an outstanding team player. You're one or the other, or both, depending on the day, conditions, and your mood. You're more inclined to join the crowd if your innovative ideas are likely to be accepted and you're in sync with the group's aims. The unusual captures your attention, and your strong mental energy is in some way unconventional, prompting a unique, imaginative approach to tasks and activities. You follow through and complete what you start. However, you may be prone to nervous tension and stress; exercise and relaxation are good antidotes.

Mars in Pisces

You are compassionate and direct much of your energy into helping others, individually or collectively, through good causes. Creativity and imagination are strengths, but it can be difficult for you to stay focused and follow through on your intentions. Disorganization disrupts your energy flow, which is enhanced by visual and aural stimulation—or even total quiet and solitude. You may have artistic or musical talent. You have far more inner strength than you give yourself credit for. This inner strength is based on a spiritual connection with the universe that promotes self-motivation and insight along with intuition. Follow your heart—with an emphasis on what's realistic. A straightforward approach gets you further than a subtle one, as does learning how to deal with confrontation.

JUPITER

Glyph: ♃

Sign rulership: Sagittarius

Natural house: Ninth house of higher education, travel, principles, philosophy

Significance: Where you can attract abundance and luck, where you're least cautious, where you want to gain knowledge and where you can benefit most from it

Rules: Luck, legal matters, higher education, clergy, religion, obesity, advertising, publishing, travel, hips, liver, arteries, thighs, horses, colleges and universities, places of worship

Mythology: Jupiter, the god of Earth and the heavens, was a protector but also the god of justice. He was associated with weather, thus the thunderbolt with which he delivered justice.

Jupiter has two faces: fun and frivolous, and thoughtful and philosophical. It's the party versus the deep discussion, the world traveler versus the serious student, the traditional religious path versus personal faith. Jupiter represents all these things, plus luck and expansion.

Jupiter expands whatever it touches. It might indicate the potential for wealth, an active social life, many children, terrific career opportunities, or loads of friends. Its sign and house position and aspects offer insight into how you can expect this abundance to manifest and what you wish for, as well as your ethics and principles, your general life philosophy.

With its designation as the "greater benefic," Jupiter is best known as a lucky charm. It is definitely that. Jupiter's position in your chart represents where your greatest luck occurs and where you're likely to be least cautious.

But Jupiter can be fickle. It's also noted for "promises, promises," so don't expect it to deliver all the time. Jupiter has a reputation for expanding everything, not just what you want to be bigger and better. It can make a mess of things!

Jupiter also is associated with higher education, travel, optimism, extravagance, opportunities, publishing, confidence, generosity, and success.

Jupiter spends about a year in a sign, touring the entire zodiac every twelve years. It's retrograde for about four months of each year.

If Jupiter was retrograde when you were born, you're more philosophical and enjoy exploring the meaning of life, but tend to keep your beliefs to yourself rather than promote them in discussion with others. You're also less objective in your thinking. If Jupiter was stationary on your birthday, you embrace good works and have strong viewpoints and principles to guide your life. (See "Retrograde and Direct Motion" on page 16 for more information on the influence of stationary planets.)

Jupiter in the Signs
Jupiter in Aries
You're an outgoing, adventuresome free spirit who spreads enthusiasm and good cheer far and wide. Challenges excite you, and there are few that you are unwilling to tackle, even those that might intimidate others. But optimism can soar and prompt you to overextend your time and energy by taking on too much. Think about the realities before you move ahead, rather than set yourself up for failure. Although you can be impulsive at times, quick action helps you snap up opportunities.

Jupiter in Taurus
You're financially lucky, plus you have the common sense it takes to successfully manage money matters to your benefit. Many people with Jupiter in Taurus amass considerable assets, and higher education further increases the odds in your favor. You also acquire and are attached to your many possessions and rarely let go of anything, even when it's outlived its usefulness.

Weight gain is possible because good food and comfort are a way of life. Your practical vision is excellent for big-picture planning.

Jupiter in Gemini
You're fun-loving and talkative, and curiosity fuels your perpetual quest for information. You know a lot about many things, but tend to scatter your mental energies rather than limit your focus to a specific area of expertise. That's the result of your versatile, intelligent mind and high boredom factor. You can turn this potential weakness into a strength by striving for excellence in a single area where you can profit from all the miscellaneous data stored in your brain. Charming and glib, you may have exceptional writing or speaking talent.

Jupiter in Cancer
Family ties are generally positive and supportive, and you cherish fond memories of special moments with close friends and loved ones. Home life is an equally important focus, and you strive to create a welcoming, warm, and caring environment. Many people with Jupiter in Cancer adopt family beliefs as their own and never waver from them, partly out of loyalty. Sympathetic and kind, you're among the first to give to those in need as well as those you love. Hunches are often on target, especially in money matters, and you may achieve wealth status.

Jupiter in Leo
You love being in the limelight and doing things on a grand scale. Generous and loving, you nevertheless expect admiration and thus can be prone to an inflated ego. Creativity, loyalty,

and leadership are strengths, as are optimism and the ability to energize and motivate others. Children delight many people with Jupiter in Leo (your own or family members'). If you're among them, you probably devote as much time as possible to these children and their interests and activities. Your taste for luxury and designer labels can become an expensive indulgence.

Jupiter in Virgo

Work can become the driving force in your life, even to the point of consuming almost all of your waking hours. Satisfaction and rewards fuel your desire for more, but you also can overextend yourself. The result, sooner or later, will be burnout, so reprogram your thinking to include regular downtime. You're excellent with details and also have an eye for the big picture, giving you a unique combination of talents. But at times you can get stuck in analysis and be overly critical. Some people with Jupiter in Virgo are actively involved in charitable organizations and other good causes.

Jupiter in Libra

Friendly, helpful, and enthusiastic, you encourage and inspire others to excel. In turn, they bring you luck, and you could benefit financially through a business or romantic partner. Relying on others can become a pattern, however, when independence would better serve your interests. You're an astute observer of human nature, and people value your advice. Although you steer clear of conflict, you will take a stand to ensure justice and fairness, and at times you put others and their needs and desires first to maintain harmony.

Jupiter in Scorpio

You delve deep into any subject that interests you, researching every facet until you've mastered the knowledge or acquired enough to suit your needs. However, you can overdo it and develop an intense emotional involvement that limits perspective. Step back periodically for a fresh look. At times, you can be secretive and suspicious of others' motives. That's an asset when used positively to protect your interests, but not if it undermines your financial objectives. Many people with Jupiter in Scorpio amass sizable assets through hard work and determination.

Jupiter in Sagittarius

Upbeat and enthusiastic, you're also a deep thinker who enjoys philosophical discussions and mental journeys as much as travel. Your lifetime quest for knowledge makes you a perpetual learner, both in and out of the classroom, and you willingly share all you know to help others. Also generous with your time and talents, you expect nothing in return for favors granted. But be careful of a tendency to put too much faith in others and their promises. Balance optimism with reality. You're lucky more often than not, and calculated risks can pay off handsomely for you.

Jupiter in Capricorn

You have an innate understanding of the principles of expansion and contraction, and a talent for practical vision. Opportunities come to you, and others are of your own making. You're somewhat cautious but also quick to follow through on anything with real potential to advance your career and status. Ambitious and success- and money-motivated, you have the common sense to know that advancement is a step-by-step process that requires goals, planning, and timing, along with your strong work ethic. Most people with this placement are conservative and traditional. Many thrive in corporate life.

Jupiter in Aquarius

You're tolerant yet unpredictable and stubborn at times, with a life philosophy that's uniquely yours. You set your own personal standards and faithfully live by them. High on your list is injustice; you see equality as the only acceptable norm. You value people—and your many friends—for their individuality and accept them as they are, even if you don't necessarily agree with their decisions and choices. Humanitarian causes, groups, and organizations appeal to you, and many benefit from your involvement and leadership. Some people with Jupiter in Aquarius are activists and instrumental in social change.

Jupiter in Pisces

You're known for your compassion and generosity. Helping others gives you great satisfaction, and people appreciate your kind and understanding nature. But these fine qualities encourage less-ethical people to take advantage of you. Be wise and good to yourself: weigh each request on its merits, and do your best to remove emotions from the equation. Not everyone is deserving of your sympathy, so temper your idealism with reality. You have an excellent imagination and are creative in some way. Many people with this placement are intuitive or psychic. Guard against self-indulgence in any form.

SATURN

Glyph: ♄

Sign rulership: Capricorn

Natural house: Tenth house of career and status

Significance: Your major life lessons, where you feel inadequate, your life ambition

Rules: Career, responsibility, ambition, hardship, obstacles, patience, chronic ailments, older people, father, politics, bones, skin, teeth, knees, gallbladder, antiques, rock, earth, property, buildings, wisdom, hard work, restriction, limitation, karma, stability, restriction, responsibility

Mythology: Saturn was the god of agriculture and the son of Uranus. Saturn ruled the feast of Saturnalia, held near the winter solstice, which later became the Christian Christmas.

Saturn needs a public relations agent. It's the planet that gets the most bad press, the one that people even somewhat in the astrological know wish didn't exist. True, it is associated with hard knocks and life lessons, but they're usually of the individual's making, one way or another. Managing Saturn takes knowledge and experience, some of which is learned the hard way. The more thoroughly and completely you fulfill Saturn's expectations, the greater the rewards.

Saturn is the planet of rewards. It recognizes hard work and brings you exactly what you deserve. And the rewards are all the sweeter because of the effort expended to achieve them. A trip down Easy Street just doesn't bring the same feeling of success.

Saturn is the universal planet of career, status, and business. Its position in your chart may or may not directly reflect your career interests, but it definitely shows what you want to achieve and be noted for and where your ambitions are focused. Saturn in your chart also shows the area of life where you have the most lessons to learn and where you feel most vulnerable and inadequate. Many astrologers associate Saturn with karma.

Besides being the planet of responsibility, Saturn represents delays, obstacles, restrictions, patience, caution, thrift, humility, endurance, and sincerity. It's also the most practical of planets, the greater teacher that imparts wisdom and helps you develop strength of character. Some people manifest Saturn's energy in narrow-minded thinking, pessimism, and stinginess.

It takes Saturn thirty years to travel through the zodiac, spending about two and a half years in a sign. This serious planet is retrograde approximately four and a half months each year. If Saturn is retrograde in your chart, you're even more responsible for your own success as well as what holds you back. Emphasize positive thinking. If Saturn was stationary when you were born, then determination, goal-setting, and self-discipline are enhanced. (See "Retrograde and Direct Motion" on page 16 for more information on the influence of stationary planets.)

Saturn in the Signs
Saturn in Aries

Saturn in Aries signifies opposing energies. Saturn represents caution, patience, and discipline, while Mars represents impulsiveness, action, and independence. Your challenge is thus to mix these diverse factors into a single unified one that can lead to personal and career success. This influence can be excellent for entrepreneur-

ial ventures, and it also lends initiative in other career endeavors. Strive for self-discipline and a steady flow of assertiveness rather than aggression or inhibition. You also benefit from working within the existing structure and company and societal rules to effect positive change.

Saturn in Taurus

You're patient and practical and have all the determination and common sense to build sizable assets. Follow-through is a strength; a goal, once identified, is pursued until it's achieved. You're a hard worker, and career and compensation advance through the years as your ambitions accelerate. Your money motivation stems from a desire for security and comfort, and you willingly spend to acquire what you want—but only if it's a good value for your dollars. You're frugal and thrifty in money matters. But your slow and steady approach, which is an asset in many areas, can also cause you to miss out on opportunities.

Saturn in Gemini

You're a logical thinker who excels at problem solving and finding practical solutions. You're highly observant, and your quick mind grasps the facts, thinks things through, and briefly sums up conclusions. You also excel at planning and organization, which are natural outlets for your realistic mindset. Many people with Saturn in Gemini enjoy working with their hands in their careers or leisure-time pursuits and are intrigued by mentally challenging puzzles and games. The communications field, including writing, is another area that attracts the interest of some.

Saturn in Cancer

You have a deep-seated need for emotional and financial security, and devote much time and effort to creating a comfortable home and family environment. You're very loyal to those you love. For some people with Saturn in Cancer, this need is the result of heavy responsibilities or a highly structured or demanding home life in childhood. You can excel at making and managing money once you gain experience and knowledge—some of which is learned the hard way. But it also may be a challenge to get beyond "austerity thinking." At times, you're ultra-cautious, and at others, you display great initiative and tenacity. Real estate could be an excellent investment.

Saturn in Leo

You have a strong need for attention and recognition, and you're truly confident only when you feel important and appreciated—and in charge. You also can underestimate your skills and talents at times. Believe in yourself and your strong willpower and determination. Tap into this ambitious energy, rise to the occasion, and maximize your practical creativity and leadership ability. Very loyal to those you love, you also expect only the best from your children and push them to succeed. Long-term investments can secure your future. Be cautious of risk taking just to satisfy your ego and desire for status.

Saturn in Virgo

Painstakingly thorough, you have practical wisdom and an orderly, analytical mind that excels at planning and organization. No detail escapes your attention, and you're a hard worker who strives for accuracy and efficiency. Routine is your comfort zone, although you can be adaptable when necessary. Even more demanding of yourself than you are of others, you can be perceived as bossy, with excessively high standards. You also have a strong belief in rules and structure, and are amazingly patient.

Saturn in Libra

Loyalty, devotion to duty, and a strong sense of justice are a few of your strengths, along with tact and kindness. You believe in fairness and impartiality and thus can be an outstanding mediator in both personal and business situations. At times, however, you can be impatient and intolerant, and you're rarely swayed by sympathy and emotions. You enjoy helping others help themselves rather than doing things for them. Many people with Saturn in Libra form romantic partnerships later in life or with someone who is older or distinguished in his or her career.

Saturn in Scorpio

Intense ambition coupled with a strong desire for a powerful position give you the drive to succeed. Your relentless staying power helps you outlast and rise above the competition, but less than ethical actions to get ahead are likely to backfire. Determination alone is usually enough to help you achieve your goals, including financial security and even wealth. Physical stamina is also an asset, but you can push yourself to the point of exhaustion. A private person, you share little about your personal and career plans and are ever alert for information that can aid your shrewd planning and moves.

Saturn in Sagittarius

You want to be known for your knowledge and expertise, and consider it your duty to share both with others. Whether teacher, mentor, or friend, you can have a positive impact on many. Some people with Saturn in Sagittarius, however, develop a know-it-all attitude that negates this potential. Honest, ethical, and principled, you have high standards from which you refuse to waver. In business, you have a knack for spotting trends, and leadership ability plus an eye for opportunities and calculated risks can take you far. You strive to achieve a responsible, honest, conscientious reputation.

Saturn in Capricorn

You're among the most ambitious people on the planet and have the self-discipline and determination to achieve every goal, along with status and recognition. A hard worker with leadership ability, you want to be in charge. But the drive to succeed can take its toll on your family and personal lives, both of which may be designed to further your ambitions. You're practical and conservative and use a logical approach in planning and problem solving. Rules are important to you, as is a structured environment. Shortcuts can bring setbacks, but you quickly regroup and move forward once again.

Saturn in Aquarius

Your ideas are a unique combination of tradition and innovation. They're also practical and enhanced by your objective, impartial viewpoint. You approach problems and decisions intellectually rather than emotionally. Projects, tasks, and goals benefit from your determination and drive, as well as your aptitude for team work and networking and your ability to see things through to conclusion. But tunnel vision can accompany stubbornness; counter it by seeking other opinions. You take friendship seriously and are congenial, if somewhat aloof, with your many acquaintances.

Saturn in Pisces

You're understanding and sympathetic, with a big heart that goes out to others. A certain sense of responsibility for humankind encourages you to help others whenever and however you can, but it's wise to remember that not everyone is deserving of your care and concern. You know how to skirt obstacles and problems and prefer to do that, rather than confront adversity. That's the outward expression of your reserved, and possibly shy, nature. Avoiding reality, however, is not always in your best interests. An inspired imagination enhances your creativity. Directing it into concrete endeavors helps you air your inner voice through artistic outlets such as photography and music, either as a career or hobby.

URANUS

Glyph: ♅

Sign rulership: Aquarius

Natural house: Eleventh house of friends, groups, goals and objectives

Significance: Where you seek freedom, opportunity, and independence, what you rebel against, where you're unconventional, where you can expect change

Rules: Friends, clubs, organizations, groups, technology, inventions, revolutions, circulatory system, ankles, shins, calves, nervous system, radiology, aerospace, divorce, homosexuality, sudden events

Mythology: Uranus was the god of the sky and the son and husband of Gaia (Earth). He was castrated by Saturn, and Venus was born as his genitals fell to Earth.

Uranus keeps life lively! It's the planet of the unexpected, the unusual, the unconventional. Wherever Uranus is placed in your chart is where you're something of a rebel, and its sign position shows what you rebel against. Its placement indicates where you seek freedom and independence, where you're a nonconformist, and where you feel free to express your individuality.

Uranus represents sudden changes, opportunities that fall in your lap, and events that happen in a flash—accidents, love at first sight, windfalls, losses, surprises, changes of plans, and computer crashes. How you react to these events has much to do with your overall chart. People who have an emphasis on fixed signs have the most difficulty because they're resistant to change. Those with an emphasis on cardinal or mutable signs are more comfortable. But does anyone really like change? Probably not, unless it's self-initiated or a lucky break. Nevertheless, Uranus's disruptive influence has a purpose: out with the old to make room for progress. Uranus is future-oriented.

Uranus represents those "aha" moments, flashes of insight and enlightenment when you just "know." That's Uranus at its intuitive best. This planet also encourages innovation, imagination, and creativity, and offers you the opportunity to express yourself in unique endeavors and ideas or through humanitarian efforts for good causes.

Uranus spends about seven years in each sign, taking eighty-four years to travel the zodiac, and its retrograde periods last about five months. Because Uranus is retrograde almost half the time, its retrograde and stationary positions in a birth chart are less significant. In general, people with Uranus retrograde are less independent and rebellious, while those with a stationary Uranus are more so. (See "Retrograde and Direct Motion" on page 16 for more information on the influence of stationary planets.)

Uranus in the Signs
Uranus in Aries

You're a risk taker who has the initiative and desire to pursue all that is new and different. Independence and confidence encourage you to promote change, and your quick mind is inventive but also impulsive. You may have entrepreneurial talent.

In the world at large, Uranus in Aries reflects a period of technological advancement, as well as new and influential or revitalized groups that promote individual rights.

Uranus in Taurus

Concrete results are your goal, and you achieve them through innovative yet practical ideas and solutions. Determination is a strength, but resistance to change can undermine your efforts. Tap into trends and take an occasional well-calculated risk.

Uranus in Taurus accents changes in financial structures and security and more concern and interest in material values, which also evolve. It may be difficult to acquire certain goods during this period.

Uranus in Gemini

Your quick, clever mind generates original thoughts and ideas, but follow-through can be a challenge. Your many interests, which some call scattered energy, net you a wealth of information—and trivia. Put all that data to work for you in your career or a moneymaking hobby.

The period with Uranus in Gemini brings changes in communication, as old forms disappear to be replaced by the new. Learning theories and concepts undergo change, and there are technological advances in vehicles.

Uranus in Cancer

Intuition helps you spot public trends, and on a personal level you sense what people think and feel. That gives you an advantage in many situations that require excellent people skills. Emotions can be erratic and unpredictable, however, and family or home life may be unusual in some way.

The concepts of home and family undergo significant changes during the period when Uranus is in Cancer as people explore and redefine the family unit and living environment. There may be a noticeable rise or fall in the birth rate.

Uranus in Leo

Willpower and creativity are strengths you use to elevate your position in life, as is your unusual leadership style that nevertheless gets results. You follow your own star and set your own rules whenever possible, and welcome change when it's your idea.

In the world, Uranus in Leo reflects changes in matters concerning children, as well as groups and organizations. Individuals are challenged to put their egos aside to join forces for the good of all.

Uranus in Virgo

You're prone to changes in employment, whether by choice or circumstance. You also can be an innovator in the workplace, with a wealth of practical yet imaginative ideas and methods. If there's an easier, simpler way, you can find it. Healing and nutrition may be of interest.

The period when Uranus is in Virgo accents changes in matters related to health care and the agricultural industries, and in the work environment, such as an increase in telecommuting.

Uranus in Libra

Independence versus togetherness is a dilemma; you want both, and with effort you can find a successful compromise to satisfy these dual needs. Some close relationships are unstable or unusual, and you have many friends and acquaintances who move in and out of your life.

Uranus in Libra, the sign of close relationships, reflects changes in existing ideas about marriage and partnership. Laws defining legal partnership may change during this period.

Uranus in Scorpio

You equate power with freedom and initiate change to achieve your goals. Friendships are deep, emotions intense, and determination unwavering. You may periodically reinvent yourself, changing life direction and physical characteristics. Willpower is strong.

Technological advances and breakthroughs in reproductive science are likely during this period, including new methods to handle infertility problems and sexual disorders. Significant changes in matters having to do with death and taxes are possible.

Uranus in Sagittarius

Everything that is new and different attracts you, and your curious mind searches for and quickly absorbs information. Travel and adventure excite you. Leadership potential and progressive ideas further your aims, as does higher education.

New thinking, concepts, and ideas accent changes in higher education and organized religion during this period. There also may be technological advances involving travel.

Uranus in Capricorn

Ambitious and well aware of how to use patience and practicality to achieve your goals, you work within the existing career structure to promote change that's based in tradition yet forward-thinking. You excel at finding logical and innovative solutions, and may be a leader in business.

Major changes in big business and government accompany the period with Uranus in Capricorn, possibly because of action on the part of groups or organizations that demand reform.

Uranus in Aquarius

An independent soul, you're unconventional in some way (lifestyle, career, interests) and at times unpredictable. Humanitarian causes draw you, and you may be involved in groups that promote change. Imagination and intuition spark innovative ideas and solutions, for which you're noted.

This period brings many technological advances, including those that change methods of communication to bring more people together in an impersonal way.

Uranus in Pisces

You're idealistic, caring, and sympathetic, and wish you could change the world. You may become involved in charitable groups and endeavors, and creativity and an active sixth sense could help you focus your life direction into worthy efforts. Inspiration, when balanced with reality, yields success.

Uranus in Pisces reflects new insights into spiritual matters and increased interest in the environment and helping those in need. The petroleum and music industries undergo significant changes during this period. A tougher stance on substance abuse also is possible.

NEPTUNE

Glyph: ♆

Sign rulership: Pisces

Natural house: Twelfth house of self-renewal and secrets

Significance: Where you're prone to illusion and deception, what inspires you

Rules: Water, hypochondria, hypnotism, con artists, music, photography, film industry, sleep, drugs, alcohol, hospitals, prisons, institutions, dreams, the environment

Mythology: Neptune was the god of the sea, freshwater bodies, and horses. He was the son of Saturn and the brother of Jupiter and Pluto.

Neptune is the planet of illusion and confusion but also vision and creativity. Most people experience all of these facets of Neptune at one time or another, in addition to other characteristics of this mystical planet. Neptune encourages self-expression through imagination, artistic endeavors, compassion, music, and spirituality. Its influence can be nebulous and difficult to define, as it represents that which is hidden or obscure. Pinpointing Neptune's influence can be a bit like trying to grab a handful of fog.

Yet like the magician's illusion, Neptune is based in reality. Discovering the reality, however, can be as difficult as spotting the magician's sleight of hand. Most often, Neptune's influence is unmasked with far too much reality, when you suddenly see that what you thought was real isn't and what you were sure was an illusion is in fact real. This, of course, can make Neptune's energy difficult to manage.

Appropriately, Neptune in your chart shows where you have a blind spot, where you're prone to illusion and self-deception or being deceived by others. Having faith in yourself and your abilities is part, but not all, of the solution. Listen to other opinions when friends or relatives suggest your thinking is off. If necessary, seek a reputable expert's opinion in financial, contractual, or legal matters.

Neptune represents romance and charm, the highest spiritual evolution, and a protective influence, as well as secrets, sleep, and dreams. It's also the planet of addiction—to alcohol, drugs, food, and other substances and situations that can take over your life.

Neptune is a slow mover. It spends an average of fourteen years in a sign, and is retrograde about five months at a time. Its retrograde and stationary influence in a birth chart is thus less influential. Retrograde Neptune, however, encourages escapist tendencies and self-delusion, and its stationary position can indicate artistic talent and profound vision or an absence of realistic thinking. (See "Retrograde and Direct Motion" on page 16 for more information on the influence of stationary planets.)

Neptune in the Signs

Neptune in Aries

You act on your spiritual beliefs, using them as a foundation for daily life and decision making as well as your overall life direction. You also inspire others to follow your lead and, by example, to express their creativity and compassion, both of which you have in abundance.

Neptune in Aries reflects an interest in exploring the world's oceans, as well as initiatives to protect the environment and water supply and to develop new sources of energy. Psychic ability may be scientifically proven during this period.

Neptune in Taurus

You're practical in money matters yet also creative, with a sixth sense about financial trends. You understand the principle of letting money circulate into the outer world and back to you, and may donate to worthy causes. Creative or humanitarian endeavors may be income sources.

With Neptune in Taurus, environmental and energy concerns may yield high financial returns, and this period will bring sizable gains for charitable organizations.

Neptune in Gemini

You may be a talented speaker or writer, which are excellent outlets for your imaginative ideas. Follow-through is your challenge, however, so train yourself to focus on one major project or interest before delving into the next. Scattered energy brings only scattered results.

There will be much questioning of learning concepts during Neptune's transit of Gemini, which also will bring further development in energy sources, primarily for vehicles.

Neptune in Cancer

Your home is your comfort zone, where you retreat to recenter, relax, and unwind. You also have a strong sixth sense. In the wider world, you have an instinct for public opinion and emerging trends that can increase financial security and career gains.

The traditional family unit will be affected by Neptune in Cancer. Families will dissolve, possibly because of a war (as during World War I, when many were killed) or a pandemic or epidemic.

Neptune in Leo

You may become a leader for a good cause, in part to fulfill your spiritual needs. Charisma and inspiration help you touch people's lives, one-on-one or on a wider scale, but you should guard against self-deception. Perceptions are not always accurate.

With Neptune in Leo, new methods of entertainment will emerge, and the film indus-

try will undergo major changes. Powerful people will be exposed for unethical behavior.

Neptune in Virgo

Although you may lack confidence in your abilities, you have a practical imagination that can create inspired ideas, and may have a talent for creative writing. Let your creative energy flow, and disregard the inconsequential details, which can block the concrete results you're trying to achieve.

With Neptune in Virgo, alternative medicine will become more widely accepted and new theories in treatment developed. Widespread unemployment is possible.

Neptune in Libra

You have an idealistic view of people and close relationships, especially romantic ones. Spiritual ties are strong with those you love, and on a wider scale you have a sense of social responsibility and sympathy for those in need. You're more inclined to help others one-on-one than to be involved in group activities for good causes.

This is a generation that will experience many changes in close relationships, including marriage and all forms of partnership. People born in the 1940s and 1950s when Neptune was in Libra were the "flower children" of the 1960s.

Neptune in Scorpio

Deep emotions and faith inspire you to achieve, and once committed, you do whatever it takes to reach your goal. You have an instinctive understanding of the life cycle, and your sixth sense is sensitive to subtle vibrations from people and places.

Drug abuse is associated with this generational influence, as well as the development of life-giving and life-prolonging drugs. Money and ethics will clash during this period, which will see the downfall of some powerful people.

Neptune in Sagittarius
Your quest for knowledge extends to a search for the meaning of life on a deeper, spiritual level. Faith is strong, and you may feel that your life is guided or directed. Other cultures intrigue you, and travel may widen your horizons as much as formal learning.

Spiritual truth and the search for the meaning of religion are associated with Neptune in Sagittarius. There may be scandals involving higher education, religion, and health care.

Neptune in Capricorn
You value and appreciate tradition but also see the wisdom in flexibility to adapt to modern times. However, change for purely idealistic reasons can result in disillusionment. Use your practical side to discover your more spiritual inner voice.

This influence generates awareness of environmental and energy concerns. The practices of big business will be challenged, although they are unlikely to undergo any significant changes.

Neptune in Aquarius
Groups and organizations are influential in your life, and you may become involved in a humanitarian effort. Your intuition is strong and sparks innovative ideas that make you an invaluable team player. Friendship is important to you.

Technology will bring advancements in science, medicine, and health care. This is also a favorable influence for new technology to benefit the environment, energy, and the sea.

Neptune in Pisces
You have a strong visual orientation, which, when combined with your creativity, can yield amazing results. Music may free your inner voice. You also sense subtle signals from people, and may have healing or artistic talent that can in some way benefit humankind.

Interest in spirituality will increase during this period, and some religious institutions will be exposed for their unethical practices. This also will bring an increased interest in the environment, alternative fuels, and alternative medicine.

PLUTO

Glyph: ♇

Sign rulership: Scorpio

Natural house: Eighth house of joint resources, inheritance, debt, insurance

Significance: Where you want power, take charge, or feel powerless; where you experience transformation and profound change

Rules: Massive change, money, power, sex, occult, recycling, inheritance, dictators, crime and corruption, research, subconscious, reproductive organs, excretory system, willpower, transformation, elimination, power, control

Mythology: The brother of Neptune, Pluto was the god of the underworld.

Tiny Pluto is anything but, astrologically. It's unforgettable and massive in its influence. Pluto is pure power and transformation. It's a tiny planet (astronomers call it a dwarf planet) that operates on a massive scale.

Although Pluto represents generations of people and the big events and trends that affect their lives, it also can manifest strongly in an individual's life when it contacts personal planets (Sun, Moon, Mercury, Venus, and sometimes Mars and Jupiter) in a birth chart. Because its major influence is generational, many people born within a few years of each other will experience its effects at about the same time.

Pluto is the great transformer. It destroys the old to make way for the new. Think of it in terms of closet cleaning. When you strip your closet of outdated or unusable clothing to make room for the latest fashions, you are "Plutoing" your wardrobe. On a larger scale, the same function is performed during company restructurings and layoffs, coups to take over countries, natural disasters that level parts of cities, and global events that affect daily life. Each is out of the individual's control, leaving hundreds and even thousands of people who feel victimized.

Yet in its wake, Pluto leaves an opportunity for change that, more often than not, turns out to be positive. You may go in directions never before considered and discover your inner strengths and hidden talents. Once Plutonian power is unleashed, there is no going back; its effects are irreversible.

On a personal level, Pluto's position in your chart represents where you choose to take charge or, subconsciously, to become a victim. There, Pluto challenges you to take a risk to initiate change at its deepest, most profound level, to exercise your personal power for the benefit of others.

Pluto creeps through the zodiac, spending anywhere from fourteen to thirty years in a sign.

Its influence when retrograde in a birth chart is negligible, although it can indicate gradual changes of your innermost beliefs and feelings. When stationary, Pluto can indicate a powerful person who chooses a positive or negative life path. (See "Retrograde and Direct Motion" on page 16 for more information on the influence of stationary planets.)

Pluto in the Signs
Pluto in Aries
Your pioneering spirit is unparalleled. Whatever is fresh and new attracts you, and you have the courage to initiate change and to explore new ideas and approaches to firmly established traditions.

Pluto was last in Aries during the nineteenth century (1823–1852). This was a period of westward expansion in the United States, when people explored new frontiers.

Pluto in Taurus
You have a strong desire for material and financial security, both of which you can achieve, item by item, dollar by dollar. Be cautious, though, about whom you trust in money matters. Let common sense prevail.

The most significant American event that occurred during Pluto's last transit of Taurus (1852–1884) was the Civil War, triggered by economic issues.

Pluto in Gemini
Your inventive mind can find a better way to do many things. Big ideas require follow-through, however. Communication and technological innovations strongly influence your life and lifestyle.

Transportation underwent significant changes when Pluto was last in Gemini (1884–1913). The Wright brothers were pioneers in flight, Henry Ford produced the first affordable car, and the telephone emerged.

Pluto in Cancer

Emotions run deep, and family ties have a profound impact on your life—positive, negative, or both. Living arrangements and property ownership may undergo significant changes as a result of societal trends.

The Great Depression occurred during Pluto's last transit of Cancer (1912–1938), as did World War I, both of which disrupted families worldwide.

Pluto in Leo

You, like your peers, represent the power of one as a force for change. Although you use this energy to affect the world around you, its primary influence is motivation for personal transformation and self-understanding.

World War II occurred during Pluto's last transit of Leo (1937–1957), along with the development of atomic power. People born during this time are part of the "me" generation, the baby boomers.

Pluto in Virgo

Existing norms of employment, health care, and service will change during your lifetime. You thus can experience a periodic restructuring of your work environment and the availability of medical alternatives. Helping others leads to personal evolution.

During Pluto's last transit of Virgo (1957–1971), there were significant advances in agriculture, food production, and medicine. The first commercial transistor radio and calculator became available.

Pluto in Libra

You're concerned with issues of personal and global justice. These beliefs also influence your view of relationships, which you believe should be mutually supportive at all times. You strive for 100 percent shared experiences in a partnership and work toward that idealistic end.

Pluto in Libra (1971–1984) featured changes in divorce laws and procedures and advances in women's rights, but the Equal Rights Amendment was defeated. The Vietnam War sparked a demand for peace, love, and harmony.

Pluto in Scorpio

Your powerful will brings strength and determination to personal and professional endeavors, along with an unwavering depth of commitment to fulfill your financial potential. Few can penetrate the depths of your soul and its mysteries.

AIDS and other sexually transmitted diseases came to attention when Pluto was in Scorpio (1983–1995), and there also was a rising crime rate and concern about atomic power and environmental pollution.

Pluto in Sagittarius

Values and ethics are prevailing themes in your life, and you're periodically faced with challenges that require values-based choices and decisions. Each is a test of your principles within the wider context of societal trends. Spirituality also is a life theme in your search for life's answers.

During the years with Pluto in Sagittarius (1995–2008), the Roman Catholic Church was faced with scandals and lawsuits involving pedophile priests, fundamentalist Christians became an influential political force, and there were religion-based terrorist acts.

Pluto in Capricorn

Business and government are likely to undergo major changes during your lifetime. While these will be on a global scale, they also will affect your personal and professional lives. Plan ahead. Protect your resources and career interests.

During Pluto's transit of Capricorn (2008–2024), there will be increasing demand for reforms in big business, corporations, and government, and long-established structures will be altered. The U.S. Declaration of Independence was signed and the United States founded when Pluto was last in Capricorn (1762–1778).

Pluto in Aquarius

You can have a profound impact on people through your efforts for humanitarian and charitable causes. You also may become involved in a group or organization where, as a leader, you can initiate positive change.

Pluto in Aquarius (2023–2043) will bring major technological advances, increased space exploration, and an emphasis on global humanitarian efforts.

Pluto in Pisces

Deeply compassionate, you have the power to change lives one by one or by the thousands. Whatever venue you choose, even on a casual, informal level you have the ability to reach out and inspire others.

During Pluto's transit of Pisces (2043–2067), environmental concerns will require major changes throughout the world, and there could be revolutionary medical advances.

PLANETARY RULERSHIP

Every planet rules, or is associated with, a particular sign. The exceptions are Mercury and Venus, each of which rules two signs. This is because there are twelve signs and only ten planets.

But throughout almost all of astrology's four-thousand-year history, there were twelve signs ruled by seven planets. These seven—Sun, Moon, Mercury, Venus, Mars, Jupiter, and Saturn—are the planets visible from Earth with the naked eye. It wasn't until the eighteenth century that telescope technology advanced enough for astronomers to see farther out into space. Uranus was discovered in 1781, followed by Neptune in 1846 and Pluto in 1930. Chart 7 shows the signs with their traditional and modern planetary rulers. Both rulers are the same except for these three recently discovered outer planets. Astrologers established the modern rulerships through experimentation and observation.

The traditional rulers definitely work today, just as they did for ancient astrologers, and are well worth studying. But because you can effectively read a chart without using the traditional rulers, this book uses only the modern ones. Traditional rulers are particularly useful in predictive astrology (because they move more quickly than the outer planets) and are used almost exclusively in horary astrology (see appendix II).

Sign	Modern Ruler	Traditional Ruler
Aries ♈	Mars ♂	Mars ♂
Taurus ♉	Venus ♀	Venus ♀
Gemini ♊	Mercury ☿	Mercury ☿
Cancer ♋	Moon ☽	Moon ☽
Leo ♌	Sun ☉	Sun ☉
Virgo ♍	Mercury ☿	Mercury ☿
Libra ♎	Venus ♀	Venus ♀
Scorpio ♏	Pluto ♇	Mars ♂
Sagittarius ♐	Jupiter ♃	Jupiter ♃
Capricorn ♑	Saturn ♄	Saturn ♄
Aquarius ♒	Uranus ♅	Saturn ♄
Pisces ♓	Neptune ♆	Jupiter ♃

Chart 7. Modern and Traditional Planetary Rulers

PLANETARY POWER

Planets are classified as *dignified*, *exalted*, in *detriment*, or in *fall* according to their sign placement (chart 8). Each planet expresses itself more freely when dignified or exalted and less so when in detriment or fall.

A planet is dignified when it occupies the sign it rules, such as Mercury in Gemini or Mars in Aries. When dignified, a planet is strengthened and functions most like its true self. A planet in its sign of exaltation functions almost as well as when dignified. A planet is exalted when it's in the sign opposite the sign of its fall. For example, Mars is in its fall in Cancer and exalted when in Capricorn.

Planets in the sign of detriment or fall are weaker and have more difficulty expressing their nature. The sign of detriment is the one directly opposite the sign of dignity. The Sun, for example, is dignified in Leo and in detriment in Aquarius (Leo and Aquarius are polar opposites in the zodiac). A planet in fall is in the sign directly opposite its sign of exaltation. For example, Saturn is exalted in Libra, so it's in fall in Aries, the polar opposite of Libra.

There is logic behind this planetary classification. Mars, for example, is pure action, energy, drive, and individual effort, all of which also describe Aries, the sign of "me first." Libra, the sign of Mars's detriment, represents partnership—two instead of one—and cooperative effort. Mars feels comfortable in Capricorn, the sign of its exaltation, because Capricorn signifies driving ambition, also a trait of Mars. Cancer represents the family group, which is energy that is foreign to independent Mars.

Planet	Dignified	Detriment	Exalted	Fall
Sun ☉	Leo ♌	Aquarius ♒	Aries ♈	Libra ♎
Moon ☽	Cancer ♋	Capricorn ♑	Taurus ♉	Scorpio ♏
Mercury ☿	Gemini ♊	Sagittarius ♐	Virgo ♍	Pisces ♓
Venus ♀	Libra ♎	Aries ♈	Pisces ♓	Virgo ♍
Mars ♂	Aries ♈	Libra ♎	Capricorn ♑	Cancer ♋
Jupiter ♃	Sagittarius ♐	Gemini ♊	Cancer ♋	Capricorn ♑
Saturn ♄	Capricorn ♑	Cancer ♋	Libra ♎	Aries ♈
Uranus ♅	Aquarius ♒	Leo ♌	Scorpio ♏	Taurus ♉
Neptune ♆	Pisces ♓	Virgo ♍	Leo ♌	Aquarius ♒
Pluto ♇	Scorpio ♏	Taurus ♉	Leo ♌	Aquarius ♒

Chart 8. Planetary Strength: Dignified, Detriment, Exaltation, and Fall

WHAT IS A PLANET?

Pluto, discovered in 1930, was considered a planet until 2006, when the International Astronomical Union demoted it to dwarf planet status. The rationale was that Pluto is too small (smaller than Earth's Moon) and too far away from Earth. Astronomers argued that if Pluto had maintained its planetary designation, then Xena, Verona, Ceres, Terran, and many others would have had to be granted the same designation.

Officially, the new definition of a planet requires that the planet orbit the Sun, be large enough to be nearly round in shape, and "clear the neighborhood around its orbit." The last requirement spelled doom for Pluto, which has an oblong orbit that overlaps Neptune's.

How does this affect astrology? It doesn't. Astrologers continue to use Pluto, having already seen its relevance in human nature, events, and societal trends.

MERCURY RETROGRADE

Many people who know nothing about astrology except their Sun sign are aware of the Mercury retrograde phenomenon, partly because it's often mentioned in published horoscopes. During Mercury's three-week retrograde period, which occurs three or four times a year, communication is disrupted, mail is misdirected and delayed, batteries quit, mechanical problems occur, and there are misunderstandings involving dates, times, places, and instructions. The general guideline during this period is to avoid making major purchases (electronics, vehicles, appliances) and to avoid signing contracts. All of this is valid, but . . .

Rarely do you see mention of the merits of Mercury retrograde. You definitely can use it to your advantage. For example, I've observed that software companies, whether by design on coincidence, often release software when Mercury is retrograde. Think about it. Part of the plan

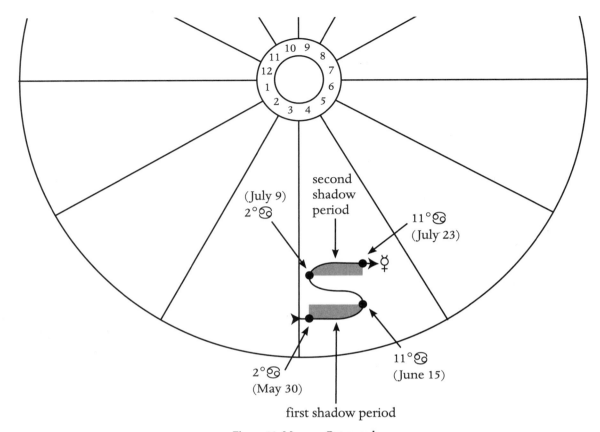

Figure 12. Mercury Retrograde

for almost any software company is to release an endless string of new versions and upgrades, each of which will add more to the company's coffers. This fits with the Mercury retrograde concept that whatever action is taken while Mercury is retrograde will have to be redone after Mercury turns direct or during a future retrograde period. Could anything make a software company happier?

Here's a trick to make Mercury retrograde work for you instead of against you. Using the ephemeris (see page 23), first locate the time period during which Mercury will be retro-

grade. Then identify the sign and degree at which Mercury will turn direct at the end of the retrograde period and look for the date when it will be at that same degree and sign before it turns retrograde. Do the same in the other direction, finding the degree and sign at which Mercury will turn retrograde and then the date when it will again reach that point after it turns direct.

For example, suppose Mercury turns retrograde at 11° Cancer on June 15 and resumes direct motion at 2° Cancer on July 9 (figure 12). Before turning retrograde, it will be at 2°

Cancer on May 30; after turning direct, it will be at 11° Cancer on July 23. These periods on either side of Mercury's retrograde period, the approach and separation, are called the *shadow periods*.

You can use this knowledge if, for example, you're looking for a job. Send out résumés between May 30 and June 15, and you may get final results (a job offer) between July 9 and July 23. Because Mercury will cover only nine degrees, between 2° and 11° Cancer, you can actually select any date on the approach when Mercury is between these degrees. When Mercury returns to that degree, either during the retrograde period or after it, you will hear news.

VOID-OF-COURSE MOON

Many people have heard of the void-of-course Moon phenomenon. This is the period between when the Moon makes its last contact to another planet and the time it enters the next sign. This is listed in many astrological calendars. The theory is that when the Moon is void of course, nothing will come of anything that occurs during this period; the matter will go on forever, in perpetuity, never reaching completion.

I've heard astrologers vehemently declare that no action should ever be taken when the Moon is void of course. Although the void-of-course Moon period is often only a matter of hours, it can be as many as two days. And that makes it tough to completely avoid, because most of us are far too busy to cease action for such long periods of time. Although you should try not to begin any major undertaking when the Moon is void of course, people do all sorts of things during these periods with absolutely no repercussions.

There's another important point to be made about the void-of-course Moon. Many people are born when the Moon is in this state. Rather than accomplish nothing, they seem to achieve more in a lifetime just because they don't know when to quit. This can be positive or negative, because there are times when the wise choice is to quit while you're ahead instead of pushing yourself too hard or pursuing a goal that has less chance of success. On the other hand, determination often breeds success.

To identify a Moon void, take a look at page 103 of the *2008 Daily Planetary Guide*, an annual publication of Llewellyn Publications (figure 13). The bracketed area on March 28 shows when the Moon is void of course after it forms its last aspect at 9:21 a.m. Eastern Time (6:21 a.m. Pacific Time) in Sagittarius and until it enters Capricorn at 10:43 p.m. (7:43 p.m.). That's a period of approximately thirteen and a half hours.

On an everyday level, you can use the void-of-course Moon very much to your advantage. For example, it's a great time to submit your tax return, deliver bad news, or schedule a routine medical appointment—all things most people want in the "nothing will come of it" category. Experiment with this. It works more often than not.

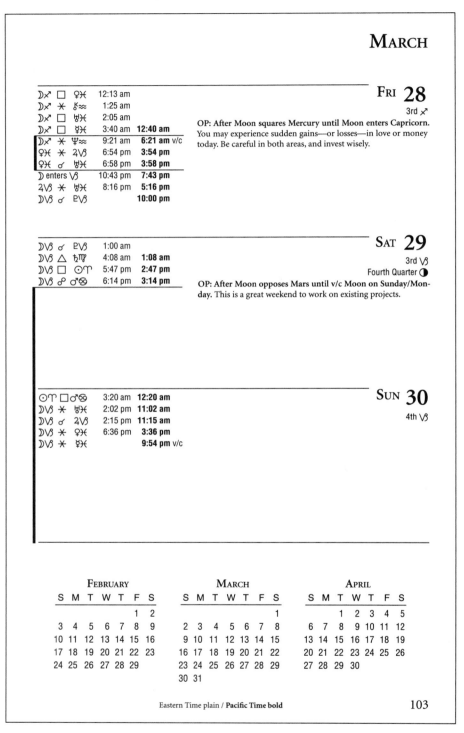

MARCH

FRI 28
3rd ♐

☽♐ □ ♀♓	12:13 am	
☽♐ ⚹ ⚷♒	1:25 am	
☽♐ □ ♅♓	2:05 am	
☽♐ □ ☿♓	3:40 am	**12:40 am**
☽♐ ⚹ ♆♒	9:21 am	**6:21 am** v/c
♀♓ ⚹ ♃♑	6:54 pm	**3:54 pm**
♀♓ ☌ ♅♓	6:58 pm	**3:58 pm**
☽ enters ♑	10:43 pm	**7:43 pm**
♃♑ ⚹ ♅♓	8:16 pm	**5:16 pm**
☽♑ ☌ ♇♑		**10:00 pm**

OP: After Moon squares Mercury until Moon enters Capricorn. You may experience sudden gains—or losses—in love or money today. Be careful in both areas, and invest wisely.

SAT 29
3rd ♑
Fourth Quarter ◐

☽♑ ☌ ♇♑	1:00 am	
☽♑ △ ♄♍	4:08 am	**1:08 am**
☽♑ □ ☉♈	5:47 pm	**2:47 pm**
☽♑ ☍ ♂♋	6:14 pm	**3:14 pm**

OP: After Moon opposes Mars until v/c Moon on Sunday/Monday. This is a great weekend to work on existing projects.

SUN 30
4th ♑

☉♈ □ ♂♋	3:20 am	**12:20 am**
☽♑ ⚹ ♅♓	2:02 pm	**11:02 am**
☽♑ ☌ ♃♑	2:15 pm	**11:15 am**
☽♑ ⚹ ♀♓	6:36 pm	**3:36 pm**
☽♑ ⚹ ☿♓		**9:54 pm** v/c

	FEBRUARY							MARCH							APRIL					
S	M	T	W	T	F	S	S	M	T	W	T	F	S	S	M	T	W	T	F	S
					1	2							1			1	2	3	4	5
3	4	5	6	7	8	9	2	3	4	5	6	7	8	6	7	8	9	10	11	12
10	11	12	13	14	15	16	9	10	11	12	13	14	15	13	14	15	16	17	18	19
17	18	19	20	21	22	23	16	17	18	19	20	21	22	20	21	22	23	24	25	26
24	25	26	27	28	29		23	24	25	26	27	28	29	27	28	29	30			
							30	31												

Eastern Time plain / **Pacific Time bold**

103

Figure 13. Llewellyn's *2008 Daily Planetary Guide*, Page 103

BRAD PITT

Brad Pitt has Mars, Mercury, Moon, and Venus in Capricorn. Besides being incredibly ambitious (Capricorn), he enjoys interior decorating and architecture (Moon, Venus) as hobbies and likes working with his hands (Mercury) and tools (Mars) to create a practical, concrete (Saturn) result.

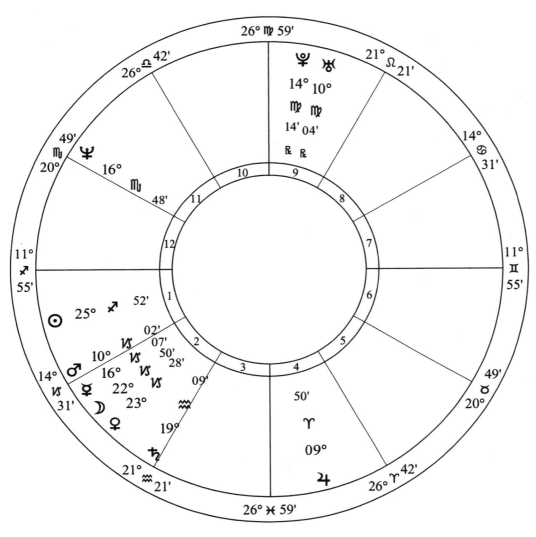

Brad Pitt
December 18, 1963 / 6:31 a.m. CST / Shawnee, OK
Placidus Houses

CONDOLEEZZA RICE

Condoleezza Rice served four years as President George W. Bush's national security director, after which she became secretary of state. She was perfectly suited for the first position, with four planets—Venus, Saturn, Sun, and Mercury—in Scorpio, which rules research, detective ability, and espionage. The same talents are useful to a diplomat (which the secretary of state is). Equally valuable is her Cancer Moon, which helps her relate well to people and the public; she's also very intuitive.

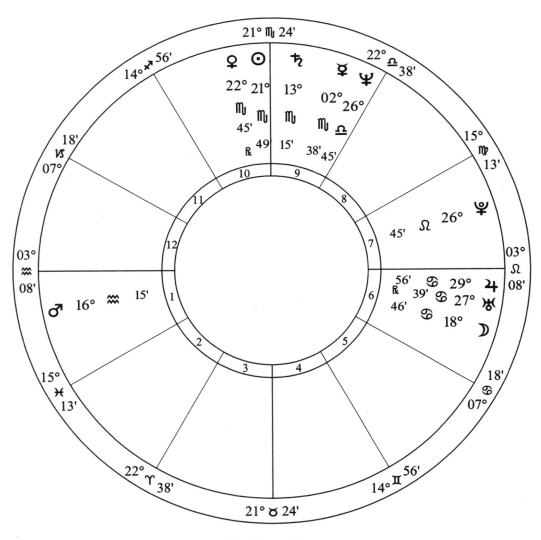

Condoleezza Rice
November 14, 1954 / 11:30 a.m. CST / Birmingham, AL
Placidus Houses

ANDERSON COOPER

Reporter and TV host Anderson Cooper is a commonsense (Saturn) risk taker (Aries), and with his Moon also in Aries, he probably follows his gut instincts and reactions. He's been in some dangerous situations as a reporter in war zones, where he undoubtedly benefited from the protection of Jupiter in Leo, a star-studded sign that's ideal for an on-air personality.

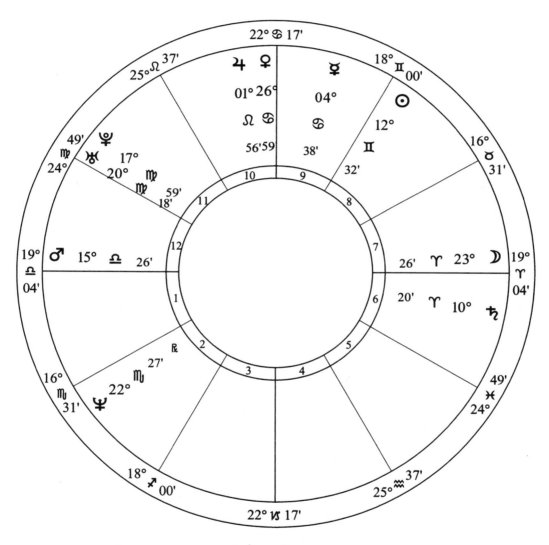

Anderson Cooper
June 3, 1967 / 3:46 p.m. EDT / New York, NY
Placidus Houses

DR. PHIL MCGRAW

With Mercury (communication) in Libra (relating), Dr. Phil easily connects with people one-on-one. Venus (popularity, relating) in Leo (showmanship) is a natural placement for a favorite TV personality.

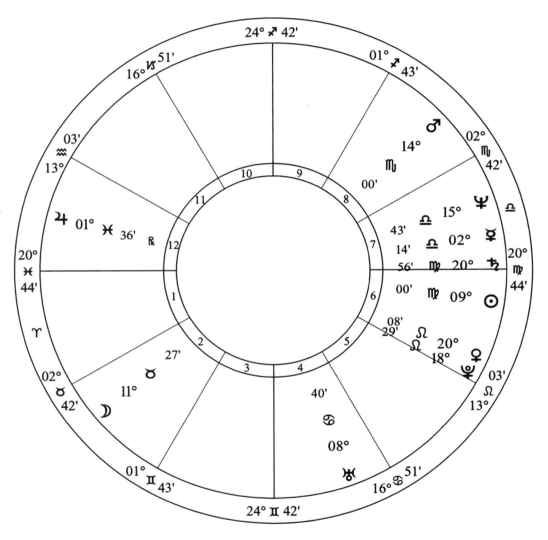

Dr. Phil McGraw
September 1, 1950 / 7:15 p.m. CST / Vinita, OK
Placidus Houses

WILLIE NELSON

Willie Nelson has Venus (and his Sun) in Taurus, the planet and sign that rule the throat and voice. He has made millions, fulfilling the wealth potential of both Venus and Taurus. Nelson's Cancer Moon, the sign and planet that rule the public, reflect his vast popularity and appeal.

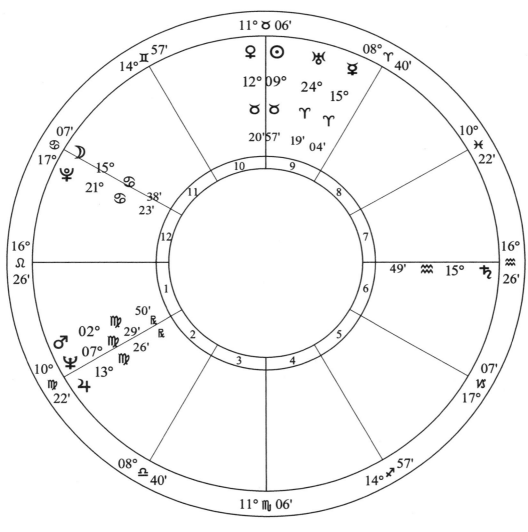

Willie Nelson
April 30, 1933 / 12:30 p.m. CST / Abbott, TX
Placidus Houses

TED KENNEDY

Ted Kennedy captures the essence of Jupiter in Leo through his position in the limelight as a U.S. senator. He has served in leadership positions (Leo). Some would call the outcome of the events in Chappaquiddick, Massachusetts, pure luck (Jupiter), as he pleaded guilty to leaving the scene after an auto accident caused the death of a campaign worker. He received a two-month suspended jail sentence and one year of probation. Jupiter rules legal matters.

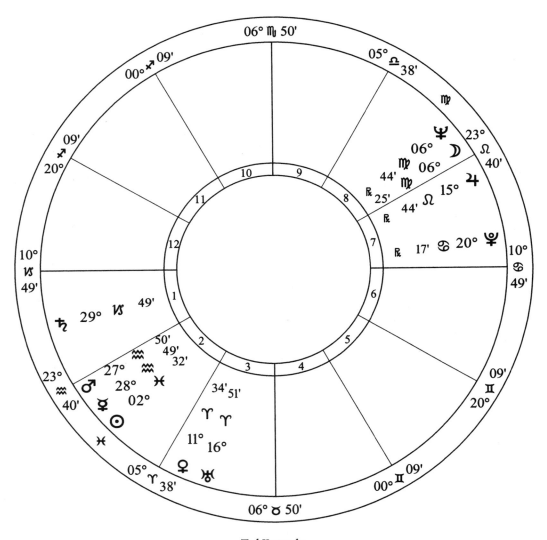

Ted Kennedy
February 22, 1932 / 3:58 a.m. EST / Dorchester, MA
Placidus Houses

TOM HANKS

Tom Hanks has the Moon (the public) in Leo (acting), which is ideal for an actor. Particularly interesting is that he has the Sun, Leo's ruling planet, in Cancer, which is the natural sign of the Moon; that is, the Sun and Moon are in each other's signs. This favorable planetary relationship is called *mutual reception* (see page 232), and it intensifies his acting talent and popularity.

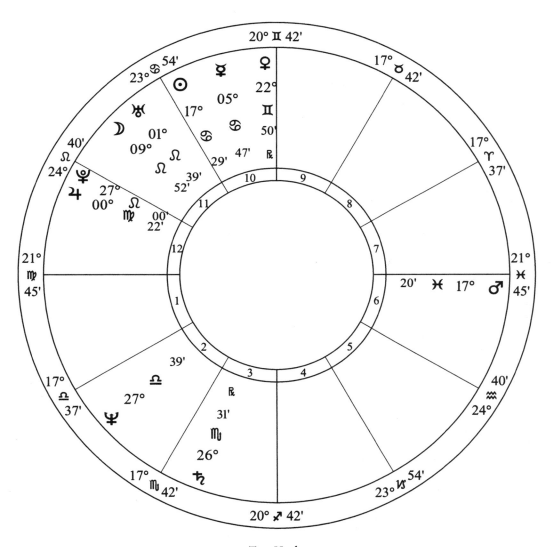

Tom Hanks
July 9, 1956 / 11:17 a.m. PDT / Concord, CA
Placidus Houses

AL GORE

Al Gore achieves emotional security (Moon) through status and career advancement (Capricorn). Although this ambitious Moon fueled his desire to become president of the United States, it also has much to do with his loss of the election. Capricorn is a serious sign, reserved and often lacking warmth. The Moon represents the public. He was unable to connect with the public and was perceived as stiff and aloof.

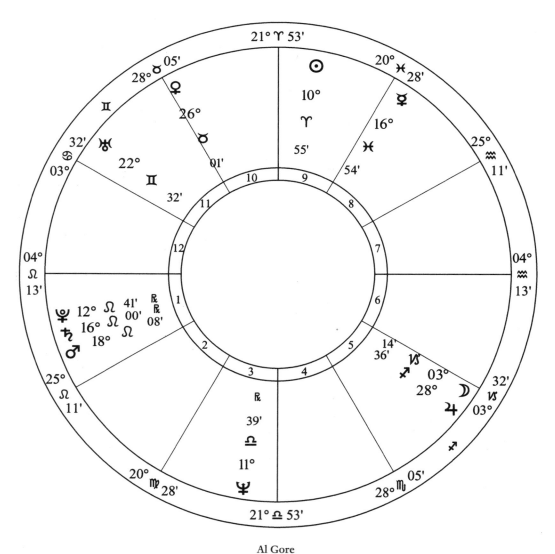

Al Gore
March 31, 1948 / 12:53 p.m. EST / Washington D.C.
Placidus Houses

TIGER WOODS

With Jupiter in Aries, Tiger Woods had the optimism and faith (Jupiter) to venture boldly (Aries) into the world of professional golf. Jupiter's expansive and lucky energy also represents his incredible talent and success in athletics (Aries).

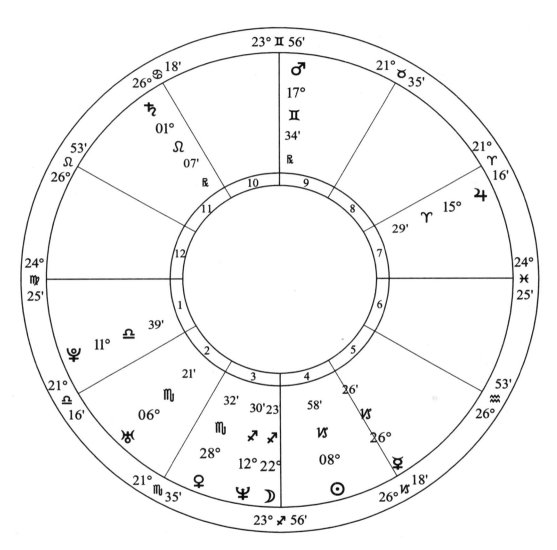

Tiger Woods
December 30, 1975 / 10:50 p.m. PST / Long Beach, CA
Placidus Houses

OPRAH WINFREY

Venus in Aquarius is an ideal influence for TV personality and host Oprah Winfrey. The magnetic, electric charm of Aquarius adds irresistible sparkle that shines through on television. She's friendly but maintains a certain distance. In a long-term relationship (Venus) for many years, she maintains her independence (Aquarius) without the need to formalize ties.

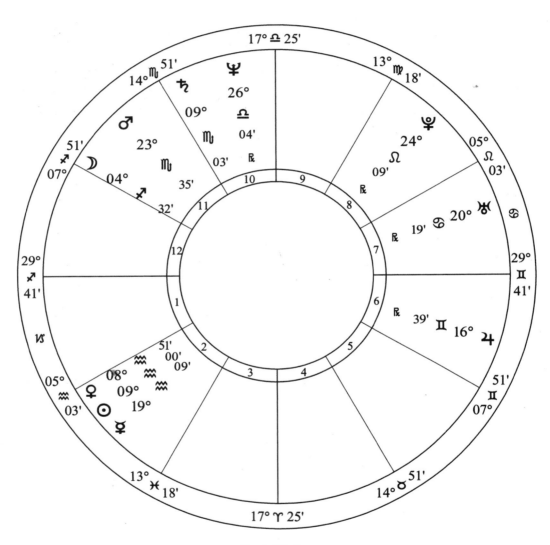

Oprah Winfrey
January 29, 1954 / 4:30 a.m. CST / Kosciusko, MS
Placidus Houses

CHAPTER FOUR

THE HOUSES

T he twelve houses are where the action is. They rule every possible area of life, including money, career, relationships, travel, and education. Think of it like this: a planet repre- sents certain energy, which is modified by its sign placement, that manifests in a specific arena—a house. As an example, consider Mercury (communication) in Aquarius (detached, inno- vative) in the seventh house (relationships). This person might have difficulty sharing his or her deepest thoughts with a romantic partner, but would excel as a negotiator, where detachment is an asset.

Each house begins and ends at the dividing line between it and the house that precedes or fol- lows it. This dividing line is called a *cusp* (figure 14). Each cusp has a sign on it. Depending on the time of year and place you were born, you could have the same sign on two house cusps with another sign *intercepted*, which means that the entire sign is wholly contained within the house and not on any cusp. If, for example, you have Aquarius on the ninth- and tenth-house cusps, then you would have Pisces (the sign after Aquarius) intercepted in the tenth house and Aries (the sign after Pisces) on the eleventh-house cusp. An intercepted sign influences the affairs of that house even though it isn't on the cusp.

A lot has been written about intercepted houses, and some astrologers consider them to be vitally important. Maybe they are, maybe they aren't. This is something you can experiment with to see if it works for you. Basically, the theory is that the intercepted sign's energy is "trapped" in the house and not as accessible as the sign on the cusp. An intercepted sign signifies something missing or energy that is stopped or put on hold. A good way to check the validity of this theory

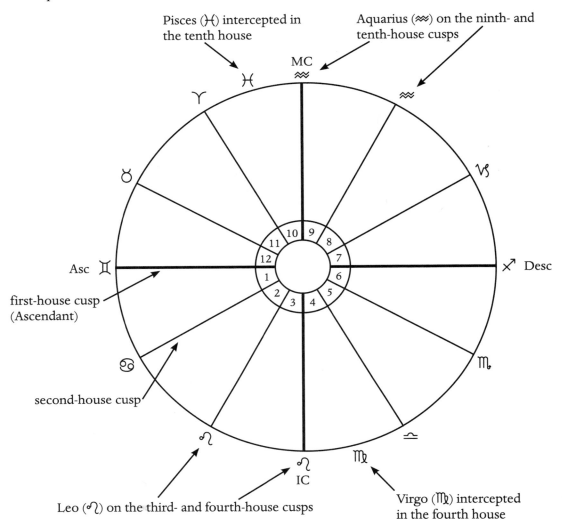

Pisces (♓) intercepted in the tenth house

Aquarius (♒) on the ninth- and tenth-house cusps

MC

Asc — Desc

first-house cusp (Ascendant)

second-house cusp

Leo (♌) on the third- and fourth-house cusps

IC

Virgo (♍) intercepted in the fourth house

Figure 14. House Cusps and Interceptions

is to study the planet that rules the intercepted sign, such as Saturn for Capricorn intercepted. The main reason I'm not an avid fan of this theory is that intercepted houses occur only when certain house systems are used. If it's not universal, it shouldn't be a valid theory.

There are nearly a dozen different *house systems*, or methods for mathematically calculating the house cusps. The angles—the Ascendant/ Descendant and Midheaven/IC—will always be the same no matter which house system you use. No one house system is better than another. It's more a matter of choice, and it's fun to experiment with the different systems. What changes with all but the Equal House system are the degrees and minutes of the *intermediate house cusps*—the cusps of the second, third, fifth, sixth, eighth, ninth, eleventh,

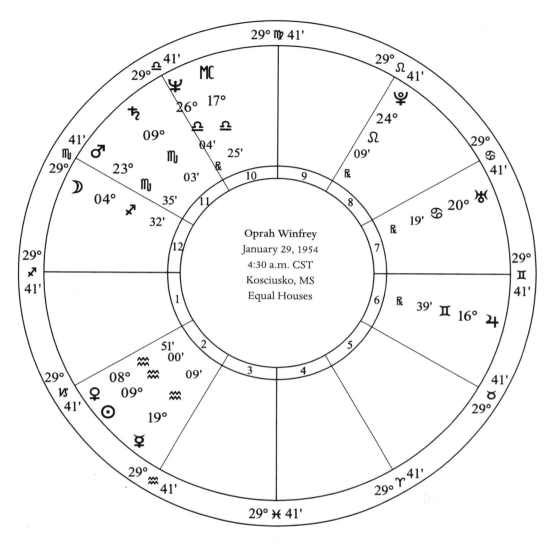

Figure 15. Equal House System

and twelfth houses. And when the house cusps change, some planets inevitably change houses too. For example, Mars in the first house using one house system would indicate high energy with lots of personal initiative. Using another house system, Mars could shift to the second house, indicating an individual who invests the Mars energy in moneymaking activities and also spends on impulse.

The Equal House system is used primarily in England. It was first used by Ptolemy in the second century and was reactivated in the twentieth century by English astrologer Margaret Hone. All the house cusps use the same degree and minutes as the Ascendant. The signs follow their natural order, as they do in all house systems. Figure 15 shows Oprah Winfrey's chart using the Equal House system.

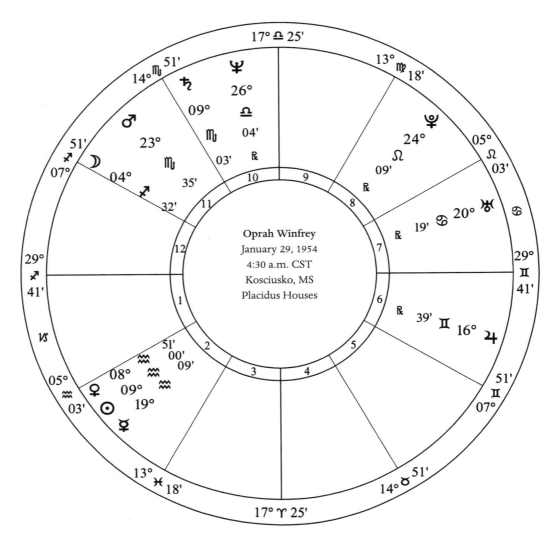

Figure 16. Placidus House System

Most Western astrologers use the Placidus system of house division or calculation (figure 16). It was developed in the seventeenth century by Placidus de Titus, an astrologer of the time, and became popular in the late seventeenth and early eighteenth centuries when it was adopted by English astrologer John Partridge. I use the Placidus system. After experimenting with several other house systems, the planetary house placements of the Placidus system seemed to be a better fit for the people I tested them on.

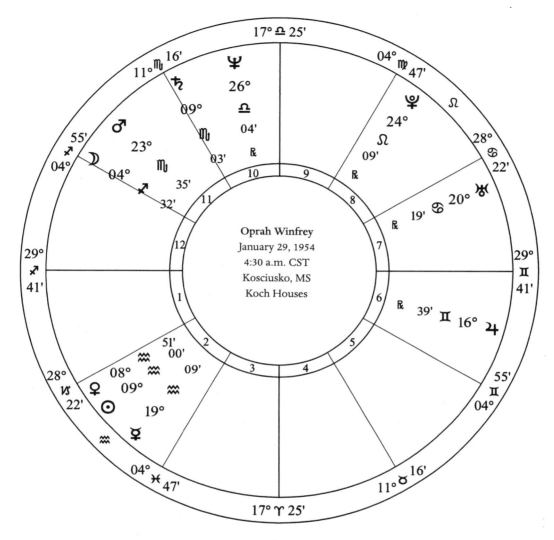

17° ♎ 25'

04° ♍ 47'

11° ♏ 16'

♄ 09°

♆ 26°
♎ 04'
℞

♇ 24°
♌ 09°
℞

♂ 23°
♍ 55'
04°

☽ 04°
♐ 32'
35'

♎ 03'

10 | 9

8 ℞

♌ 28°
♋ 22'

☿ 19' ♋ 20° ♅

29°
♐
41'

12
1

Oprah Winfrey
January 29, 1954
4:30 a.m. CST
Kosciusko, MS
Koch Houses

7

6 ℞

29°
♊
41'

39' ♊ 16° ♃

51'
00'
♒ 08°
09°
♒ 09°
♒ 19°
♀
☉
☿

2

3 | 4

5

55'
♊
04°

28°
♑
22'

04°
♓ 47'

11° ♉ 16'

17° ♈ 25'

Figure 17. Koch House System

The Koch house system is used by some Western astrologers (figure 17). It was developed by German astrologer Walther Koch in the twentieth century.

Some of the other house systems are Regiomontanus, Alcabitius, Campanus, Meridian, Morinus, Porphyry, Solar Sign, and Topocentric.

Because of its popularity and widespread use by Western astrologers, Placidus is a good choice while you are learning astrology. Later, you can experiment with other house systems. Or, if you're daring and want to be different, choose one of the others. What's important is to stay with one house system until you're more

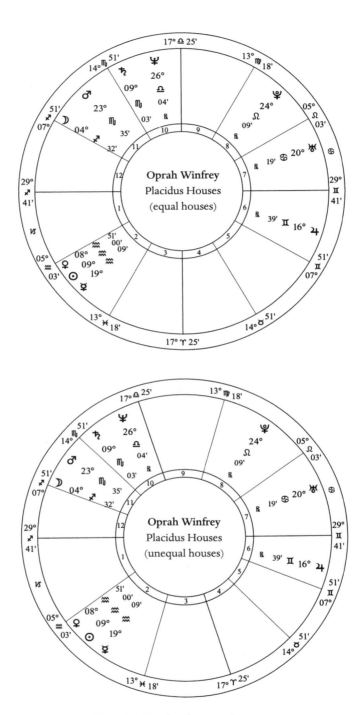

Figure 18. Equal and Unequal Houses

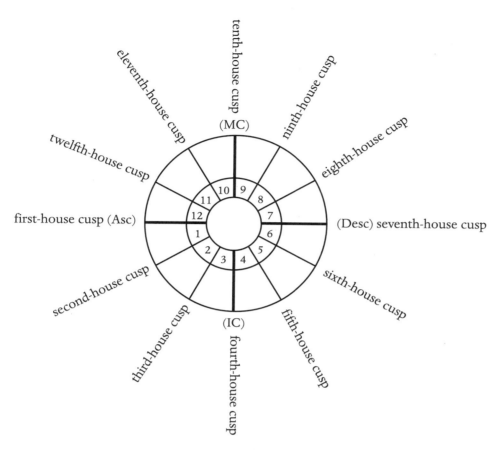

Figure 19. House Cusps

experienced with astrology. Consistency makes it easier to understand how a planet manifests its energy in a house.

Figure 18 shows Oprah Winfrey's chart with equal and unequal houses. This is not the same as the Equal House system. Rather, the chart is displayed with all houses of an equal size (equal houses) or all houses proportional to the number of degrees in each house (unequal houses). Neither one is better than the other. It's a matter of personal preference. I always use equal houses because I find them easier to read. Try both and decide which you like.

THE HOUSES

The chart begins with the first-house cusp, on the left side of the chart, followed by the second through twelfth houses in a counterclockwise direction (figure 19). The Ascendant is the sign that was rising over the horizon at the time of your birth and as viewed from your place of birth.

The Ascendant, together with the IC (fourth-house cusp), Descendant (seventh-house cusp), and Midheaven (tenth-house cusp), are collectively referred to as *angles*, because they are the

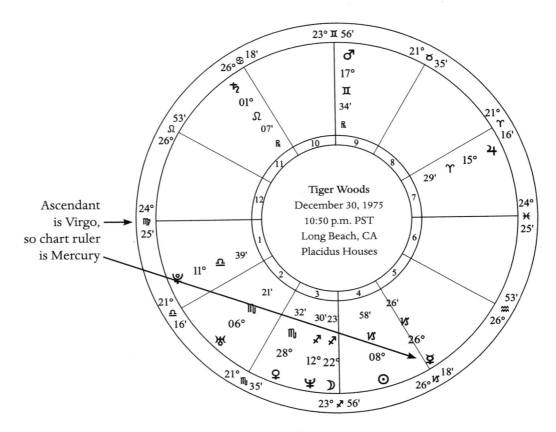

Figure 20. Chart Ruler

cusps of the angular houses (which will be discussed in the "House Classifications" section on page 151). The angles are all-important points in a horoscope and are powerful tools in predictive astrology.

Because there are twelve houses but only ten planets, it's impossible for a person to have a planet in every house. This is also true because the Sun, Mercury, and Venus are always orbiting near each other; Mercury and Venus are thus always in the same house as the Sun or within one or two houses of the Sun. This doesn't mean that two and probably more areas of

life are missing from yours! They're just not as prominent in your life as others.

There are two simple and easy ways to learn what those empty houses say about you and your life. The first is to learn about the influence of the sign on that house cusp (which provides valuable information even when there are planets in the house). The second is to interpret the influence of the planet in your chart that rules that house (as well as the sign the planet is in). For example, if Aries is the sign on your third-house cusp, then you would study Mars, the planet that rules Aries. Some of the example charts at the end of this chapter illustrate how this works.

The planet ruling the sign on the first house (on the first-house cusp) is called the *chart ruler*. This important planet says much about your reason for being and your mission in life. Its house placement also reflects an area that will be emphasized throughout your lifetime. You should carefully study this planet, its sign and house placement, and the aspects it makes (see chapter 5).

Mercury is the chart ruler in Tiger Woods's chart because his Ascendant is Virgo (figure 20). Both Virgo and Capricorn are practical earth signs, so the Ascendant and Mercury (the chart ruler) are especially compatible. Both Mercury and Virgo indicate a strong mental orientation, and Mercury in Capricorn reinforces this, giving Woods a sharp, goal-oriented mind, with strong powers of concentration. He directs this energy and himself (Ascendant) into a fifth-house activity—sports.

Before delving into the individual houses and their meanings, you can learn a lot about your basic personality from the four hemispheres and four quadrants.

HEMISPHERES AND QUADRANTS

The chart can be divided into four hemispheres: the *northern hemisphere* (houses one through six), the *southern hemisphere* (houses seven through twelve), the *eastern hemisphere* (houses ten through three), and the *western hemisphere* (houses four through ten). Notice that these directions are different from a traditional map orientation (figure 21). This is because the chart is calculated from the perspective of the North

Pole to the equator, as if your head were at the North Pole looking past your feet toward the equator. If your birth place is in the Southern Hemisphere, then the view is reversed, looking from the South Pole to the equator.

If the majority of your planets are in the...

- northern hemisphere, you're introspective and rely on yourself for solutions more than you consult with others. You're usually more comfortable operating out of the public eye.
- southern hemisphere, you're outgoing and involved with people, consulting them for opinions and solutions. You probably enjoy being in leadership positions.
- eastern hemisphere, you focus more on your needs and desires and are self-motivated and self-reliant.
- western hemisphere, your focus is on other people, and you're responsive to their wants and needs.

The chart also can be divided into four quadrants: the *first quadrant* (houses one, two, and three), the *second quadrant* (houses four, five, and six), the *third quadrant* (houses seven, eight, and nine), and the *fourth quadrant* (houses ten, eleven, and twelve). Each quadrant is a combination of the influences of two hemispheres (figure 22).

If the majority of your planets are in the...

- first quadrant, you're independent, action-oriented, and self-absorbed.
- second quadrant, you're self-directed but also receptive to others.
- third quadrant, relationships are important to you and you're a people person.

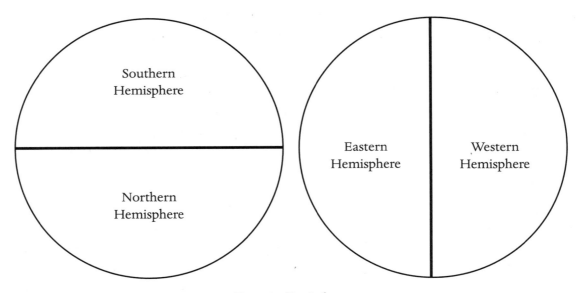

Figure 21. Hemispheres

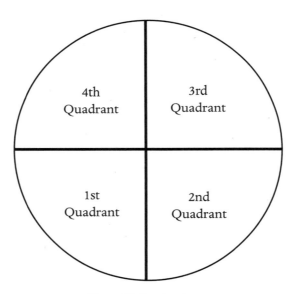

Figure 22. Quadrants

• fourth quadrant, you're self-motivated and ambitious and value teamwork.

HOUSE CLASSIFICATIONS

The individual houses are classified according to their general type of activity. There are three classifications with four houses in each one. The three classifications are *angular, succedent,* and *cadent.*

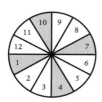

Angular houses (houses one, four, seven, and ten) are the strongest and correspond to the cardinal signs (Aries, Cancer, Libra, and Capricorn). Each angular house represents action, motivation, and initiative in the four main areas of life represented by these houses. Action is initiated in these houses. Having many planets in angular houses indicates a person who is a go-getter with a high level of initiative. These people often achieve prominent positions.

As already discussed, the angular house cusps each have a special designation: the first-house cusp is called the *Ascendant*, the fourth-house cusp is the *IC (Imum Coeli)*, the seventh-house cusp is the *Descendant*, and the tenth-house cusp is the *Midheaven*.

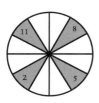

Succedent houses (houses two, five, eight, and eleven) are similar to the fixed signs (Taurus, Leo, Scorpio, and Aquarius). These houses represent steady, thorough action and follow-through on what was begun in the angular houses. Having many planets in the suc-

cedent houses indicates a person who is stubborn and resists change, but also one who has excellent follow-through. These people often outlast the competition and succeed through determination and willpower.

Cadent houses (houses three, six, nine, and twelve) operate much like the mutable signs (Gemini, Virgo, Sagittarius, and Pisces). They represent completion and distribution of what was begun in the angular houses and developed in the succedent houses, and people with many planets in these houses are adaptable and like variety. They are curious and are perpetual learners with a vast mental knowledge bank.

ELEMENTAL HOUSES OF FUNCTION

The houses also are categorized according to elemental function. They are divided into sets of three houses each, often called the *trinities.* Each set of three houses is associated with one of the four elements: fire, earth, air, and water. The houses are the natural houses of these four elements.

The first (self), fifth (children), and ninth (life philosophy) houses are called the *trinity of life.* They are the fire houses, representing the ego, creativity, and adventure. Having many planets in these houses indicates self-expression, enthusiasm, high energy, and leadership ability.

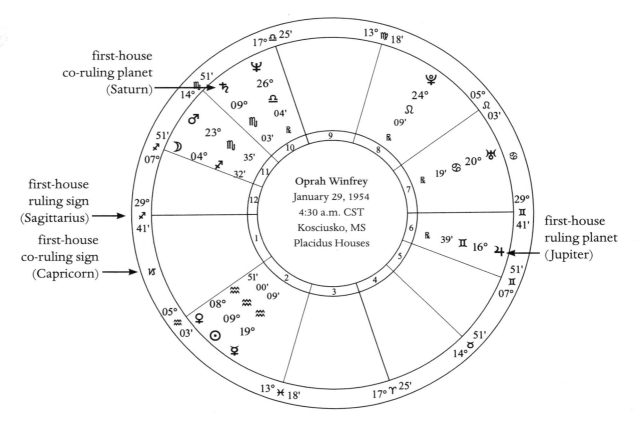

first-house
co-ruling planet
(Saturn)

first-house
ruling sign
(Sagittarius)

first-house
co-ruling sign
(Capricorn)

first-house
ruling planet
(Jupiter)

Oprah Winfrey
January 29, 1954
4:30 a.m. CST
Kosciusko, MS
Placidus Houses

Figure 23. Sign and House Rulers and Co-Rulers

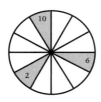

The *trinity of wealth* comprises the second, sixth, and tenth houses. The second house rules personal resources, the sixth house rules work and service, and the tenth house is career and recognition. These are the earth houses. Having many planets in these three houses indicates a hard worker who achieves personal recognition and financial success.

The *trinity of association* focuses on relationships through the air houses: the third house (neighbors and relatives), the seventh house (business and personal partners and other close relationships), and the eleventh house (friends and groups). People with many planets in these houses need and want to interact regularly with others; they dislike being alone.

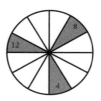

The water houses compose the *trinity of endings*: the fourth house (the latter years of life), the eighth house (regeneration and death), and the twelfth house (the subconscious, karma). Having many planets in these houses indicates compassion, intuitive or psychic ability, and the desire to delve deep into the mind and other areas of life through research.

INDIVIDUAL HOUSES

The sign on the cusp of a house is its *ruling sign*, and the planet that rules that sign is the house's *ruling planet*. For example, if Gemini (which is ruled by Mercury) is on the seventh-house cusp, then Gemini is the seventh-house ruling sign and Mercury is the seventh-house ruling planet. Intercepted signs and their ruling planets are *co-rulers* of the house.

Outgoing, enthusiastic Sagittarius is the Ascendant in Oprah Winfrey's chart (figure 23), which makes Jupiter the first-house ruling planet. This chart has Capricorn intercepted in the first house, so Saturn (Capricorn's ruling planet) is the co-ruler of the first house. Both of these signs and their ruling planets are thus strongly emphasized in Winfrey's personality. But because Sagittarius is on the cusp, that sign represents more of her outward expression than does serious, ambitious Capricorn.

The houses in your chart that contain planets are the strongest, and especially so if they are angular houses. Each has a major influence on your life.

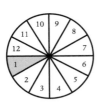

First House

The first house represents you—your personal ambition and drive, your body, and the face you present to the world. The Ascendant (the cusp of the first house) is a strong personality influence, along with the Sun and Moon. The Ascen-

dant, or rising sign, reflects your general temperament, likes and dislikes, personality traits, appearance, mannerisms, and how you project your personality. In a sense, the rest of your chart is filtered through your Ascendant.

Natural rulers: Aries and Mars

Represents: you—your body and personality

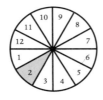

Second House

The second house reflects your materialistic attitude, income, money, spending habits, and whether you're a giver, a receiver, generous or stingy. It also represents your overall financial attitudes, including those toward debt, budgeting, savings, and investments. The second house indicates whether you're thrifty, extravagant, or somewhere in between. Possessions and earning potential also are ruled by this house.

Natural rulers: Taurus and Venus

Represents: personal income and spending habits, possessions, gifts given and received

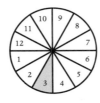

Third House

This house governs all forms of communication, including mail, blogs, calls, speaking, writing, and conversation. It's also the house of learning and describes your learning style and study habits, as well as your thinking process. Cars, errands, contracts, bicycling, skating, walking, and weekend trips are associated with the third house. This house rules your siblings and relatives in general (other than parents), plus your neighbors and neighborhood.

Natural rulers: Gemini and Mercury

Represents: communication, quick trips, thinking process

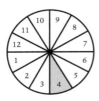

Fourth House

The fourth is the house of domestic affairs, including your home life, family, and physical home. Your roots, childhood, and parents are associated with this house, as well as your father or mother. (Some astrologers believe that the fourth house represents the father and the tenth house represents the mother, while others believe the opposite is true. Decide for yourself which works best for you and your chart. I use the fourth house for the father and the tenth house for the mother.) The fourth house can indicate what you inherit from your family, including money. It also reflects the waning, or elderly, years of your life, including a general indication of what you can expect from retirement in terms of daily life.

Natural rulers: Cancer and Moon

Represents: home, family, parents, roots, property, father (or mother)

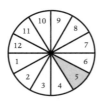

Fifth House

Fun and pleasure are the main focus of the fifth house. The fifth rules your leisure-time pursuits, love life, dating, creativity, sports, hobbies, socializing, and games. Your children, especially your first child, are associated with this house, although some people instead have children of

the mind—creative projects. The fifth house also governs gambling and other games of chance, including investments and anything speculative that involves money.

Natural rulers: Leo and Sun

Represents: creativity, children, hobbies, social life, love life, sports, speculative ventures

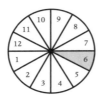

Sixth House

The sixth house governs your specific job (your career is symbolized by the tenth house), work habits and attitudes, working environment, and coworker relationships. This is also the house of service and thus rules volunteer activities. The sixth house rules health, specifically diet, eating habits, hygiene, medical tests and personnel, chronic health conditions, and minor illnesses. Pets also are ruled by this house.

Natural rulers: Virgo and Mercury

Represents: work, service, health, diet, nutrition, coworkers, pets, volunteer activities

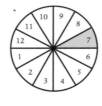

Seventh House

The seventh house represents close relationships and business and romantic relationships, as well as how you interact with other people and the public at large. This house also rules your best friend, rivals, and known adversaries. Lawsuits, agreements, and contract negotiations are seventh-house matters.

Natural rulers: Libra and Venus

Represents: partners (business and romantic), close relationships, known adversaries

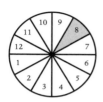

Eighth House

The eighth is the house of joint resources and other people's money. It represents your partner's (business or personal) earning potential, income, and spending habits, and your and your partner's combined total assets. Taxes, inheritance, insurance, loans, and mortgages are ruled by this house, as are spousal maintenance and child support. The eighth is also the house of sex.

Natural rulers: Scorpio and Pluto

Represents: joint resources, debt, loans, mortgages, investments, sex, death, inheritance, insurance, partner's income

Ninth House

Spirituality, religion, morals and ethics, and higher education are ruled by the ninth house, which indicates your life philosophy and the value you place on postsecondary learning. Long-distance travel and communication fall here, as do publishing and the Internet. Legal matters, courts, and judges are ninth-house matters. This house also rules your relationship with in-laws.

Natural rulers: Sagittarius and Jupiter

Represents: higher education, life philosophy, long-distance travel, religion, spirituality

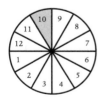

Tenth House

The tenth is the house of achievement, recognition, prestige, and status. It rules your career and your career ambitions, honors, and promotions. The tenth house represents what you want to be noted for and thus also indicates fame—or infamy. Your relationships with your boss and other authority figures (including parents) are represented by this house, as is the government. The tenth house also represents your mother or father (see the fourth house for an explanation). I use the tenth house for the mother and the fourth house for the father.

Natural rulers: Capricorn and Saturn

Represents: career, status, achievement, honors, recognition, ambition, mother (or father), superiors, and authority figures

Eleventh House

The eleventh house describes your approach to friendship, your friends and acquaintances, and your interest in groups, clubs, and organizations. This house also rules your hopes and wishes—your personal and professional goals and objectives—and the networking contacts that can help you achieve them.

Natural rulers: Aquarius and Uranus

Represents: friends, acquaintances, groups, organizations, goals and objectives

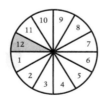

Twelfth House

This is the house of self-renewal, as it rules your subconscious and self-talk. It indicates intuitive, or psychic, ability and your inner, spiritual self. But it's also the house of self-undoing or karma and indicates where you can be your own worst enemy. The twelfth house rules secrets, worries, confidential information, and private matters, as well as

SUN SIGN TIP

Here's how to get the most from Internet, magazine, newspaper, and other Sun sign astrology columns and publications: read the write-up for your rising sign (Ascendant) as well as the one for your Sun sign. You'll gain additional insights because these horoscopes are written using a solar chart, where the Sun sign is the first house. So if you have a Libra Sun and a Cancer Ascendant, you would read both Libra and Cancer.

If relationships, for example, are mentioned in the horoscope, this usually means that a planet or planets are in your solar seventh house, or the sign opposite your Sun or Ascendant sign. In the Libra-Cancer example, this would mean that there are planets in Aries (the polar opposite of Libra) and Capricorn (the polar opposite of Cancer). As another example, money would be mentioned when planets are in your solar second house, or the sign after your Sun or rising sign.

DERIVATIVE HOUSES

Derivative houses (also called derived houses) is a technique used to gain information about other people through your own chart. For example, you can learn about your child's preferred choice of friends, or your mate's coworker's sister. You can even carry this so far as to discover information about your boss's nephew's child's career, if you're really that interested.

This is a simple concept that involves moving from house to house in your chart, counting off the appropriate number of houses. Always begin with your first house, counting it as number one.

Here's an example:

Your child's friend

Your—First house.

child's—Your child is the fifth house in your chart, or five houses counted forward, beginning with your first house.

friend—This is your child's friend, so count forward eleven houses from the fifth (your child), which results in your third house. The sign and ruling planet of your third house, plus any planets in your third house and the aspects these planets make, will give you insights into your child's choice of friends.

EASY INTERPRETATION

Keywords make chart interpretation easy. Here are a few examples of planets in signs and houses to get you started.

Mercury + Cancer + second house =
Thought process + emotional + money = emotionally based thinking influences spending habits

Mars + Leo + eleventh house =
Drive + ego + groups = leadership boosts ego in group activities

Jupiter + Taurus + fourth house =
Abundance + money + family = material security through family

Saturn + Aquarius + first house =
Restriction + independence + self = self-reliance

---

deception and unknown enemies. Also ruled by the twelfth are institutions (such as hospitals, jails, prisons, and nursing homes), charitable organizations, and government relief.

Natural rulers: Pisces and Neptune

Represents: subconscious, self-renewal, self-undoing, unknown adversaries, health, secrets, behind-the-scenes events

SIGNS ON THE HOUSE CUSPS

The sign on each house cusp (and/or the sign intercepted in the house) indicates how you express the affairs of the house, much as planetary action is colored by sign placement. Aquarius on the sixth-house cusp, for example, is similar to but not as influential as Uranus (Aquarius's ruling planet) placed in the sixth house. Your preferred work environment (sixth house) would be one that allows a high level of independence (Ura-

nus, Aquarius) in daily work and that encourages innovation (Uranus, Aquarius).

The difference between a sign on the cusp and a planet in the house is a subtle yet important point to grasp. If Aquarius is the Ascendant (first-house cusp) and Uranus is in the sixth house, then the energy of Uranus would manifest through the sixth house, and workplace changes would affect the individual (Ascendant). Reversing this, with Uranus in the first house and Aquarius on the cusp of the sixth house, changes initiated by the individual would affect his or her job.

You can gain additional insight into a house by reading the sections about the ruling planet in that house. For example, if Sagittarius is on the third-house cusp, you would read the description for Jupiter (Sagittarius's ruling planet) in the third house. You can do the same to learn more about your communication style

157

by reading about the influence of Mercury in the house in your chart that has Gemini on the cusp. Be sure to read about the Sun in the house in your chart with Leo on the cusp; you'll learn more about your ego needs and what can help fulfill them.

Aries House Cusps—Ruling Planet, Mars

Aries First House (Ascendant)

You're a starter, not a finisher, the first one out of the gate on your way to the next competitive achievement. A leader, you can motivate and inspire others to emulate your drive and ambition. High energy and physical stamina are assets that complement your confidence and extroverted, upbeat personality.

Aries Second House

You direct much energy into moneymaking activities and have the initiative to pursue them with the highest potential return. Impulsive spending, however, can leave you with little to show for your efforts. Put yourself on a budget that includes monthly savings goals and contributions to your retirement account.

Aries Third House

You're a decisive, quick thinker, an idea person who avidly expresses thoughts and opinions. You can be argumentative at times and make snap decisions when caution would be a better choice. Although concentration is a challenge, you're also a quick study, a rapid and active learner. Sibling rivalry is the norm.

Aries Fourth House (IC)

Home life is never boring, as Aries promotes a lively environment and a busy family. However,

there could be conflict with Aries here, either during your childhood or adult life, because everyone wants to be in charge. You might become the mediator, the one who promotes compromise to ensure peace.

Aries Fifth House

You express your individuality through leisure-time activities—creative pursuits, athletics, socializing, and a lively, ardent romantic life. Playing the field excites you, as does the thrill of new love. If you're a parent, you're actively involved in your children's lives, although at times you're impatient with them.

Aries Sixth House

You're a hard worker. You also want to be the boss and can become impatient and move on if promotions are delayed. A fast-paced work environment is a must to keep your interest, and you might prefer physical work to a desk job. Safety precautions are important because Aries here can be accident-prone.

Aries Seventh House (Descendant)

You're attracted to dynamic people, go-getters with a passion for life. Your desire for a mate, however, can prompt an impulsive union, which may or may not stand the test of time. Some close relationships are prone to conflict, which unsettles you. Nevertheless, voice your opinions and stand up for what you believe.

Aries Eighth House

You're in charge (or want to be) of family funds, an area that can trigger conflict over debt. Either or both of you can be impulsive spenders, buying on credit. Budgeting is thus as important as shared responsibility and compromise. You also should think long term and emphasize savings, investments, and retirement funds.

Aries Ninth House

Your spirit of adventure spans the globe, and you'd like to explore every location and culture. Knowledge and information stimulate you, but you can become bored with the slow pace of a college curriculum; accelerated learning thus might be a good choice. In-laws can test your patience. When necessary, you actively seek legal solutions.

Aries Tenth House (Midheaven)

You may be the consummate entrepreneur. If that's not your bent, then you have the incentive, initiative, and persistence to aim for and achieve a top spot. But be cautious and tactful with supervisors, who might feel you're after their jobs . . . which you are! Impatience and slow advancement can trigger a job search.

Aries Eleventh House

Your active social life includes many opportunities to meet new people, whom you quickly welcome into your circle. In any group activity, you quickly take the lead and, if you're involved in an organization, are the first to initiate new endeavors. This influence also can prompt conflict with friends and groups.

Aries Twelfth House

You have the internal motivation to launch new personal endeavors. But initiating them can be a challenge because you prefer established routines and dislike change. Once you jump that hurdle, however, what's new becomes the norm, and you embrace it with relentless determination and usually succeed.

Taurus House Cusps—Ruling Planet, Venus
Taurus First House (Ascendant)

You love habits and routine, rich food, and serenity, and you hate change. That's your comfort zone, and you see no reason to have it any other way. Determination, practicality, and slow, steady progress are part of your makeup. Used positively, these traits give you a strong commitment to goals and willpower to overcome obstacles.

Taurus Second House

The need for financial security and a comfortable lifestyle motivates you to maximize your excellent earning potential. Practical and realistic in money matters, you're also thrifty and have a sixth sense for bargains. Good value is important to you and the deciding factor in most purchases. You have a taste for luxury.

Taurus Third House

You're a patient, thoughtful thinker and planner who won't be rushed into decisions. Once your mind is made up, you rarely change it. Your powers of concentration are excellent, and what you learn, you learn thoroughly. Relationships with siblings are generally close and affectionate, and you're a helpful neighbor.

Taurus Fourth House (IC)

You want a home designed for comfort and practicality and one with plenty of space for all your possessions, including collectibles. Your place is also something of an artistic showplace, with artwork and décor. Family relationships under Taurus are generally favorable, and you could benefit from a relative's legacy.

Taurus Fifth House

You want a stable, supportive, and sensual romantic relationship, and when dating, you focus exclusively on your current love interest. Hands-on hobbies are among your favorites, and you also might enjoy cooking and artistic projects. You're fond of children, although you insist on order and discipline.

Taurus Sixth House

A hard worker, you're methodical, thorough, and reliable. You want a steady, slower-paced environment and one that's comfortable and pleasing to the eye. Routine is your comfort zone, so you resist procedural and other changes, preferring to do things the old way. You may be susceptible to sore throats and sensitive to dust.

Taurus Seventh House (Descendant)

In love, you're loyal but also possessive, and your insecurities can trigger unwarranted jealousy. Learn to trust and have faith in your partner. Partnership is very important to you, and when you commit, you intend it to be for a lifetime. You could profit financially from a business or personal relationship.

Taurus Eighth House

A business or romantic partnership, investments, and an inheritance are all potentially lucrative sources of financial gain. Except when absolutely necessary or practical, you avoid debt, and you shop for the best bargains and interest rates. You could do well with real estate, antiques, and collectibles.

Taurus Ninth House

Higher education can increase your earning potential, and you're likely to pursue subjects that are practical and useful. Vacation trips are a good tension reliever, although you prefer to travel in comfort or not at all. Your code of ethics and spiritual beliefs are conservative, and your relationships with in-laws are congenial.

Taurus Tenth House (Midheaven)

Once you find your niche, you're likely to stick with a career path and preferably the same company, advancing through the ranks. Money is a strong motivation and probably the only reason you consider changing jobs. Even then, you hesitate to move on, preferring your established routine and what's familiar.

Taurus Eleventh House

You attract wealthy and influential friends, many of whom are for a lifetime. Membership in an investment club can be profitable and link you with other moneymaking opportunities, as can friends and organizations. You're goal-oriented, and once committed, you rarely waver from your objectives.

Taurus Twelfth House

You're here, there, and everywhere on a daily basis, and some people perceive you as scattered and inconsistent, which you are at times. Yet on a deeper level, you have a strong need for security and stability, especially in relationships, finances, and material gains. Let this side of yourself emerge and pursue your dreams.

Gemini House Cusps—
Ruling Planet, Mercury

Gemini First House (Ascendant)

You're fun and flirtatious, lively and popular, curious and interested in most everything. Focus is a challenge, as you tend to scatter your energies, partly out of boredom prompted by a short attention span. Mentally stimulating activities—reading, games, puzzles—hold your interest.

Gemini Second House

You have plenty of moneymaking ideas and want to pursue them all. Be selective and do one or two well to increase income potential, possibly through a sideline or freelance work in addition to your day job. Earnings fluctuate, so budgeting and regular savings are to your advantage to meet the inevitable unexpected expenses.

Gemini Third House

You're a natural communicator, curious, logical, and quick-thinking. Ideas are your specialty, but a short attention span can make depth of learning a challenge except in areas that capture your passionate interest. Phones and electronic devices are among your favorite possessions, and you enjoy puzzles and games.

Gemini Fourth House (IC)

There's nothing constant about your home life. Activities, entertaining, and coming and going are the norm, along with a lively intellectual atmosphere. You may have an extensive library in addition to the latest technology. Relationships with siblings and other relatives are changeable.

Gemini Fifth House

You're fun and flirtatious and delight in playing the field, sometimes with two simultaneous romances. Once committed, your playfulness helps keep love alive, along with long walks and talks. Your many hobbies are creative outlets, and you could have writing talent. Twins are possible with Gemini here.

Gemini Sixth House

You enjoy work where you can use your hands almost as much as your mind, but your short attention span can lead to job hopping. You're happiest in a fast-paced, active work environment with lots of variety. Some people with Gemini here have two jobs. Nervous tension requires daily stress relief.

Gemini Seventh House (Descendant)

It takes a special person to capture your heart, someone who's as free-spirited and curious as you are. You may never commit or do so only later in life. Some people with a Gemini Descendant have multiple long-term relationships. People with quick, lively minds attract your interest.

Gemini Eighth House

Family funds fluctuate, as do investments and retirement accounts. Information-based decisions help maintain stability if you take time to gather data. Also make financial organization a priority, and be cautious with credit as debt can mount quickly. You could gain through a relative's legacy.

Gemini Ninth House

Learning satisfies your curiosity, as does travel. You might be a perpetual student, taking classes for fun, to advance your career, or both. In-law relationships are friendly but not close, and you keep in touch with faraway relatives and friends. Your spiritual and ethical beliefs evolve throughout your life.

Gemini Tenth House (Midheaven)

Your ideal career is one that features communication and includes varied responsibilities. As an excellent multitasker, you easily juggle many projects and prefer it that way to stave off boredom. Career matters fluctuate. You might pursue two careers simultaneously—a day job and a freelance one.

Gemini Eleventh House

You're popular with a wide variety of people and easily make new friends, who come and go, in and out of your life. Your fondest friendships are with lively, witty people who complement your playful spirit and enjoy weekend getaways. Personal goals fluctuate, changing with your current interests.

Gemini Twelfth House

You collect gossip and secrets. You also maintain confidences, which is why people freely share information with you. However, you may not—but should—do the same with personal information and feelings, which less-honorable people might use to their advantage. Put in writing only what you want others to read.

Cancer House Cusps—Ruling Planet, Moon
Cancer First House (Ascendant)

The quest for emotional and financial security is a strong theme in your life. You're well liked, but may be shy, and prefer time with family and close friends to socializing. Highly receptive and intuitive, you're also sensitive; your feelings are thus easily hurt, although you hide it well from outsiders.

Cancer Second House

Emotional security is linked to material resources —money, investments, home ownership, and possessions. But you may have difficulty setting limits and never feel that enough is enough, no matter the size of your bank account. If so, examine your fears and motives. You're thrifty but generous with loved ones.

Cancer Third House

Feelings affect your thoughts and decision making, which are subjective and often based on family influences. You're intuitive and have an active imagination and excellent memory. Learning and concentration depend on your mood and level of interest. Emotional ties with relatives run deep.

Cancer Fourth House (IC)

You desire a traditional home and family life. Time with loved ones brings out your nurturing qualities, and you have strong emotional ties with immediate and extended family. A warm home environment pleases you, and you want it and its contents to reflect your career and community status.

Cancer Fifth House

Sentimental and romantic, you invest your emotional self in your love life. But your feelings also are easily hurt and breakups difficult. Most people with Cancer here want children and instinctively nurture and protect them, sometimes too much so. Your home is a reflection of your creativity, in terms of both home décor and improvements and of leisure-time activities and hobbies.

Cancer Sixth House

You need a calm and supportive work environment with congenial coworkers and one that emulates a family atmosphere. But you can be so emotionally tied to your job and colleagues that it can be tough to move on when change would be advantageous. Nervous tension can trigger stomach ailments.

Cancer Seventh House (Descendant)

Some people with this influence delay commitment until they feel their careers are well under way, and most seek a partner who is family-oriented. You attract people who freely express their emotions and who share your desire for financial and material security. You also relate well with people in general.

Cancer Eighth House

Joint resources, although subject to fluctuation, are generally favorable if carefully managed. Intuition can be an asset when backed by facts, not emotion. You could gain through a family inheritance, and it's important to you to ensure the same for your children. Home ownership could be an excellent investment.

Cancer Ninth House

You're emotionally tied to your life principles and beliefs, which are based on feelings and family tradition. Vacation travel may be with or to visit relatives, including in-laws, whom you consider to be part of the family. Higher education may be funded by parents or relatives, and you strive to provide the same opportunity for your own children.

Cancer Tenth House (Midheaven)

A glowing reputation is important to you, and you have a strong emotional investment in your career life. You may be involved in a family business or work with the public or out of your home. But your career ebbs and flows, with many changes over the years. Listen to your sixth sense.

Cancer Eleventh House

You enjoy entertaining friends at home, the closest of whom are like family. If you're involved in groups or organizations, you're emotionally connected to them and choose those that foster close relationships. Goals are changeable, subjective, and linked to your feelings and family influences.

Cancer Twelfth House

You hesitate to freely express your deepest emotions until you feel totally secure in a relationship. Few people know this, however, because you're outwardly confident and upbeat. This may be the result of your family environment or conditioning or self-talk. Your sixth sense often yields hunches.

Leo House Cusps—Ruling Planet, Sun
Leo First House (Ascendant)

You're the life of the party, the one who energizes any gathering, business or pleasure. Confident and outgoing, you're a natural leader who revels in the limelight and does most everything with a flair that attracts attention. But you also can be egocentric and dramatic, blowing small things out of proportion.

Leo Second House

You have a taste for luxury, designer labels, and jewelry. You also have excellent earning potential. Keep the two in line rather than finance your desires through credit, and take pride in saving, investing, and providing for your retirement. You're likely to splurge on entertainment, romance, and children.

Leo Third House

You're open-minded but also opinionated, and express your creativity, thoughts, and ideas with flair. You also have a gift for motivating others and could be an inspirational speaker or writer. Learning motivates you if you're interested in the subject or consider it one for personal gain. Sibling relationships are affectionate.

Leo Fourth House (IC)

You want a beautifully decorated and furnished home, one that boosts your ego and reflects your success—a royal palace to call your own. Size, however, isn't as important to you as the right address. Family loyalty is strong, and you're influential in family affairs, although these relationships may not be especially close.

Leo Fifth House

You're a true romantic—dramatic, affectionate, and passionate about your love life from the first date through long-term commitment. Although you're fond of children, you may have none or only one of your own. You take pride in your creativity and fill your leisure hours with hobbies and an active social life.

Leo Sixth House

You take pride in your work and are conscientious, doing the job to the best of your ability. Criticism is thus unwelcome and can dent your ego, even if it's just business and nothing personal. You dislike being in a subordinate position and see yourself as a boss. Education, patience, and experience can fulfill that goal.

Leo Seventh House (Descendant)

You're not in favor of or against commitment. The challenge is in finding the right person who can accept and embrace your independence as a quality to be treasured. Do that, and you're a loyal, generous mate who attracts the same sort of person. Be prepared, though, to stroke your partner's ego.

Leo Eighth House

Joint resources benefit from your hands-on involvement, but ego-based decisions regarding debt and investments can undermine your financial goals. Put your pride on hold and consult your partner and reputable experts rather than go it alone. An inheritance could considerably improve your financial position.

Leo Ninth House

Your ego is closely aligned with your beliefs and educational success, and you might pursue an advanced degree simply to boost your status. Spirituality is viewed from a personal perspective, and your faith ultimately might be solely in yourself. You could excel in a career in the legal field or higher education.

Leo Tenth House (Midheaven)

You crave a star-studded life, complete with an important position, recognition, and respect.

Determination is strong, so you can achieve what you set out to do career-wise. But a big ego can trigger setbacks, as can slipping into a dictatorial role. Encourage and support others; share the credit.

Leo Eleventh House

You're popular, with a wide circle of friends and many acquaintances, and invest much time and effort in maintaining these contacts. Organizations that offer leadership and recognition opportunities appeal to you. But if participation is ego-centered, you could lose supporters and credibility.

Leo Twelfth House

Personal recognition may be on a private rather than public level, which you prefer because you're more comfortable out of the limelight. This position also strengthens your position behind the scenes, where your personal power is at its most influential. People sense your inner strength and look to you for support, but rarely return the favor. Self-reliance is part of your life mission.

Virgo House Cusps—Ruling Planet, Mercury
Virgo First House (Ascendant)

You're reserved, even shy, and although this diminishes with age and experience, you'll always feel most comfortable with people you know well. Work is a dominant theme in your life, and everything is filtered through your practical mind. You even analyze how you feel, and can be your worst critic.

Virgo Second House

You're financially thrifty and practical. You pay close attention to budgeting and keep meticulous records and files. Credit is rarely a problem because you live within your means and save regularly. Although occasionally extravagant, you prefer to shop sales and outlets to get quality at a reasonable price.

Virgo Third House

You're an excellent planner and organizer, giving every detail equal attention. You take the same approach with decision making; you gather information and carefully weigh the pros and cons. Chitchat isn't your style except with those you know well, and you enjoy puzzles and games. At times, you can be critical of people, especially relatives.

Virgo Fourth House (IC)

Whether your home is neat or messy, it's undoubtedly clean and ultimately practical and functional. Many people with a Virgo IC enjoy working around the house, gardening and doing home improvement projects. One of your parents may be highly critical, a factor that shaped your childhood foundation.

Virgo Fifth House

You're discriminating in love, choosy about whom you date. It's great to maintain high standards, but finding someone perfect is impossible. Many people with Virgo here fill their leisure hours with gardening, games, puzzles, needlework, and woodworking, all of which your friends may define as work, not pleasure. But not you!

Virgo Sixth House

You have the ultimate work ethic, much to your employer's delight. Every task is completed with accuracy and attention to detail, and you put in long hours when necessary. In return, you expect to be well paid and have a clean, although not necessarily upscale, working environment. Nervous tension and intestinal upsets are possible.

Virgo Seventh House (Descendant)

You're drawn to practical people, and a mate who fits that description could be an excellent match. The right person can help you see the details, as you encourage vision and faith in return. People respond to your charm and humor, and you have a gift for adapting to any situation or group.

Virgo Eighth House

You and/or your partner gather all available information and details as part of the decision-making process for loans, mortgages, insurance, and investments. At times, you worry unnecessarily about money, playing the "what if" game. Think positive and invite the abundance you deserve into your life.

Virgo Ninth House

You relate to concrete, black-and-white principles rather than all the shades of gray, and your spiritual beliefs are down-to-earth. Higher education is valuable to you for its practical use in the work world and only as far as it will further your ambitions. Relations with in-laws range from tolerant to critical.

Virgo Tenth House (Midheaven)

You're work- and task-oriented and believe your work should speak for itself. You also strive for perfection and expect the same from others. That's unrealistic, which you learn with time and experience. A career that emphasizes communication, planning, and organization, possibly in a service industry, may be ideal for you.

Virgo Eleventh House

You're content with a few close friends (some may be coworkers) rather than being part of the wider social scene, and are quick to lend a hand when needed. If you're involved in an organization, it's probably as a volunteer for a good cause. You track goals—daily, weekly, monthly, and long-term—through list making.

Virgo Twelfth House

You worry and dream about the small stuff, much of which is inconsequential. But your hidden talent for detail and your sixth sense are definite pluses because you often see what others miss. You may work behind the scenes or on your own as an independent contractor.

Libra House Cusps—Ruling Planet, Venus
Libra First House (Ascendant)

With Libra, the universal sign of relationships, as your Ascendant, you're a people person who wants and needs a partner. Charm and diplomacy are strengths, and socializing is your comfort zone. Many people with Libra rising are exceptionally attractive and have a taste for luxury and an eye for beauty.

Libra Second House

You have excellent earning potential, but also like to spend. That makes it a necessity to budget and use credit wisely. Do so consistently, and you can build sizable assets to fund a comfortable lifestyle and the quality goods you desire. You also have an eye for value and a sixth sense for bargains.

Libra Third House

Tactful and considerate, you have a sharp mind that's especially attuned to other people. You're also an excellent conversationalist and enjoy lively talk and debate. Many with Libra here are avid readers but lazy students, unless the subject is of interest. Sibling ties are close and neighbor relationships congenial.

Libra Fourth House (IC)

Family relationships are close and congenial, with an emphasis on communication, although even minor conflict is avoided. You want your home to reflect your good taste with the latest in décor and furnishings, and you may collect artwork or china and decorate in white and various pastels.

Libra Fifth House

Romance is high on your priority list, but you may stick with a relationship just for the companionship. You have an active social life to fill evening and weekend hours, along with a variety of hobbies and interests. You and/or your children may have artistic talent or an interest in the arts.

Libra Sixth House

A job in anything but an attractive, congenial, cooperative environment is not for you. Any-thing else reduces productivity and elevates stress. Working with others is equally important, and you have the people skills to be an excellent manager. Many people with Libra here are fond of dogs as pets.

Libra Seventh House (Descendant)

You seek a true partnership, one that's loyal and 50–50, where you can share equally in each other's successes and disappointments, the little things and the big things. A sense of fairness and justice surrounds all your close relationships, and you appreciate the balance and support they bring to your life.

Libra Eighth House

You see family finances as a shared responsibility and are uncomfortable making decisions on your own. Together, you and your partner have good earning potential, but one or both of you could be extravagant at times. You could gain financially through a professional or personal partnership.

Libra Ninth House

Fairness and equality are your guiding principles, and you're intolerant of hypocrisy and bigotry, which are foreign to your way of thinking. You're interested in people and what motivates them to act as they do, and also enjoy traveling with your mate or friends. Higher education can increase career earnings.

Libra Tenth House (Midheaven)

You're well liked by many and popular in social and business circles. Your career may involve working closely with other people or the public, and you strive for high earnings and recognition.

Networking—whom you know, not necessarily what you know—is an important success factor.

Libra Eleventh House

You're popular and have a wide circle of friends and acquaintances and an active social life, possibly from your involvement in cultural organizations or the arts. Above all, though, you want your partner to be your best friend. Goals and objectives are influenced by those closest to you, and their needs and desires.

Libra Twelfth House

Although most people describe you as intensely self-reliant, which you are, you have a softer inner self that gains strength from a partner. Time together in a romantic location recenters you. Some people with Libra here are heavily in debt because of their expensive tastes, and others have secret affairs.

Scorpio House Cusps—Ruling Planet, Pluto

Scorpio First House (Ascendant)

You have an intense, magnetic aura that many find irresistible. Only those who know you very well glimpse your internal motivations and read your subtle signals. Determination is your strength. Nothing comes between you and your goal. But you also can be incredibly stubborn and unyielding.

Scorpio Second House

You have an intense drive not only to make money but to amass wealth, which is highly possible. Secretive about finances, you consider money matters to be personal and private. You're also a saver and can do well with invest-ments. When you spend, you do it on a grand scale. Power shopping is your specialty.

Scorpio Third House

Anyone who tries to change your mind quickly learns that you rarely do so. You're also secretive about your life and plans and often withhold information for no reason other than privacy. A shrewd, intense mind gives you a talent for research, and you often sense what others are thinking but not saying.

Scorpio Fourth House (IC)

You're loyal and highly protective of loved ones. Family feelings run deep, although a parent may have been demanding. You prefer to keep family matters private, even those that are inconsequential, and impromptu visitors are discouraged. Home improvement projects are favorite weekend activities.

Scorpio Fifth House

You take romance seriously, investing your heart and soul in a relationship. Breakups are difficult, so much so that you can hang on in order to avoid the inevitable. You're sometimes jealous, although it's usually unwarranted. As a parent, you can be demanding and pressure your children to achieve.

Scorpio Sixth House

You're a responsible hard worker who pushes yourself to the extreme because you want to finish what you start. Although you have incredible stamina, overdoing it can result in injury or illness. You take charge of projects and prefer solo work to teamwork in order to maintain control.

Scorpio Seventh House (Descendant)

Love relationships are stormy and intense, loving and passionate, sensual and kind. Romance is a natural state for you, and once committed, you aim for a lifetime of togetherness. Friends and business associates find you warm and supportive, and they value your calming energy and solid support.

Scorpio Eighth House

Joint resources are generally favorable, and you have wealth potential. But sometimes debt becomes an issue, especially if you, your partner, or both of you are secretive about money matters. Be up-front and share all the information. It's also important to be current on taxes. A family inheritance could be sizable.

Scorpio Ninth House

You strive for depth of understanding in any subject that interests you and thus can be an excellent student who earns advanced degrees. Travel may or may not appeal to you; if it does, you're likely to combine pleasure with learning. Highly principled, you have strong spiritual and ethical beliefs.

Scorpio Tenth House (Midheaven)

There are no in-betweens concerning your career. You strive for a power position and can achieve it if your intentions are honorable. Manipulation and shortcuts, however, can wipe out potential gains. At various times you'll initiate major career changes or have them thrust upon you because of uncontrollable events.

Scorpio Eleventh House

You're content with a few close friendships, people with whom you develop long-term ties based on trust. They may think they know you well, but you hold back in some way, never telling all. Friends are likely to be influential or powerful people who can help advance your status. You commit fully or not at all to goals.

Scorpio Twelfth House

You're well aware of the power of the mind and the subconscious. With practice, you can effectively program your thinking to achieve personal change and goals through self-understanding. On a practical level, however, you can be your own worst enemy and possibly become involved in power struggles.

Sagittarius House Cusps— Ruling Planet, Jupiter

Sagittarius First House (Ascendant)

You're an independent free spirit who embraces each day with optimism and a spirit of adventure. Everyone knows where you stand because you express your opinions without reservation. You're also motivated by knowledge and information, and can be an outstanding leader and an excellent joke teller.

Sagittarius Second House

Although you attract material abundance, you might do the same with debt, spending as fast as—or faster than—you earn. Good luck usually sees you through lean times, but not always. Tap into your common sense, save, budget, and replace shopping with a creative hobby that can net a sideline income.

Sagittarius Third House

Curiosity and a broad range of interests make you a perpetual student, although not necessarily of the classroom variety. Conversation and technology keep you in the know. People enjoy your wit and optimism, but at times you can be blunt and outspoken. Tactful comments net more positive results.

Sagittarius Fourth House (IC)

Home is one of your favorite locations, and you simply enjoy being there. Large, open rooms appeal to you, and you usually have many domestic projects in various stages of completion. With so much going on, your home is likely to be messy. Family relationships are close, loving, and beneficial.

Sagittarius Fifth House

Your playful spirit delights in romance and enjoys each moment to the max. Commitment deepens your passions. You also enjoy an active social life and have many leisure-time interests. As a parent, you're your children's number one cheerleader, encouraging them to explore and develop their talents.

Sagittarius Sixth House

You're an enthusiastic employee and often the first to take on extra work. In exchange, you expect a reasonable amount of freedom to do your job without supervision. A hovering boss is not for you. You also prefer a spacious work environment and one that offers plenty of opportunities to interact with coworkers.

Sagittarius Seventh House (Descendant)

You seek independence and optimism in a partner and shun anyone who expresses jealousy or possessiveness. Some people with a Sagittarius Descendant have a series of long-term partnerships, each fading away as their interests change. You excel at communication, although you could be overly talkative.

Sagittarius Eighth House

Money flows in your direction through a partner, inheritance, insurance, or lucky break. But it also can flow in the other direction if credit is mismanaged or your partner is a big spender. Emphasize budgeting, saving, and long-term investments and retirement funds. Windfalls periodically come your way.

Sagittarius Ninth House

You seek not just information but knowledge through higher education and lifelong learning. Highly principled and deeply spiritual, you live your beliefs and may teach them to others. You probably travel at every opportunity (or wish you could) and take mental journeys in between through books and technology.

Sagittarius Tenth House (Midheaven)

Whether by vocation or avocation, learning and teaching are linked to your career success. Higher education will help you develop your full potential, as will sharing your knowledge with others. You're luckier than most in career matters, where you benefit from abundant opportunities to learn and grow.

Sagittarius Eleventh House

You're an outstanding and popular friend, with an ever-expanding circle of people to fill your weekend hours with an active social life. You're probably also drawn to group activities and organizations, where you can be a leader and inspire others. Goals focus on the big picture, and you usually achieve them.

Sagittarius Twelfth House

Optimism can get the best of you at times, when you take on more than is realistic or make well-intentioned but unrealistic promises. Yet you also benefit from a fortunate protective influence that usually sees you over hurdles. Your dreams can be prophetic, sometimes years in advance.

Capricorn House Cusps— Ruling Planet, Saturn

Capricorn First House (Ascendant)

You view just about everything in life as serious business. Although reserved, cautious, and conservative, you're also very ambitious and willing to work hard to get where you want to go. Common sense and a practical mindset keep you on track, along with patience and perseverance.

Capricorn Second House

You're thrifty and cautious, but some people with Capricorn here are miserly. It all depends on your mindset and your security needs. Your ambitions are directed toward materialistic gain, and with careful, realistic money management and the right attitude, you can amass sizable assets in your lifetime.

Capricorn Third House

Your powers of concentration are among the best, as are your planning and organizational abilities. As a student, you can excel, especially in subjects that are of practical use. Cautious in speech, you voice your ideas only when you're positive they're accurate. There may be a wide age span between you and your siblings.

Capricorn Fourth House (IC)

Your childhood environment may have been highly disciplined, with little time for frivolity, although you have deep ties to loved ones and feel a sense of responsibility for your parents. Traditional décor probably appeals to you, along with accents of dark colors that are unusual but stunning.

Capricorn Fifth House

You take matters of the heart seriously and see no reason to date just to date. Once committed, however, your sensuality emerges and you love with all your soul. Hobbies are likely to be practical and useful, such as gardening, home improvement, woodworking, and furniture refinishing. If you're a parent, you're a responsible one.

Capricorn Sixth House

You're an efficient, organized, and ambitious hard worker who expects the same from coworkers and supervisors alike. Work hard, play hard, is your ethic, and you live up to and often exceed your responsibilities before taking well-deserved time off. Your social and business lives are usually separate.

Capricorn Seventh House (Descendant)

You want a mate who's as security-conscious as you are and one who's ambitious and responsible. Some people with a Cancer Ascendant commit long after their peers or unite with a mate who's older. Your partner is likely to be a true soul mate from whom you can learn a lot, and vice versa.

Capricorn Eighth House

You, your professional or personal partner, or both of you are financially cautious and conservative and anywhere from thrifty to miserly on the spending scale. However, a few with Capricorn here stretch debt to the limit. Long-term investments, including possibly real estate, can help you achieve financial security.

Capricorn Ninth House

You're traditional and possibly even narrow-minded regarding religion and ethics. Although you'd never compromise your principles, listening to other opinions could be surprisingly enlightening. You may travel on business and prefer to spend vacations at home. Higher education is one path to career success.

Capricorn Tenth House (Midheaven)

You're among the most ambitious people out there, with your sights set on a top position where you can be in charge. A slow, steady climb brings success, and you have the patience and determination to outlast and exceed the competition. Some people with a Capricorn Midheaven excel in the corporate world.

Capricorn Eleventh House

Your friends represent almost every age group—older, younger, and peer. Close friendships with a few can last a lifetime, and you have many business acquaintances. If you're involved in an organization, it's likely to be professional in nature or one through which you can advance your career ambitions.

Capricorn Twelfth House

If your career ambitions include high visibility, you may experience frustration. With Capricorn here, your strongest position is behind the scenes, either in a supporting role or in an institutional career. You're also dependable, with a strong inner drive to do the right and responsible thing.

Aquarius House Cusps— Ruling Planet, Uranus

Aquarius First House (Ascendant)

You're friendly but aloof, free-spirited yet traditional. You also have a magnetic charm that intrigues people. Individuality defines you, and you can be both determined and stubborn, spontaneous and staid. Change excites you when it's your idea, and sometimes you initiate change for the sake of change.

Aquarius Second House

Your imagination sparks innovative moneymaking ideas, both practical and impractical. Follow through on the most realistic ones. Money matters fluctuate from windfalls to unexpected expenses and everything in between, so make savings and budgeting priorities. Build a personal nest egg.

Aquarius Third House

You're a lively conversationalist and an independent thinker, with a wealth of unique, farsighted ideas. Intuitive and innovative, you spot easier, simpler ways to do things. As open as you are to what's new and different, you're also stubborn and opinionated at times. Study habits are inconsistent.

Aquarius Fourth House (IC)

Your home is a gathering place for friends, and you may favor contemporary furnishings. Home and family life, both as a child and an adult, is unusual in some way, including frequent moves. Parental relationships are friendly but not necessarily close unless you view them as friends.

Aquarius Fifth House

A romance that's also a close friendship is your ideal, and commitment may evolve over time with someone who is first a friend. You also enjoy an active social life and leisure-time activities with friends. Hobbies and interests may be unusual. You and your children are close friends as adults.

Aquarius Sixth House

You need a high degree of independence in your daily work, the freedom to organize and prioritize tasks. Rules and procedures are fine if you agree with them; otherwise you make your own. So it's imperative that you establish the level of independence and autonomy you desire before accepting a job.

Aquarius Seventh House (Descendant)

Friends are near and dear to you, and friendship is the quality you most desire in a partner. Although this Descendant sign increases the odds of multiple committed relationships, that's ultimately up to you. Spontaneity helps keep the spark alive, as does accepting your mate's need for independence.

Aquarius Eighth House

You benefit from periodic windfalls, including the possibility of a lucky win or an inheritance from a friend or mentor. Unexpected expenses also pop up, and you or your partner may be extravagant at times. Long-term investments are a good choice; adjustable rate loans and mortgages probably aren't.

Aquarius Ninth House

You're curious about the unique and unusual and delve deep into whatever captures your interest. In formal education, you might do well with distance learning instead of instruction in a traditional classroom. You're intolerant of prejudice and injustice but also believe others are entitled to make their own choices.

Aquarius Tenth House (Midheaven)

Your career is prone to the unexpected—both gains and losses, sudden changes, and instant fame. Networking brings you luck and helps you land on your feet, as do professional groups. Your challenge is to maintain your independence and be a team player. It's doable if you give a little to get a lot.

Aquarius Eleventh House

You make friends with ease, each unique in some way. "Normal" people don't interest you. Your friends come from all walks of life. Most people with Aquarius here are involved in and are also leaders in clubs or organizations, both charitable and professional. You're an excellent networker.

Aquarius Twelfth House

You rely on friends for emotional support, but when this becomes one-way, even those closest to you can tire of the sympathetic role. But you're also loyal and go out of your way to help friends as well as those in need. Dreams offer insight into your subconscious needs and desires, as does your intuition.

Pisces House Cusps—
Ruling Planet, Neptune

Pisces First House (Ascendant)

You're creative, intuitive, sensitive, and romantic. At times, you may view the world through rose-colored glasses, hoping that if you believe strongly enough, all your wishes will come true. They might or they might not. Protect yourself. Be realistic when necessary, and compassionate only when it's also best for you.

Pisces Second House

You can be impractical in money matters, but also inspired and intuitive. Tap into your common sense, and consult someone trustworthy about major financial decisions. Also plan, develop, and implement realistic, practical money-making ideas, and avoid those that promise quick returns.

Pisces Third House

You're intuitive, imaginative, and creative, with a strong visual orientation and possibly a photographic memory. But concentration and study are often interrupted by daydreams and wishful thinking; music may help overcome this. You're also a charmer with a knack for promoting your ideas.

Pisces Fourth House (IC)

Your home is your haven, the place where you feel comfortable and totally yourself. Family relationships, however, can be murky and prone to misunderstandings. One of your parents may have been absent or a substance abuser. You have strong emotions, positive or negative, about your childhood.

Pisces Fifth House

Loving and sentimental, you're a true romantic. You follow your heart and believe love conquers all, but this also can make you vulnerable to disappointment and disillusionment. Children are something of a mystery to you, although emotional ties are strong. Your creative talent may be exceptional.

Pisces Sixth House

A calm and congenial working environment is a must for job happiness and productivity. In the right job and the right situation, you're easygoing and adaptable and among the most helpful of employees. It's equally important that you have the freedom to use your creative energy; routine work is not for you.

Pisces Seventh House (Descendant)

Although outsiders might never suspect it, you're a sensual romantic who responds favorably to charm and attention. But you also can be idealistic about love, seeing what you want to see instead of what's real. Close personal and business relationships can be prone to deception. Protect yourself.

Pisces Eighth House

With careful money management, you can remain debt-free. It's also possible you or your partner could run up debt by viewing credit as "free" money. Develop budgeting and savings habits and a policy of mutual decision making. Avoid deals that sound too good to be true; they probably are.

Pisces Ninth House

Your life principles are based on an innate, emotionally based faith and spirituality. They may be traditional or your own inspired view. You see the value of higher education, but pursue it only after you've found your true calling. Vacation travel calms and soothes your inner soul.

Pisces Tenth House (Midheaven)
You have the magical, mystical charm shared by many movie stars. This can take you a long way in the work world when combined with creativity and hard work. But it may take you a while to find your career focus, your passion. Explore—within reason—until you find your perfect niche. Aim for public acclaim.

Pisces Eleventh House
You're compassionate, caring, and sympathetic to your friends and lend a hand whenever possible. This is a wonderful quality when shared with true friends, but some only appear that way and expect far more than they give. Advice from friends could be well-intentioned but misleading or even deceptive.

Pisces Twelfth House
You have a depth of feeling that many people never see and often do random acts of kindness. This comes from your innate understanding of the underdog and the wisdom that comes from knowing that one person really can make a difference. Be cautious, however, with alcohol; you may be sensitive to drugs.

PLANETS IN THE HOUSES

Although you experience every area of life represented in your chart, the houses that contain planets are those of higher interest and greater activity. Take an overall look at your chart and take special notice of those houses (and hemi-spheres and quadrants) that contain the most planets. For many people, this is the house with the Sun. This will tell you more about your life mission and its potential challenges and successes. Also note the house that contains your chart ruler (the planetary ruler of your Ascendant), as this can offer more clues into your life path.

Sun in the Houses
Sun in the First House
You have the energy, confidence, and willpower to stand out and rise well above the norm. Persistence and initiative are yours, and your warm, friendly, outgoing personality and vitality help you gain supporters to further your aims. Highly individualistic, you're a leader who craves attention and being in charge and wants to be known and recognized for your accomplishments. That's almost as easily said as done because you set definitive goals and have the determination to achieve them. Some of your finest moments are those in which you motivate others to do and be their best. But you're also prone to an inflated ego and a self-centered view of events and situations. Be generous. Share the limelight and the credit, welcome other viewpoints, and be open to compromise.

Sun in the Second House
Your ego and confidence are linked to financial success, and you invest a great deal of energy and initiative in moneymaking activities. Your goal is financial independence. But your excellent earning potential might be matched by equally extravagant spending habits. Luxury and designer goods attract you, and owning them boosts self-esteem. Use your exceptional

willpower to resist what you can't really afford, and seek the self-gratification that comes from saving and long-term investments. Learn to use assets constructively rather than solely to meet your immediate needs. You also have strong values and expect others to live according to your code of ethics. That's an ideal, albeit an unrealistic one, so do what's right for you and let others follow their own path.

Sun in the Third House

You take great pride in your mind and want to be recognized and honored for your mental achievements. Learning inspires you and satisfies your ever-active curiosity; education is a necessary step toward achieving your life goals. You're up on the latest news, using technology as a tool for information. You may be an outstanding speaker, with the flair and presence to motivate others. But some people with the Sun in the third house are know-it-alls with big egos who seize every opportunity to voice their opinionated views. Sibling relationships are generally favorable, and siblings may look to you for advice. The same is true of neighbors, and you could be a community leader or be involved in local politics or education.

Sun in the Fourth House

You're a loyal and loving family member who's actively involved in the lives of your children, parents, mate, and extended family. You're proud of your roots and may have an interest in tracing your family tree. A secure, stable home environment is as important to you as owning your own home. Nearly everything domestic interests you, and you may be an outstanding cook. Your home is an ideal outlet for your creativity—decorating, remodeling, hobbies, and crafts. Do-it-yourself is both satisfying and a great way to create the showcase home you want on a budget. You also enjoy entertaining friends and family in the starring role as king or queen of your castle, whatever its size.

Sun in the Fifth House

You're playful and fun-loving, with plenty of hobbies, friends, and other activities to fill your leisure hours—your favorite times of the week. Spectator and competitive sports, theater, and the arts also attract many people with the Sun in the fifth house. You like children but may have none or few of your own. If you're among those without offspring, you instead have children of the mind—creative projects through which you "voice" your self-expression. You can, however, be self-centered, dramatic, and ego-centered at times. An active romantic life is important to you, whether single or committed, and you know how to romance a date or your mate with all the pizzazz of Hollywood. You can win or lose with investments, so test your luck and skill before you plunge in a big way.

Sun in the Sixth House

You identify strongly with your work, which is probably at or near the top of your life priority list. An eye for details, pride, and the goal of perfection make you a valuable employee. You expect to be recognized and rewarded for your efforts and enjoy the satisfaction that comes from a job well done. You can be an excellent manager, although a demanding one. But all work and no play, as well as your tendency to worry, can trigger nervous tension. If necessary, force yourself to program daily relaxation time into your hectic schedule. This will help you maintain good health and a strong immune system, as will a nutritious diet. Many people with the Sun in the sixth house are involved in service and charitable organizations and are animal lovers.

Sun in the Seventh House

You invest a lot of yourself, your time and energy, in other people. They're a major focus in your life, personally and professionally, and your ego and drive are directly linked to them and especially to your partner. This is due partly to your desire for approval and partly to your need to have a close one-on-one relationship. Yet investing too much of yourself in another person can undermine your strengths and independence. Many people with the Sun in the seventh house plunge into a partnership just to fulfill their need to "have" someone when they first should develop self-reliance. This placement can be excellent for sales and other positions where success depends on self-expression and people skills.

Sun in the Eighth House

You're driven to make money and probably have the willpower and determination to realize your financial goals. Wealth is more than a possibility with careful management of income and investments. You also may gain through an inheritance or insurance and possibly through a partner. But putting too much faith in someone else's abilities rather than developing your own can have a negative financial impact. You may become involved in handling another person's (friend, parent, relative) funds at some point or do that regularly through your career. Some

people with the Sun in the eighth house insist on absolute control of partnership or family funds, much to the detriment of the relationship. You also may have an interest in metaphysical subjects.

Sun in the Ninth House

Knowledge is your main motivation in life. In some way, formally or informally, you learn something every day and probably have a long mental list of topics you hope to explore someday. That could take several lifetimes! Include higher education in your life goals, and freely share with others what you know. You have high principles against which you measure ethical and philosophical questions as well as important decisions. Spirituality may be another theme in your life, along with frequent travel. Many people with the Sun in the ninth house have extensive involvement with in-laws and, at some point, in legal matters. Some with this placement, however, are narrow-minded and egotistical know-it-alls.

Sun in the Tenth House

You thrive on hard work and success and want to be noted and recognized for your career achievements and status. You also want a position of authority, preferably a powerful one. Public life is a natural for many people with the Sun in the tenth house who enter politics to use their leadership skills; others choose careers that involve high visibility and working with the public. You also have the management skills to advance your ambitions, which are far above the norm. But you're hardly one who grabs the glory at the expense of others—or you shouldn't be. Pitch in and be a team leader as well as a team player rather than adopt a heavy-handed, demanding attitude, which some with this placement do.

Sun in the Eleventh House

You take friendship seriously and treasure these special relationships, some of which last a lifetime. Your friends come from all walks of life. Some are influential, and others are an unlikely match or unusual in some way. All that's necessary is that you click with someone; then you welcome him or her into your ever-widening circle. You have a knack for networking, both for yourself and others, and can be the consummate team player. Many people with this placement are joiners, involved in and leaders of organizations, good causes, and other group activities. You're far more goal-oriented than many realize and usually achieve your aims. Overscheduling can be a challenge, however. Don't spread yourself too thin in an attempt to do it all.

Sun in the Twelfth House

You may be shy and reserved and lack the confidence to pursue your desires, or you may be confident but have difficulty making your presence known. Either way, that will change at some point in your life, probably before age thirty. Your strongest position, however, will always be behind the scenes, where you can achieve great things and be recognized, even if only privately. Inner strength is one of your outstanding traits, and it gives you the power and drive to overcome obstacles. You're a private person who needs and enjoys plenty of time alone (sometimes too much). Contemplation is natural because much of your energy is directed inward. Compassionate and caring, you get great satisfaction from helping others.

Moon in the Houses

Moon in the First House

You're guided by your emotions and feelings, and an active sixth sense helps you "read" people. You often know who's truthful, who's lying, and who has ulterior motives. But it's vital that you protect yourself from negative energy, which your receptive nature easily absorbs. (Learn to use metaphysical techniques, such as visualizing yourself surrounded by protective white light, to shield yourself.) Sympathetic and sensitive, your feelings are easily hurt. You're also susceptible to peer pressure because being accepted is as important to you as being up to date with the latest phases and fads. You're in tune with trends and can spot emerging shifts in public opinion. Most people with the Moon in the first house are family-oriented and have a strong desire for children and close ties with loved ones.

Moon in the Second House

You're emotionally involved in money matters, primarily because you equate assets with security. Money in the bank, investments, and possessions all contribute to this feeling, which encourages you to accumulate and seldom let go. You hold on to what you have, especially when you experience (or sense approaching) periods of financial fluctuation. You will spend on your home and loved ones, but your wallet opens most freely when you're feeling low, a trait of the changeable lunar energy. This may give you a "feel good" moment, but it hardly promotes the financial security and stability you strive for. Direct your feelings instead into a hobby or creative project or time with family.

Moon in the Third House

Your thoughts and feelings are interwoven, with one influencing the other. You think what you feel, and feel what you think. This strong interplay limits objectivity but heightens intuition and imagination. You have an excellent memory. Used productively, daydreaming can trigger clever ideas and solutions; however, it also can interfere with concentration. You're easily bored and need a high level of mental stimulation to remain focused and steer your attention away from unimportant details. Background music may be helpful. You have deep emotional ties with siblings and some family members. If these relationships are positive, then you see and communicate with them regularly. Neighbors are often included in gatherings, as members of your extended family.

Moon in the Fourth House

Family relationships are an important part of your life and probably the most dominant influence on a daily basis. Your emotional security and well-being are closely tied to home and family, and even minor upsets with loved ones can throw you off-kilter. Most people with the Moon in the fourth house create warm, comfortable, inviting homes, both for their own pleasure and to entertain friends and family. You might remodel and/or redecorate regularly to keep up with the latest interior design trends, and some people with this placement move frequently. At some point you may become interested in tracing your family tree, visiting your ancestral home, or creating an oral history for future generations.

Moon in the Fifth House

If a get-together involves fun or romance, you're there! With the Moon in the fifth house, both are high on your life agenda and necessary to your emotional well-being. You feel at one with the universe when your love life is active and fulfilling, whether you're caught up in the thrill of a new romance or in a long-term relationship. It's possible, though, that parents or other relatives could interfere with your love life. Children warm your heart, and many people with this placement have (or want) a large family to satisfy their nurturing instincts. Hobbies and other leisure-time pursuits are ideal creative outlets, and friends ensure a lively social life. Investments can be lucrative, and home ownership may net the highest return.

Moon in the Sixth House

Your work life fluctuates, sometimes day by day or even hour by hour. On a broader scale, your job does the same, and you could find this area of life to be unstable. If you're among those on an almost perpetual job search, ask yourself why. There is no perfect job; satisfaction ultimately comes from within, not without. Coworkers are part of your extended family, and you go out of your way to help them. You also may work with the public and women more than men. Emotional well-being is linked to physical health. When you feel low or dissatisfied, you're more likely to pick up a virus. Some people with this placement are prone to psychosomatic illnesses or hypochondria. Most are neat and fastidious about cleanliness, order, and food safety.

Moon in the Seventh House

You're highly sensitive to other people, their feelings and moods, and often know intuitively what they're really thinking, despite outward appearances. But energy flows two ways, so you're also easily swayed by other viewpoints. Besides being mentally and emotionally receptive, you strive for acceptance, to be part of the crowd. Having the Moon in the seventh house is excellent for dealing with the public, such as working in retail, the food industry, or government service. Happiness and emotional security are strongly tied to close relationships, and most people with this placement seek a mate and want to have children. It's possible that you see your partner as a mother or father figure who fulfills your need for a supportive, nurturing environment.

Moon in the Eighth House

Few people experience the depth of feeling and emotion that's life as usual for you. You care deeply and passionately about those you love, as well as building the financial security that's vital to your emotional well-being. But the more tightly you hang on to what belongs to you and yours, the greater the chance you will lose what you're trying to gain. Money matters fluctuate with this Moon position, so by accepting that change is the norm, you actually encourage more of life's abundance to flow your way. Security is just as much a state of mind as it is dollars and cents. Your sixth sense can be an asset here—in terms of career earnings and benefits, and investments—when matched with facts and figures. You may gain financially through a family inheritance or partnership.

Moon in the Ninth House

Your life is a quest for knowledge and experience. Travel, education, and mental journeys inspire you and fulfill many of your emotional needs. Optimism and a spirit of adventure encourage you to investigate and explore, and you may live in or emigrate to another country to discover your familial and psychological roots. The Moon in the ninth house indicates strong ethics and principles as well as a deep interest in spirituality. Your beliefs may reflect those of your family, or at least until you've been exposed to a wider range of opinions and information. Some people with this placement are deeply involved in the religious life as clergy or laypeople. If in-law relationships are positive, then your ties are as close as family.

Moon in the Tenth House

You want and need to be recognized for your career efforts and contributions. The same applies to life in general, where status is your goal. Your family may be prominent in the community and your mother your biggest supporter, pushing you to achieve even as an adult. Some people with the Moon in the tenth house are involved in politics or a career focused on working with the public. But you can expect changes in your career life that range from an unexpected rise or fall to switching to a new field. Intuition helps you spot emerging interests and trends, sometimes years in advance; use this information to advantage to advance your aims. You also may work from home or have a home-based business.

Moon in the Eleventh House

Close friends are like family to you, and emotional ties with some may be deeper than those with relatives. Although these friendships are often for a lifetime, you also have many acquaintances who move in and out of your life. They seem to arrive for a purpose; once it's been fulfilled, they fade away. Many people with the Moon in the eleventh house are involved in groups and organizations (often as leaders) that also provide a sense of family. You enjoy entertaining at home and have a knack for networking. Your goals and objectives fluctuate according to your mood, so it can be difficult to maintain focus and direction. Yet you're not easily sidetracked when passion motivates you to achieve.

Moon in the Twelfth House

You're ultrasensitive and compassionate. Your heart goes out to those in need, and you can almost feel their pain as your own. Yet you effectively mask your emotions, partly as a defense and protection mechanism and partly because of family influences. Only in the most secure relationships do you share your feelings, and then only with some hesitancy. You're closely attuned to your subconscious (if you let the messages emerge into your conscious thinking), and dreams may be prophetic. The same is true of your sixth sense, which can be insightful and motivational. Many people with the Moon in the twelfth house spend a great deal of time alone—possibly too much.

Mercury in the Houses
Mercury in the First House

You spend a lot of time thinking about yourself—your goals, hopes, wishes, plans, and activities. This doesn't necessarily mean you're self-centered (although you may be). It's just that you're self-absorbed, focused on yourself and your many interests, which you're quick to talk about. Remember that you can learn as much—maybe more—by listening to others. Your inquiring mind and strong mental focus are scattered at times because almost everything piques your curiosity. Decisions are based on logic and facts, and you may be an excellent writer or speaker. An outstanding multitasker with a high need for communication, you make the most of the latest technology at work and to keep in touch with friends and relatives.

Mercury in the Second House

Moneymaking ideas attract your interest. You're ever-alert for a new opportunity to fatten your bank account and may have the insight and creativity to dream up clever ideas of your own. Follow-through, however, could be a challenge, as some people with Mercury in the second house scatter their financial energies. The solution: take moneymaking endeavors one at a time; explore and research each and weigh the pros and cons. Knowledge and information increase earning potential, and your shrewd mind is an advantage in money management and financial decision making. Chances are, your financial records are carefully organized and you track expenses and income and regularly update budgets.

Mercury in the Third House

Your communication skills are excellent, and you may be a fast talker, quickly sizing up the facts and presenting your views. Sometimes, though, you omit the "middle" and fail to fully explain yourself—your mind moves faster than your mouth. Ever curious, you have a strong need to be in the know and thus usually are up on the latest news and gossip. (Some people with this placement are notorious gossips.) Many people with Mercury in the third house are avid readers and among the first to acquire the latest technology. You enjoy learning, have good hand-eye coordination, and often change your mind. Relationships with siblings, extended family, and neighbors are usually favorable with this placement, and you keep in touch with everyone in your phone book.

Mercury in the Fourth House

You put great emphasis on family communication and generally know exactly what's going on in the lives of your immediate and extended families (and roommates). Family and domestic news is the first you share when seeing friends. You may work fully or in part out of your home or have a sideline home-based business to supplement earnings. Most people with Mercury in the fourth house have extensive libraries and up-to-date information and entertainment technology to stay in touch with people and the world. With so much domestic activity going on, your home may quickly—and even perpetually!—become messy and cluttered. The best policy is to get in the habit of putting everything away when you're finished with it.

Mercury in the Fifth House

You enjoy the challenge of mental and electronic games and also fill your leisure hours with reading, socializing, quick trips, and activities with your children, if you're a parent. Your many and varied interests, which are ever-changing, keep your life—and the lives of those close to you—

lively and fascinating. Boredom is your enemy. Mercury's intellectual emphasis also makes a mental connection a must in romance. You can fall in love with someone's mind, and delight in long, stimulating talks. Romance without communication is unthinkable to you. Some people with Mercury here are parents of twins, and others excel at creative writing or motivational speaking. Be cautious with investments. What looks good today may not tomorrow, so you might do best with a conservative, long-term investment policy.

Mercury in the Sixth House

You need a job with plenty of mental stimulation, variety, open communication, and possibly the opportunity to express yourself as a writer or speaker. You also enjoy working with your hands and excel at multitasking. Boredom and a slow-paced workplace, however, can send you quickly in search of a new position. That can lead to job hopping, which is not the best for your résumé. Take the time to assess all facets of the position before you accept. At your best, you're organized, efficient, and detail-oriented, and can zip through tasks in record time. Gadgets and technology intrigue you, and you might excel at fixing things. Accuracy is your goal. Most people with Mercury here are informed about the latest health trends. Nervous tension is common.

Mercury in the Seventh House

Communication is a must in any close relationship, especially with a personal or professional partner. You need someone who shares your interest in news and events and also enjoys lively conversation and debate. But if you tend to talk more than you listen, you should adjust your communication style. You'll acquire more information and build solid, supportive relationships. You want to know what others think and have a strong need for acceptance not only of your ideas and thoughts but also as a person. An inclination to compromise and cooperate can make you an excellent mediator, and you have an innate understanding of human nature. (You could be an excellent psychologist.) Some people with Mercury in the seventh house enter into a romantic partnership at a young age or with someone who is younger.

Mercury in the Eighth House

You have the mind of a detective—suspicious, clever, inquisitive, and a little conniving. You're also an excellent researcher and strategist, with the ability to sift through and analyze data, facts, and figures and then to form an accurate and succinct conclusion. Intrigue excites you, and you're secretive, sharing little personal information. You almost never repeat a confidence. In money matters you're an organized planner with firm financial goals. You think about money a lot—how to acquire more and use it to best advantage—and usually succeed in finding or negotiating the best deals and the most favorable rates. You could benefit financially through a sibling or another relative. Some people with Mercury in the eighth house hold grudges, sometimes for years as they await an opportunity to seek revenge.

Mercury in the Ninth House

You're a seeker of knowledge and information, on a perpetual, lifelong quest to learn as much as you can. Higher education attracts you, and you may have several advanced degrees in addition to being a perpetual student in the classroom or on your own. You're also a natural teacher and step into that role with ease, either professionally or informally with friends and colleagues. You're ever curious, and your search for knowledge may include learning other languages and exploring other cultures, past and present. Lively discussion stimulates you, and you base your decisions on facts as well as ethics. However, some people with this placement are opinionated and have closed minds. You have a strong sense of justice and are intolerant of those who cross the line. You may enjoy travel or travel extensively in connection with your job, or have an interest or career in the legal field.

Mercury in the Tenth House

Education is your door-opener to career success and achievement, and strong communication skills add the finishing touch. With both, you can make the most of your leadership ability and excel in a career that involves contact with the public. Your challenge, however, may be to define a career focus, because your interests are so broad-based. The best career choice is one in which you can use your diverse skills and talents. Multitasking is a strength, along with organizational and planning abilities. Some people with Mercury in the tenth house pursue two careers at once—a day job that allows them the financial security to pursue their true passion. This placement favors politicians, writers, speakers, and other positions in the communications field.

Mercury in the Eleventh House

Your address book is packed with names and numbers. Among them are a few close friends and many acquaintances. They're people from all walks of life, because you're very much an equal-opportunity friend who enjoys people who are unique or unusual in some way. Each friend is also a potential contact for networking—something at which you excel. You learn a lot from friends and also share your knowledge and advice during long chats and get-togethers that satisfy your need for an active social life. But you're strongly influenced by the opinions of friends and may adopt their ideas when independent thinking would serve you better. You may be involved in groups or organizations with a humanitarian emphasis or that stimulate your mind and add to your knowledge bank.

Mercury in the Twelfth House

You're a deep thinker who's somewhat secretive; you share little personal information and rarely reveal your innermost thoughts. That's your comfort zone. But there are times when a lack of confidence prevents you from saying what you really think in favor of going along with the crowd. Your decisions often are based more on feeling than fact, and also on intuition. People share confidences with you, with the assurance that you almost never repeat what you hear. You also have an excellent imagination and vivid dreams that can be insightful, revealing images from your subconscious. Always read the fine print in contracts or credit agreements. Doing so could save you many future headaches, worries, and hassles.

Venus in the Houses

Venus in the First House

Charming, popular, and gracious, you're a people person who instantly puts others at ease. You're a natural diplomat and mediator, the one who promotes cooperation and compromise. What you're definitely not is a pushover, despite what others may think. You know that the art of finesse—not aggression—is the way to win battles and wars. Image-conscious, you understand that perception is reality and thus strive to look your best at all times. But designer clothing and jewelry can stretch your budget when you feel extravagant and self-indulgent. Most people with Venus in the first house are attractive, and some have artistic talent. All have an eye for beauty and symmetry. This placement also encourages laziness.

Venus in the Second House

Money, money, money! You attract plenty of it during your lifetime, and probably got started in childhood with odd jobs for family and neighbors (and fast deals with friends!). You value your possessions and also want life's luxuries and top-of-the-line quality. At times extravagant, you're generally thrifty but willing to splurge occasionally on yourself and loved ones. You won't, however, pay more than a fair price, and almost always find the bargains that elude others. You could profit financially from a business or personal partnership. Some people with Venus in the second house seek a mate who is wealthy or one with social status, which you value highly. You also have strong ethics, principles, and a sense of justice.

Venus in the Third House

You're a charming conversationalist with a talent for subtle persuasion. At your best, you can convince anyone of almost anything and make them believe it's their own idea. You're also tactful and gracious and rarely utter unkind words. This is as much a reflection of your communication style as it is your dislike of conflict. At times you'll concede a point just to maintain harmony. Socializing is high on your priority list, and you mix and mingle and circulate with ease, leaving everyone feeling like they're the center of your universe. Reading, the theater, music, and the arts appeal to many with this placement. You also like to travel in comfort and will stretch your budget to acquire a luxury vehicle. Relationships with siblings and neighbors are favorable, and regular communication with them is important to you.

Venus in the Fourth House

You home is (or you want it to be) beautifully decorated with artwork and the best furnishings you can afford. It's a showplace that reflects your financial success, as well as a place to entertain friends, which you do frequently. Many people with Venus in the fourth house lavishly decorate their homes inside and out for every holiday and are avid gardeners. Clutter is a challenge for some people with this placement, who save everything and cover every surface with knickknacks, photos, and other possessions and paraphernalia. You're close to family and loved ones and do all you can to maintain family harmony, which is vital to your happiness. You may inherit a sizable sum from your parents or other relatives.

Venus in the Fifth House

Charm, popularity, and charisma are yours, along with an active social life and many admirers. You're a romantic who loves to love as much as you need to be loved. This is true whether you're single and dating or in a long-term commitment. Love notes delight you, and you're fond of surprising your partner with heartfelt expressions of TLC. Most people with Venus in the fifth house are fond of children, and many are the parents of talented, creative offspring. Fun, leisure time, and hobbies have a prominent place in your daily life. You may have artistic or acting talent or support the arts. Without a doubt you're creative in some way and have a sense of balance and an eye for beauty and harmony.

Venus in the Sixth House

You enjoy your work life most of the time—when you're in the right position at the right company. Pleasant surroundings are a must. You won't consider a job where you'll be in a run-down or strictly utilitarian environment from 8 to 5. If you work in an office setting, you personalize your workspace with photos, knickknacks, and mementos. You're well liked by coworkers, and these congenial, harmonious relationships boost productivity. You promote cooperation and compromise, partly to limit conflict, which upsets you more than most people. Many social and romantic opportunities come through coworkers. Most people with Venus in the sixth house are fond of pets, and some are susceptible to sore throats.

Venus in the Seventh House

You're a people person who's popular, tactful, and charming. People flock to you, which suits you fine because you dislike going anywhere alone. Companionship is a natural state for you, and you have a knack for bringing people together. Many people with Venus in the seventh house have such a strong need for a mate that they form a union at an early age. Although this placement generally indicates a happy partnership, you should be sure you're in love—not in love with love—before you commit. Business relationships and partnerships also benefit from this placement, and financial gain can come to you through a personal or professional relationship. But you can be too trusting at times, taking people at face value when a closer look would be to your advantage. Be selective. Don't let people use you for their own ends.

Venus in the Eighth House

Joint resources are generally favorable when Venus is in the eighth house. You can benefit through a partner's money, inheritance, or insurance, as well as your own high income potential. Some people with Venus in the eighth house choose a mate for status and money as much as (or sometimes more than) for love. This placement also can indicate intense emotions, possessiveness, and jealousy. You can run up considerable debt if you're an extravagant free-spender. Save first, budget, and plan for the future; allow yourself an occasional self-indulgent splurge. A career in the financial arena, such as banking, investments, or fundraising, might interest you.

Venus in the Ninth House

Education has a dual purpose in your life: in addition to its obvious merits, education can open up more lucrative career opportunities and connect you with potential partners who

have above-average earning potential. Some people with Venus in the ninth house are linked romantically or professionally to someone from a different culture, country, or background. Your interest in other cultures extends to travel that mixes pleasure and learning—almost always with a partner—and usually in the most luxurious accommodations you can afford. The arts also attract many people with this placement, as a career or hobby or as a supporter. Justice, equality, and spirituality are prominent themes in your life.

Venus in the Tenth House

Although you have career ambitions, they're not associated with the drive and determination typical of high achievers. They don't have to be. With Venus in the tenth house, your charm, charisma, and people skills give you a head start over many. Popular with coworkers and managers alike, you have an excellent image and reputation as a hard worker who's congenial and cooperative and supportive of team efforts. However, some people with this placement are decidedly lazy social climbers who expect others to carry their load. Others form romantic partnerships for social or financial gain. Venus here is a plus for a career in the arts, financial fields, and beauty and fashion industries, as well as those with public contact.

Venus in the Eleventh House

Socializing with your many friends is a favorite evening and weekend activity. Many people with Venus in the eleventh house are actively involved in organizations, including those that support the arts. You could benefit financially from an investment club, and many of your friends are likely to be financially secure. Your popularity is linked to your charming and gracious personality and your effortless ability to put others at ease. However, you're overly generous with friends at times, doing too much for them and investing too much of your time, effort, and money. Sometimes this placement indicates a partnership through or with a friend. Many people with Venus here are inveterate matchmakers.

Venus in the Twelfth House

You enjoy peace, quiet, and time alone, yet at the same time you can be lonely. This dichotomy is tough to resolve, especially if you're essentially shy. You thus can be highly susceptible to anyone who showers you with attention. Be cautious. He or she may be the real thing or one with ulterior motives. When a union is at its best, you love to the depths of your soul. Some people with Venus in the twelfth house have a succession of secret love affairs. Others choose a mate who emulates a parent. You're creative and may have artistic talent and a highly developed sixth sense. You're also compassionate and willingly share time and resources with those in need. This placement can indicate a shopping/spending addiction.

Mars in the Houses
Mars in the First House

Many people saunter through life. You dash! And you can do most things in half the time it takes others. High energy and stamina combined with initiative and confidence and a competitive edge make you an odds-on favorite to be a high achiever. As an active participant in life, you're well placed to be a leader who attracts

and seizes opportunities. But you also can be impulsive and headstrong and charge ahead without considering possible consequences. Learn to temper your zeal and discover the fine line that separates aggression from assertiveness. Vitality and physical strength encourage risk taking—and also increase accident potential. You love whatever is new and fresh and always want to be first.

Mars in the Second House

You have the initiative and incentive to make money. Financially competitive in every way, you're quick to snap up any potentially lucrative opportunity. But at times you can leap without considering the potential for loss. It's thus a good idea to risk only what you can live without. Although Mars in the second house boosts earning potential, it also encourages impulsive spending; outgo can equal income. That can leave you with a budget crunch when unexpected expenses arise, so pay yourself first—save and make wise investments—and be cautious with credit. Some people with this placement have entrepreneurial talent.

Mars in the Third House

You're noted for your enthusiasm and quick mind, which can grasp concepts and absorb information in a flash. Debate stimulates you, and you passionately express your opinions and ideas. But you also jump to conclusions at times and make snap decisions you soon regret. Train yourself to think, listen, and read before you speak and act. That will save you lots of time, hassle, and money in the long run. Your competitive spirit may emerge in full force with siblings, where conflict is also possible; these relationships could be difficult, as could those with neighbors. Some people with Mars in the third house are aggressive drivers with a heavy foot—and the traffic tickets to prove it. Slow down. Stay safe.

Mars in the Fourth House

Your domestic dilemma is independence versus security. You want the freedom to come and go and do as you please and the security of a stable home and family life. This becomes more manageable with time and experience, although frustration can manifest as family conflict. (Some people with Mars in the fourth house grow up in a tension-filled atmosphere dominated by a controlling parent.) Do-it-yourself home improvements are a good outlet for this Martian energy. If you're handy (or have the interest to acquire the necessary skills), you could profit from buying, improving, and selling property. Home life is active with this placement, with people coming and going and many projects in various stages of completion. Finishing what you start, however, can be a challenge.

Mars in the Fifth House

Some people want a life of leisure. What you want is a life of leisure time, hours to fill with hobbies, socializing, sports, and creative projects. Your romantic life gets equal billing, and you love the thrill of the chase and keeping the spark of passion alive throughout many years of togetherness. Competitive in sports, you may be an outstanding athlete who's also involved in youth sports as a coach or organizer. Electronic gaming is popular with many people with Mars in the fifth house, as are games of strategy such as chess and bridge. Although you can do well

with investments, impulsive risks can result in loss. Some people with this placement are single parents. If you have children, your tendency may be to push them too hard; ease up and let them find their own pace and interests.

Mars in the Sixth House

You're noted for the enthusiasm and initiative you bring to the workplace. It's tough for anyone to match your pace, although speed isn't everything. Without attention to details and follow-through, your competitive nature may go unrewarded. Learn to be almost as good a finisher as you are a starter and you'll increase the odds of winning a good number of the promotions you desire. The rules change somewhat if your focus is physical or mechanical work, which this placement favors; Mars indicates stamina and high energy. But always follow safety guidelines. Whatever your job, impatience can get the best of you. You're intolerant of anyone who's lazy, and can push others when tact and finesse would produce better results and limit potential conflict.

Mars in the Seventh House

You're impulsive, falling in and out of love and friendship in the time it takes others just to get started. The same is true of relationships with coworkers and other business associates. Simple solution: don't commit until you've thoroughly tested your compatibility and life and/or business philosophy. In love, you excel at keeping the passion alive, which is reminiscent of your initial competitive quest to win the heart of your mate. You're equally competitive in other relationships and have a strong desire to be the first and the best and to be in charge. However, some people with Mars in the seventh house find themselves always giving in. If you're among them, learn to voice your opinions and settle only for a compromise. This placement also can indicate conflict in close relationships.

Mars in the Eighth House

It's only natural that you take charge of joint resources and family finances. Even if that's okay with your mate, it's still smart to discuss and compromise on budgeting, savings, major expenditures, and other money matters. Mars in the eighth house indicates financial gain—or loss—through a partner, and you could benefit from an inheritance or insurance, possibly only after conflict or complications. Overall, you have above-average financial potential, although some people with this placement feel they're owed a fat paycheck rather than having to earn it. You also can be impulsive with spending and credit. Your excellent research skills are a plus in decision making regarding investments and in shopping for the best prices and interest rates.

Mars in the Ninth House

You might be a leader who champions a cause, or do the same one-on-one or on behalf of a worthy organization that represents your ideals. However, some people with this placement are narrow-minded and overly zealous in promoting their beliefs. Even at your best, impatience and strong convictions can prompt you to tune out other viewpoints. Listen and think before you reject other opinions. A true adventurer, you emulate an ancient conqueror in the modern-day world, seeking new experiences and information. You're restless and independent and place high value on freedom as both

a concept and a lifestyle. Many people with this placement are avid travelers, while others prefer mental journeys. Legal matters are generally positive or negative; compromise is seldom an option.

Mars in the Tenth House

Everyone who spends even a few minutes in your presence quickly realizes they've encountered a dynamic soul who's a very competitive go-getter. "No" isn't in your vocabulary; in fact, it's one word that can launch you into high gear if for no other reason than to prove something can be done. Mixed in is an impulsive mindset that can land you in hot water. Any attempt to manipulate events to suit your purposes can have a similar outcome. It's a choice between fame and infamy. Because you're ultra-ambitious, it's easy for you to step on toes without realizing it, and this can trigger conflict with supervisors. This is one reason some people with Mars in the tenth house prefer to be their own boss or an entrepreneur. As a boss, you can be demanding. Be a leader, not a dictator.

Mars in the Eleventh House

You invest considerable time and energy on friendship, so it's only natural that you have a wide circle of social and business contacts. Highly confident and outgoing, you take the initiative to introduce yourself to new people and make friends on impulse. You easily rise to top positions in clubs and organizations, and in any group activity other people look to you to take the lead. That's also true even when you're on a casual outing with close friends. Many people with this placement have more male than female friends. This position, however, can indicate conflict with friends and within groups, possibly because of your competitive spirit. In humanitarian efforts, you can be a driving force for positive, progressive change.

Mars in the Twelfth House

Mars in the twelfth house requires careful handling. Much depends on your comfort level with operating behind the scenes or from the sidelines. It can be tough to maximize your initiative, which can trigger frustration and impulsive actions resulting in instant karma. Some people with this placement find it difficult to stand up and defend their views, in part because they go out of their way to avoid conflict. If this describes you, then start small and build your confidence, voicing your opinions in "safe" situations before attempting to do so in others. You can be a champion for the underdog, devoting considerable energy to good causes. This is an excellent use of Mars's energy. Some with this placement benefit from anger management therapy.

Jupiter in the Houses

Jupiter in the First House

You look to the future and greet most days with enthusiastic optimism. Popular and outgoing, you're friendly and generous, glad to lend a hand when someone needs your help. You seek knowledge and truth and motivate others to do the same, along with setting an example for high ethical standards. Jupiter brings you luck and is a protective influence. Yet this expansive planet can encourage a love of calorie-rich foods, resulting in weight gain. Jupiter also promotes overoptimism and exaggeration, so you can easily overprogram yourself. Do a reality check before you begin—or promise to deliver—a major project. Most people with Jupiter in the first house have excellent leadership potential and a talent for joke telling.

Jupiter in the Second House

You have an almost magical ability to attract money and other resources, and you often receive gifts from friends and relatives. With this abundance comes good fortune and business know-how, as well as a talent for securing funding whenever you need it. But as much as Jupiter expands income, it can do the same with spending. Money may disappear as fast as it appears, or gains could be on paper but inaccessible (retirement funds, investments, property). So even when money continues to roll your way, it's wise to build cash reserves for the unexpected. Lucky Jupiter doesn't always deliver as promised or hoped for. Most people with Jupiter in the second house are inveterate shoppers; some have a shopping addiction.

Jupiter in the Third House

It's important to you to be well informed and knowledgeable on a wide variety of subjects. Learning stimulates you, so you may be a perpetual student, formally or informally, for fun or for profit. You're a talker who enjoys sharing what you know, and you're quick to offer advice. But some people with this Jupiter placement talk excessively when they should listen. You're noted for positive thinking, although sometimes to your detriment. Realistic thinking is a wiser choice in many situations; look at the cons as well as the pros. Relatives and possibly neighbors bring you luck, and you may have a talent for writing, teaching, or motivational speaking.

Jupiter in the Fourth House

You place great value on family relationships, which generally are happy and upbeat. This is true even if you live far away from your roots, as some people with this placement do. Wherever you are, the basic principles instilled during childhood stay with you as a family legacy. In essence, you come from a "good" family. A large and impressive home is your goal, but you may stretch your budget rather than wait until your dream home is fully affordable. Take care, because that can strain your resources sooner or later. Generous with loved ones, you're likely to benefit from an inheritance or life-changing opportunity through a relative.

Jupiter in the Fifth House

Your creative energy is among the best, whether you express it through ideas, artistic endeavors, hobby projects, or sports. The biggest challenge may be to decide exactly where to focus your efforts because you have so many leisure-time interests. You're also fond of children and may become involved in youth activities as a way to better the lives of young people. Your own children are likely to excel. Investments can be profitable if decision making includes facts, figures, and information in addition to luck, which is definitely with you. You also could benefit through games of chance, but caution is advised; know when to walk away. Jupiter in the fifth house also indicates a happy love life and extensive social opportunities as well as an interest in sports and theater.

Jupiter in the Sixth House

Need a job? No problem. Need a favor from a colleague? Ditto. Although life guarantees nei-

ther, Jupiter in the sixth house puts the odds in your favor. There is a challenge, however, in that there are so many job opportunities and so many available projects and tasks. You easily can take on too much and promise more than you can deliver, all with the best of intentions. Curb your enthusiasm a little and go for only the best of the best. You can play this Jupiter position to advantage and gradually expand your responsibilities until you've created your ideal (and close to irreplaceable) job. You're well liked by coworkers and supervisors, some of whom bring you luck. Some people with this placement are natural healers.

Jupiter in the Seventh House

Other people are your lucky charm, with your partner and closest friends heading the list. In addition to overall good fortune, you could benefit financially through a professional or personal partnership. You also attract abundant opportunities through both social and business contacts. Ultimately optimistic and fair-minded, you tend to see the best in people even when a more realistic view might be in your best interests. Everyone has faults, some more than others. Less-honorable people can take advantage of your good nature. Some people with Jupiter in the seventh house have multiple long-term relationships, and others link hearts with someone who was previously married or involved in a long-term partnership.

Jupiter in the Eighth House

Your powers of attraction are at their best when it comes to money. Jupiter in the eighth house is one of the best placements for high earnings, gifts, inheritance, and grants such as scholarships.

Money comes easily to you and probably also to your partner, but so does spending. Set a percentage aside every month for savings, investments, and retirement. You also can successfully negotiate employee benefits and could receive sizable bonuses. Most people with this placement are attuned to generosity, partly because they understand a basic principle: what goes out comes back many times over. Education can increase your overall lifetime earnings. You also excel at research and finding the knowledge and information you need.

Jupiter in the Ninth House

You're a perpetual student, whether in or out of the classroom. Knowledge and information excite you, and some people may call you a walking encyclopedia. You enjoy discussing ideas and concepts, and you're as much a natural teacher as you are a learner, sharing what you know to benefit others. Some people with this placement hold several advanced degrees. You're adventuresome and outgoing and travel regularly, taking trips that add information to your vast knowledge bank. Highly principled, you have a clearly defined code of ethics from which you never waver. You expect others to do the same and have little tolerance for those who don't. Relationships with in-laws are generally positive, and you could benefit financially through them.

Jupiter in the Tenth House

Lucky you! Career success, an honorable reputation, and recognition are matched by abundant opportunities to make a name for yourself. You're popular with coworkers and supervisor and as a manager yourself, and can benefit financially from your career efforts. But your optimism can be a challenge when high hopes shove reality aside. Weigh the pros and cons of an opportunity before diving in with enthusiasm. It will help prevent headaches and regrets when the bloom wears off, as it inevitably does even in the most positive career endeavors. You're also inclined to take on more than you can reasonably handle—the downside of enthusiasm. Again, be realistic and promise only what you're sure you can deliver.

Jupiter in the Eleventh House

You never lack for friends, thanks to the expansive influence of Jupiter. Popular and outgoing, you have an active social life and an extensive network of personal and professional contacts. Good fortune and opportunities come through friends and groups. Many people with Jupiter in the eleventh house are involved in clubs and organizations, and some find themselves with too many commitments. Be selective and practical about time constraints and accept only the most rewarding leadership positions. You're also among the first to help friends, generously sharing your skills and talents. Enthusiastic goals guide your life, but here, too, you can overdo it. Optimism is an asset if it's tempered with realistic thinking.

Jupiter in the Twelfth House

You're deeply spiritual and have strong faith in the universe and life itself. You also feel protected, which you are. Jupiter in the twelfth house functions like a guardian angel who watches over and protects you. You can no doubt cite many instances where your luck turned for the better and good fortune arrived at the eleventh hour—just as you were about to lose all hope. But don't make the mistake of relying on Jupiter to bail you out of every tight spot. It's usually reliable, but not always. You're generous with your time, talents, and money in helping others. Just be sure the recipients are worthy of your gifts, because you have a tendency to "give yourself away," to do more than you should. Some people with this placement dream in full color.

Saturn in the Houses
Saturn in the First House
People might see you as aloof and reserved, when in actuality you're shy or lack self-confidence. This is more often the case in your younger years; with experience, you learn to let the lighter facets of your personality emerge. Even so, you're far more comfortable with familiar situations and people. Serious and conscientious, you live up to your responsibilities. You're also an ambitious, self-disciplined worker who seeks status and recognition and always wants to be in charge. These qualities were also a dominant theme during your childhood. You want people to think highly of you, but a tendency to be bossy can create the opposite outcome. Success usually comes later in life to people with Saturn in the first house, and obstacles overcome make achievements all the sweeter. Main message: lighten up and enjoy the little things.

Saturn in the Second House
Like all else in the zodiac, this placement has its pluses and minuses. It all depends on how you use the energy. Some people with Saturn in the second house are cheap and greedy. Others are cautious and conservative, frugal, and financially risk-averse. Some are penny wise and pound foolish; others are shrewd money

managers. Your challenge is to talk the fine line that separates the two and to embrace the principle that money that circulates returns to you many times over. Also ban all austerity thinking. Accomplish these things and you can achieve great wealth, little by little, and with increased earnings later in life. Your patience and perseverance will be rewarded.

Saturn in the Third House
You're practical and serious-minded, with excellent reasoning ability and powers of concentration. Learning is to your advantage, and many people with Saturn in the third house are excellent students who return to school later in life to increase the chance for career gains. Education plus experience is the formula to fulfill your ambitions. You approach life and career advancement with the same methodical mindset you use in everything from daily tasks to major projects, and you have outstanding organizational and planning skills. But you're also a worrier and sometimes borrow trouble rather than rely on your superb analytical skills. Relationships with some neighbors and siblings are likely to be distant and could be problematic. You may be responsible for handling a relative's affairs at some point.

Saturn in the Fourth House
Your childhood may have been less than lighthearted and easygoing. Although conflict probably was part of the environment, the dominant influence was an emphasis on responsibility, achievement, discipline, and structure. Even playtime had a useful purpose. You may not have enjoyed the experience, but it did provide a strong foundation and sense of family

that contributes to your desire for a stable and secure home and family life. Home ownership is a priority and a status symbol, and you could do well with long-term real estate investments. Some people with Saturn in the fourth house are self-employed or work from their homes. Family obligations continue throughout much of your life, and you may be involved in caring for an older parent or relative.

Saturn in the Fifth House

You take matters of the heart seriously and may be more attracted to people who are older or more mature than your peers. Some people with Saturn in the fifth house are content with a long-term (even decades-long) relationship without the need for formal commitment or even living together. You may have few or no children or have them later in life. Much of your creative output is practical and useful, and you enjoy leisure-time hobbies such as woodworking, furniture refinishing, crafts, and other activities that some people see more as work than play. Long-term investments may be the best choice for your generally risk-averse mindset. You also could do well with real estate.

Saturn in the Sixth House

Given a choice, you'll do the responsible thing rather than the frivolous one, putting work before play. Reprogram your thinking to allow a periodic impulsive and carefree moment, if for no other reason than to release tension. Pursue hobbies and volunteer activities, which are excellent stress relievers. You're the one who willingly (or sometimes grudgingly, because you think it's your karma) does all the tasks no one else wants to do. Ditto with any extra

available unassigned work. Somehow it'll all be completed even if you don't do it. Long hours fall in the same category. The work will still be there tomorrow and the next day in an unending supply. Most people with Saturn in the sixth house limit coworker relationships to business. Some are prone to chronic ailments.

Saturn in the Seventh House

Whether you should or shouldn't, you feel responsible for your partner and other people with whom you have close ties. Therein lies Saturn's lesson for your lifetime: relationships. You may view these people as burdens or soul mates, as teachers or students, or some of each. Letting go of a close relationship or putting one in perspective is difficult for you at least until you feel you've gained all you can from it in practical or esoteric terms. On another level, you may choose a mate who's older or commit later in life. You and/or your partner may need considerable time alone. You also have an innate understanding of what it takes to build and maintain a successful relationship. Choose wisely in business partnerships; they're likely to be long-lived.

Saturn in the Eighth House

Although Saturn in the eighth house can indicate less rather than more money in the bank, its predominant influences are perfection and a cautious mindset. You or your partner, or both of you, are thrifty and financially conservative. But you also might be downright cheap, with an austerity mentality. Live a little! Denying yourself at least some of the pleasures money can buy is less than you deserve, so strive to keep finances in perspective. Realistically, you can expect joint resources to increase later in life. The same time frame could bring an inheritance, although possibly less than hoped for. Some people with this placement work for companies that offer poor compensation. You could profit from real estate and long-term investments.

Saturn in the Ninth House

Higher education is an essential factor in career success and advancement when Saturn is in the ninth house. You might, however, delay your schooling until later (or complete it later), in your thirties, forties, or fifties, for any of several reasons: parental influence or family circumstances, as a result of being passed over for promotion, or when you discover that job qualifications require a degree. Some people find their true calling only after entering the workforce. The guiding principles in your life are generally conservative, time-tested ones. Anything less than ethical, honest action can trigger karma, possibly through the legal system. Many people with this placement travel only reluctantly, or when necessary, but others are frequent business travelers. You could take responsibility for an in-law's affairs at some point.

Saturn in the Tenth House

The facts: you're an ultra-ambitious status seeker who will accept nothing less than worldly success and recognition for your efforts. You have an innate understanding of what it takes to rise to the top, although it may take until about age thirty for you to fully realize this. Once you do, you then embrace the strategy of slow, steady, step-by-step advancement to achieve your goals. Along the way, you gain wisdom and hone your leadership skills. Use both

and remind yourself of what it was like to be the "little guy." Anything less—or cutting corners—will undoubtedly have repercussions. A responsible hard worker, you could find career success in the corporate world, business, or politics. Whatever your career field, obstacles that would throw others off course are merely temporary setbacks for you.

Saturn in the Eleventh House

You cherish your few close friends, the people with whom you can be completely at ease and totally yourself. They refresh and renew your spirit, especially because much of your social life is business-related. If you're involved in organizations, as many with this placement are, they're likely to be professional groups or those that can otherwise advance your career and status. However, your sense of responsibility could encourage you to try to "do it all" in any group. That might also be because you believe you're the most qualified for any task. You excel at goal setting and have the patience and wisdom to work long and hard to achieve your objectives. Networking is part of your path to success, and you may have some close elderly friends or mentors.

Saturn in the Twelfth House

You may work behind the scenes for the greater good of a few or all of humankind with little expectation or desire for recognition. However, if you're otherwise ambitious, especially in your career, then you may experience frustration when honors arrive only years later or not at all—too little, too late, in your estimation. That's because this placement is one of service and a responsible, committed work ethic. The more you follow Saturn's "rules," the greater your achievements will be with this potentially karmic influence. Some people with Saturn in the twelfth house have "secret enemies," or believe they do. If you're among them, look within to seek answers and solutions. This placement is as much about right action as it is about understanding your motivations and ambitions.

Uranus in the Houses

Uranus in the First House

Independence and unique individuality set you apart from the crowd. You embody both of these traits in some way, even if it isn't immediately obvious to others, who are intrigued by your magnetic charm. Some people with Uranus in the first house are rebels who pursue an unconventional lifestyle. Often unpredictable, you keep people guessing and sometimes even surprise yourself. You initiate change for the sake of change. Friendship is important to you, and you may be actively involved in clubs, organizations, and good causes. Many with this placement are sensitive to electronics (phones, computers and other technological gadgets, and even appliances), which mysteriously shut themselves on and off, work some times and not at others. Be cautious with electricity.

Uranus in the Second House

You're prone to unexpected financial gains and losses and thus should make budgeting a priority. Saving is equally important so you're covered when extra funds are needed. Yet you're also innovative in moneymaking and have clever, inventive ideas to increase income. Follow through on the most promising opportunities, which may come through friends, networking, and groups or organizations. Spending habits also vary; one day you're impulsive and the next you're thrifty (or even cheap). You have an unusual code of ethics in that you set your own standards, which may or may not be in line with traditional values—but they work well for you.

Uranus in the Third House

You're intelligent and may be a genius. At the least you have a quick, inventive mind that sparks clever, original ideas. Some are ingenious because you have the ability to view problems from a unique viewpoint. You're also future-oriented in your thinking and sense coming trends. Some people with Uranus in the third house use this imaginative planetary energy in writing or public speaking, and others are amateur or professional inventors and technological wizards. Chances are, you're among the first to acquire the latest electronic gadgets. Siblings are also friends, and you're well acquainted with neighbors and may be involved in community groups. Impromptu weekend getaways are among your favorite activities.

Uranus in the Fourth House

A stereotypical domestic life is not for you. If you live in a traditional home, the décor is sure to reflect your unique style and have plenty of space for the latest gadgets and electronics. Unexpected disruptions and friends dropping in are common. One (or both) of your parents is unusual in some way—interests, activities, career, background—and your relationship is likely to be more one of friendship than parent-child. In your younger years (and possibly as an adult), you may have rebelled against parental controls and family thinking. The freedom to come and go at will is important to you, and you may move frequently.

Uranus in the Fifth House

Attending social events and spending time with friends are among your favorite evening and weekend pastimes. You also have unusual hobbies (and frequently pursue new ones that catch your interest), may be an amateur inventor, and want all the latest in entertainment technology. Your love life is lively, albeit unpredictable, and spontaneity keeps the romance alive in a long-term commitment. If you're a parent, your children (or first child) are likely to be independent, intelligent, and somewhat rebellious, and may be gifted and even brilliant. You may be lucky in games of chance and with investments, but unexpected losses can undermine gains. Take well-calculated and informed risks.

Uranus in the Sixth House

If you feel like your work life is often in a state of flux, you're probably correct. Uranus in the sixth house indicates unexpected developments on an almost daily basis and periodic major changes such as layoffs, mergers, and buyouts. Be wise; make networking a priority and stay on top of job trends. You need the freedom to structure your daily work to suit your needs. A job with flexible hours is your ideal and satisfies your need for autonomy and independence. You're a conscientious hard worker who also needs the freedom to try new techniques in search of a better, faster way. Uranus here favors high-tech jobs or those that depend on technology. Nervous tension can be an issue. Add daily relaxation to your schedule.

Uranus in the Seventh House

You attract unusual and interesting people. That's no surprise because you're probably the same. Although you may feel misunderstood in your younger years, maturity brings an appreciation for your uniqueness. Friendship and romance are spontaneous events more often than not with this placement, including love at first sight. That very spontaneity—and impulsiveness—is why Uranus in the seventh house is associated with divorce and breakups. You need a partnership where you can maintain your individuality. In fact, any attempt to curb your independence triggers a rebellion. You simply won't stand for it. Your ideal mate is also your best friend, a person who touches your soul. Friends play a major role in your life.

Uranus in the Eighth House

Where there's an upside there's usually a downside: Uranus here indicates unexpected financial gains—and losses. The odds, however, favor gains if you use common sense and resist impulsive money moves. In the eighth house, Uranus can be the classic rags-to-riches story. It can trigger a surprise inheritance from a long-lost rich relative, a big lottery or contest win, or a fabulous bonus. Those government lists of unclaimed funds? Check them out. On a practical level, be smart and be involved in family and/or business finances and decisions, as this placement can indicate a loss because of someone else's actions. Always read the fine print in loan documents and consumer credit applications.

Uranus in the Ninth House

Injustice goes against all your beliefs, as does inequality. Although your personal code of ethics might be somewhat unusual, you won't bend on those two principles and are intolerant of anyone who disagrees. Given the right circumstances, you might even become a rabid reformer with what others view as revolutionary ideas. Offbeat topics and the unusual attract your interest, and you study the most intriguing ones in depth. In formal higher education, you might find distance learning more effective than classroom instruction. Some people with this placement have difficulty focusing on a single area of study and perpetually change majors in search of one that will hold their interest. Career counseling may be helpful. In-laws may be unusual in some way and your contact with them intermittent.

Uranus in the Tenth House

Your career life is subject to sudden changes—positive and negative. Uranus here also indicates sudden fame (or infamy), a flash in the pan that fades fast. Even more typical is a certain fated quality. Your career life may feel somehow guided in that you're usually in the right place at the right time, presented with an exciting opportunity that fits your current circumstances. If you try to direct your energies elsewhere, you're stymied. More often than not, the unseen hand that pushes you this way or that lands you where you should be. Each career opportunity brings with it the freedom to direct all or a large part of your daily activities. But because you want total control, you can find yourself at odds with supervisors. You also have a talent for innovation.

Uranus in the Eleventh House

You're the consummate friend and networker, a team player who appreciates the value of group effort. Socializing with your many acquaintances and spending time with close friends are favorite leisure-time activities. You might be involved in organizations, because this placement is one of a joiner. Groups are also excellent outlets for your leadership skills. Here, you can make a significant difference in people's lives. Humanitarian efforts may interest you. In any group you're likely to initiate change, rebelling against the old ways in your role as a future-oriented visionary. You're innovative, with imaginative yet realistic ideas. Change for the sake of change, however, can be unproductive. Some people with this placement are rebels, championing causes to bring about society reforms.

Uranus in the Twelfth House

Independence is one of your defining traits, although only those closest to you may appreciate the true depth of your individuality. You might assert your independence in an unusual way, such as through a hobby like astrology or computer games that most friends and colleagues would never associate with you. Many people with Uranus in the twelfth house are intuitive and can sense coming events and what others are thinking. Hunches are often on target. The most powerful use of your sixth sense, however, is insight for positive personal change. Friends share secrets with you, and you could form lasting friendships through charitable organizations in which you're involved.

Neptune in the Houses
Neptune in the First House

One of your most defining traits is a chameleon-like ability to adapt to any situation and fit in with almost anyone at any time. That's a perfect match for your charming personality and your knack for subtle persuasion. You're very creative but probably underestimate your talents; your confidence level thus ebbs and flows. It's tough at times to view yourself objectively, so it's important to emphasize realistic thinking and to ask someone trustworthy for another viewpoint. You're also compassionate and caring; helping others inspires you. Intuition is strong, and you easily pick up vibrations from people and places. Metaphysical techniques, such as visualizing yourself surrounded by protective white light, are good ways to protect yourself from negative energy.

Neptune in the Second House

You can be financially impractical and unrealistic, but also astute and on target, partly because of your sixth sense. A hunch often tells you when to plan ahead, when it's wise to save, and when it's okay to splurge a little. Think twice, however, before you buy on credit. Payments might seem doable at the time but stretch your budget later. Yet you almost always generate the income you need (and can even achieve wealth) to cover expenses, even though at times money seems to disappear as if into thin air. Be cautious, though, of anything that sounds too good to be true; it probably is. You have strong emotional ties to possessions, especially those that were gifts from loved ones and things that are linked to memorable moments.

Neptune in the Third House

You have a strong visual orientation, and your thoughts probably are often in the form of pictures rather than words. Daydreaming is a favorite pastime, and some of your vivid night dreams could be prophetic. You may have a photographic memory or at least the ability to recall a great deal by seeing things in your mind's eye. Your sixth sense is active and usually reliable. Your ideas are imaginative and even visionary, yet not always practical and realistic, so you should seek and listen to other opinions. Some people with Neptune in the third house are gifted creative writers or inspirational speakers. Although you're emotionally tied to siblings and other relatives, contact with them is infrequent, as it is with neighbors.

Neptune in the Fourth House

Your domestic goal is serenity—calm and quiet, with artistic décor that soothes your soul. You see your home as a haven and do all you can to ensure that it's conflict-free. That, of course, can interfere with family communication, which focuses on tough decisions and practical realities at times. You may be intuitive about family matters and certain relatives. Emotional and spiritual ties with loved ones are strong, yet you view these relationships somewhat idealistically. That's pleasant while it lasts; sooner or later, however, you're sure to see them as they really are, not as you wish them to be. You inspire loved ones as they inspire you. Some people with this placement have a parent (or parents) who is a substance abuser.

Neptune in the Fifth House

Your creative energy is exceptional. It might manifest artistically or in hobbies and crafts, photography, music, or dancing. Most important is that you find an outlet for your imagination, which not only brings pleasure but also nurtures your spirit. Your first child also may have this talent. As a parent, either you're very tuned in (possibly through your sixth sense) to your children or you put them on an idealistic and unrealistic pedestal. You're also idealistic and a romantic in matters of the heart. That's a wonderful influence for true and lasting love, but one that can lead to disillusionment in dating relationships. Although wishful thinking can prompt unwise investments, you might profit from your ability to sense trends and thus build a sizable portfolio.

Neptune in the Sixth House

A congenial, cooperative environment is vital to job happiness and success, as are close relationships with coworkers. The opportunity to use your creativity is equally important. When these elements are missing, productivity suffers, followed by disillusionment and possibly illness, real or psychosomatic. Blind trust in coworkers is inadvisable, however, as some could prey on your compassionate nature and willingness to help; some may have a hidden agenda. Give only a little more than you get and save the rest for volunteer activities and good causes. You're spiritual and intuitive and may have an interest in nutrition and alternative healing. Use caution with medication. Some people with Neptune in the sixth house react negatively to prescription drugs and are sensitive to alcohol.

Neptune in the Seventh House

You're a true romantic, idealistic in love and attuned to the thoughts, feelings, and moods of your partner. Although your love is unconditional, you're prone to disillusionment when reality trumps your perfect-world perception. Consider it a learning experience in spirituality

and one that can bring new insights into yourself and relationships. Intuition adds finesse to your people skills, an extra level of charm that attracts others into your orbit. But you're just as easily charmed by other people, some of whom could try to mislead or even deceive you. Be especially cautious with business deals and partnerships and contracts; read the fine print. The caring and concern you show for others encourages some to take advantage of you. Be selective. A grandparent might be your biggest fan and inspiration.

Neptune in the Eighth House

You or your partner, or both, may be secretive about personal and joint resources. Although that may work temporarily for some couples, in the long run it can undermine trust. Unfortunately, Neptune in the eighth house indicates the possibility for deception in partnership (business and personal), so be cautious and aware of shared financial responsibilities. The same applies to loans and consumer credit; always concern yourself with the details and read the fine print before you sign your name. Get in the habit of protecting personal information and regularly checking your credit report for errors. Be sure your home and property are adequately insured. Your active sixth sense can be an advantage in money matters, including investments, and if you're creative, you could be highly paid for your skills and talents.

Neptune in the Ninth House

You strive for knowledge and a depth of understanding that transcends mere information gathering. Spirituality is equally important. Your challenge, however, is focus. Although knowledge for its own sake is valuable, unless you narrow your scope—at least in the realm of higher education—you may never be able to fully utilize what you know. And that would be unfortunate because many people with Neptune in the ninth house are visionaries who can spot future trends and capitalize on them. At your very best you inspire others to touch the untouchable and reach the unreachable. Travel, possibly on or near water, touches your soul and recenters you. Relationships with in-laws are likely to be highly emotional or nebulous.

Neptune in the Tenth House

Some people with Neptune in the tenth house are successful actors, musicians, or artists. Others are spiritual leaders, pursue careers in medicine or the healing arts, or use their charm and charisma in business or sales. Whatever your chosen field, you have the power to inspire others, collectively and individually. However, it's also possible that you could undermine yourself by setting unrealistic and impractical goals that result in disillusionment. If you drift from job to job or move on without first securing a new position, examine the reasons why. The ideal job is nonexistent, despite your wishes to the contrary. Be sure all actions are honest and ethical, and protect yourself against those who try to place blame on others. You'll probably be honored many times for good deeds—things done solely out of the goodness of your heart.

Neptune in the Eleventh House

You can be idealistic regarding friends, seeing what you want to see rather than all their human failings. Some are well-intentioned, true friends who will do anything for you, as you will do for them. Others, however, are false friends, interested only in what you can do for them. Be cautious, not trusting, until you're sure of a new friend's motives. You can gain great satisfaction from involvement in charitable organizations, where your vision is an example for others to follow. Yet personal goals can be a challenge. You're a dreamer with high aspirations, but may have difficulty following through on your intentions. Focus on one goal at a time, and define measurable objectives. Be a dreamer and a doer, not just a wishful thinker.

Neptune in the Twelfth House

You're in touch (or can be) with your subconscious, a deep part of the mind that some people never access. With this awareness comes the ability to sense the unseen through psychic impressions. You're also creative and may express this talent with the help of your sixth sense in words, pictures, ideas, or another medium. Vivid dreams, sometimes accompanied by sound, can be prophetic and insightful. Solitude recenters you. Although you're a private person, you're also a charmer who attracts people. But you can be equally susceptible to the charms of others, who lull you into a false sense of security. Be aware: others may try to shift the blame to you as they take advantage of your caring nature. Some people with this placement are healers.

Pluto in the Houses
Pluto in the First House

Few can match your willpower and determination. Relentless and incredibly patient once your mind is set, you're unwavering and willing to invest years to achieve a goal. Your ultimate desire is to be in a powerful position where you can be fully in charge. Controlling in some, if not all, areas of life, you dislike surprises and do all you can to avoid the unexpected. When it inevitably occurs, you're thrown off center, at a loss until you can regroup, which you inevitably do. Your powers of personal transformation are outstanding. Once committed, you follow through with the desired personal change, such as weight loss, an exercise program, or shedding a habit.

Pluto in the Second House

You're money motivated. Your goal is not just a comfortable lifestyle but true wealth, with all the freedom and power that accompanies it. That can encourage some people with Pluto in the second house to be ruthless in their financial quest, and others to cut corners to realize their goals. Doing either can backfire because this placement is usually one of boom or bust. Calculated risks matched with your potential for high earnings can yield the financial rewards you seek. Spending is generally in line with income, although you have a taste for quality and want the biggest and the best. Do so when you can afford it.

Pluto in the Third House

Your intense and focused mind and penetrating insight, along with your ability to outthink the competition, give you an edge over many people. Complement this talent with education to realize your full potential. You excel at research and are rarely caught unprepared, without all the facts and figures to back up your conclusions. Secretive by nature (and at times rightly or wrongly suspicious of others' motives), you amass a wealth of information because people

feel comfortable sharing confidences with you; they know you don't repeat what you hear. You express your thoughts in a few words or phrases, and could be a powerful and commanding speaker. Emotional ties with siblings run deep, but these relationships may be difficult, complete with power plays.

Pluto in the Fourth House

Your home is your power base, the place where you feel in charge and in control—or want to be. This may be the result of a childhood influenced by a difficult and demanding parent. (In some instances, Pluto here indicates a mentally or physically abusive family environment.) Domestic privacy is important, and you keep family business within the family. Invited guests are welcome; impromptu ones and spur-of-the-moment gatherings are not. Some people with Pluto in the fourth house are avid do-it-yourselfers. Even if you aren't, you consider your home to be a work in progress. Renovations, major and minor, are ongoing, and you periodically conduct a clean sweep to eliminate clutter and unneeded items. You could inherit a substantial legacy from a family member.

Pluto in the Fifth House

You have a deep well of emotional expression just waiting to be released. This can occur on several levels: through creativity, hobbies and leisure-time pursuits, children, or romance. All can be a positive part of your life in some way. In love you can be possessive and jealous and try to hang on to a relationship that's outlived its potential. You're also protective of those you love, which could stifle your children's independence and creativity. Nurturing support is more effective, albeit more difficult for you, but definitely one way to encourage strong ties. You could do well with investments but also incur losses, so you might fare better with those that are more conservative and long term.

Pluto in the Sixth House

You're passionate about your work life and excel at finding easier, better, and more efficient procedures. Convincing others to follow your lead, however, could be a challenge because your natural inclination is to take charge. Ease up on the intensity and get them involved; people support what they help create. Pluto in the sixth house also increases the chance for layoffs and other similar job-related developments as a result of global changes. Use networking and ongoing training to increase marketability. With your strong willpower, you're usually successful at making needed changes to ensure a healthy lifestyle. You also have above-average stamina. Some people with this placement get great satisfaction from helping others improve their lives.

Pluto in the Seventh House

You're attracted to strong-willed people who have a commanding presence. Their powerful energy intrigues and stimulates you. But Pluto here also can indicate a partner who is controlling and domineering—or you might fit that description yourself. Either way, your life is sure to be profoundly influenced and changed through close relationships. Your challenge is to promote cooperation and unity, which are enhanced by your intuitive understanding of people. You're probably an excellent amateur, if not professional, psychologist. This can make you an excellent manager if you emphasize

guidance and support over your desire to be in charge. You also could find yourself caught in a power struggle from time to time. Overall, you can be a major force for positive change in people's lives.

Pluto in the Eighth House

You have the talent to transform what others see as junk into something useful. This ability can manifest in everything from home improvements, to finances, to job tasks. It's your unique inventive perspective in action. Your strong willpower encourages an all-or-nothing attitude. Halfhearted attempts are left to those you consider to be weaker souls who lack your determination and stamina. An active sixth sense (you could be psychic) gives you added insight that can benefit money matters. Many people with Pluto in the eighth house experience a major life change because of substantial financial gains—or, unfortunately, losses. Your largesse could come through a family legacy, career success, or even a lucky win. This placement also indicates research ability and a secretive nature.

Pluto in the Ninth House

Higher education has a twofold purpose in your life: career achievement and knowledge. Your powerful need to know is closely linked to your morals and sense of justice. Hypocrisy goes against your deep-seated beliefs, and some people with Pluto in the ninth house become crusaders for a cause. You have the power to initiate ethical change for society or on an individual basis by sharing your knowledge and encouraging others to strive for high standards. Spirituality is also a strong theme, and you may have strong religious convictions. Legal matters may or may not work out to your advantage, and relationships with in-laws can be positive or negative. Travel can be life-changing through exposure to other cultures.

Pluto in the Tenth House

You have the ambition and drive to achieve the top career position you desire. It could be a powerful one where your leadership skills—used ethically—create an environment of healthy change and personal and professional growth. Use them unwisely, however, and you risk losing all you've gained. There is rarely any in-between when transformative Pluto influences the career. Much the same applies to people you encounter through your career, as well as in other activities. They fall primarily in two categories: friend or foe. Supporters help further your aims, while adversaries try to undermine your efforts. Knowing who's who is part observation, part intuition. Some people with this placement are masterful politicians and executives.

Pluto in the Eleventh House

Friends are a major influence in your life. Some are wealthy, powerful, or have the right connections when you need a networking contact for personal or professional reasons. You know or have met more famous people than most. Your leadership skills are influential in group activi-

ties, clubs, organizations, and humanitarian efforts, where you have the potential to affect the lives of many. In those venues you can be a catalyst for positive and monumental change. Stress cooperation and share the work and the credit. Should ego replace good intentions, however, you could quickly come into disfavor. Some people with Pluto in the eleventh house fall in with the wrong crowd instead of using this planetary energy to better society or a small segment of it.

Pluto in the Twelfth House

You're contemplative at times and enjoy time alone to explore the inner workings of your mind. Thoughts and your sixth sense prompt insights into the world at large and the psychology of human nature. You're interested in what makes people tick. Depth of spirit adds compassion and motivates you to help others to better their lives. Some people with Pluto in the twelfth house make significant contributions in medical research, hospice work, or prison reform. Your most influential position may be behind the scenes, where you have the ear of powerful people who seek out and respect your advice. Be cautious, though, about whom you trust; this placement indicates both hidden supporters and adversaries. Also use common sense and steer clear of any potentially unsafe area.

AL GORE

True to his Sun in the ninth house of publishing, foreign countries, higher education, and teaching, Al Gore was an Army reporter in Vietnam before entering politics. After the 2000 presidential election, he accepted a position teaching a university journalism class and wrote *An Inconvenient Truth*, a book about global warming. Mercury (writing) is in his eighth house of research and investigation and in Pisces (environment).

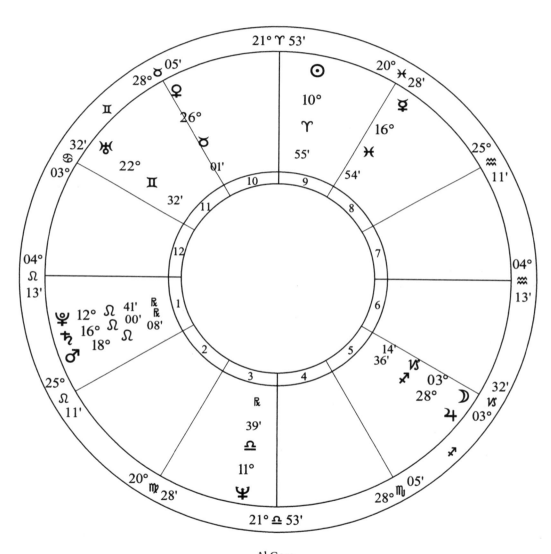

Al Gore
March 31, 1948 / 12:53 p.m. EST / Washington D.C.
Placidus Houses

TIGER WOODS

Tiger Woods is noted not only for his phenomenal golf talent but also for his ability to focus, to tune out the environment and zero in on the game. He has Mercury (thinking process) in Capricorn (concentration, discipline) in the fifth house (sports). Woods's chart is an excellent example of house rulership. Mercury rules the Midheaven (career) through Gemini and also the Virgo Ascendant (self). He is thus extremely career-oriented and ambitious.

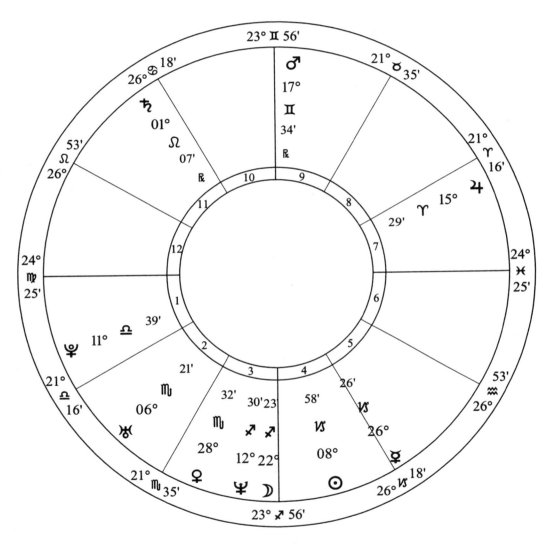

Tiger Woods
December 30, 1975 / 10:50 p.m. PST / Long Beach, CA
Placidus Houses

OPRAH WINFREY

With freedom-loving Uranus in the seventh house of partnerships, Oprah Winfrey's long-term relationship without marriage is perfect for her—independence (Uranus) and commitment (seventh house). With six planets in the trinity of wealth houses (second, sixth, and tenth), she has fulfilled her high earning potential. Aquarius on the second-house cusp indicates unexpected gains and, with Venus (universal money planet and Midheaven ruler), the Sun (self and eighth-house ruler), and Mercury (communication and sixth-house ruler), reinforces the wealth potential. Pluto in the eighth house represents big money.

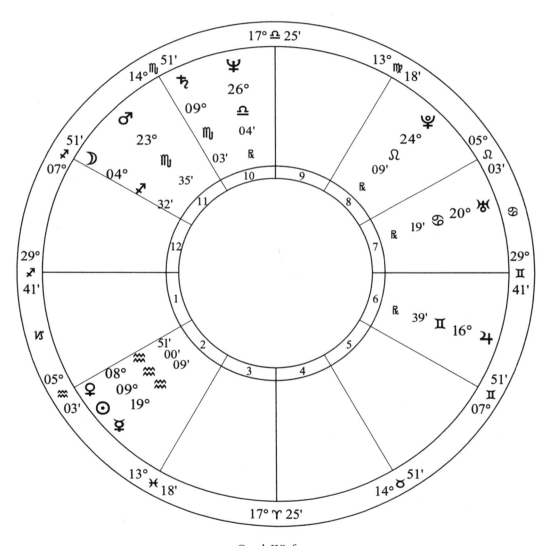

Oprah Winfrey
January 29, 1954 / 4:30 a.m. CST / Kosciusko, MS
Placidus Houses

TED KENNEDY

Ted Kennedy's chart has Saturn (karma) in the first house (self), with Saturn also as the chart ruler because Capricorn is the rising sign. Two well-known instances of irresponsibility have occurred: his suspension from Harvard when a classmate took an exam for him, and the Chappaquiddick event. Yet he emerged from both relatively unscathed: he received what some people consider an inappropriately light sentence for Chappaquiddick, and his college suspension was followed by a two-year Army stint (shortened from four because of his father's influence), his return to and graduation from Harvard, and then law school. Why? The answer is in the aspects, as will be seen in the next chapter.

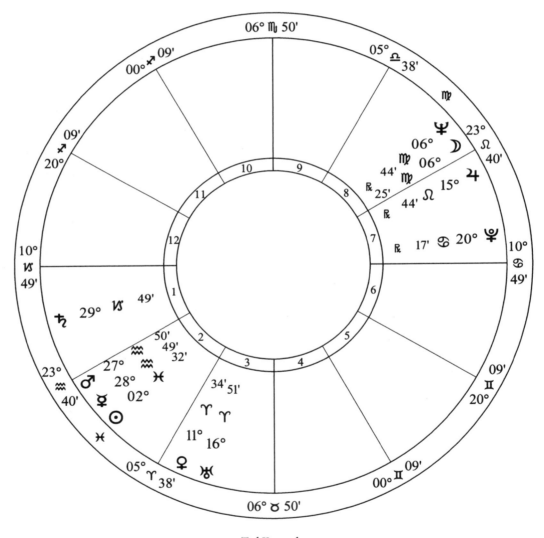

Ted Kennedy
February 22, 1932 / 3:58 a.m. EST / Dorchester, MA
Placidus Houses

WILLIE NELSON

With Venus in the tenth house, Willie Nelson's chart is a natural for popularity, career success, and high earnings. The latter is reinforced by Jupiter in the second house of income. Venus is in Taurus, his Midheaven sign, as is the Sun; Venus and Taurus rule the voice, and the Sun rules the Ascendant in Leo, the sign of the performer. Saturn in the sixth house indicates a hard worker. Saturn in Aquarius is a dichotomy; it's both traditional and unique, which his music definitely is. He also has freedom and independence (Aquarius) in his work (Saturn in the sixth house).

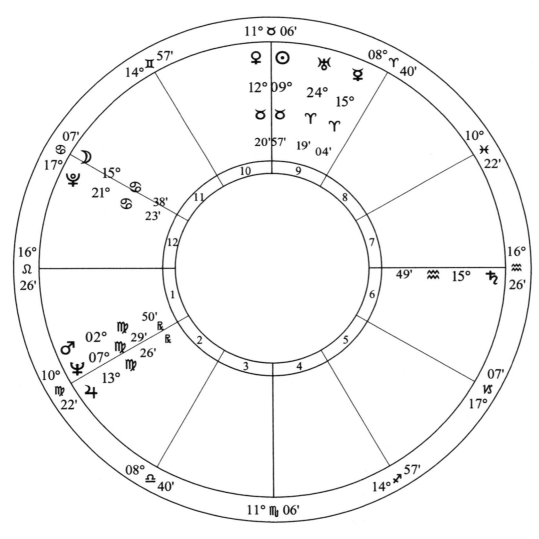

Willie Nelson
April 30, 1933 / 12:30 p.m. CST / Abbott, TX
Placidus Houses

TOM HANKS

Although Uranus in the eleventh house indicates many friends, they're more likely to be acquaintances because of other influences in Tom Hanks's chart. He probably has a much smaller group of close friends whom he considers family. Cancer (family) is on the cusp of the eleventh house, and the Moon (family, emotions), Cancer's ruler, is in the eleventh house in Leo (loyalty).

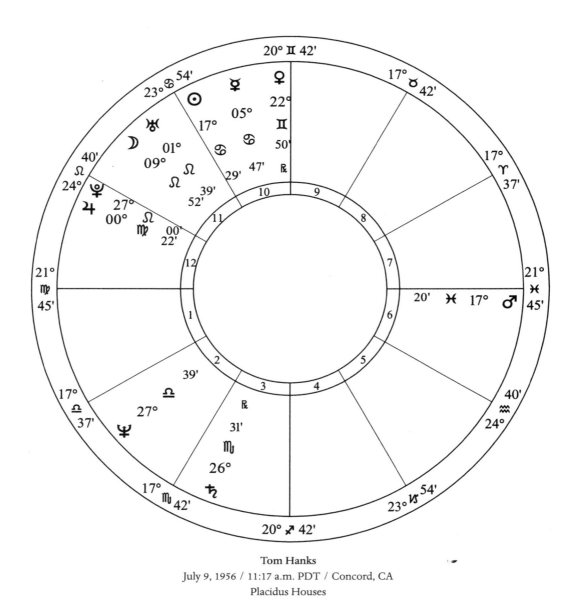

Tom Hanks
July 9, 1956 / 11:17 a.m. PDT / Concord, CA
Placidus Houses

ROBERT REDFORD

An acclaimed actor and director, Robert Redford's true passion may be the many charitable causes in which he's involved, including the Sundance Film Festival for independent filmmakers, raising money for SIDS (Sudden Infant Death Syndrome) research, and many environmental efforts. His chart has five planets in the sixth house of service and volunteer work. Four of the planets, including Neptune (environment), are in Virgo, the sign of service. Karmic Saturn (earth) in Pisces (environment) is in the twelfth, the natural house of compassionate Pisces.

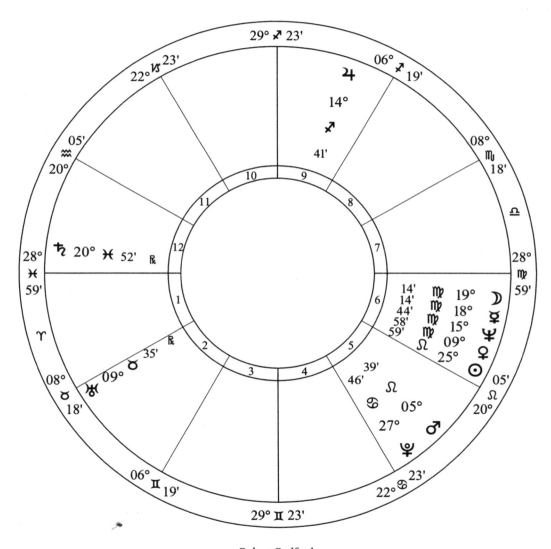

Robert Redford
August 18, 1936 / 8:02 p.m. PST / Santa Monica, CA
Placidus Houses

DR. PHIL MCGRAW

TV personality and self-help guru Dr. Phil is a psychologist who uses his practical, no-nonsense Virgo Sun in the sixth house of work to deliver realistic advice focused on responsibility and hard work. With Mercury in the seventh house of relationships, he easily connects with people. Also notice Uranus in the fourth house; Dr. Phil's family moved often during his childhood years.

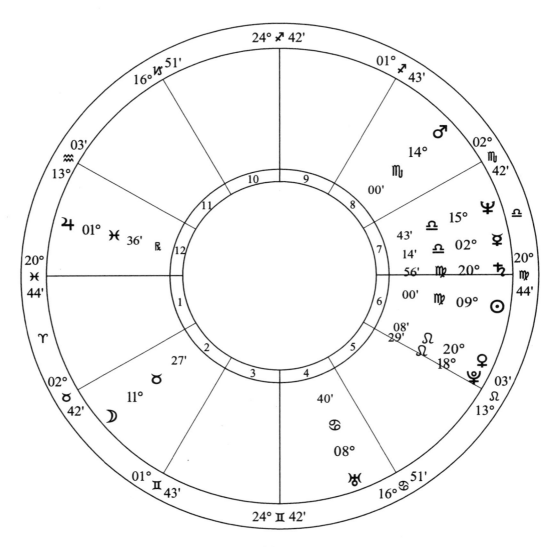

Dr. Phil McGraw
September 1, 1950 / 7:15 p.m. CST / Vinita, OK
Placidus Houses

CONDOLEEZZA RICE

Before entering public service in the Bush administration, Condoleezza Rice earned bachelor's, master's, and doctorate degrees, after which she was a professor and provost at Stanford University. All of this is an obvious fit with her chart, which has Saturn, Mercury, and Neptune in the ninth house of higher education. Venus, which rules the ninth house, is in the tenth house of career along with the Sun—a position that indicates high achievement.

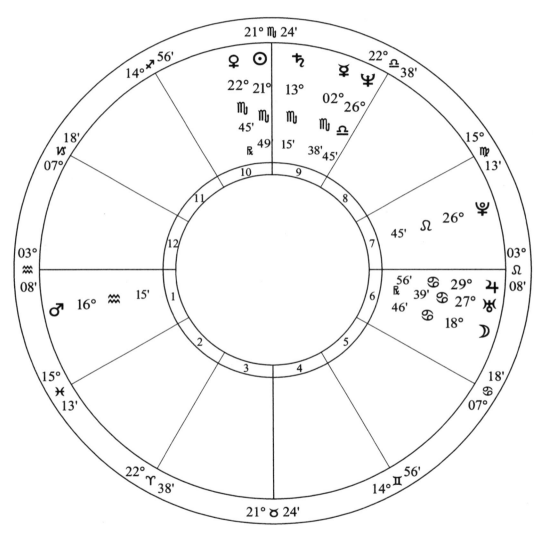

Condoleezza Rice
November 14, 1954 / 11:30 a.m. CST / Birmingham, AL
Placidus Houses

ANDERSON COOPER

Like Willie Nelson, TV reporter and host Anderson Cooper has Venus in the tenth house (popularity), as well as Jupiter (good fortune). Jupiter rules the third house of communication through Sagittarius on the cusp. The Sun (self) is in Gemini (communication) in the eighth house (research, investigation), and Mercury (communication) is in the ninth house of publishing and travel (he often reports from other countries).

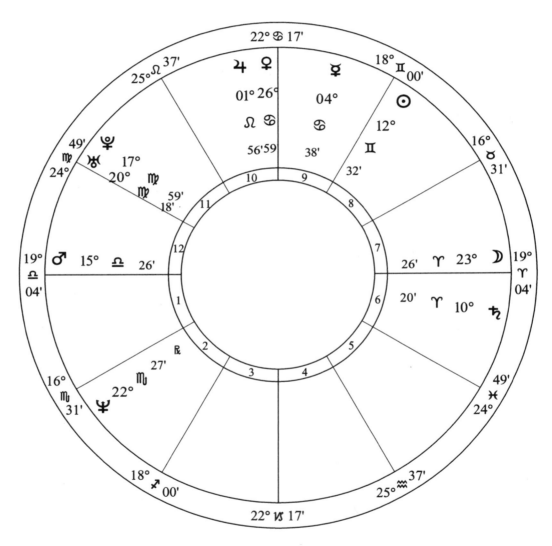

Anderson Cooper
June 3, 1967 / 3:46 p.m. EDT / New York, NY
Placidus Houses

BRAD PITT

Brad Pitt attended college to study journalism. His ninth-house (higher education) ruler, the Sun, is in Sagittarius, the sign of publishing. His Ascendant is also in adventuresome Sagittarius. He quit school on a whim (Uranus in the ninth house) in his last semester and headed to Los Angeles to pursue an acting career. Four planets in the second house, including Midheaven ruler Mercury and Saturn (second-house ruler), reflect the mega-millions he's earned. With the strong Capricorn and Saturn influence in the second house, he's undoubtedly thrifty and an excellent money manager.

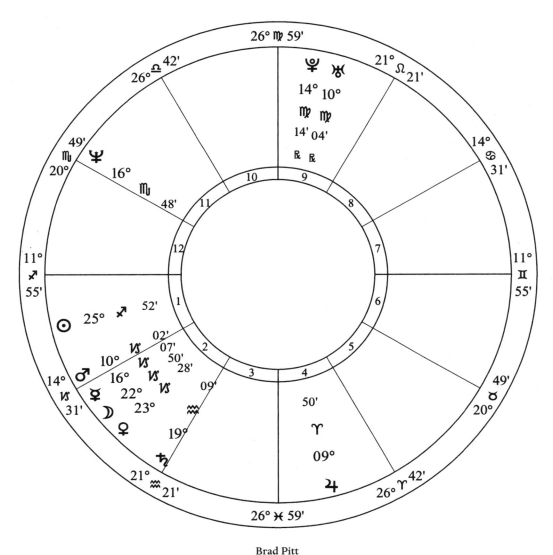

Brad Pitt
December 18, 1963 / 6:31 a.m. CST / Shawnee, OK
Placidus Houses

DALE EARNHARDT JR.

Dale Earnhardt Jr., a winning stock car driver, has ambitious Saturn in the tenth house of career. Saturn rules his fifth house, linking sports and career. Mercury, which rules both the Virgo Ascendant (self) and the Gemini Midheaven (career), is in the second house of money, reflecting his high earnings. Mercury in Scorpio is excellent for strategic planning, an asset for a race car driver.

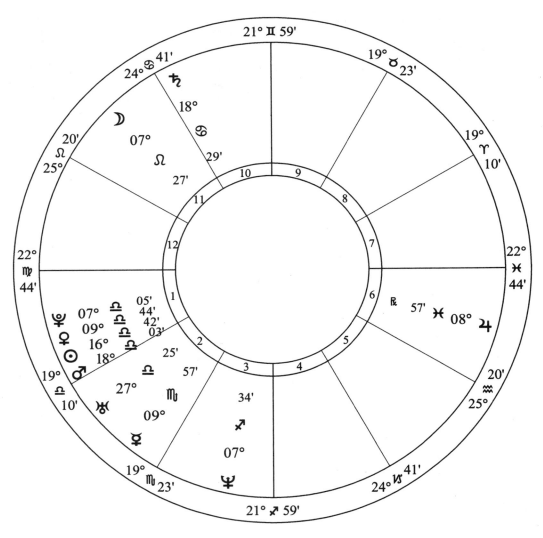

Dale Earnhardt Jr.
October 10, 1974 / 5:33 a.m. EDT / Concord, NC
Placidus Houses

CHAPTER FIVE

THE ASPECTS

A spects are the fourth factor in reading a chart: sign, planet, house, and aspect. Without aspects, every planet would operate completely on its own, like someone going through life in a cocoon, never interacting with anyone. Aspects provide the means for the planets to interact with each other.

Life would be boring if people didn't express their emotions (Moon) and thoughts (Mercury), and even periodically let their tempers emerge (Mars). What if everyone liked spicy food (fire sign) or enjoyed the exact same reading material (Mercury) or the same leisure-time pursuits (Sun)? Boring! When planets link their energies, life is anything but.

You reflect many—or most—of the qualities of your Sun sign. The differences between one Gemini and another, or one Virgo and another, are partly reflected in the aspects that each person's Sun makes to other planets. If your Sun contacts Saturn, you might like to build things in your spare time. If your Sun aspects Mars, sports may be more to your liking. This type of modification occurs with all the planets in your chart.

Aspects between planets (or between planets and angles—Ascendant, Descendant, IC, Midheaven) influence each other's expression depending on the aspect, the planets involved, and the sign and house each planet is in. In some cases, aspects bring out the best in the planets; in others, they represent obstacles or challenges for personal growth. Aspects, like planets, signs, and houses, mirror life: some things are easy, and others are difficult.

Aspects are geometric angles, such as 90° or 120°. There are many aspects, some of which are obscure and seldom used. The most common are the five major aspects (figure 24) called the *Ptolemaic*

Aspect	Glyph	Degrees	Orb	Keywords
Conjunction	☌	0°	8°	Intensity
Sextile	✶	60°	6°	Opportunity
Trine	△	120°	8°	Ease, luck
Square	□	90°	8°	Action, obstacle
Opposition	☍	180°	8°	Separation
Inconjunct	⚻	150°	3°	Disharmony
Semisextile	⚺	30°	3°	Mildly beneficial
Semisquare	∠	45°	3°	Friction
Sesquisquare	⚼	135°	3°	Aggravation
Parallel	‖	0°	1°	Unity
Contraparallel	⸾	0°	1°	Separation

Chart 9. Aspect Glyphs, Degrees, Orbs, and Keywords

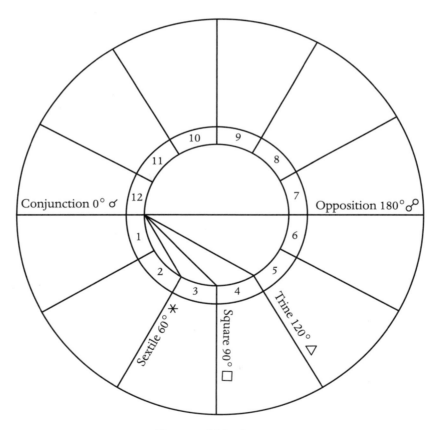

Figure 24. Major Aspects

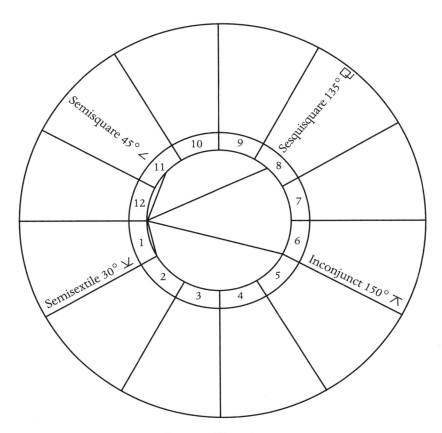

Figure 25. Minor Aspects

aspects: the *conjunction*, *sextile*, *trine*, *square*, and *opposition*. In addition, there are several minor aspects (figure 25) that are commonly used, including the *semisextile*, *semisquare*, *inconjunct*, *sesquisquare*, *parallel*, and *contraparallel*. Of these, most astrologers consider the inconjunct (also known as the *quincunx*) to be the strongest, and some view it as a major aspect. The semisquare and sesquisquare are particularly useful in predictive astrology. Use of the parallel and contraparallel (illustrated in figure 29 on page 223) continues to increase. You can glean a tremendous amount of information from the major aspects, which are used in this book, but you should definitely test the influence of the minor aspects in your chart.

Although the angle of each aspect is a precise number of degrees, only rarely do you find two planets exactly in aspect. (Take note when you do, because that aspect is extremely powerful in the chart.) Because of this, each aspect has an allowable *orb of influence* within which the planetary energies can interact (chart 9). Orbs work in two directions, both before and after the aspect would be exact.

For example, the orb for a sextile (60°) is 6°, so the two planets must be between 52° and 68° apart. So the Moon at 10°25' Aquarius in the

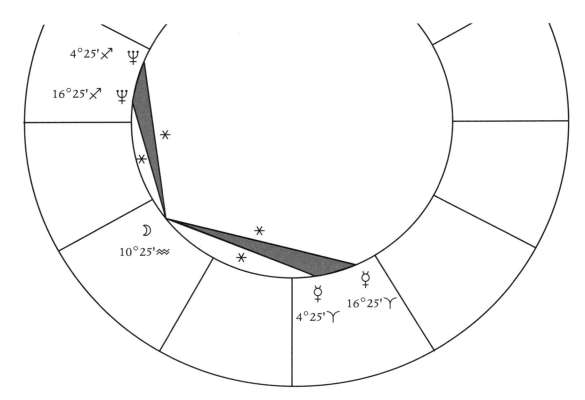

Figure 26. Orb of Influence

second house would be sextile Mercury in Aries in the fourth house if Mercury were anywhere between 4°25' and 16°25' Aries, which is the 6° allowable orb in either direction (figure 26). The Moon also would be sextile a planet (Neptune, in figure 26) between 4°25' and 16°25' Sagittarius, which is two signs before Aquarius. The Moon in aspect to Mercury between 4°25' and 10°25' would be called an *approaching aspect* (approaching the exact sextile), while the Moon in aspect to Mercury between 10°26' and 16°25' would be called a *separating aspect* (separating from the exact sextile). An approaching aspect is generally stronger than a separating one.

The conjunction (0°) symbolizes intensity because the two planets are next to each other,

in the same sign and at the same degree, plus or minus an 8° orb (anywhere between 0° and 8° apart). The energies of the two planets are united and blended into one entity, with each taking on some of the characteristics of the other (figure 27). This aspect can be *positive or negative* depending on the planets in the conjunction. A Venus-Jupiter conjunction is beneficial and lucky because these two planets represent good fortune; however, this conjunction also can promote laziness and self-indulgence. A Venus-Neptune conjunction represents idealistic love and possible deception in romance and money matters, but it also can enhance creativity and imagination.

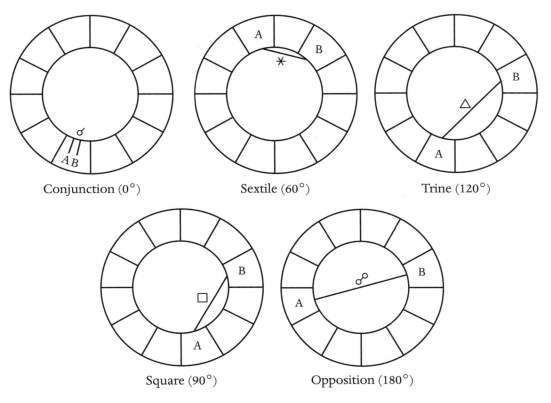

Figure 27. The Five Major Aspects

The sextile (60°) and trine (120°) are classified as *easy aspects*. The sextile is formed between two planets that are 60° apart, plus or minus a 6° orb (anywhere between 54° and 66° apart), and the trine is formed between two planets that are 120° apart, plus or minus an 8° orb (anywhere between 112° and 128° apart). Planets involved in trine aspects represent areas of good luck and the ability to overcome difficulties, usually with little or no effort on your part. Trines also indicate natural talents and areas where you achieve the greatest success. The sextile is similar to the trine, although weaker. It represents opportunity, but unlike with the trine, you must initiate action to reap the benefits of a sextile.

The square (90°) and opposition (180°) are called *hard aspects*. The square is formed between two planets that are 90° apart, plus or minus an 8° orb (anywhere between 82° and 98° apart), and the opposition is formed between two planets that are 180° apart, plus or minus an 8° orb (anywhere between 172° and 188° apart). Planets in square aspect represent obstacles to be overcome; things never come easily here, and conflict is likely. But squares also represent action that, when used positively, can yield amazing results and more rewarding achievements than experienced with the easygoing trine. The key is to learn to constructively manage the energy of the two planets in the square.

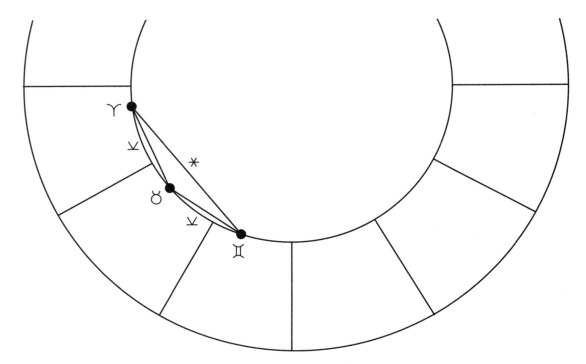

Figure 28. Two Semisextiles

The opposition represents separation—two opposing forces at odds with each other. Oppositions often involve relationships, personal or professional, and indicate confrontation. The goal is cooperation and compromise, the happy medium that balances the two energies so they can meet in the middle and work together.

People tend to celebrate their trines and sextiles and to view their hard aspects and some conjunctions as trials and obstacles. That's a simplistic view and in many respects an erroneous one. Think about it. Life is nice when everything is going smoothly, but would a life of leisure really satisfy you? Most people would answer no to that question, because humans are at least somewhat competitive by nature, if for

no other reason than to experience the ego gratification that accompanies an achievement.

In some ways, the trines and sextiles (and some conjunctions) are more difficult. Because things usually go smoothly and come easily in the areas represented by the easy aspects, it's just as possible to squander the energy. What a waste! This is why some very talented people fail to reach their potential, while others with more difficult aspects achieve phenomenal success. The latter are the ones who have the incentive that comes with 10 percent inspiration and 90 percent perspiration. The best combination of aspects is a mix of both—some hard aspects to get the easy aspects moving.

The minor aspects add further depth to a chart. They're not at all necessary in order to

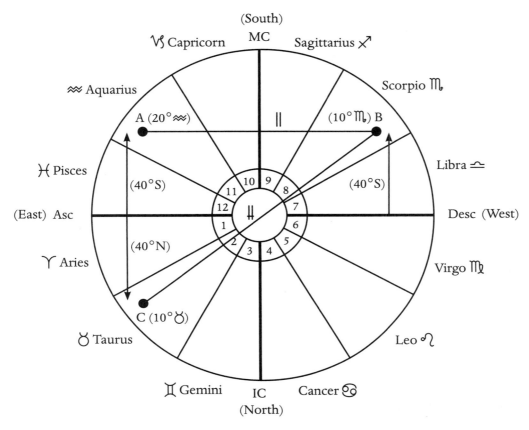

Figure 29. Parallel and Contraparallel

read a chart, but they can reveal subtle yet active influences or reinforce the influence of major aspects.

The semisquare (45°) and sesquisquare (135°) are hard aspects that manifest in ways similar to the square, but with less forcefulness. Mercury square Mars, for example, is associated with snap decisions and a short temper. These two planets in a semisquare or sesquisquare would be less volatile—a medium temper instead of a short one.

The semisextile (30°) can function like a weak sextile (the aspect of opportunity), but overall the energies of the two planets in the semisextile don't blend very well with each other. Aries is sextile Gemini, a fire sign with an air sign. These two signs are compatible; both are outgoing and active, albeit in different ways. Aries is semisextile Taurus, a fire sign with an earth sign. The energies are diverse, with Aries representing impatience and pure action, while Taurus is slow, steady, and thorough. Suppose, though, that there is a sextile between planets in Aries and Gemini, and both are semisextile another planet in Taurus (figure 28). In this case, the tension represented by the semisextiles (from Taurus) would help to provide the follow-through necessary to make the most of an opportunity represented by the sextile.

Planet	*Orbital Cycle*
Sun ☉	1 year
Moon ☽	27.33 days
Mercury ☿	88 days
Venus ♀	225 days
Mars ♂	1 year, 11 months (688 days)
Jupiter ♃	12 years
Saturn ♄	29½ years
Uranus ♅	84 years
Neptune ♆	165 years
Pluto ♇	248 years

Chart 10. Planetary Speeds

As with the semisextile, planets in an inconjunct represent diverse energies. But this aspect is stronger than the semisextile and thus more apparent in a person's life. Planets in an inconjunct are 150° apart, halfway between a trine (120°) and an opposition (180°). A trine is an easy aspect that represents free-flowing energy, while an opposition is a hard aspect that indicates action. The inconjunct, placed in between these two, is an aspect of disharmony that requires an adjustment to deal with the two planets in the aspect. Things don't go smoothly with it (trine), and it's difficult to take action (opposition). This triggers the feeling that something is about to happen, but it never quite does. For example, action-oriented Aries is inconjunct practical, meticulous Virgo. Aries is ready to move ahead, while Virgo wants to get organized, analyze the facts, and double-check the details. With these two diverse forces at work, you can get stuck, taking no action but feeling you should.

The parallel is similar to a conjunction, and the contraparallel is similar to an opposition. These aspects are formed not by longitude but by declination.

To better understand the concept of declination, imagine that the Ascendant/Descendant axis is the celestial equator, which is the imaginary line that represents Earth's equator extended into space (see figure 29). Planets A and B are 40° south of this line, while planet C is 40° north. Notice that planets A and B do not form a longitudinal aspect (square, opposition, sextile, and so on), but because they are both 40° south of the celestial equator, they are in parallel aspect and thus operate somewhat like a conjunction. Planets B and C, which are contraparallel each other, are also in (longitudinal) opposition aspect. Because a contraparallel is similar to an opposition, this strengthens the opposition.

Specific terminology is used when describing planets in aspect. With one exception, the

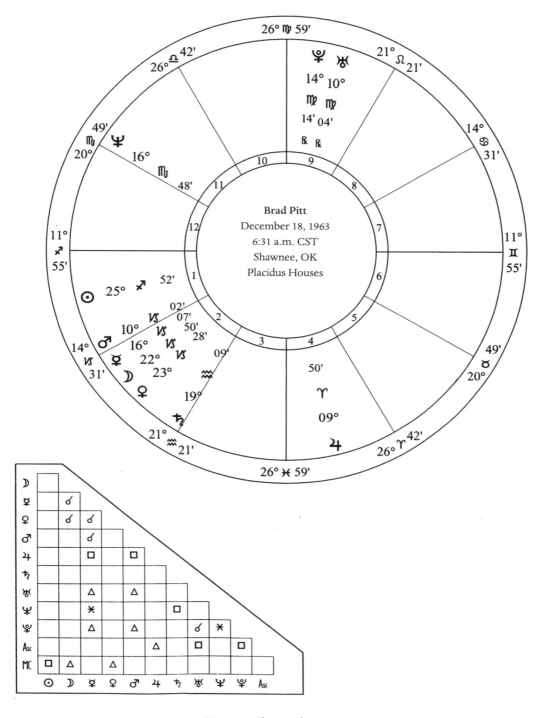

Figure 30. Chart with Aspectarian

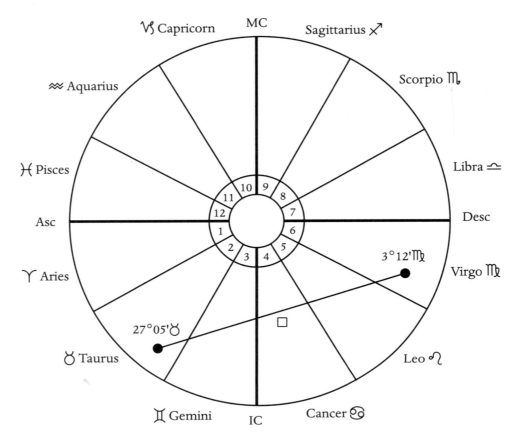

Figure 31. Out-of-Sign Aspect

faster-moving planet is listed first, then the aspect, and finally the slower-moving planet (see chart 10). For example, you would say or write "Mercury conjunct Saturn," not "Saturn conjunct Mercury." Solar aspects are the exception. Even though the Moon is the fastest-moving planet, an aspect between the Sun and Moon is listed as, for example, "Sun conjunct Moon," not "Moon conjunct Sun."

Identifying the major aspects is simple with a little practice, even if you're not a math whiz. You can learn to eyeball most of them by using the elements (fire, earth, air, and water) and the modes (cardinal, fixed, mutable).

Figure 30 shows Brad Pitt's chart with an *aspectarian*, or aspect grid, which lists the major aspects in his chart. This is a handy tool that makes it easy to see the aspects without individually calculating each one. All chart calculation software programs include this option.

To read the aspectarian, first look down the far left column where all the planets plus the Asc (Ascendant) and MC (Midheaven) are listed. Notice that the same list in the same order is also on the bottom of the aspect grid. The aspect symbols throughout the grid show which planets are in aspect.

For example, look at the Mercury symbol (☿) on the left and follow it across the row to the right to the second box, where there is a conjunction symbol (☌). Now look down the column to find the planet at the bottom of the aspect grid, which is the Moon (☽). So you know that the Moon is conjunct Mercury in Brad Pitt's chart. Mercury is also conjunct Mars, which you can see by following the Mars row over to the Mercury column.

Aspects can form in either direction—clockwise or counterclockwise. A sextile can thus, for example, be from a planet in the second house to a planet in the fourth house or one in the twelfth. A planet in the first house can be square a planet in the fourth house or one in the tenth.

Conjunctions are easy to spot because the planets are close together, often in the same house. Planets in trine aspect are in the same element, such as both in air signs. Gemini is trine both Libra and Aquarius.

You can use the modes (qualities) to see squares and oppositions. Planets forming either of these aspects are in the same mode, such as both in cardinal signs. Aries is square Cancer and Capricorn and is opposite Libra.

Out-of-sign aspects, or dissociate aspects, occur in some charts. An example of this would be the Sun at 27°05' Taurus square Uranus at 3°12' Virgo (figure 31). The two planets are within the 8° allowable orb but are in different modes; Taurus is a fixed sign and Virgo is a mutable sign.

Out-of-sign aspects are generally, but not always, weaker. In this case, the square is weaker because of the different modes, and it's also easier to resolve the obstacle indicated because both Taurus and Virgo are earth signs and therefore compatible. But because it's weaker, it also

would be more difficult to tap into the action energy of the square.

The reverse would be true with a dissociate trine, such as the Sun at 26° Libra trine Mars at 2° Cancer. Although the signs are trine by degree (a 6° degree orb), they are square by mode because they are both cardinal signs. So while the trine would encourage high energy and risk taking, a person with this aspect would be more inclined to take unwise risks and engage in impetuous behavior because the signs are square. On the other hand, the trine indicates luck, which at times, but not always, will save the day and thus encourage more risk taking.

Occasionally you will see a planet that forms no aspects to other planets. Because unaspected planets are not influenced by other planets, they are true to their nature, expressing the planetary energy in its purest form in the area of life represented by the house placement. This can be more or less positive or negative depending on the planet and its sign and house placement. This is one area where planetary dignity, debility, fall, and exaltation can be useful in judging how the planet will operate (see "Planetary Power" on page 126). Someone with an unaspected Mars in Cancer (fall) would have a tougher time taking action because Mars gets no assistance from other planets. An unaspected Mars in Capricorn (exaltation), however, would fuel ambition and success.

ASPECT CONFIGURATIONS

There are four *aspect configurations* involving the major aspects. These configurations are called the *stellium, grand trine, T-square* (or *T-cross*), and *grand cross.* Each involves multiple planets.

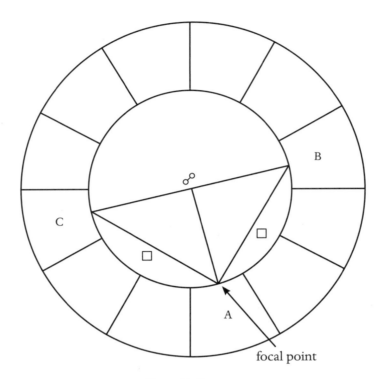

Figure 32. T-square

A stellium is a group of three or more planets, all of which are conjunct, or next to, each other in a row (see figure 27 on page 221). The planets in a stellium are usually in the same sign, but they also can span the last degrees of one sign and the first degrees of the next. So, for example, you could have a stellium formed by planets at 27° Gemini, 29° Gemini, and 2° Cancer. Sometimes the first and last planets in the stellium aren't within orb, but they're still considered to be conjunct because the planet(s) between the two bridges the gap.

The same is true of another planet within aspect orb to a planet(s) in the stellium; if it aspects one, it aspects them all. For example, if a stellium comprises planets at 10°, 14°, and 19° Gemini, then all three are conjunct. Another planet at 20° Aquarius is trine all three even though technically it's out of orb to the first planet in the stellium.

A stellium represents intense, powerfully focused energy that's a major personality component. The house(s) of the stellium indicates an area of life that's a major theme for the person, and the sign(s) shows how the stellium is expressed. A stellium in the tenth house, for example, indicates someone who is ambitious, career-focused, and status-motivated.

A T-square is formed when two (or more) planets in opposition are square a third planet, forming the letter *T* (figure 32). Drive and ambition are associated with the T-square. The same orb flexibility used with the stellium applies to this configuration. The planet that is square the

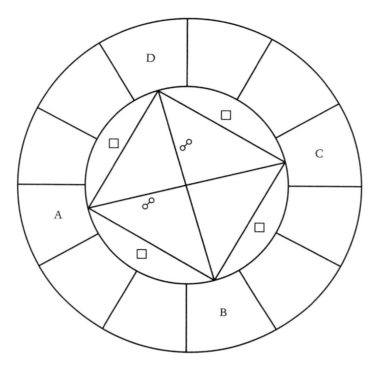

Figure 33. Grand Square

two planets in opposition is the *focal point* of the T-square, the outlet through which the opposition can be managed or resolved. For example, someone with Mercury opposition Mars probably has a temper and is prone to snap decisions. With the Moon as the planet square Mercury and Mars, the natural inclination would be to react at times with emotional outbursts and to make decisions based on erroneous intuitive feelings or peer pressure. A better use of the T-square would be to ask for and listen to other opinions and to direct this strong emotional energy into passionately constructive learning and leadership.

T-squares almost always occur in the same mode—cardinal, fixed, or mutable—but they can be dissociate, with one or more planets in the last degrees of one sign and one or more planets in the first degrees of the next sign. A *cardinal T-square* indicates impulsiveness, impatience, and drive. A *fixed T-square* is associated with endurance, determination, and stubbornness. A *mutable T-square* benefits the individual with flexibility, but it also encourages him or her to avoid obstacles rather than take action to resolve them.

A grand square, or grand cross, is formed by two oppositions and four squares, with the oppositions forming a cross (figure 33). As with the T-square, the planets in a grand square are usually, but not always, in the same mode. The grand square, which is an uncommon configuration, represents tension, obstacles, and turmoil and is difficult to handle. In fact, it's one of the toughest configurations. Challenges come

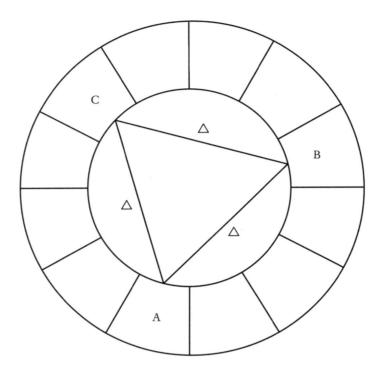

Figure 34. Grand Trine

in groups, one thing after another, as if you're the universe's main target. Then calm returns and life is easygoing. This pattern repeats over and over.

Resolution of the difficulties and challenges associated with the grand square is possible through the planet(s) that has the most trines and/or sextiles in aspect to it. (Use the same orb flexibility as with the stellium.) If one planet isn't within the allowable 8° orb to another planet in the grand square, then look for a third planet that's in aspect to both, such as planets at 2°, 5°, 10°, and 12° in the same mode. The 5° planet, which is within orb to the 10° and 12° planets, would pull in the energy of the 2° planet, forming an operative T-square. Also look at the order of the planets by degree (not sign)

and make a list of them from the lowest degree to the highest.

For example, suppose the four planets in the grand square are Mars at 14° Aries, Uranus at 11° Cancer, Neptune at 17° Libra, and Mercury at 20° Capricorn. You would list them in this order: Uranus, Mars, Neptune, Mercury. When the chain of events occurs, it often will begin with something sudden and unexpected (Uranus), after which you take impulsive action (Mars), then question your act or decision (Neptune), and finally resolve the matter through communication (Mercury). How much easier would it be if you were to change the order of your responses? That's very possible because the four planets work in tandem. You could follow up on the unexpected event (Uranus) with com-

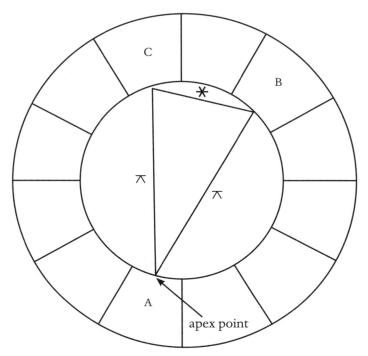

Figure 35. Yod

munication and fact-finding (Mercury), then develop an inspired and creative solution (Neptune), and, finally, take action (Mars).

A grand trine is three (or more) planets trine each other, forming a triangle or pyramid shape (figure 34). This configuration is fortunate and indicates areas where life goes smoothly, but it also can manifest as laziness and a tendency to take these areas for granted. The squares and oppositions that contact the planets in the grand trine are the way to make the most of this fortunate configuration. I think of a grand trine as a gerbil wheel that goes around and around and around, going absolutely nowhere. The goal is to jump off the wheel into the hard aspects in order to make forward progress.

A grand trine also can indicate specific talents or gifts and can help alleviate the stress associated with squares, oppositions, and some conjunctions. The planets in a grand trine are almost always in the same element—fire, earth, air, or water—but can be dissociate, as is also the case with the stellium and T-square. *Fire grand trines* represent creativity, leadership, and inspiration; *earth grand trines* indicate material prosperity; *air grand trines* strengthen the intellect; and *water grand trines* encourage compassion and indicate psychic ability.

A yod is formed by two inconjuncts and a sextile. Often referred to as the "Finger of God," the yod configuration is more easily managed than a single inconjunct. An example of a yod is a planet in Libra that is inconjunct one planet

MUTUAL RECEPTION

Mutual reception occurs when two planets in aspect are each in the sign that the other rules. For example, the Moon in Leo sextile the Sun in Cancer are in mutual reception because the Moon rules Cancer and the Sun rules Leo. Another example of planets in mutual reception is Jupiter in Virgo square Mercury in Sagittarius (because Jupiter rules Sagittarius and Mercury rules Virgo), or Mercury in Scorpio sextile Pluto in Virgo (because Mercury rules Virgo and Pluto rules Scorpio). Mutual reception can occur with any aspect, easy or hard.

Planets in mutual reception support each other, sort of trading their energy back and forth so each can draw on the other. This strengthens both planets and their influence in the chart. If the aspect is a square or opposition, then mutual reception eases the tension between the two planets so that they operate more like an easy aspect. As is true with other aspects, the closer the aspect, the stronger the influence.

Take special note of any planets in mutual reception, as well as their house placements, the houses they rule, and the aspects they make with other planets. Such planets usually have a major influence on the individual's life.

in Taurus and one in Pisces, with the planets in Taurus and Pisces sextile each other (figure 35). The sextile provides a way to handle the disharmony of the two inconjuncts. But remember that although a sextile represents opportunity, it is static energy that requires the individual to take action to reap the potential rewards.

In this example, the Libra planet is the *apex planet*, the one that is the key to resolving the tension and lack of ease of the two inconjuncts. With Taurus and Pisces sextile, there might be an opportunity to develop a practical yet creative talent; with the apex planet in Libra, the sign of relationships, another person will be instrumental in the individual developing the talent.

PLANETARY ASPECTS

On the following pages are descriptions of each planet in major aspect to every other planet and each of the four angles. Because of space limitations, the square and opposition are grouped together, as are the sextile and trine. Although the energies of the aspects are different, both easy aspects are similar, as are both hard aspects. The aspects are listed in astrological planetary order, beginning with the Sun.

You'll find the write-ups helpful as a starting point in your study of astrology, but they are by no means the equivalent of a full chart interpretation. The difficulty with these descriptions is that they represent the planetary and aspect energy in its purest form. This is seldom seen in an actual chart, where the planets are modified by sign and house placement and, most importantly, by aspects to other planets.

So, for example, while Sun trine Mars represents self-confidence and initiative, if the Sun is also square Saturn, then the individual will have less confidence and at times will hesitate to take action. But by blending both aspects through maturity and experience, and learning to work with the energy, the three planets can fuel the individual's drive and ambition. This person would benefit from goal setting and from pursuing activities and relationships that boost self-esteem.

Taking all these factors and conflicting energies into consideration is called astrological *synthesis*, which becomes easier and easier to do with practice. Start with your own chart and the planet or planets that have the most aspects. You'll discover that you express all the various energies at various times, depending on the situation. This will give you additional insights into your personality, your hot buttons, your skills, and your talents, and help you learn to emphasize the positive, minimize the negative, and use the hard aspects to maximize the energy represented by the easy aspects.

Sun Aspects

Sun Conjunct Moon

Even though you may not be an Aries, this aspect gives you an Aries influence because you were born around the time of the New Moon. This gives you extra energy, motivation, and drive, as well as a pioneering spirit. You approach life with enthusiasm, energy, and confidence, and you excel at new endeavors, which benefit from your initiative. But at times you're so self-absorbed and wrapped up in your own activities that you appear to be self-centered. Make it a point to include others, especially loved ones, who are very important to you.

Sun Conjunct Mercury

Although objectivity is limited, you have the initiative to act on ideas, to put plans in motion. Your thoughts are often ego-driven and your decisions based on what's best for you and you alone. That's great if you plan to live in a mountaintop cave, but not so good if you expect relationships to thrive. Your challenge is to see yourself as others do and to be considerate of their needs, wishes, and desires. At its best, this planetary energy adds determination to meet goals and an excellent mind, plus a talent for speaking or writing.

Sun Conjunct Venus

You're friendly, outgoing, and popular, with a love of life, romance, pleasure, and socializing. Charm, charisma, and an attractive appearance add to your people skills. Most people with this aspect feel incomplete without a partner, and dislike going anywhere and doing anything without other people. You have excellent earning potential, but you're also prone to extravagance, especially with those you love. Some people with this aspect are self-indulgent, vain, or lazy and expect the universe to grant their every wish.

Sun Conjunct Mars

Your high energy is matched by an equal level of drive, initiative, courage, and perseverance. Each of your goals is pursued with enthusiasm, although sometimes without consideration of potential consequences, which can be your downfall. A risk taker, you enjoy physical activity, which is an excellent way for you to release stress and tension; but be careful and be smart because you're also accident-prone. Aggression and a hair-trigger temper are possible with this aspect, and anger management training could be beneficial.

Sun Conjunct Jupiter

Optimistic and confident, you approach life with enthusiasm and high hopes. You attract abundance and good fortune, which could manifest as money, career success, and lucky breaks, and through business and personal relationships. But overoptimism can be a challenge when you take on more than you can reasonably handle. That's because you think big and do almost everything in a grand way. Teach yourself to scale back when it's to your advantage. Excesses, such as weight gain and extravagance, are possible.

Sun Conjunct Saturn

You're the epitome of responsibility (or should be, with this aspect), an ambitious hard worker who respects and values rules and procedures. Anything else more often than not results in repercussions, sometimes within minutes. You're the one who takes on all those extra jobs, including what coworkers and family members would rather avoid. That's positive if it advances your aims, but you really don't have to do everything yourself, despite what you may think. Frustration and setbacks are likely, yet with age and experience you learn to overcome them and also gain self-confidence.

Sun Conjunct Uranus

You're an independent free spirit who's unusual in some way, perhaps in terms of interests, career, or hobbies. Change and spontaneity stimulate you if they're your idea, but you're often resistant if others initiate the same. You have a magnetism that attracts others who value your insights and objectivity. You only appear to be unpredictable; you think things through, saying nothing, and act when the time is right. Intuition is strong. This is the aspect of the eccentric and the rebel, but also the consummate friend and networker.

Sun Conjunct Neptune

You're both inspired and inspirational, with a gift for motivating and encouraging others. Creative, intuitive, and visionary, you have a strong imagination and visual orientation. However, you can be impractical, idealistic, and unrealistic, and some people with this aspect tend toward escapism and self-deception (as well as drug or alcohol abuse). Overall, your physical energy may be low in comparison to others; the twenty-minute power nap was designed just for you. Learn to be cautious when you meet new people; not everyone is honest and ethical.

Sun Conjunct Pluto

You have the willpower and determination to accomplish almost anything. Others sense this intensity, your underlying strength and control, which can be a great source of comfort to those who need someone to lean on. You're also intuitive and relentless and a natural psychologist who understands what makes people tick. This aspect can indicate control issues, and some people with this combination are ruthless and power hungry. If you use this aspect positively, you can be a force for incredible personal and worldly change, and can rise to a powerful position of influence.

Sun Conjunct Ascendant

Confident and outgoing, you embrace life with a positive attitude and a strong belief in your abilities. You're ambitious and self-directed and strive for recognition and achievement. But at times you can be self-centered, interested only in your own agenda. Most people with this aspect are healthy, with strong recuperative powers. The more you develop your people skills, the further you'll go in life. Be especially aware of the traits you dislike in others; they may be your own.

Sun Conjunct Midheaven

Much of your energy is directed toward career achievement and attaining high honors, recognition, and status. A positive public image is likely, and fame is possible. However, some people with this aspect believe they deserve accolades without effort or pursue the wrong avenues for the wrong reasons. Career satisfaction is more than money and a place in the limelight. Follow your passion. Maximize your talents. Realistic expectations get you much further and bring the self-satisfaction you desire.

Sun Square/Opposition Moon

It's tough to find the emotional satisfaction you desire, mostly because you're self-critical. This in turn can block your creative energy and create relationship conflict. It can be difficult to connect emotionally with others unless you feel totally secure, which these aspects challenge you to do. Develop your self-esteem and learn to treat yourself with TLC. Everyone is human; no one is perfect, including you, so go easy on yourself. Childhood home life may have been dominated by parental discord, or you could have grown up in a single-parent household.

Sun Square/Opposition Mars

You can benefit from the high energy and initiative of this aspect if you channel it in positive, constructive directions. Otherwise, you encounter obstacles created through impulsiveness, aggression, anger, and argument. This, of course, only antagonizes other people, who could be valuable supporters in your personal and professional lives. Examine your motives when you find yourself reacting negatively. With careful thought, you'll discover a central issue to be resolved, possibly involving self-esteem and your view of authority figures.

Sun Square/Opposition Jupiter

You can be extravagant and excessively optimistic, betting (literally or figuratively) on what's to come. It's also possible that you have an unrealistic view of yourself and your abilities. Directed in constructive avenues, however, these aspects indicate success and achievement. Seek and listen to objective advice, and learn to temper your high hopes with common sense and reality. Wishes alone won't make something come true. For that you'll have to plan, work, and make your luck by following through on the opportunities that come your way.

Sun Square/Opposition Saturn

At times you probably feel that life is one obstacle after another. Facing each head-on, however, can bring well-deserved but hard-earned success because you're an extremely hard worker, sometimes to the point that others take advantage of you. By learning to work with others, rather than doing it all yourself, you can achieve far more and with less effort. You're reserved and conservative, and others may perceive you as shy or aloof. The opposition, especially, indicates potential conflict with superiors and other people who stand between you and your goals.

Sun Square/Opposition Uranus

You're a free spirit, an independent soul with a rebellious streak who believes rules were made for other, more conservative people. This philosophy and a lack of self-discipline can create problems with relationships, employment, and life in general. The solution is to channel your energy into constructive change within existing structures; for example, run for office rather than march on city hall, or be a leader and team player at work rather than organize a campaign to oust a supervisor. With the opposition, especially, relationships can begin and end suddenly.

Sun Square/Opposition Neptune

You're a dreamer who's prone to self-deception and being deceived by others. You look for the best in people and too often you see what you want to see, not what's really there. This can present challenges in relationships, as well as in personal, life, and career goals. Although life takes you in interesting directions, a lack of focus can have you wandering in circles. Learn to set clear, measurable goals. Also protect yourself with expert legal and financial advice, when necessary. Your major strengths include creativity and intuition, and you're sometimes secretive.

Sun Square/Opposition Pluto

You can be forceful, relentless, and demanding because of your drive to achieve personal power and success. Some people with these aspects may be ruthless in the face of obstacles and try to control everyone and every situation in their lives. If you're among them, sooner or later you'll learn the hard way that smiles, people skills, and knowledge better complement your quest for success. Used constructively, this is powerful energy that can be used for personal change and achievement in almost any area you desire. You have the willpower, self-control, and inner strength to maximize your potential and life success.

Sun Square/Opposition Ascendant

Relationships are a central focus in your life. Some are positive and some are negative, and the closest ones have a major influence on your personality and personal goals. You may need to assert your independence more freely or, conversely, learn to be less domineering in the lives of other people. The lessons here are cooperation and compromise. Once you master those, you'll have the ability to meet everyone's needs, including your own. If you have family issues that hold you back, strive to understand why. Until you do, they can affect business and personal relationships.

Sun Square/Opposition Midheaven

Time management is vital to handle this planetary energy, which challenges you to devote equal time to career and family life. Doing it all might seem, well, doable, and at times it is, but you can quickly stretch yourself too thin. Aim for balance even if that means occasionally scaling back your ambitions. A key factor is to ask those close to you for help and advice, when necessary, and to include your mate in decision making. Do the same in your career to promote positive relationships with coworkers and supervisors.

Sun Sextile/Trine Moon

You have the confidence and people skills to move through life with ease and also to achieve whatever you set out to do—if you invest your skills, talents, and effort. You could do well working with the public, and are well liked by friends and coworkers. Home life is upbeat and family relationships are positive. Your home and children are positive extensions of your ego, which is in sync with your emotions, at least in part because of a supportive and nurturing environment during your childhood.

Sun Sextile/Trine Mars

Dashing and daring, you're a leader who has the courage, confidence, and enthusiasm to forge new territory and generate plenty of support along the way. You're ambitious and self-motivated, but it's easy to forget that not everyone has your indomitable energy and stamina, so go easy on those around you as you push yourself to succeed. Most people with these aspects enjoy good health, physical strength and coordination, regular exercise, and competitive sports, as a participant or spectator.

Sun Sextile/Trine Jupiter

You were born lucky. But there's more to it than that. You also make your own luck by spotting and following up on opportunities. Confident and self-assured, you're honest and reliable and gain life benefits through education. The potential downside with this planetary energy, however, is that overoptimism can encourage you to take on more than you should. But this protective influence usually sees you through and helps you navigate difficulties. Overall good health and happiness usually accompany these aspects.

Sun Sextile/Trine Saturn

You're conservative, patient, and responsible and have the wisdom and ambition to steadily pursue and ultimately achieve any goal you set. These qualities are backed by personal commitment, determination, and hard work, all of which can lead to career and life success, recognition, and status. You have an excellent work ethic and really enjoy work and the satisfaction and pride that come from a job well done. Relationships with supervisors and other authority figures generally are favorable, and mentors can smooth your rise to higher positions.

Sun Sextile/Trine Uranus

You have a unique, indefinable magnetic aura that intrigues many. And that's your entrée into many situations where you can capitalize on your strengths and talents. Traditional yet a little eccentric in some way, you see things from a different perspective, and look for and find new and better ways to do most anything. That's your inventive nature, which benefits from your imagination, intuition, and originality. As a friend, you're among the best, loyal to those in your circle. Teamwork comes naturally.

Sun Sextile/Trine Neptune

You're intuitive—even psychic—and thus can sense what others are thinking and how events might unfold. But that also means you're receptive and can easily absorb energy—both positive and negative—from people and your environment. Your compassionate soft spot makes it tough to say no even when you know you should. Change that pattern. Give more weight to what's in your best interests, even if it's not what the other person desires. Be true to yourself. Spirituality and faith are strong themes in your life.

Sun Sextile/Trine Pluto

You're noted for your willpower and ability to tune out the world to concentrate on the matter at hand. At times you can be intense, which is the outward reflection of your inner strength and vitality. People sense these qualities in you and are drawn to them, looking to you for answers, solutions, and emotional support. One of your greatest strengths is the potential to be an outstanding leader who's influential in the career arena and community activities. Confidence and determination breed success.

Sun Sextile/Trine Ascendant

People rightly see the confidence, optimism, and enthusiasm you bring each day to your personal and professional relationships and goals. You're a people person with a knack for gaining supporters and help when you need it, and you're usually among the first to lend a hand when needed. Close relationships and partnerships (business and romantic) are fulfilling and generally favorable with this influence, and you have an easygoing way that puts others at ease and encourages them to back your endeavors.

Sun Sextile/Trine Midheaven

A happy home life and supportive family members give you the freedom to pursue your career interests and ambitions. Worldly success comes fairly easily, and you could be involved in a family business or achieve your career goals through the influence or networking contacts of a relative. As you work your way up the career ladder, confidence and talent bring you to the attention of decision makers. You're also popular with colleagues and supervisors; these relationships can pay off handsomely.

Moon Aspects

Moon Conjunct Mercury

An excellent memory gives you an advantage throughout life. You can, however, have difficulty separating facts from feelings and thus base decisions on emotion rather than what's logical and realistic. This can be a challenge if you let others sway your thinking one direction when you should head in another. You're also intuitive and receptive, but be cautious when in the presence of negative people because you can easily absorb their energy. Tension can trigger excessive talk, and at times you're overly sensitive to criticism.

Moon Conjunct Venus

You enjoy the company of other people, especially loved ones, and are emotionally involved with those closest to you. Partnership comes naturally to you, and you're known for your charm and social skills. But a strong mating desire can prompt you to commit your heart on impulse. Conflict may be difficult for you to handle. You're drawn to the finer things in life and have an eye for beauty, which can encourage extravagance and self-indulgence. Some people with this aspect are lazy, and others have artistic or musical talent.

Moon Conjunct Mars

People rarely mistake how you feel in any given situation. You're up-front with your emotions—intense at times, easygoing at others. This can be positive or negative: passion versus temper, courage versus recklessness, aggression versus assertiveness, love versus hate. Make it a policy to think before you speak and act, especially with those closest to you; it's tough, if not impossible, to retract what's said or done in a heated moment. Try to cultivate patience and tolerance, and emphasize logic rather than pure emotion.

Moon Conjunct Jupiter

Generous and good-natured, you go out of your way to help others and have strong emotional ties to home and family. But your big heart and concern for others can encourage you to be overly generous with people who don't truly appreciate your time and energy. Be selective; put you and yours first. You can do well working with the public because people usually take an instant liking to you. For you, emotional security is based in knowledge, education, and spiritual beliefs; the more you know, the more comfortable you feel.

Moon Conjunct Saturn

Whatever the reason—possibly because of family influences—it's difficult for you to freely express your emotions. Others may see you as aloof, and home life is (or was) dominated by rules and discipline with this aspect. At times you may feel lonely even when among people, and you could be prone to depression. A mentor, or being one for others, can change your life perspective. By developing safe, supportive, and nurturing relationships—and letting others into your life—you'll find yourself opening up more and, in turn, you'll feel your ambitions coming alive.

Moon Conjunct Uranus

No one, least of all you, can guess what your mood of the day might be. Your feelings are in continual flux, unpredictable and changeable, depending on current conditions. Intuitive and imaginative, you thrive on excitement and the unusual, but can suffer from nervous tension. Home life is likely to be extraordinary in some way, in terms of your physical space, relationships, or both. The best influence of this aspect is that you're often in the right place at the right time to seize opportunities.

Moon Conjunct Neptune

You're receptive, intuitive (possibly psychic), and sympathetic to the needs, moods, and feelings of others. Tears come easily to your sensitive soul. Inspired and inspirational, you usually see the best in people (even when undeserved) and gently encourage them to live up to their potential. Most people with this aspect are creative and imaginative. You undoubtedly are, even if you haven't yet discovered this side of yourself. Explore the possibilities. You may have a talent for photography, art, graphic design, or dancing.

Moon Conjunct Pluto

Your emotions are intense and your will strong, and you often make your presence known wherever you go. This aspect can indicate a tendency to engage in subtle emotional manipulation, consciously or subconsciously, to maintain control; some people with this combination are overbearing and even pompous, expecting others to listen with rapt attention as they pontificate. You initiate sweeping changes at times, especially in your home life, and you may be psychic. The most positive use of this powerful energy is to influence public opinion and policy. You can do this one-on-one with friends, through organizations, or on a community or national scale.

Moon Conjunct Ascendant

You're approachable, warm, and responsive to others and their needs. Highly impressionable and receptive, you sense how others feel and pick up the subtle vibrations in your environment. You're also moody and sensitive, and your feelings are easily hurt. It's important to you to be well liked and accepted by your peers, but try not to let that influence your decisions. It's far more important to honor your values and ethics and to do what's right for you, even if that means you're temporarily not a part of the crowd.

Moon Conjunct Midheaven

You might be drawn to a career that involves working with the public, such as in government, retail, or a service industry. What gives you the edge over others career-wise is your sixth sense about trends, fads, and public opinion. You feel secure when all is well with your career life, your status is on the rise, and your stellar reputation is intact. Many fifteen minutes of fame are likely with this aspect, but career fortunes fluctuate and you can expect major changes about every seven years. Be proactive; initiate change before others do it for you.

Moon Square/Opposition Mercury

Concentration can be difficult at times because your mind wanders and thoughts are strongly influenced by your mood of the moment. You also have a tendency to second-guess yourself and play the "what-if" game. With the opposition, especially, fluctuating emotions can add stress to relationships because your partner never knows quite what to expect from you. You also have a mind that responds well to positive self-talk. Learn to replace negative thoughts with uplifting ones, and make it a policy to focus on the positive. Give meditation a try.

Moon Square/Opposition Venus

Your family and romantic relationships ebb and flow, with frequent ups and downs as needs and desires conflict. So these aspects are all about blending your wishes with those of others and striving for compromise. It doesn't take much for you to feel neglected or rejected, whether that's perception or reality. Spending is another challenge associated with these aspects. If you shop to feel better, to lift your mood, then take practical steps to break this habit. Otherwise, extravagance and debt could undermine financial security.

Moon Square/Opposition Mars

This aspect can indicate a hair-trigger temper and emotional outbursts sparked by what in reality are inconsequential events or comments. Yet each touches a nerve that's very real to you, if not to others. Conversely, you might internalize your anger, letting it build into resentment. Either way, impulsive reactions can create obstacles to life and relationship success. Used constructively, this aspect indicates positive energy and passion for life, love, and personal and professional success. Find the stress reliever that works for you and incorporate it into your daily life.

Moon Square/Opposition Jupiter

There's nothing subtle about your emotional expression. No one around you can mistake exactly how you feel, whether you're upbeat and excited or feeling low. You're overly sympathetic and generous, which are fine qualities in and of themselves, but you're also prone to "hard luck" stories. Some people are deserving of your kindness and concern, but many are not. Learn to be selective, and question any deal (or person) that sounds too good to be true. Chances are it is, and you'll soon regret the decision.

Moon Square/Opposition Saturn

You're prone to negative thinking and depression, possibly because you lack the confidence to pursue and realize your dreams. This can lead to a tendency to give up and accept life as

a permanent obstacle with all the accompanying burdens. When you replace pessimism with optimism through positive self-talk, this aspect becomes a major motivator, an indicator of unmatched, relentless ambition and the incentive to achieve all that you desire and deserve. Your relationship with your mother might be chilly or based on responsibility, or she could be a soul mate who pushes you to succeed.

Moon Square/Opposition Uranus

For you, life is perpetual motion. Your need for an almost constant supply of change, stimulation, and excitement is the outward manifestation of your restless and high-strung nature. Of course, this makes it difficult to focus on one major interest at a time, which can be your downfall. Search for and find your one true passion (okay, maybe two or three) to truly maximize your many talents. Change also extends to relationships, including friendships, all of which are prone to sudden beginnings and endings.

Moon Square/Opposition Neptune

You can get lost in daydreams and fantasies as a way to protect your sensitive soul and to weather the ups and downs of relationships. Unfortunately, some people with this influence resort to substance abuse as an escape mechanism. Sure, it might be easier to live in a world of illusion, isolating your emotions from reality and the inevitable hurts that result when humans interact, but that's both impractical and unproductive. Accept that life and people are what they are, and direct this energy into nurturing your creativity and intuition.

Moon Square/Opposition Pluto

You're emotionally intense, with a powerful desire to be in charge and in control. This can be a real plus when directed toward yourself and your ambitions. The outward manifestation, however, may not be so positive. When others are involved, a tendency to dominate, to be in control, can emerge, because you dislike being confined by someone else's rules, desires, or authority. (This aspect can be associated with emotional or physical abuse, given or received.) Look to your childhood and early family environment for the root cause and then address the issues.

Moon Square/Opposition Ascendant

You have strong feelings about loved ones and others who are close to you. All of these relationships are part of your identify and affect your mood of the day. You usually express your emotions with passion and intensity—sometimes too much so. But there are some topics you prefer to avoid, and others are perplexed when you suddenly cut talk short. This is a self-defense mechanism, the way you protect your feelings. You also should guard against a tendency to subtly manipulate others as a way to establish control.

Moon Square/Opposition Midheaven

You have a tough time handling career and domestic conflict, and sometimes the more you try to keep the peace, the more stressful situations become. Try not to let things get to that point, because career stress can affect family life and vice versa. You'll find these situations easier to deal with if you learn conflict-resolution skills and emphasize open communication,

cooperation, understanding, and support. Let others know how you feel, and ask them to do the same. All this will help stabilize your career and personal life.

Moon Sextile/Trine Mercury

You're comfortable expressing your thoughts, feelings, and emotions, and an active sixth sense gives you the ability to tailor your comments to specific people and situations. That, of course, enhances your terrific people skills. Learning is generally easy for you, partly because of your excellent memory, and you're curious and interested, up on the latest news—and gossip. If there's news to be known, you're usually the best source. Family communication is upbeat, and you have strong ties with relatives.

Moon Sextile/Trine Venus

You're kind, thoughtful, and considerate of others and have a knack for putting people at ease. Noted for your charm, good taste, and social skills, you also attract material abundance. But extravagance and a love of luxury can lead to debt if you're not careful with easy credit. You're a natural when it comes to romance and attract admirers at every turn before settling in to what you expect to be a lifetime commitment. You may have artistic or acting talent or an interest in the arts. But laziness and self-indulgence are potential weaknesses.

Moon Sextile/Trine Mars

Passionate ambition and imagination are yours, along with the determination and persistence to achieve whatever you set out to do. That's easily accomplished if you back it up with a solid plan and then focus your energy. As an involved participant in life, you benefit from initiative, assertiveness, and a talent for energizing and motivating others. Your enthusiasm is contagious, and you can generate a lot of excitement with your words and actions. Family life is active, and you could benefit financially from an inheritance. Athletic talent is possible.

Moon Sextile/Trine Jupiter

You're lucky to have one of these fortunate aspects, which provide a protective influence. Good fortune surrounds you, and you usually come out on top, avoiding many of life's obstacles. This is partly because of your upbeat, optimistic attitude and your rarely wavering faith in yourself and the universe. Highly principled, you support good causes and enjoy warm and loving family relationships. Material abundance, including an inheritance, is likely, as wealth flows in your direction. Even so, remember that much of it has to be earned!

Moon Sextile/Trine Saturn

Practical and realistic, you have a strong sense of responsibility that complements your excellent planning and organizational abilities and business sense. Logic and common sense appeal to you, which is great, but there are times when you let both rule your emotions. Gut feelings and spontaneity can be just as valid; give this approach a try. Although you're less demonstrative in expressing your feelings, you open up more with people you know well and those you love. Make that a habit. Even though your security is based on material success, others need the human touch.

Moon Sextile/Trine Uranus

Boredom is never an issue for you. When life becomes mundane, you do or say something unpredictable just to keep things lively. That's part of your charm and your unique individuality that's a magnet for many. A consummate networker, you also have a wide circle of friends and acquaintances and delight in putting people in touch with each other. In any group situation you can be both a team player and a leader who inspires others to use their imagination just as you do. You also have a knack for spotting future trends.

Moon Sextile/Trine Neptune

You have great faith in yourself and the universe, and a spiritual depth that encourages you to believe that everything eventually will work out for the good. That's usually true for you, even if the end result is not immediately apparent. But you also can be naive in your compassion and caring for others; at times you give far more than you should and then wonder why others don't appreciate your efforts. Take heart. Good works earn rewards. You're also imaginative, intuitive, creative, and highly receptive to your environment.

Moon Sextile/Trine Pluto

You have a natural talent for psychology and an underlying emotional strength that encourages others to lean on you. This personal power, combined with intuition and a natural understanding of people, is an asset in any leadership position, as well as in family affairs and relationships. Anything to which you commit your passion and determination usually succeeds, although success comes so easily that you can coast along when you should give it your all. You also could benefit from a family inheritance.

Moon Sextile/Trine Ascendant

You have a wonderful way with people and a talent for putting them at ease. No small part of this is your sixth sense, which also helps you to adapt to any situation and environment. This is true of every relationship in your life—business, personal, romantic, and family. But there are times when you go along with the crowd rather than take a stand because it's important to you to be well liked and to fit in with your peers and colleagues. You're also sensitive to the needs of others and respond with a helpful, caring attitude.

Moon Sextile/Trine Midheaven

Career success comes easily if you put forth even modest effort. Go all out and you could earn a top position as well as significant recognition. Part of your success formula is your ability to establish and maintain positive, productive relationships with coworkers, superiors, career contacts, and the public. These aspects favor an upbeat home and family life and close ties with relatives and parents, who encourage you to explore and develop your talents.

Mercury Aspects

Mercury Conjunct Venus

With your excellent communication and conversation skills, you could become an outstanding speaker or writer. Friendly, popular, and sociable, your words are charming and tactful, and you can talk almost anyone into almost anything with your innate sales ability. You're also a natural diplomat who excels at smoothing

things over, initiating compromise, and helping others reach consensus. Ever the flirt, no matter your age, you also might be a bit vain and put pleasure ahead of work.

Mercury Conjunct Mars

You have a quick mind, but also a quick temper. Decisiveness is a plus; snap decisions are not when careful thought would serve you better. Plain talk is your style, but tact often will get you much further; add the fluff and precede negatives with positives. The best of this influence can make you an excellent debater and public speaker. Learning brings out your competitive side, and you're fortunate to be a quick study who absorbs information faster than most. Mental challenges, such as games, appeal to you.

Mercury Conjunct Jupiter

You have excellent reasoning ability along with a talent for grasping facts as well as concepts. You're probably an outstanding student who learns easily and knows the value of higher education. You might be a perpetual student, earning advanced degrees, or an outstanding teacher. Knowledge satisfies your curiosity, as do travel and other cultures. Your ideas are big picture, even visionary, but not necessarily practical, so study all the pros and cons before moving forward with important life decisions.

Mercury Conjunct Saturn

Your mind is undoubtedly the envy of many. Besides being a logical, practical thinker, you have a disciplined mind and a talent for planning and organization. Hard work furthers your ambitions, and you're willing to do whatever it takes to achieve success. Your powers of concentration are exceptional, and what you learn, you learn thoroughly and completely. Chitchat is not for you. This aspect can indicate pessimistic thinking and worry, but with your fine mind, you can train yourself to emphasize the positive.

Mercury Conjunct Uranus

People marvel at your quick mind, which sparks original and progressive ideas because you're an innovative, future-oriented thinker. Accepting things at face value is not your style; you need proof and all the facts. Your communication style is unique in some way—phrasing, presentation, word choice—and designed to stir the pot, all of which fascinates listeners. But concentration can be a challenge for your restless, curious mind, so find what works to help you focus, such as music or an ergonomic chair.

Mercury Conjunct Neptune

Where other people think mostly in words, you think in pictures. That's your fertile imagination and creativity at work. You're naturally intuitive, with an active sixth sense, and you may have talent in the visual arts or creative writing. But difficulties can arise in decision making, with contracts, and with the practical details of daily life. Always read the fine print and, if in doubt, consult an expert in order to protect you and yours and your resources. Dreams can be prophetic. Some people with this aspect are deceptive or easily deceived.

Mercury Conjunct Pluto

You have the mind of a detective—shrewd, intense, suspicious, and penetrating. Few can match your ability to keep a secret, of which you know many, gathering information that might be to your advantage someday; it usually is. You're an excellent strategist and researcher who can outthink and outwit adversaries and competitors, often before they even realize your considerable mental strength. But this aspect is also noted for manipulation, whether subtle or overt, either by you or those around you.

Mercury Conjunct Ascendant

You're a talker, a writer, a thinker, a communicator. Logic, thought, curiosity, and a perpetual quest for information and news guide your life. But restlessness can make it tough to focus your energy both on a daily basis and in meeting goals. Organization can be helpful here, as can list making. Nervous tension can be an issue, so find the best stress outlet for you—exercise, gaming, reading, gardening, puzzles, or another hobby. Your car may be your second home, and both car and home are equipped with the latest gadgets and technological wonders.

Mercury Conjunct Midheaven

Your thoughts, ideas, and life plans center around career ambitions and making your mark on the world. Communication plays an important role in your career and can be the make-it-or-break-it factor. Polish your speaking, presentation, and writing skills until you're among the best. Also get the education you need to pursue your dreams; without it you're unlikely to go as far and to maximize your potential. Many people with this aspect pursue a career in the communications field, and others are professional public speakers.

Mercury Square/Opposition Mars

Snap decisions and impulsive actions can undermine even your best efforts, as can impatience and a short temper. You'll get further in life if you learn to think before you speak and act, and take the time to weigh the pros and cons before making important life decisions. Also remember that people respond more favorably to tactful requests; no one likes to be pushed, least of all you, so you can easily imagine how this would make others feel. Put your quick mind to work for yourself in positive endeavors.

Mercury Square/Opposition Jupiter

You're an optimist who views life from the bright side, ever ready to snap up an opportunity. But at times you go overboard and promise more than you can deliver. Take time to look at the downside as well as the upside. Before dashing blindly into a new endeavor, consider potential stumbling blocks that could sidetrack you. Although the big picture is your comfort zone, the practical details are also necessary to success. Some people with this influence talk too much and have a tendency to exaggerate, boast, and tell all, even secrets.

Mercury Square/Opposition Saturn

Tradition is important to you, and your thoughts tend to be conservative, cautious, and conventional. You prefer the known to the unknown and find it difficult to break with established routines. Although you lack confidence in your brain power, possibly because of early learning experiences, most people with any Mercury-Saturn aspect are highly intelligent. If you have yet to discover this side of yourself, develop the learning and communication skills you need to succeed in life. Also emphasize positive thinking and face challenges and worries head-on.

Mercury Square/Opposition Uranus

You often take the opposite view in discussion and debate just to exert your individuality and independence. Stirring the pot excites you, and you enjoy seeing people's reactions. But your ideas are also a valid expression of your intelligent, inventive mind, even if some are impractical or ahead of their time. That can make it tough for others to follow your lead. The trick here is to deliver your message in terms that others can accept; reference the past and present. Your quick mind is prone to snap decisions, which can backfire; think things through.

Mercury Square/Opposition Neptune

Yours is a creative mind, not a focused and logical one. This is terrific for an active imagination and brilliant ideas, but it can be tough to deal with life's practical realities. This aspect encourages blind faith, so be cautious about what and whom you believe. Others may try to take advantage of your good nature or even try to deceive you. Indecisive at times, you can be absentminded and forgetful. You dislike pointed questions and can be artfully evasive when you choose to be. That's a distinct talent in some situations.

Mercury Square/Opposition Pluto

You reveal little about what you know, and keep your thoughts, plans, and ideas to yourself. You're wary and watchful, suspicious until you have all the facts, and have a deep and penetrating mind. All of this is excellent for research and amassing information, and you could excel in an investigative career. But these traits can be detrimental to relationships, where open communication is vital. Once set, you rarely change your mind, even when new information becomes available. Some people with this aspect are vengeful and manipulative.

Mercury Square/Opposition Ascendant

You may lack confidence in your speaking or writing ability or simply prefer to keep private matters private. Either way, lack of communication can interfere with and limit success in business and personal relationships. Yet you have a powerful mind with a depth of understanding and insight about the world and people that few can match. Learn to more freely express yourself and your ideas and opinions, and increase your comfort zone of trust with those who are deserving of it.

Mercury Square/Opposition Midheaven

Communication can be a stumbling block in family and/or career relationships. Take an objective look at your written and verbal skills and make improvements where necessary as an investment in yourself. With practice and polish, you could become a successful public speaker or attain a well-respected position in the communications field. Also emphasize open communication with supervisors and loved ones—even if they don't do the same. At least you'll be doing the right thing, which will pay off in the future.

Mercury Sextile/Trine Mars

Much of your energy is directed into intellectual pursuits. You enjoy challenges, puzzles, and mentally competitive games, and may be an outstanding writer or charismatic speaker. You

quickly grasp information and can size up situations in a flash, which also makes you an active, quick, lifelong learner. These aspects indicate excellent hand-eye coordination and athletic ability, which you probably take for granted. Make the most of these talents.

Mercury Sextile/Trine Jupiter

You're wise beyond your years, intelligent, open-minded, and a seeker of knowledge. Noted for your honesty, integrity, and sense of humor, you're popular within your social and career circles. Almost any topic grabs your interest, and you enjoy discussing everything from the latest news to philosophical concepts. Most people with this aspect learn easily and pursue higher education. If you haven't yet fully discovered this side of yourself, you should, because education can boost your life success potential. You also might excel in teaching, publishing, or the communications field.

Mercury Sextile/Trine Saturn

Your outstanding memory and practical, logical, intelligent mind are two of your best life assets. You can plan and organize anything, which you do on a daily basis for yourself and your family—sometimes to their distraction. Few can match your mental discipline, powers of concentration, and attention to detail, all of which can make you a top student, and you approach decision making with a realistic, commonsense attitude. Your excellent manual dexterity makes working with your hands a pleasure.

Mercury Sextile/Trine Uranus

You're a quick study, witty, intelligent, and intuitive, attuned to trends and the future. All this means you think outside the norm and form your own opinions rather than always go with the crowd. You see things from a different perspective and reach valid conclusions that at times amaze others. That's because innovative ideas are your specialty, and you might even have the talent to be an inventor. Technology intrigues you, and you're usually among the first to have the latest gadgets. You could do well in a high-tech career.

Mercury Sextile/Trine Neptune

A master of persuasion, you immediately sense what others need and want. This, of course, gives you a talent for subtly influencing others with all the right words, and they often think your ideas are their own. Creativity is a strength, and you may have a talent for writing, poetry, music, art, dancing, or writing. You're also intuitive, possibly even psychic, and thus benefit from insights into human nature as well as practical matters involving your career and everyday life. Many people with these aspects have a strong spiritual connection to the universe.

Mercury Sextile/Trine Pluto

You have a shrewd mind and the ability to delve deep into and master any subject that interests you. This powerful mental energy also gives you the ability to program your thinking in any way you choose, and the determination to commit and follow through on any goal you set. Mysteries intrigue you, and you could have a talent for writing, research, or public speaking. It's also easy for you to subtly maneuver, and sometimes manipulate, people and situations to fit your needs.

Mercury Sextile/Trine Ascendant

People listen to what you say and look to you for information and ideas. You have the potential to be an excellent writer, speaker, or both, and should develop these talents in order to maximize your ability to influence others, both one-on-one and in your career and community. You're also an excellent networker, with all the finesse and social skills to fit into almost any situation. The communication emphasis extends to personal relationships, where you place a high priority on an open and lively exchange of ideas.

Mercury Sextile/Trine Midheaven

Communication skills and networking are key factors in career success. At least as important, and maybe more so, is education. With all three in place and your best effort, you can achieve your worldly goals. You understand the importance of developing strong ties with supervisors and keeping them in the loop. In turn, they listen to your observations and suggestions, and adopt many of them. Your family life is lively, with an emphasis on the free expression of ideas, an extensive library, and up-to-date communication technology.

Venus Aspects
Venus Conjunct Mars

You have a passionate personality, especially when it comes to love, romance, and money. Moneymaking endeavors can be lucrative if you stick with them, but the temptation to move on to something new—job, career, or entrepreneurial venture—is an ever-present challenge. If you stick with one main endeavor, your finances will reflect the effort. But you're also a spender, often buying on impulse, which quickly can put finances in the red. Learn to live within your means and within a budget. And be sure love is the real thing before you commit.

Venus Conjunct Jupiter

You attract material abundance and share it generously with loved ones, friends, and good causes. Well liked by those in your circle, you have an active social life, many leisure-time interests, and an active and happy love life. You may become involved in the arts, as a performer, supporter, or volunteer. Although your earning power is well above average, at times you spend to excess, especially for quality clothing, home furnishings and décor, and jewelry. Some people with this aspect are lazy and extravagant, both of which are a poor use of this lucky influence.

Venus Conjunct Saturn

You're an excellent money manager who's thrifty and saves and invests for the long term. Highest earnings come later in life, when you also could receive a family legacy. But it's also easy to slip into austerity thinking, and some people with this aspect are stingy and even miserly. You take romantic relationships seriously and expect a commitment to last a lifetime, although you probably find it difficult to express your feelings, at least until you feel totally secure in a relationship. Talent in the arts or music is possible, and social status is important to you.

Venus Conjunct Uranus

You crave excitement in social and romantic relationships, and endings are often as sudden as attractions. A magnet for unusual people (you wouldn't have it any other way), you could profit financially through friends, networking, and groups. Income and spending habits may be erratic, although you also luck into sudden windfalls; with this aspect, finances are often way up or way down. A strong independent streak prompts some people with this aspect to remain single. But even if you find your soul mate, you insist on a certain level of independence.

Venus Conjunct Neptune

You're a true romantic, idealistic about love, devoted and sensitive to your partner's needs and wishes. But this also opens you up to disillusionment in all but the very best relationships, which have a deep spiritual connection. You have a magical, mystical aura that attracts many and may be a gifted artist, dancer, or creative writer. Finances require care, as you can be impractical in money matters. So be cautious about whom you trust, especially when love is involved, and deal only with the most reputable of financial institutions.

Venus Conjunct Pluto

You have a subtle yet powerful magnetic aura that attracts admirers and money. Love can be all-consuming, and jealousy and possessiveness are probably an issue. Learn to trust, and build self-esteem through your own activities and career endeavors. Wealth is within your lifetime reach, but overconfidence can lead to financial reversals. Manage funds wisely and with all the financial shrewdness you possess. This aspect also indicates the potential for power plays involving family funds with your partner or a relative.

Venus Conjunct Ascendant

You're charming and gracious, warm and friendly—a true people person who instantly puts others at ease. This makes you popular with your peers and well liked by almost everyone. The potential downside, however, is that you can be a people pleaser, going along with the crowd just to fit in; you shy away from conflict even when it's a necessary part of life. Partnership is important to you, and you feel complete only when with a mate; rarely do you go anywhere alone. Many people with this aspect are physically attractive and rarely leave the house without looking their best. Carried to the extreme, vanity and laziness become a challenge.

Venus Conjunct Midheaven

Born with this enviable career placement, you can start and stay a step ahead of many as you rise through the ranks. Just don't rely totally on your popularity and people skills; it takes effort, too, in order to maximize your potential. Relationships are a key component of success, so network and get to know decision makers who can help advance your aims. Status is equally important to you, and some people with this aspect are obvious social climbers. Others form partnerships based almost solely on money and community standing.

Venus Square/Opposition Mars

You do almost nothing halfway. You either go all out or don't bother. That's the passionate nature of this planetary influence, which also indicates a temper with a short fuse. This, of course, increases the potential for relationship conflict in a highly charged atmosphere. Finances can be an issue if you give in to extravagance and impulse spending. Yet you can just as easily channel this dynamic energy into constructive moneymaking activities and, possibly, entrepreneurial success. Learn to think before you act and speak.

Venus Square/Opposition Jupiter

You're charming and affectionate and enjoy an active social life. But some people with these aspects are vain and extravagant, indulging in life's pleasures and luxuries with little regard for the possible consequences. With hard work and wise decisions, however, this potentially fortunate planetary energy can significantly increase your earning potential and net worth. In business and personal relationships, you may be drawn to those who can enhance your financial picture and status, as well as those who are exceptionally attractive. Look beyond the packaging.

Venus Square/Opposition Saturn

Although you may lack social and romantic opportunities in your younger years, this is likely to change as you mature. It's as much about gaining confidence in yourself as it is about gaining the people skills that will make you more comfortable interacting with others. Finances take a similar path, with the potential for higher earnings later in life. Both, of course, depend on your mindset and willingness to welcome love and money into your life. More than most people, you reap what you truly believe you deserve. A business or romantic partner may be a soul mate, and you could delay commitment or unite with someone older.

Venus Square/Opposition Uranus

You're attracted by the thrill of new love and the excitement of romance. Long-term commitment is thus at odds with your independent nature, which can prompt you to leap from one relationship to the next. These planetary alignments are known as "divorce aspects," but you can choose a different outcome by keeping the spontaneity and freshness of new love alive. Money is in a similar category; income and spending are erratic, and some people with this energy take unwise financial risks and invest in impractical moneymaking ideas.

Venus Square/Opposition Neptune

You have a deep reservoir of creative energy, and using it is a positive outlet for either of these aspects. Think beyond art and music to crafts, photography, and graphic design (and others), any of which might be your talent. In relationships, you're idealistic and susceptible to charm; you see what you want to see and ignore the faults—until your vision eventually clears. Financially, you can be impractical and unrealistic and thus prone to deception. Always read the fine print, ask questions, and check credentials. Some people with this influence have secret love affairs.

Venus Square/Opposition Pluto

Both business and personal relationships are prone to power struggles, as either you or the other person, or both of you, attempts to control finances and each other. Manipulation can be subtle or overt, and jealousy can be an issue. (In some instances this aspect indicates physical, emotional, or mental abuse, or romantic ties with people who are unavailable, such as those who already are committed.) Yet when this energy is used constructively and cooperatively in tandem with a partner, you can realize the potential for financial security and deep, loving ties.

Venus Square/Opposition Ascendant-Descendant

You may be ultrasensitive and lack confidence in romantic and business partnerships, at least until you gain life experience and have a chance to develop your interpersonal skills. Do that and you will put luck on your side. Take your time before committing to a partnership; if you jump in, you could realize too late that what seemed like a good match needs significant work to survive. Money matters can be a source of conflict if your financial attitudes differ; compromise, honesty, and written goals are the best solution.

Venus Square/Opposition Midheaven-IC

Take charge and take action if at times you feel like you're on the outside looking in, careerwise. Your chances for success increase dramatically if you network and develop positive relationships with coworkers and superiors, in addition to having the right skills, education, and experience. Family ties benefit from a similar level of time and attention; here, too, the more you give of yourself, the more you're likely to receive in return. But also take care not to become a total people pleaser who goes along with the crowd just to fit in.

Venus Sextile/Trine Mars

You usually surround yourself with all the right people, which is a plus for business and romantic partnerships. Both are likely to be personally and financially profitable, and you enjoy an active, fun-filled social life with many friends. Your earning potential is among the best, but you're also a spender and can be extravagant just to satisfy the urge to splurge; what you want, you want now. Switch your focus to a long-term view, including investments, retirement, and savings for unexpected expenses. Do that and you can build significant assets in your lifetime. You also might benefit from an inheritance.

Venus Sextile/Trine Jupiter

You attract money, good fortune, and lucky breaks that can prompt a life of leisure or one of high achievement. The choice is yours whether to be lazy or productive, to fulfill your potential in the fast lane or to be content with letting life coast along. Partnerships (business and personal) are for the most part easygoing and upbeat and have the potential to increase your lifetime net worth. Education also can boost your earning potential. Most people with these aspects support good causes, both financially and as volunteers.

Venus Sextile/Trine Saturn

You take commitments seriously and readily contribute and accept your share of the responsibility to ensure business and relationship success. A loyal friend and partner, you form long-lasting ties with ease, and attract people whose knowledge and experience benefit your own, as well as those who can advance your career. You're thrifty and practical in money matters, living within a budget and saving a percentage of your earnings. A family inheritance is pos-sible, coming later in life to benefit your retirement years.

Venus Sextile/Trine Uranus

You have a unique, magnetic aura that attracts admirers, friends, and business contacts. Many of these people are as lively and interesting as you are and probably unusual in some way. They're also your lucky charms, and chance encounters can bring unexpected opportunities. You see commitment not as a threat to your independence but as a complement to your individuality. Money matters are generally favorable, with the bonus of periodic windfalls and contest wins.

Venus Sextile/Trine Neptune

You have an irresistible, alluring, and indefinable charm that makes you a magnet for romance. That's fine with you, because love and part-nership bring happiness and a good chance for financial security. You have a talent for inspir-ing others and have a spiritual connection with those closest to you. Although money matters aren't your strength, you usually attract what you need—an unexpected expense is offset by an unexpected gain. You're creative and might express that energy through art, music, danc-ing, or theater.

Venus Sextile/Trine Pluto

You form close ties with a select few, and your romantic partnerships are deep and intensely emotional, with a strong and usually unbreak-able commitment. You and your partner fuel each other's drive and determination and prob-ably have a powerful psychic connection. These aspects favor wealth because of your financial savvy and the potential for a sizable inheritance, both of which you generously share with friends, loved ones, and those in need. You understand the principle that when money circulates, it returns to you many times over.

Venus Sextile/Trine Ascendant-Descendant

You're easygoing, fun-loving, and likable, and enjoy a wide circle of friends and an active social life. Relationships are congenial and upbeat, and romantic ties close and loving, with each of you enhancing the other's skills, talents, and overall life success. You could benefit financially through a business partner or committed relationship. Most people with these aspects are attractive, dress well, and use their easygoing people skills to advantage in personal and business endeavors. Whom you know is sometimes more important than what you know.

Venus Sextile/Trine Midheaven-IC

Worldly success is almost yours for the asking if you put forth the effort. Direct your energies toward career gains, tap into your natural good fortune, and see how high you can go by giving it your all. You gain many supporters in your life journey, many of whom contribute to your success, and you could benefit from family connections. Domestic life is pleasant, with solid, loving relationships, and your goal is a comfortable, beautifully decorated home that also reflects your status and material achievements.

Mars Aspects

Mars Conjunct Jupiter

High energy, ambition, enthusiasm, optimism, and an adventurous spirit fuel your desire for success, so you achieve your goals more often than not. You're a go-getter and a risk taker and could succeed as an entrepreneur, but impatience and recklessness can trigger setbacks. Teach yourself to pause and think things through, weighing the pros and cons, before you act. And don't hesitate to get another opinion when necessary. Physical activity agrees with you, and some people with this aspect are outstanding amateur or professional athletes.

Mars Conjunct Saturn

You're an exceptionally hard worker who has the added advantages of endurance, discipline, and the determination to meet every goal you set for yourself. However, you're likely to react with frustration when obstacles block progress and your initiative and momentum are stalled. This can prompt rash actions you'll later regret and that could have a negative impact on your career and personal ambitions. Physical activity is an excellent outlet during these times, a way to direct your need for action in a positive and healthy direction.

Mars Conjunct Uranus

Given the slightest opportunity, you initiate sudden, sweeping change, both to counteract boredom and because you delight in stirring the pot. But you give little thought to the outcome before you act, so some initiatives work out and some don't, depending on the luck of the day. With even a little forethought, however, you can increase your success quotient. Teach yourself to think before you act in important matters, and find other outlets to satisfy your rebellious, independent soul that won't tempt fate and your accident-prone nature.

Mars Conjunct Neptune

You have a subtle allure that's indefinable and immensely intriguing. It draws people to you and gives you the persuasive edge in almost any situation. But at times you find it difficult to define exactly what you desire, to zero in on goals and take definitive action. You prefer indirect to direct action, which isn't always the best choice because you can miss out on opportunities and leave people wondering where you stand. You have a spiritual nature and intuitive or psychic ability, and could be a natural healer.

Mars Conjunct Pluto

Your drive, ambition, and willpower are in a class of their own, and you have a powerful and lasting influence wherever you focus your energies. Bold and relentless, you have a magnetic personality that attracts followers for you to lead. But you need to guard against a tendency to take control in every situation; sometimes it's better to sit back and let others have their moment in the sun. You also have exceptional physical stamina. Some people with this aspect are dictatorial and use intimidation or force to achieve their goals.

Mars Conjunct Ascendant/Opposition Descendant

You make your presence known wherever you go, arriving with a burst of energy that attracts a lot of interest both socially and professionally. Competitive and outgoing, you're a leader who immediately jumps in and takes charge. Try not to push others, though; tact and diplomacy will get you further. You plan as you go and prefer action to organization, but impulsiveness can land you in a tight spot. Learn to consider consequences before you act. You're also impatient and at times reckless, which increases the potential for accidents.

Mars Conjunct Midheaven/Opposition IC

You're driven to succeed, focusing much of your energy on career ambitions and the rise to a prominent position. Your zeal, however, can put you at odds with superiors who've earned their way up over time and expect you to do the same. Long work hours can result in domestic difficulties, so aim for a balanced lifestyle with time for loved ones as well as your worldly ambitions. You might have a desire for self-employment or an aptitude for entrepreneurial ventures. Plan carefully before you make the leap to increase your odds for success.

Mars Square/Opposition Jupiter

Enthusiasm and optimism are your strengths but also your weaknesses. At times you jump in without regard to consequences, and also can overestimate your ability to complete a project on time, meet a physical challenge, or generate income to cover an extravagance. Learn to think and plan before you act; replace reckless, impulsive actions with productive ones that will result in financial, career, and personal gains throughout your lifetime. Follow a similar path in matters of the heart. Leap only after you're sure; true love will wait.

Mars Square/Opposition Saturn

Your challenge is to develop greater perseverance and endurance. Rather than give up and view obstacles as blockages or someone else's fault, learn to see and use them as the incentive and motivation to succeed. This is a great use of your ability to initiate action that yields productive solutions and practical results. So choose to make the most of your steady energy and what can be incredible staying power. Otherwise, anger and resentment will build over time and a stubborn refusal to bend will limit your worldly achievements.

Mars Square/Opposition Uranus

Too often you act on impulse without considering potential consequences—usually much to your regret. This trait is linked to impatience, recklessness, and your freedom-seeking need for action and excitement. Find other, and safe, outlets to satisfy your independent nature and thirst for adventure. Also emphasize common sense and caution when driving and in athletics and other activities with high accident potential. And, if you're short-tempered, consider taking a self-help course to gain the management skills you need.

Mars Square/Opposition Neptune

Your definition of action is different from that of most people. For you, it's subtle and indirect moves that often occur behind the scenes. That's your comfort zone, but sometimes you miss out on opportunities that go to more assertive people. Get the skills and confidence you need to join them on the front lines, at least in important matters. You'll go further and gain more from life as a result. You live and act on your spiritual beliefs and may have a strong sixth sense. Some people with these aspects suffer from hay fever or are prone to substance abuse.

Mars Square/Opposition Pluto

Giving up or giving in is foreign to you. Only in the most unusual circumstances will you concede defeat to yourself or to someone else—even when you should. This indomitable will can see you through many obstacles to success. But there are times when retreat is the best option, because doing so can save you from unneeded frustration, stress, and tension. You run the risk of alienating people if you push too hard. Some people tap into the negative energy of these aspects and resort to manipulation and intimidation, especially when relationship conflict arises.

Mars Square/Opposition Ascendant-Descendant

Close relationships can be a challenge with these aspects, which increase the potential for conflict and control issues. (This may have been your family experience during childhood.) You, your partner, or both of you may try to dominate the partnership and important decisions. Tact and compromise are the solution, but that's only possible if both of you are open to the idea and then commit to a 50–50 shared relationship. This also applies to business partnerships, which can undergo difficulties when one partner acts on behalf of both.

Mars Square/Opposition Midheaven-IC

Career and domestic conflicts are associated with these aspects, with difficulties in one arena compounding problems in the other. These aspects also increase the potential for conflict with superiors, because you speak your mind and rarely hesitate to question authority. Success in family and career relationships requires finesse, tact, compromise, and the ability to think before you act and speak. Learn to be a team player and develop your potential for motivational leadership. If you accomplish that, then your high energy, motivation, and ambition can yield the highest levels of success.

Mars Sextile/Trine Jupiter

You have the energy, initiative, and enthusiasm to fulfill your many personal and professional ambitions. Opportunities flow in your direction, and whatever you follow through with is likely to develop to your advantage. The challenge here is to choose only the best ones and to pursue them fully rather than coast along. You're also financially lucky but extravagant at times, and known for your honesty and integrity. Physical coordination is usually excellent with these aspects, so you could be an outstanding amateur or professional athlete.

Mars Sextile/Trine Saturn

You get the best of both Mars and Saturn: initiative and practicality. A hard worker, you pursue your ambitions with common sense, determination, and a realistic, responsible attitude. Your shrewd assessment of any situation helps you work it to advantage, and you're cool and calm under stress, which makes you a good candidate for high-level career positions. Calculated risks rather than chancy moves are your style, and they usually pay off well, personally and financially.

Mars Sextile/Trine Uranus

You're innovative and resourceful, and if there's a better way to do something, you're usually the first to spot it. Your outlook is unconventional, although not eccentric, which makes your ideas easy for others to accept. If you're like most people with one of these aspects, you're outgoing and highly energetic, with the adventuresome mindset of an explorer who has the confidence and courage to fearlessly explore new territory. Yet the risks you take are calculated rather than reckless, which increases your odds for success.

Mars Sextile/Trine Neptune

Aware of and in sync with your highly spiritual inner voice, you benefit from a strong and active sixth sense. Your actions sometimes are based on hunches and gut feelings, and you're at your best in a creative environment where you have the freedom to express yourself. People are attracted to your sensual, mystical aura, which inspires them to trust you with secrets. You also benefit from people skills that are enhanced by your unconscious observation of body language, as well as listening between the lines.

Mars Sextile/Trine Pluto

Your policy is to never, ever give up. When that attitude is matched with your incredible willpower and drive, you have all the determination needed to achieve whatever goals you set for yourself. People sense your inner power and lean on you for strength as they look to you for advice and solutions. But in certain situations you can be domineering and ruthless; you also have a long and vengeful memory. These traits can undermine the very success you desire, so use your power wisely to better yourself and those around you.

Mars Sextile/Trine Ascendant

You're an action person who also has a sharp mind and a dynamic personality. This combination makes you a natural leader, assertive and direct. Actively involved in life, you meet challenges head-on with energy and initiative and no thought of failure—it simply isn't an option that you ever consider and thus you usually succeed in life. Partnerships and other close relationships stimulate you, and you do the same for others. Business partnerships can be profitable if you first weigh the risk-reward ratio.

Mars Sextile/Trine Midheaven

You understand and fulfill the need for a balanced lifestyle that includes time for family as well as career; overall, you're successful at both. When focused on the outer world, you pursue your ambitions with an easygoing yet focused drive and determination that can mislead the competition. Your natural leadership ability offers many opportunities to further your aims. You bring the same energy and optimism to domestic and family activities, and may be an active weekend home improvement do-it-yourselfer.

Jupiter Aspects

Jupiter Conjunct Saturn

Your challenge is to balance the optimism of Jupiter with the responsibility of Saturn. You can achieve financial and career success through hard work and an appreciation for slow but steady progress. Even though you experience setbacks along the way, you also benefit from good fortune and a protective influence. Keep that in mind when you're tempted to give up or, conversely, when enthusiasm encourages you to ignore the realities. Determination is very much your ally.

Jupiter Conjunct Uranus

You're lucky in unexpected and unusual ways. Financial windfalls, including big wins, are possible. But consistent good fortune is more likely to come in the form of networking, knowing the right people, and being in the right place at the right time to snap up beneficial opportunities. Even in the face of an unpleasant situation, you usually emerge with the best possible, but not necessarily the ideal or perfect, outcome, while those around you marvel at your ability to land on your feet most of the time.

Jupiter Conjunct Neptune

You're idealistic, imaginative, and creative and may have a strong sixth sense—even psychic ability. Although luck is associated with this aspect, you realize its full potential only if you also use your common sense and have realistic expectations. It's easy to see the bright side of things, while ignoring potential pitfalls. At times you may—with the best of intentions—promise more than you can deliver, believing that faith and the universe will see you through. That's true sometimes, but not always. Be practical too.

Jupiter Conjunct Pluto

You thrive on power and the opportunity to initiate major change. With the good fortune indicated by this aspect, the odds are that you will have many opportunities to do both throughout your lifetime. What is most important is to use this forceful energy honorably to benefit not only yourself but others, through willpower and determination. Faith and spirituality are major themes in your life, or will be at some point when you experience an ultimately positive period of personal transformation.

Jupiter Conjunct Ascendant/Opposition Descendant

You're a fun-loving optimist who exudes confidence and enthusiasm, spreading cheer wherever you go. This makes you a natural for a career in a teaching or healing profession or for simply inspiring others to do and be their best. Close personal relationships also benefit from this planetary influence, and throughout your life most are happy, upbeat, and loving. But Jupiter also increases the chance for excess, such as weight gain, exaggeration, or misplaced optimism. Strive to keep things in perspective, and temper your zeal with reality.

Jupiter Conjunct Midheaven/Opposition IC

You're eligible for the some-people-seem-to-have-it-all category—career and personal success, a loving family, an honorable reputation, and a comfortable home. Getting there takes luck, which you have, but also determination and hard work. Cutting corners, taking it easy, and drifting through life might yield success, but nowhere near what you can achieve if you give it your all. Do that, but also strive for balance; family life could become a distant second if your worldly ambitions become all-consuming.

Jupiter Square/Opposition Saturn

You can be tremendously successful depending on your life choices. Although that's true of everyone, it's more so with you. Where others can coast along at times, your mission is hard work, responsibility, and perseverance. Periodic setbacks test your commitment, but the rewards are far more satisfying than those experienced by many because for you, each is a major personal achievement. Good judgment, planning, and organization in any endeavor help you build confidence in your skills and talents.

Jupiter Square/Opposition Uranus

You might feel that luck is with you most of the time, but chances are it's not nearly as often as you'd like to believe. To fully realize the potential of this planetary energy, you need to learn to be less impulsive, less the thrill seeker, and less impatient for the next exciting adventure. Steady effort yields the most positive results, as does promising only what you can realistically deliver, even when presented with an irresistible opportunity. Be selective and make your luck work for you rather than against you.

Jupiter Square/Opposition Neptune

Your life challenges, as well as your obstacles to success, are faith, trust, and reality. Idealistic and well-intentioned, you can miss the mark by putting your faith in unrealistic and impractical endeavors and untrustworthy people whose intent is to deceive. Business partnerships require ultimate caution, as do financial and legal matters. Even though the lure of easy money and guaranteed success can be strong, most endeavors do not pay off. Travel a higher, more spiritual road: share yourself and your talents with those who deserve them.

Jupiter Square/Opposition Pluto

You see no reason to bend, change, or compromise on anything that separates you from a goal. This can be positive or negative depending on your approach. When this energy is used unethically or even ruthlessly, you may achieve temporary success, but eventually it will catch up with you. Working within existing structures may not be as easy, or your first choice, but it's potentially more lucrative, both financially and in terms of overall life success. Be a leader and a team player who empowers others.

Jupiter Square/Opposition Ascendant-Descendant

It's admirable, although idealistic, to believe you can do it all and please everyone all the time. Not possible. Be selective and resist the temptation to spread yourself too thin, to promise far more than you can reasonably deliver. That and a practical, realistic approach will increase your odds for success and make the most of your enthusiastic optimism. Also accept the reality that not every relationship is positive and upbeat all the time. People are human and imperfect, no matter how much you wish otherwise.

Jupiter Square/Opposition Midheaven-IC

Your career ambitions may be realistic, but how you approach them may not. Despite your wishes or what you believe you deserve, rising to the top requires hard work, common sense, time, and education. Do your fair share, be a team player, and deliver on promises. You can be overly generous with loved ones and might be tempted to live a lifestyle beyond your means. Buy only what you can afford, including your home and furnishings, and build financial security for the future and retirement.

Jupiter Sextile/Trine Saturn

This planetary influence accents optimism, responsibility, common sense, organizational ability, and a talent for money management and business. Earning potential is thus excellent. You take the inevitable setbacks in stride, overcome obstacles with a fresh approach, and function well under stress, all of which make you an outstanding candidate for an executive position. People respect your honesty and integrity, practical vision, and conservative values, and you enjoy a high reputation.

Jupiter Sextile/Trine Uranus

You're independent and free-spirited. Yet you're also a responsible team player who lives up to expectations if given a high level of autonomy. Without that, you have a tough time functioning at your best. Under the right conditions you can not only achieve your goals but exceed them. You're attuned to trends and have success in initiating positive change, especially in group endeavors. These aspects also indicate luck through sudden opportunities, and you may enjoy travel and be involved in humanitarian efforts.

Jupiter Sextile/Trine Neptune

Deeply spiritual, you have an innate understanding of the universe and a strong faith in yourself and humankind. You look for the best in people; unfortunately, this trait can blind you to the realities of human nature. Choose your friends and business acquaintances with care, and refrain from sharing your kind, compassionate, generous nature with just anyone, including good causes and those in need. You're also intuitive and at times may feel your life is directed and protected by a guardian angel.

Jupiter Sextile/Trine Pluto

You have the charisma and the leadership ability to effect positive change within your environment—home, community, and workplace—and in the lives of those around you. Your visionary ideas and ability to see the big picture are no small part of this, and you have a talent for attracting powerful people who support you and your efforts. On a wider scale, global and societal changes can be to your advantage personally and professionally. These aspects also have wealth potential, with gains coming through high earnings, inheritance, or windfalls.

Jupiter Sextile/Trine Ascendant

You attract opportunities and good fortune through other people—colleagues, friends, relatives, and partners—and business and personal alliances can be lucrative. No small part of this success with and through others is due to your infectious optimism and enthusiasm. People respond instinctively to your upbeat aura and feel great just being in your presence. You also have the innate confidence to test your talents with new endeavors, which are successful more often than not. Higher education furthers your life success, and you may travel extensively.

Jupiter Sextile/Trine Midheaven

A combination of factors brings you career luck. You're optimistic, a team player who's well liked by coworkers and superiors, who appreciate your honesty and ethics. All are helpful as you rise through the ranks to ever-increasing positions of trust and status. You're a risk taker, but within reason, and a leader whose enthusiasm inspires others to give their all. This fortunate planetary influence also favors a happy home life and financial benefits from family members.

Saturn Aspects
Saturn Conjunct Uranus

At its best, this aspect indicates a knack for innovative yet practical ideas, as well as the ideal personality mix of responsibility and independence. But at times, the push-pull of this diverse planetary energy makes it tough to find that perfect mix, which comes with maturity and experience. You have the ability to use the past as a foundation for the future because of your unique perspective on both. Being a team player and a champion networker rather than doing everything yourself is your route to life and career success.

Saturn Conjunct Neptune

You're a creative thinker, an idea person who can see the difference between what's real and what's merely an illusion. You also have a talent for practical, realistic, inspired planning. But it can be a challenge to have faith in the outcome because concepts are intangible, not something you can see, feel, or touch. Leap that hurdle and you will have the ability to act on your dreams and develop logical steps to achieve them. Some people with this aspect have artistic or musical talent, or excel at photography or graphic design.

Saturn Conjunct Pluto

This dynamic planetary combination gives you the ability to initiate powerful, constructive change and the determination to achieve your ambitions. But power plays also are possible, and it can be tough to wait your turn to be the boss. Your career is prone to shifting global conditions. This makes it wise to remain alert to what's happening in the wider world as well as in your immediate environment. Look for developing trends and acquire the necessary skills to adapt and therefore help minimize the impact if your field or industry is affected.

Saturn Conjunct Ascendant/Opposition Descendant

You're cautious and conservative, the epitome of responsibility, hard work, and self-discipline. However, it may take you until about age thirty to embrace these realities and fully determine your life direction. You know the meaning of "instant karma"—consequences that occur, sometimes within minutes, when you've stepped out of line. Other people can get away with a lot; you, however, can get away with almost nothing. Remember that there's no need to work constantly and to take life seriously all the time. Teach yourself to play and add some fun to your life!

Saturn Conjunct Midheaven/Opposition IC

You're among the most ambitious people on the planet. The quest for status, recognition, career achievement, and rewards motivates you to pursue your goals with drive and determination, trying again and again until you succeed. This aspect is also a test of integrity. Any-thing less than completely honorable actions can negate your efforts, usually very quickly, but this can happen even years later. Home and family life can suffer because you're so focused on your worldly ambitions, and at times you'll be faced with tough decisions regarding priorities.

Saturn Square/Opposition Uranus

Your challenge is to find the middle ground that satisfies your need for freedom as well as your desire for stability. Increased self-discipline helps you achieve this goal, as does accepting the fact that life goes much more smoothly if you play by the rules. Rebellious and impulsive actions can affect your career and also result in accidents and physical injury. It can be tough to find a positive, productive outlet for the frustrations indicated by this planetary energy, yet that's exactly what you need to do. Find a good fit with a hobby or sport that's not high-risk.

Saturn Square/Opposition Neptune

Insecurity and low self-esteem are associated with these aspects. The difficulty lies in blending reality with the mystical side of life and may be most apparent in career matters and relationships. Accept the fact that many people are less than honorable or at least will put their ambitions ahead of yours. Strive to see the true person rather than your ideal, and protect your own interests. Legal and financial dealings also require caution and awareness to help prevent deception. Creative endeavors are good outlets for this planetary energy, especially those that result in a tangible finished product, such as woodworking, gardening, or sculpting.

Saturn Square/Opposition Pluto

These aspects indicate heavy responsibilities in relationships and career matters. Your challenge is to learn to weather disappointments with determination and to rise above the temptation to take the easy way out. The more effort you put in to pursuing your worldly ambitions and developing positive relationships, the more success you will achieve. This also will help you learn to better manage difficulties with authority figures as well as power plays. Some people with this influence are relentless in their pursuit of money and control.

Saturn Square/Opposition Ascendant-Descendant

Relationships can be a challenge with these aspects, and you might find it difficult to warm up to people. While others might see you as aloof and unresponsive, the reality may be that you're shy and lack confidence. It's also possible you prefer your own company to that of others and enjoy time alone. Yet it's people skills that will help you achieve your ambitions. These aspects also can indicate a career focus that leaves little time for or interest in a romantic commitment until later in life. Business partnerships can be positive or negative; be cautious.

Saturn Square/Opposition Midheaven-IC

Career advancement may be slow in coming, or you might focus all your energies on achieving your ambitions to the exclusion of other facets of life. Either way, you are likely to shoulder heavy family responsibilities and have a strained relationship with parents or other close relatives, possibly because of childhood experiences. Your challenge is to identify and learn from what holds you back and then move beyond it. Doing so will ease the way to the status and worldly success you crave and covet.

Saturn Sextile/Trine Uranus

You're as attuned to tradition as you are to innovation and thus have a talent for building on the past to embrace the future. Technology intrigues you, and you see it as a tool for career success. If you have an inventor's mind, you could create the next must-have gadget, the better mousetrap that sets the world on fire. In a traditional career, you can earn high praise for your clever, creative, time-saving ideas. Best of all, you benefit from lucky opportunities that seem to appear out of nowhere. Follow through on them.

Saturn Sextile/Trine Neptune

Creative yet practical energy is associated with these aspects, which also indicate a sixth sense that's useful in planning, organization, and analysis, and the vision to take an idea from concept to reality. You may prefer to work behind the scenes in a quiet atmosphere conducive to concentration, or to use this planetary energy to enhance success in a career in sales, marketing, working with the public, or a creative field. Some people with these aspects are involved in charitable organizations as professionals or volunteers.

Saturn Sextile/Trine Pluto

You might feel as though your life is predestined, fated, or guided by the universe on a path of constructive achievement. If you have the desire and the passion, you can attain powerful positions as well as wealth and security. You initiate change when it has a practical purpose and when it will further your aims. You also cultivate powerful friends and networking contacts, many of whom are attracted by your compelling energy that indicates you're a strong contender for an influential position in the world, your community, or your career.

Saturn Sextile/Trine Ascendant-Descendant

You're patient, practical, and conservative in outlook and dress. People value your common sense and wise advice and look to you to be a steadying influence in stressful situations. You're a rock in a world of change, and have an innate understanding of the laws of the universe. Business and romantic partnerships are usually stable and successful with these aspects, although you might postpone commitment until later in life. People, some of whom are soul mates, seem to enter your life for a purpose and then depart when their mission is complete.

Saturn Sextile/Trine Midheaven-IC

Career gains are rarely sudden with these aspects; slow, steady progress is more the norm, and you fully appreciate the concept that hard work and responsibility are what reap the greatest rewards. Because of this, you have an easier path to career achievement if you give it your all. Family ties are usually strong and supportive, even if they're not warm and lighthearted, and your parents instilled good values to last a lifetime. You prefer a quiet domestic life and a traditional home that reflects your status.

Uranus Aspects
Uranus Conjunct/Square/Opposition Neptune

These are generational aspects that on a personal level inspire creativity and imagination but also indicate confusion and the potential for disillusionment in the face of change. You probably will experience all of these in your lifetime, primarily in the house(s) where the aspect is located. Adaptability and inventive solutions are the way to maximize the opportunities presented.

Uranus Conjunct/Square/Opposition Pluto

These generational aspects indicate that you will experience many changes in your lifetime as a result of the shifting global environment. These changes will affect you directly or indirectly in the area of life represented by the aspect's house locations. The most profound developments in your adult life are likely to occur around ages forty and fifty-five.

Uranus Conjunct/Square/Opposition Ascendant-Descendant

You're a free spirit, an independent soul who follows your own path. Unique and unconventional in some way, you have an irresistible magnetism that intrigues people, but you may find a committed relationship too confining. You take immediate action when you decide it's time for change, even if that means moving cross-country. Try to teach yourself to step back and take an objective view before you make life-changing decisions. Given time and perspective, the urge may pass, to be replaced by something that's potentially more constructive. Be cautious around electricity.

Uranus Conjunct/Square/Opposition Midheaven-IC

These are "flash in the pan" aspects—sudden fame or infamy. You're likely to experience this phenomenon periodically throughout your life. Sudden career changes—up, down, or out—are likely, either through your initiative or global conditions. Each represents another opportunity to claim your temporary place in the spotlight. Many changes of residence are also possible, and you may have had an unusual home environment or upbringing as a child. Try to channel your energy into worldly success rather than indulge in impulsive career decisions.

Uranus Sextile/Trine Neptune

Innovation and creativity flow smoothly between the houses where these planets are located. Your sixth sense is especially active in these areas of life, giving you the advantage in almost any situation. Many people with this planetary energy have an interest in and support humanitarian and charitable causes as volunteers or career professionals. Others are successful in the tech industry in positions that benefit from creative, future-oriented thinking.

Uranus Sextile/Trine Ascendant-Descendant

You're a trendsetter, a true original with a unique style and a magnetic personality. Unusual hobbies, interests, and people attract you, and your favorite friends, among the many, are those who share your spontaneity and unconventional attitudes. With the right person, this influence indicates a happy and long-lasting romantic (or business) partnership. But that's only possible with someone who values and shares your need to maintain your independence within a mutually supportive relationship.

Uranus Sextile/Trine Midheaven-IC

You're a magnet for opportunities, any of which could suddenly elevate your status and advance your career ambitions. Entrepreneurial talent is possible; if this describes you, look to technology to help carve out your niche. If you work for a company, you need the freedom to prioritize your own work and to implement new ideas without a hovering boss who's sure to stifle your productivity. Some people with these aspects favor contemporary homes and furnishings in an eclectic environment.

Neptune Aspects

Neptune Square/Opposition Pluto (no one alive today has the conjunction)

These aspects represent a generational influence during which health care and institutions undergo massive changes. On a personal basis, these aspects can indicate disillusionment and the potential for deception in the areas of life represented by the houses involved. Be especially cautious if this affects career or finances.

Neptune Conjunct/Square/Opposition Ascendant-Descendant

You have a subtle intriguing allure, an active sixth sense, and the ability to blend in and adapt to almost any environment—if that's your desire. However, you're equally susceptible to the charms of others, all of whom may not be well-intentioned. Ask questions, learn to be skeptical, and let people earn your trust. Practicality and common sense are often lacking with these aspects, so protect yourself and your resources with expert legal and financial advice when necessary.

Neptune Conjunct/Square/Opposition Midheaven-IC

This aspect often indicates unrealistic career ambitions or entering the wrong (for you) career field because of family influence. But it's also one that enhances a career in film, photography, and other creative pursuits, as well as sales, advertising, marketing, medicine, and the beverage industry. Your childhood may have been influenced by substance abuse in the home or an absent parent. Because Neptune rules water, flood insurance for your home is a wise idea, even if you're not in a designated flood zone.

Neptune Sextile/Trine Pluto

You, and others born during the same time frame, have the ability to tap into your own personal spiritual consciousness to effect change within your community or the world at large. Although some of your aims are lofty and idealistic, you have an amazing ability for personal transformation in the areas represented by the houses involved in this planetary influence.

Neptune Sextile/Trine Ascendant-Descendant

You have a glamorous aura that's both fascinating and irresistible, matched by a charming way with words and people. Strong intuitive insights make you sensitive to subtle vibrations and the needs and concerns of others, a trait that favors romantic partnerships and involvement in humanitarian causes. You're also creative and may have considerable artistic, musical, or dancing talent. Best of all, you have the ability to eas-ily fit into any situation, quickly adapting to the environment and people around you.

Neptune Sextile/Trine Midheaven-IC

Charm is no small part of your career success, especially when backed up by hard work, ambition, and relationships with all the right people. Your intuition is an asset, and you often sense trends and developments long before they become public. But it's all too easy with either of these aspects to drift along, content with the status quo, which is definitely not the best use of your talents. Most people with these aspects have strong emotional and spiritual ties with parents, immediate family, and other relatives.

Pluto Aspects
Pluto Conjunct/Square/Opposition Ascendant-Descendant

Power plays are associated with these aspects; they're either initiated by you, aimed at you, or both. Learn when to take a stand and when to back off and compromise, as well as to recognize your or someone else's controlling behavior. Relationships, especially business and romantic partnerships, benefit from a give-and-take attitude, with you initiating the give and the take. Handled with tact and diplomacy, these aspects can bring positive, uplifting learning experiences through relationships.

Pluto Conjunct/Square/Opposition Midheaven-IC

Pluto in any of these positions powerfully influences your career and home life, positively or negatively. Although your childhood environment may have been difficult, with a demanding, controlling parent, you can reverse the influence and build a stable, loving, and supportive home and family life. You have the determination to rise to the top of your career and to become a well-respected leader if you draw on your inner strength and empower others rather than taking charge in every situation.

Pluto Sextile/Trine Ascendant-Descendant

Your strength and stamina are notable, and people are drawn to the inner power they rightly sense in you. You thus can be influential in the lives of many people, a positive force for change and inspiration. And you can do the same for yourself with all the determination this planetary influence signifies. Although yours may be the dominant voice in a business or personal partnership, you're also attuned to the needs and wishes of others. Take care, though, not to shoulder all the responsibility; share the load.

Pluto Sextile/Trine Midheaven-IC

Your natural leadership skills bring many opportunities to excel in the wider world, your career, and your community. People look to you to take charge, which you do effortlessly, using each situation to advantage to advance your standing. Many people with this planetary influence rise to the top of their career fields. Home life is intense at times, but these ties are strong, lasting, and generally unbreakable, because part of your outward success is based on the support you receive from loved ones.

AL GORE

As a presidential candidate, Al Gore found it difficult to—and never really did—connect with the public, as indicated by Sun (self) square (obstacle) Moon (public). He gave it his all with the Pluto-Saturn-Mars stellium in the first house (self), an aspect that represents a hard worker who has ambitious drive but also is prone to frustration (Mars-Saturn) and uncontrollable career setbacks (Saturn-Pluto). The Sun is trine the stellium, so he had political success, serving as a senator and vice president of the United States. The trine with the ninth-house (publishing, teaching) Sun is a natural outlet for him, and he is working for constructive change (Saturn conjunct Pluto) regarding environmental issues.

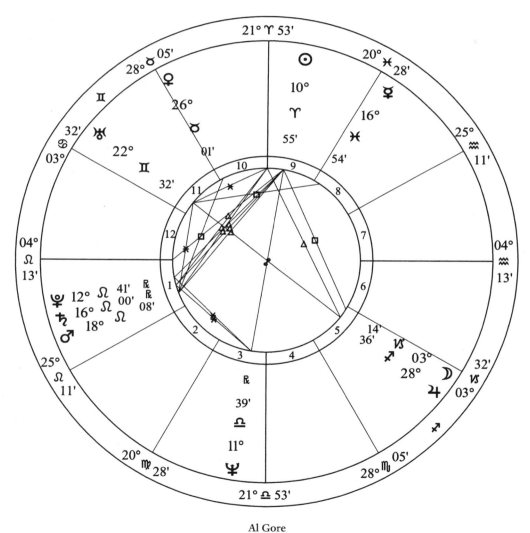

Al Gore
March 31, 1948 / 12:53 p.m. EST / Washington, D.C.
Placidus Houses

TIGER WOODS

Mars conjunct Midheaven is an entrepreneurial aspect, which Tiger Woods certainly is as a self-employed athlete. He easily taps into the willpower and determination of the Mars-Pluto trine, which links self (first house) with career (Midheaven). This chart is an example of how one planet within orb of aspect to two others pulls the two other planets together into a conjunction. The Moon and Neptune are out of orb of a conjunction, but Mars is opposition both planets to bring the energy of the three into a working relationship. People with Moon conjunct Neptune are highly intuitive and excellent at visualization. With the Moon and Neptune opposition the Midheaven and Mars—and sextile Pluto—Woods uses these talents to fuel his passion for career success. Media sources report that he meditates, which is another excellent use of this configuration.

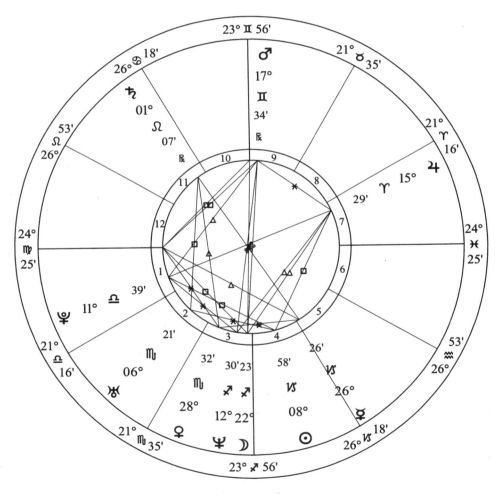

Tiger Woods
December 30, 1975 / 10:50 p.m. PST / Long Beach, CA
Placidus Houses

OPRAH WINFREY

Oprah Winfrey is an attractive person, as is often true of those with a Sun-Venus conjunction. At first glance, it would be easy to assume that she is friendly but distant, even aloof, with the Sun, Venus, and Mercury in Aquarius. She may be at times. These are valuable qualities for a TV host, who must maintain perspective. Her chart is an example of the importance of the rising sign. Her Ascendant is outgoing, enthusiastic Sagittarius, the same sign as the emotional, public-oriented Moon. Winfrey's chart is also an example of someone who overcame the odds and obstacles represented by a Sun-Saturn square, who worked hard to achieve her ambitions. Venus square Saturn indicates her reluctance to—or choice not to—marry her longtime friend. But a happy relationship is nevertheless indicated by Mercury (seventh-house ruler) trine Jupiter (Ascendant ruler).

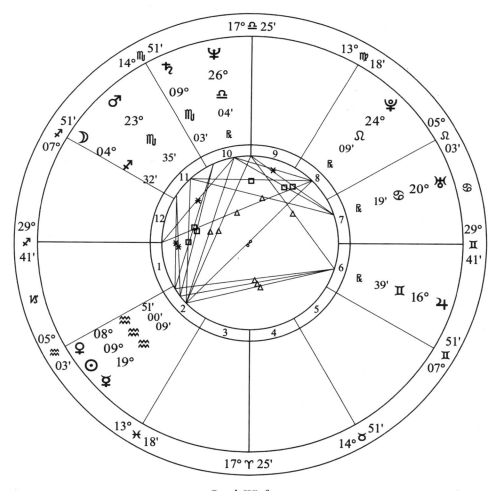

Oprah Winfrey
January 29, 1954 / 4:30 a.m. CST / Kosciusko, MS
Placidus Houses

TED KENNEDY

The Venus-Uranus conjunction in Ted Kennedy's chart reflects his divorce and remarriage. Because Uranus is within orb of a square to Pluto in the seventh house of relationships, it pulls Venus into the square. With Pluto in the seventh house and ruling the tenth (career), and square Venus-Uranus, this indicates that a relationship could have a detrimental effect on his career and reputation, which the Chappaquiddick event did—it ended his chances for a presidential bid. Venus also rules his ninth house (legal system). Yet with Jupiter also trine the Venus-Uranus conjunction, he has a strong luck element, which came into play in the aftermath of Chappaquiddick. It has been reported that his second marriage is happy and successful, as would be expected with the trines.

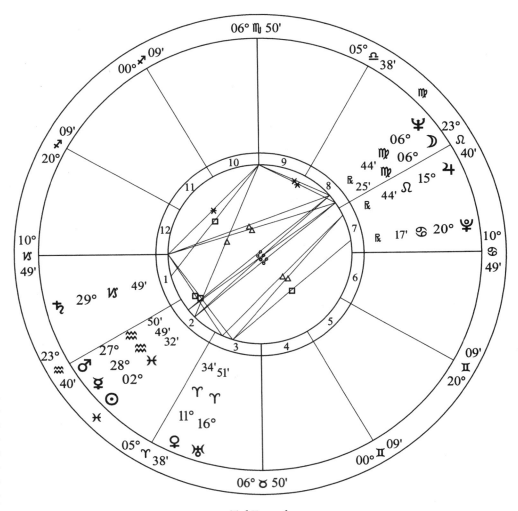

Ted Kennedy
February 22, 1932 / 3:58 a.m. EST / Dorchester, MA
Placidus Houses

WILLIE NELSON

Willie Nelson has experienced the upside and the downside of the Jupiter-Neptune conjunction in the first and second houses. Jupiter is in the second house of personal money, and Neptune rules the eighth house of other people's money (Pisces on the cusp). His IRS problems resulted from overconfidence (Jupiter) and misplaced trust (Neptune) in those who were handling his finances. Yet with both planets trine the fortunate Sun-Venus-Midheaven stellium, friends and farmers raised money for him and purchased some of his property and returned it to him. He also has used his talents and popularity to found Farm Aid and raise money to help small farmers stay in business.

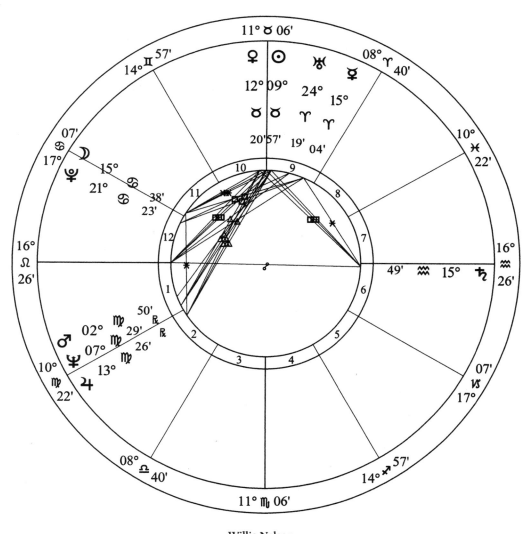

Willie Nelson
April 30, 1933 / 12:30 p.m. CST / Abbott, TX
Placidus Houses

TOM HANKS

Charisma—the "it" factor—can make the difference between phenomenal and mediocre success as an actor. Tom Hanks has it, with Venus conjunct the Midheaven and Neptune trine both. Neptune is also the planetary ruler of film. Note that Venus is retrograde, indicating Hanks's preference for time with family and close friends rather than the party scene. This retrograde influence also reflects delayed earning power; he was about thirty-seven before he gained stardom and the matching paycheck. With a grand trine in water signs, he is probably highly intuitive.

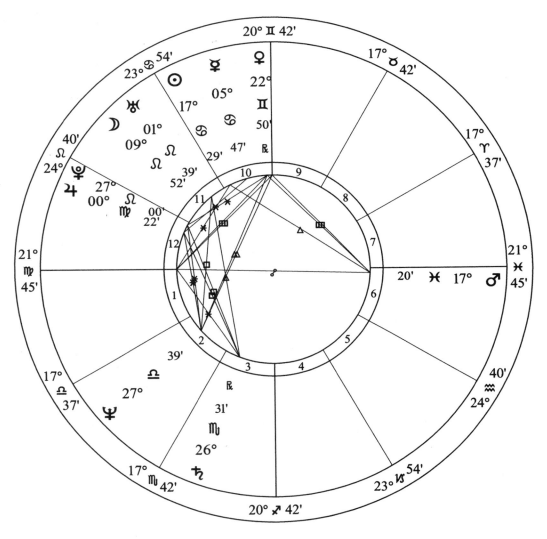

Tom Hanks
July 9, 1956 / 11:17 a.m. PDT / Concord, CA
Placidus Houses

ROBERT REDFORD

Robert Redford's chart has a T-square with Jupiter as the focal point square Saturn opposition a Venus-Neptune-Mercury-Moon stellium. He disliked the regimentation of school and said he was always bored, daydreaming of life beyond the town of Van Nuys, California, where he grew up. This is a perfect description of adventuresome Jupiter in the ninth house of travel and education. Redford attended the University of Colorado on a baseball scholarship (Mars in the fifth house is often an indication of athletic ability), but quit after the death of his mother and hopped a freighter to Europe. Upon his return, he became a highly successful actor. The best uses of the T-square, however, are his work for the environment, fundraising for SIDS, and support of independent film-makers. All are positive uses of the T-square, which in his earlier years lacked a constructive outlet. He went from irresponsibility to responsibility. Saturn in the twelfth house is often a karmic influence, the sixth is the house of service and voluntary efforts, Virgo and Neptune are associated with the environment and health, and Jupiter rules teaching—he is doing his part to educate the world.

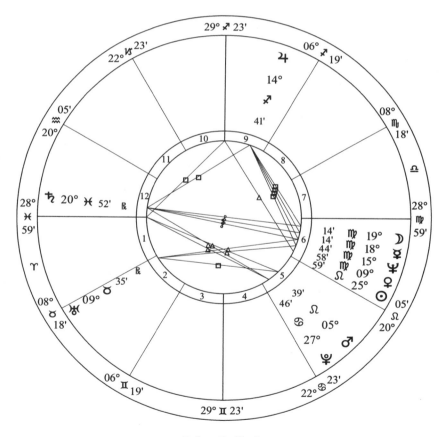

Robert Redford
August 18, 1936 / 8:02 p.m. PST / Santa Monica, CA
Placidus Houses

DR. PHIL MCGRAW

Dr. Phil has Uranus in the fourth house, an indication of frequent moves, especially in childhood. Reinforcing it is fourth-house ruler Mercury (Gemini on the cusp) square Uranus. This same aspect (Mercury square Uranus) indicates a highly intelligent, inventive mind and a person who enjoys stirring the pot, which he certainly does by challenging people to break out of their ruts. With Mars in the eighth house of money trine Uranus, he has a talent for turning his innovative ideas into riches, which he first did when he established Courtroom Sciences to assist lawyers with courtroom strategy and jury selection. It was through this company that he met Oprah Winfrey, who made him a regular on her show. Mercury in the seventh house square Uranus also indicates sudden opportunities through other people.

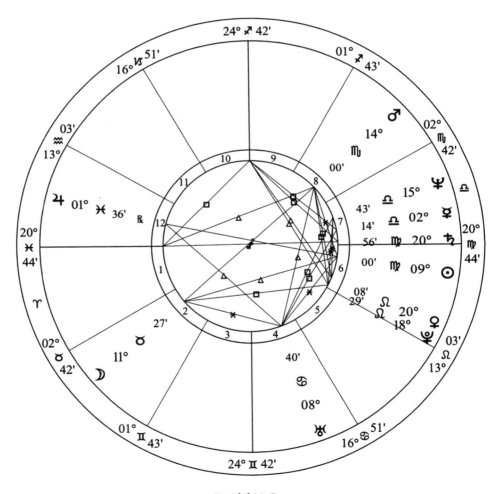

Dr. Phil McGraw
September 1, 1950 / 7:15 p.m. CST / Vinita, OK
Placidus Houses

CONDOLEEZZA RICE

Condoleezza Rice's close family ties are reflected in the Sun- (self) Venus (fourth-house ruler) conjunction trine Moon (family) in Cancer (family). These aspects, which involve the Midheaven (career and status) and the sixth house (daily work), also indicate the potential for a highly success-ful career, which she has earned. Her true passion, however, is probably higher education, because the Moon is trine Saturn in the ninth house. With a Mercury-Neptune conjunction (out-of-sign) in the ninth house, she has the visionary ideas to improve higher education. Sun conjunct Midheaven square the first-house Mars gives her drive and ambition and also reflects her athletic ability and interest; she was a competitive figure skater as a teenager and is an avid football fan.

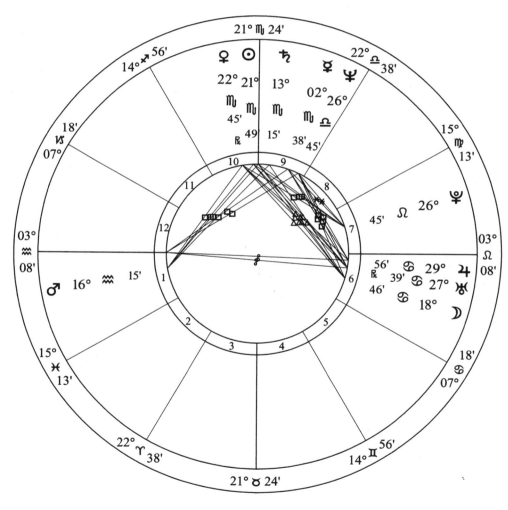

Condoleezza Rice
November 14, 1954 / 11:30 a.m. CST / Birmingham, AL
Placidus Houses

275

ANDERSON COOPER

Reporter and TV host Anderson Cooper has the Sun in the eighth house of research, investigation, and undercover activities—an ideal influence for someone who digs out the facts. The Sun is sextile Saturn in the sixth house of daily work, so this talent for research is one he capitalized on. Mercury is square Saturn, reflecting his sharp mind and thorough thinking process. (Any Mercury-Saturn aspect is indicative of intelligence.) He benefits from the Venus-Jupiter conjunction in the tenth house (also conjunct the Midheaven), which reflects popularity and luck (he was in and survived some risky situations when reporting overseas) and the potential for fame.

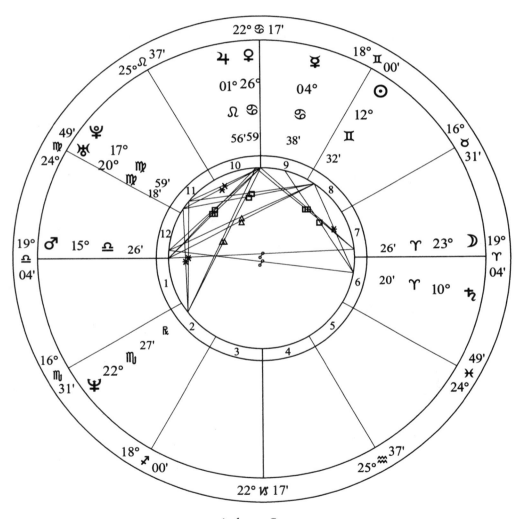

Anderson Cooper
June 3, 1967 / 3:46 p.m. EDT / New York, NY
Placidus Houses

BRAD PITT

Brad Pitt's chart has Mercury conjunct Mars (quick mind, snap decisions) trine Uranus conjunct Pluto in the ninth house of publishing and travel, so his first career choice (journalism) was a natural fit. With the trine, it was easy for him to take what turned out to be a calculated risk (Capricorn), quit school, and head for Los Angeles. The Moon-Mercury-Venus stellium trine the Midheaven reflects his tremendous success as a Hollywood sex symbol.

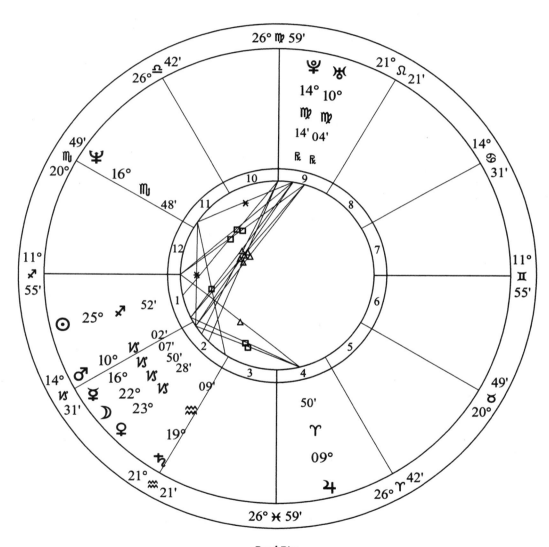

Brad Pitt
December 18, 1963 / 6:31 a.m. CST / Shawnee, OK
Placidus Houses

DALE EARNHARDT JR.

Cooperative Libra is one of the signs least likely to be associated with an award-winning race car driver. But Junior is well suited for his chosen career because of the very close (fewer than two degrees) conjunction of the Sun and action-oriented Mars. Libra gives him the people skills to be a crowd and media pleaser, as does the Sun-Mars conjunction trine the Midheaven. His chart also has a Mars-Saturn square, which tempers the impulsiveness of Mars while providing staying power and ambition (Saturn in the tenth house). Libra is also an excellent strategist, a desirable quality for a race car driver, and Junior has the ability to see the big picture with Mercury trine Jupiter.

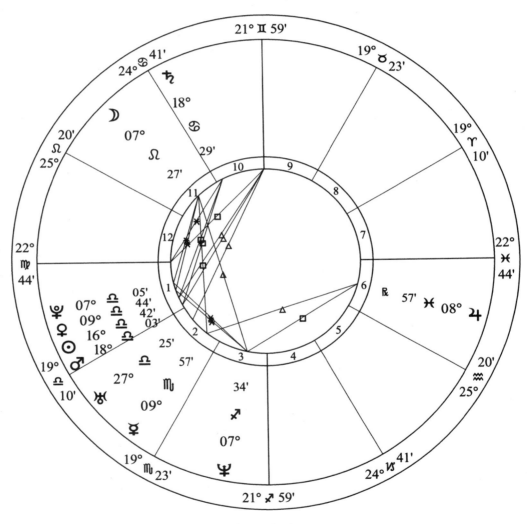

Dale Earnhardt Jr.
October 10, 1974 / 5:33 a.m. EDT / Concord, NC
Placidus Houses

CHAPTER SIX

ASTROLOGY IN ACTION

READING THE CHART

Now that you have all the pieces of the puzzle—the signs, planets, houses, and aspects—how do you fit them together into a complete picture? Synthesis.

Synthesis is part of the art of astrology. It's how you blend all the various, and conflicting, factors in a chart in order to accurately reflect the personality. This takes practice and, again, it's far easier to learn if you work with your own chart and those of friends and family members you know well. Then you can see how all the components work together.

Using the chart of Dale Earnhardt Jr. (page 281), who's called "Junior," I'll explain how I read a chart. This isn't the only way to do it, although my method definitely covers all the basics of synthesis. As you begin reading charts, you'll develop your own variations of this method as you discover what works for you in practice. Don't be surprised if this chart analysis seems confusing at first. Chart interpretation takes practice, and it will get easier in time. You'll find the concepts easier to grasp if you read this analysis several times and study each component.

I begin by looking at the Sun, Moon, and Ascendant signs, as this gives a quick look at the personality. Junior's Ascendant is practical, reserved Virgo. However, his Sun is in Libra, the sign of people skills, and his Moon is in Leo, an outgoing, fun-loving sign. He reflects all of these in media interviews, where he comes across as an aw-shucks guy next door (Virgo) who's a nice guy (Libra) and knows how to self-promote (Leo). This man is definitely a crowd pleaser and probably the most popular NASCAR driver. Interestingly, Kelley, Junior's sister, said in an interview that he was shy in his younger years; that's pure Virgo.

Now that we have some clues into his personality, let's look at the hemisphere and quadrant emphasis. Earnhardt has eight planets in the northern hemisphere, which means he's introspective, self-reliant, and more comfortable out of the public eye (this is similar to the Virgo Sun). Nine of his planets are in the eastern hemisphere, so he's self-motivated and self-reliant and focuses on his needs and desires. The third quadrant has seven planets, indicating that he's action-oriented and self-absorbed. From this we know that Junior is very much the master of his own cylinder, an action-oriented man with high initiative. This reinforces the Libra (cardinal sign) and Leo (fire sign) energy, so already we can tell that he's not the typical reserved Virgo rising. But he was until he grew into himself and gained the confidence indicated by his Sun and Moon signs.

Junior has the trinity of wealth, with planets in the second, sixth, and tenth houses. This indicates a hard worker who strives for recognition and financial success, all of which he's already accomplished. Here's an example of a judgment call an astrologer often has to make. Mercury in the second house is in a close trine to Jupiter in the sixth. Both planets are technically out of orb to a trine to Saturn in the tenth house. Because this would be a grand trine, we can use a little wider orb. In this case, we know he is a multimillionaire, so the energy is probably working that way. If you didn't have this information, you would ask the client some pertinent questions about financial status in order to determine if he was merely well-off and financially

secure or truly wealthy, either of which is indicated by the trinity of wealth.

Junior also has a weaker trinity of association, with planets in the third and eleventh houses. The other house of this trinity would be the seventh, but because he has a Libra Sun (the natural sign of the seventh house), this energy is available to him and important (and visible) in media and fan relations.

After getting this overview of the chart, I begin with the first house and work counterclockwise around the chart through the twelfth house.

Junior has a packed first house! The four planets there definitely reinforce what we already saw in the hemisphere and quadrant emphasis. This is a man in charge of himself.

There are two conjunctions in the first house: Venus-Pluto and Sun-Mars. On its own, the Venus-Pluto conjunction indicates the potential for big money through individual effort (first house). Note also that Venus rules his second house through Libra on the second-house cusp. With Pluto ruling the third house, he can profit substantially through a business partnership (Venus) with a sibling (Pluto), with Venus-Pluto sextile Neptune in the third house, ruler of the seventh house of partnerships. And that is exactly what he has done. He is in business with his sister, who successfully manages his JR Motorsports. (With this Venus-Pluto-Neptune configuration, however, he would be wise to sign a pre-nuptial agreement prior to marriage, because it also indicates the potential for loss through a romantic partnership.) Venus-Pluto are also sextile the Moon in the eleventh house of friendship, and all his employees were friends before he hired them.

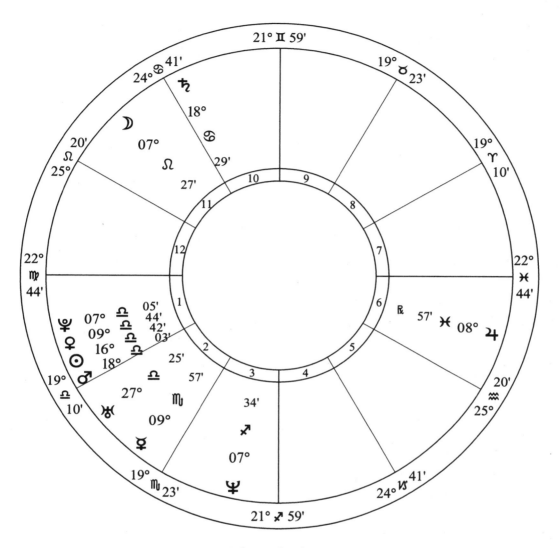

Dale Earnhardt Jr.
October 10, 1974 / 5:33 a.m. EDT / Concord, NC
Placidus Houses

The most fascinating aspect in Junior's chart is the Sun-Mars conjunction in Libra in the first house. Libra is not a sign one would normally associate with an aggressive race car driver, but with the Sun conjunct Mars (which rules Aries), it takes on the flavor of Aries. And remember, the first house is the natural house of Aries, so this is an even stronger influence. It provides all the assertiveness and risk taking necessary for a race car driver. What Libra gives him is the strategic mind that is invaluable for a race car driver, and, of course, the people skills to please the media and the fans.

Even more fascinating is that Dale Earnhardt Sr., his father, also had Sun conjunct Mars, but in Taurus. Senior was known as "the Intimidator." He was not only an aggressive driver, but one who was noted for ramming other cars to get them out of the way. That is pure Taurus determination—the Bull who plows ahead, set on a goal, who won't be deterred. So while Senior used brawn to succeed, Junior uses his brains, analyzing the situation (Virgo) and strategizing (Libra).

The Sun-Mars conjunction is square Saturn in the tenth house, which presents obstacles (square) to success (tenth house) but also the ambition and incentive to succeed. It also indicates that he had to pay his dues to reach the top, which he definitely did, receiving help from his father (Saturn and tenth house) only after he had somewhat proved himself as a driver.

Libra on the second-house cusp is excellent for money, and Uranus in the second house indicates unexpected gains and losses. In his younger years, Junior worked at his father's Chevrolet dealership changing oil in cars in order to fund his weekend race activities. Obvi-ously, Uranus in the second house has been far more of a boom rather than a bust placement for him. Note that Uranus makes no aspects to other planets in his chart, but because it's in Libra, it also indicates that money can come to him from partnerships.

Mercury in the second house is part of the trinity of wealth, so it also indicates the potential for big money. Mercury's placement in Scorpio, the natural sign of the eighth house of money, confirms this.

Mercury is also the communications planet. With this planet in Scorpio, the sign on the third-house (communication) cusp, Junior is somewhat secretive. Libra reflects his public persona, but he's undoubtedly a very private person who shares little of his inner self with anyone other than those closest to him. The Mercury-Scorpio influence is another indication of a strategic mind that outwits the competition. Neptune in the third house is terrific for creative thinking and charming words, especially with the sextile it makes to the first-house planets. But Neptune also can invite deception and wishful thinking. Its square to Jupiter in the sixth house of work could be used for visualization as one technique for job success. This is reinforced because these planets (Jupiter in Pisces and Neptune in Sagittarius) are in mutual reception (since Jupiter rules Sagittarius and Neptune rules Pisces), and thus the square functions more like an easy aspect.

The fourth house (IC) has Sagittarius on the cusp. Because there are no planets in that house, we look to its ruler, Jupiter. This is a beautiful example of the effectiveness of rulerships. With Jupiter in the sixth house and ruling the fourth house, Junior works for the family business.

The fourth is the house of parents, so we'll look at his relationship with his mother and father here. They were divorced when he was three years old. Junior and his sister lived with their mother for a while, and then with his father and stepmother. The Moon (mother) is favorably aspected except for its square to Mercury. Note that Mercury rules the tenth house; this indicates some difficulty between his parents and a separation at some point from his mother. Jupiter (fourth-house ruler) square Neptune also indicates difficulty between the parents, and an absent (Neptune) father, which he was, either because Junior lived with his mother or his father was rarely home.

His mother is obviously a rock in his life (they are reportedly very close) because of Saturn in Cancer (the Moon's sign) in the tenth house. But the Sun and Saturn are also the universal rulers of the father, which makes the Sun-Mars square Saturn a revealing aspect. Junior had tremendous respect for his father, whom he probably viewed as a taskmaster; his father also pushed him to succeed, and Junior responded by pushing himself in order to prove himself to his father.

Saturn is also the ruler of the fifth house, with Capricorn on the cusp. With Saturn in the tenth house, it's a perfect fit for a career in sports (fifth house), and with Saturn in Cancer, again we see the family-business influence. Because the fifth is the house of leisure, Junior probably socializes with colleagues who are also friends. Capricorn here sometimes indicates a person who has no children or only one and usually later in life.

Aquarius on the cusp of the sixth house reflects Junior's unusual job and also that he would be satisfied only with one in which he had a lot of freedom and autonomy. He definitely has that. With Jupiter in the sixth, he also wants and has a "fun" job.

The Descendant, the cusp of the seventh house of relationships, is Pisces. Junior is idealistic about love. He's in search of the perfect mate, who doesn't exist. But with the Jupiter-Neptune aspect, he's ever hopeful. When he meets the right person, he'll no doubt be totally consumed and madly in love because of his intense Venus-Pluto conjunction (Venus is the universal ruler of partnership). He also has an innate understanding of partnership because of his Libra Sun, which is idealistic.

Mars rules the eighth house of joint resources and other people's money through Aries on the cusp. This is particularly interesting because of Junior's Sun-Mars conjunction, which indicates conflict involving these funds. He had difficulties in working out an ownership arrangement of Dale Earnhardt, Inc. (DEI), for which he drove through the 2007 season. He ultimately left DEI to pursue other opportunities. DEI is managed by his stepmother, and the media has reported that their relationship is less than positive. The tenth is the house of his stepmother, and difficulties are reflected in the Sun-Mars conjunction square Saturn, and the Moon square Mercury (the first- and tenth-house ruler).

The ninth is the house of travel, knowledge, philosophy, spirituality, and ethics. With Taurus on the cusp, we look to Venus as the ruler. Venus's conjunction to Pluto, ruler of the third house, indicates that Junior is a deep, introspective thinker (which he has said he is) who has clear, unbending ethics and a strong personal life philosophy. He should, however, be cautious when traveling, because this aspect (Venus-Pluto) and the houses ruled by these planets (second, third, and ninth) increase the possibility of accidents.

Anyone with Saturn in the tenth house is ambitious to the max, but it also takes them a while to settle in and get on the right path. Junior did this when he was almost thirty, at the time of his Saturn return. (The Saturn return occurs about every twenty-eight years, the period during which Saturn moves through the entire zodiac and returns to its natal place to form a conjunction with natal Saturn. The first Saturn return is a coming-of-age aspect, the time when most people grow up and fully move into an adult life of responsibility.) Saturn in the tenth house is one of the best placements for career success, but only if the rules are followed. As long as Junior does that, he will have a long and successful career and in time become a NASCAR legend.

With Cancer on the eleventh-house cusp, Junior considers his friends to be family. He's also popular among his group and enjoys socializing, with the Moon in this house in Leo, the sign of play. This is where he's comfortable being a star and the center of attention, and he's also very generous with his friends. Junior has also had some success as an actor; Leo is the sign of the actor.

The twelfth is the house of self-renewal and the hidden, secluded side of life. With Sun-ruled Leo on the twelfth-house cusp, Junior enjoys time alone to re-center and simply enjoy his own company. This is another indication of his need for private, introspective time.

Don't be concerned if you feel confused or overwhelmed at this point. Reread this section several times, studying each aspect, and your comfort level will begin to rise. Remember also that like anything else, astrology and chart analysis and synthesis take practice and more practice.

LOVE, MONEY, AND SUCCESS

Love, money, and career success are major interests for most people and among the most frequent reasons people consult an astrologer or decide to study the subject. Astrology is an invaluable tool in all these areas in terms of self-understanding, talent and skill recognition, and maximizing your potential.

You already know a lot about yourself and these areas of life from the signs, planets, houses, angles, and aspects in your birth chart. The following sections include more detailed information that can give you added insights.

LOVE

The best romantic relationship is all about chemistry, that indefinable something that attracts two people to each other. Sometimes it's love at first sight, sometimes it's a flash of passion, sometimes it's a slow discovery that leads to deep love, and sometimes it's a friendship that grows into a romance.

You'll find write-ups of Venus and Mars in the signs on pages 285 and 286. The Venus sign will tell you more about your (and a romantic interest's) approach to dating and romance, as well as what can be a deal breaker. Mars is all about passion and sex, and Mars in the signs

VENUS, THE LOVE PLANET

- *Venus in Aries* is impulsive and competitive and loves the thrill of the chase and playing the field. The main motivation is the equal thrill that comes from the first rush of new love.

- *Venus in Taurus* wants a partner with whom to share a comfortable life, right through old age. Affectionate, thoughtful, and possessive, this person loves romance but finds spontaneity unappealing.

- *Venus in Gemini* is a charming, sociable flirt who loves spur-of-the-moment dates and socializing. To this person, feelings are more thoughts than actual feelings, and a lack of communication is a deal breaker.

- *Venus in Cancer* wants a happy family, including a partner, children, and in-laws. Sometimes clingy, always sensitive, this person needs emotional and material security to feel self-assured.

- *Venus in Leo* is outgoing, warm, generous, and extravagant, but also wants to dominate the relationship and be the center of attention. Romantic to the max, this person knows how to set the stage for love.

- *Venus in Virgo* is choosy, so it often takes persistence to (a) get a date with someone who has this placement and (b) move the relationship along. A mental connection is a must and is the path to winning this person's heart and mind, which can be critical at times.

- *Venus in Libra* feels incomplete without a partner and can fall into the trap of being in love with love. Harmony is a must, along with strong communication skills. Compromise makes this person smile.

- *Venus in Scorpio* is intense, passionate, and possessive in love. Sometimes a jealous streak can mar the harmony of a relationship, as can deep, all-consuming emotions. A healthy motto for this person to adopt: live and let live.

- *Venus in Sagittarius* finds excitement in romantic moments, variety, and the chase. This person's honesty and high ideals and principles are qualities to be admired, but bluntness can nix a promising partnership before it gets started.

- *Venus in Capricorn* sees love as love but also as business. Finances and status are practical and necessary realities, and feelings are expressed only when emotional security reaches its peak.

- *Venus in Aquarius* wants a friend possibly even more than a lover, along with a high level of freedom and independence. Possessiveness is totally unacceptable to this person, while communication and spontaneity are winners.

- *Venus in Pisces* needs a partner to romance, but also frequent reassurance that all is well. Sensitive and sentimental, this person seeks a spiritual connection with a true soul mate.

MARS, THE SEX PLANET

- *Mars in Aries* is passionate, impulsive, and spontaneous, with a strong sex drive. Taking things a little more slowly, including plenty of TLC, is partner-pleasing and the way to enjoy the moment, not just the result.

- *Mars in Taurus* is sensuality at its best. The power of touch, chocolate, and a comfortable, romantic environment ignite a passionate yet gentle response, with plenty of affection.

- *Mars in Gemini* is lighthearted and playful. The perfect mix for this person is flirting, sex, and talk. Mental stimulation is a true turn-on, and without it, sex is just sex without the passion. Variety adds spice.

- *Mars in Cancer* is passionate when feeling emotionally secure and safe, needed, and protected. Then the spark flashes brightly, with all the emotional sensitivity of ultimate satisfaction.

- *Mars in Leo* has a strong sex drive that glitters as pure pleasure when mixed with romance in just the right setting. Rejection is especially tough to take for one who's so generous and considerate of a partner's needs.

- *Mars in Virgo* might appear to be prim and proper. Not so. Sensuality emerges with the confidence of experience and in the right atmosphere with the right person. Enjoying the moment is the biggest challenge.

- *Mars in Libra* sees romance and togetherness as being as important as sex itself, with the partner's desires the most important. Giving is better than receiving as long as all the niceties are observed.

- *Mars in Scorpio* wonders, is there anything else in life?! A powerful sex drive, intense emotions, and a magnetic charisma put this person in contention for the Best Lover Award if possessiveness and jealousy don't become an issue.

- *Mars in Sagittarius* is turned on by what's fun, different, and an adventure, and enthusiasm and pure enjoyment can be partner-pleasing qualities if both people are in sync with each other's feelings and needs. Share the experience.

- *Mars in Capricorn* takes sex seriously, maybe too much so. Sensual and ardent when feeling secure, this person will find that sex is at its best without the structure. Skip Saturday night and try Wednesday, or Thursday, or . . .

- *Mars in Aquarius* lives according to this formula: friendship plus a meeting of the minds equal memorable sex. Spontaneity counts too. Otherwise, a take-it-or-leave-it attitude can prevail, and sex is impersonal and unfulfilling.

- *Mars in Pisces* knows how to keep the romance alive with affection, attention, and plenty of TLC for the adored partner. Sex is one of this person's ultimate fantasies and is the deepest link to a spiritual connection.

tells you much about the steamy side of a relationship and how to keep the sizzle alive.

When attraction becomes love, astrology can help you assess compatibility—where the two of you are in sync and where you're prone to clash. This is called *synastry*: the comparison of two charts and how the planets in both charts interact with one other. But before getting to that point, astrology can help you identify who has romantic potential and who doesn't.

Opposites Attract, Like Attracts Like

It's a cliché that opposites attract, but it's also true. And by using a simple technique, you can quickly and easily identify which men or women are worth a few more dates. Before that, though, you're sure to feel at least some level of chemistry, whether a subtle twinge or a rush of passion. You can confirm the feeling with this technique. Although not foolproof—nothing is—it's a reliable test in the majority of cases. Here's how it works.

You know the sign on your Ascendant (on your first-house cusp), your Sun sign, and your Moon sign. Chemistry happens when any of these signs are the opposite of someone else's Sun, Moon, or Ascendant. For example, if you have a Virgo Ascendant, Sun, or Moon, then take a second look at anyone who has a Pisces Sun, Moon, or Ascendant.

How do you know? It's easy to ask anyone you've just met what his or her Sun sign is. And within a few dates you probably can discover the person's birth date and maybe the place, if not the time. Once you have that information you can calculate what's called a *solar chart*.

A solar chart is a birth chart with the time set for noon. The advantage of using a noon birth time is that it's easier to see the days on which the Moon changes signs, which it does every two and a half days. The Moon advances approximately twelve degrees in a twenty-four-hour period, so by using noon you can subtract and add six degrees from the noon position to determine if the Moon was in the same sign all day. For example, if the noon chart shows the Moon at 12° Leo, then you know that anyone born that day has the Moon between 6° and 18° Leo. But if the noon chart has the Moon at 3° Leo, then someone born that day could have the Moon anywhere between 27° Cancer (the sign before Leo) and 9° Leo. In such a case, you would need the exact time of birth to determine the Moon sign.

A solar chart usually has the Sun in place of what would be the Ascendant, because without a birth time there is no Ascendant (or any of the other angles).

So for this quick chart comparison, you have three factors from your chart—Ascendant, Sun, and Moon signs—and two factors from the other person's chart—Sun and Moon signs. The odds are you'll have one or two matches with anyone who has relationship potential. Later, when you get the person's birth time, you'll have even more to work with.

Al and Tipper Gore are a good example of a couple with strong relationship potential. If Al had been aware of his birth chart when he met Tipper at his high school senior prom (and who knows, he might have been), he would have known that there was a possibility she would become his wife. Al's Ascendant is Leo, his Descendant is Aquarius, and his Moon is in Capricorn. Tipper's Moon is in Aquarius (Al's Descendant), and her Sun is in Leo (Al's Ascendant). Another connection is

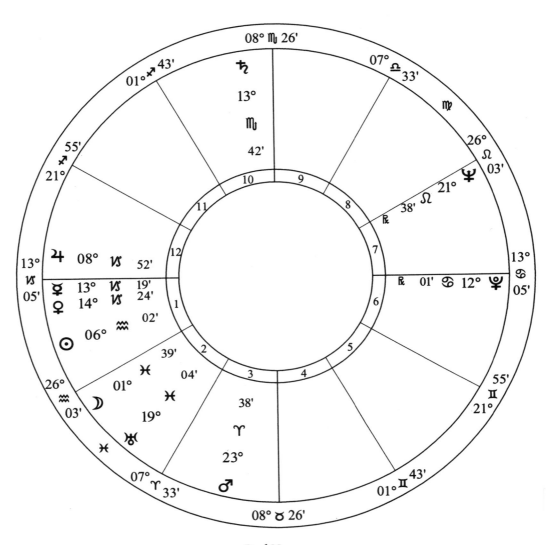

Paul Newman

January 26, 1925 / 6:30 a.m. EST / Cleveland, OH

Placidus Houses

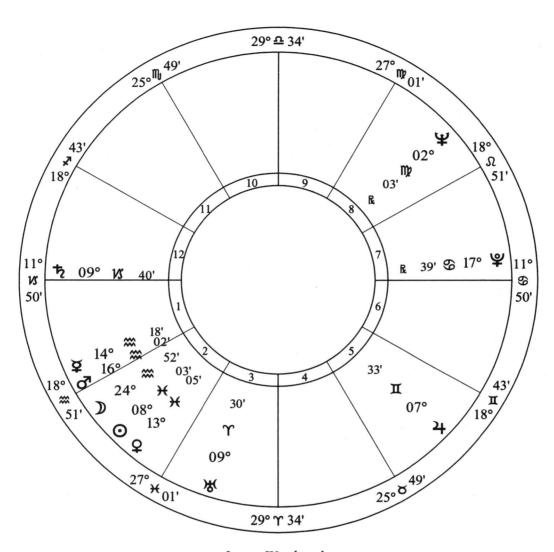

Joanne Woodward

February 27, 1930 / 4:00 a.m. EST / Thomasville, GA

Placidus Houses

her Capricorn Descendant, which is Al's Moon sign.

Another cliché that's also true is that like attracts like. People who have the same Sun, Moon, and/or Ascendant sign either are strongly attracted to each other or intensely dislike each other. Sometimes too much of the same thing can be too much of the same thing! But when these relationships click, they're some of the strongest possible matches.

The charts of Paul Newman and Joanne Woodward are a good example of like attracts like. Defying the Hollywood odds, this couple has been together since their 1958 marriage. This is no surprise to an astrologer. They both have a Capricorn Ascendant (pages 288–289). He has the Sun in Aquarius; she has the Moon in Aquarius. She has the Sun in Pisces; he has the Moon in Pisces. Even without the Ascendant, they're a match.

Synastry

Synastry, the compatibility comparison of two charts, is useful in assessing romantic relationships as well as other personal and business relationships, such as those with family members, coworkers, and friends. This technique can be quite complex when all factors are taken into consideration, but you can get a good idea of how well you fit with someone through some simple aspect comparisons.

All that's necessary is to find the aspects between the planets in both signs. More advanced techniques involve orbs, and the closer the orb, the stronger the influence, just as in a birth chart. But there's also validity in looking at the aspects by sign only, such as any planet in Aries is sextile any planet in Gemini.

In general, the sextile and trine mean a harmonious mix of personalities, and the square increases the potential for conflict. The conjunction varies according to the planets involved; a Mars-Saturn conjunction promotes conflict, while a Venus-Jupiter conjunction indicates happiness. Aspects between the personal planets (Sun, Moon, Mercury, Venus, and Mars) yield the most valuable information.

Communication difficulties are likely when Mercury in one chart is square, opposition, or conjunct Mars, Saturn, Uranus, Neptune, or Pluto in the other chart. Money is often an issue when Venus forms the same aspects to those planets, and Mars can spark conflict when square, opposition, or conjunct Saturn, Uranus, Neptune, or Pluto. Any personal planet in difficult aspect to Pluto usually indicates control issues. Easy aspects to any of these connections can help alleviate the tension.

Look again at Paul Newman's and Joanne Woodward's charts. Chart 11 lists the aspects by sign between them.

Most of the aspects are favorable or of little consequence; however, there are a few potentially problematic ones. Newman's Mercury and Venus square Woodward's Uranus and opposition Pluto can indicate communication difficulties and control issues. But notice that his Sun is sextile her Uranus and his Moon is trine her Pluto. These easy aspects provide an outlet, a way to resolve or work around the difficulties that occur. The same applies to the squares between Mars, Saturn, Mercury, Moon, and Pluto. For each there is a favorable aspect to ease the tension.

No relationship is perfect or ideal, which these synastry aspects illustrate. Yet when there are more positive than negative ones, along

Newman Planets	Aspect	Woodward Planets
Sun ☉	Conjunction ☌	Mercury ☿, Mars ♂, Moon ☽
Sun ☉	Sextile ⚹	Uranus ♅
Sun ☉	Trine △	Jupiter ♃
Moon ☽	Conjunction ☌	Sun ☉, Venus ♀
Moon ☽	Sextile ⚹	Saturn ♄
Moon ☽	Opposition ☍	Neptune ♆
Moon ☽	Trine △	Pluto ♇
Moon ☽	Square ☐	Jupiter ♃
Mercury ☿, Venus ♀, Jupiter ♃	Square ☐	Uranus ♅
Mercury ☿, Venus ♀, Jupiter ♃	Opposition ☍	Pluto ♇
Mercury ☿, Venus ♀, Jupiter ♃	Trine △	Neptune ♆
Mercury ☿, Venus ♀, Jupiter ♃	Conjunction ☌	Saturn ♄
Mars ♂	Square ☐	Saturn ♄, Pluto ♇
Mars ♂	Conjunction ☌	Uranus ♅
Mars ♂	Sextile ⚹	Jupiter ♃
Saturn ♄	Square ☐	Mars ♂, Mercury ☿, Moon ☽
Saturn ♄	Trine △	Sun ☉, Venus ♀

Chart 11. Synastry for Paul Newman and Joanne Woodward

with the sizzle of love, most couples find ways to minimize the weaknesses and maximize the strengths of their relationship.

But even the best synastry between two charts can't negate the indications of relationship difficulties in one or the other, or both, individual birth charts. This makes it important to evaluate each person's birth chart for how he or she handles conflict, compromise, communication, and relationships in general. You also should assess the potential and desire for long-term commitment, children, immediate family and in-law relationships, and life priorities. A realistic assessment can help avoid major challenges in future years.

MONEY

Money, money, money! Most people get it by earning it, yet it's the rare person who doesn't wish for a little or a lot of easy money—an inheritance, lottery win, or other windfall.

Your birth chart doesn't tell you when or for sure if you'll be lucky. What it indicates is the potential, and the stronger the potential is, the greater the chance you'll realize your financial wishes. Your birth chart also reflects your ability to earn your way to wealth.

Because every birth chart is unique, it's difficult to generalize about financial potential, but there are certain factors that increase the odds for high earnings:

- a grand trine in earth signs (Taurus, Virgo, Capricorn)
- a grand trine that includes planets in the second, sixth, and tenth houses
- a grand trine in water signs (Cancer, Scorpio, Pisces)
- a grand trine that includes planets in the fourth, eighth, and twelfth houses
- Jupiter and/or Neptune in the second or eighth house
- planets in the second and/or eighth houses

Even with one or more of these factors active in your birth chart, you still will need to put forth the effort to realize your financial potential. Money will just come more easily to you.

The possibility for an inheritance is easier to find in a birth chart, mostly because this is something decided by someone else. It requires no or little effort on your part, unlike personal earnings.

Finding your inheritance potential requires the use of house rulerships—the planet that rules the sign on the house cusp. These are the factors to look for that can indicate a family inheritance:

- the eighth-house ruler in the fourth house; for example, Aries on the cusp of the eighth house with Mars in the fourth house
- the fourth-house ruler in the eighth house; for example, Libra on the cusp of the fourth house with Venus in the eighth house

- the second-house ruler in the eighth house; for example, Leo on the cusp of the second house with the Sun in the eighth house
- the fourth- and eighth-house rulers sextile or trine one another
- the second- and-eighth house rulers sextile or trine one another
- planets in the second house and/or fourth house and/or eighth house in aspect to one other
- Neptune in the second house in aspect to the eighth-house ruler or planets in the eighth house
- Moon in aspect to a planet in the second house or the second-house ruler

When many of these factors are active, it often indicates a larger inheritance or one that will make a significant difference, whatever the amount. The aspects, easy or difficult, don't indicate the size of the inheritance. Trines, sextiles, and favorable conjunctions (such as Venus-Jupiter or Moon-Mercury) reflect ease in assets passing from one generation to the next. Squares, oppositions, and some conjunctions (such as Mars-Saturn) indicate difficulties surrounding the inheritance or that the amount received is ultimately less than what was expected or hoped for.

Everyone is lucky in some way, usually in the birth-chart areas influenced by Jupiter. For some, it's career, relationships, or right timing. For others, it's games of chance.

Almost everyone dreams about winning tens of millions in a lottery or thousands from gambling. Few do. More people have an almost perpetual lucky streak that nets them small winnings, raffle prizes, or a few hundred from a slot machine.

The following birth-chart indicators increase the chance for a lucky win:

- planets in the fifth house (speculation)
- aspects between planets in the second, fifth, and eighth houses and/or the rulers of these houses
- a prominent Jupiter—many aspects to Jupiter, Jupiter in one of the angular houses, or Jupiter in aspect to the Sun or Venus
- Jupiter in the fifth or eighth house
- a Jupiter-Uranus conjunction or these planets in or ruling the fifth and eighth houses
- a Venus-Jupiter conjunction

Give speculation a try if you have a number of these factors in your chart. But start small and test your luck, risking only what you can afford to lose.

CAREER SUCCESS

Many people drift into jobs and careers, while others know from a young age where they want to direct their energies. For some, career and job are the most defining factors in their lives, but for others, a job is merely a life necessity. Finding the right career field and the right job within that field can turn even the most half-hearted worker into an ambitious one.

Now that you've explored your birth chart, you undoubtedly have an even clearer idea of your strengths, talents, and skills and the areas of your life that present challenges. You probably discovered things about yourself that you never knew or were only vaguely aware of. All of this information and knowledge can contribute to your career and job success.

The tenth house and Midheaven represent your career field—the big picture area of focus, such as medicine. The sixth house is linked to your specific job, which might be nursing, pharmaceuticals, nutrition, or one of many others, and to your preferred working style and best working environment. (See chapter 4 for descriptions of the signs on your sixth- and tenth-house cusps.) The signs on the cusps of the sixth and tenth houses, their ruling planets, and any planets in these houses also influence your career and job choice.

The career fields listed here for each sign and its ruling planet represent only a smattering of possibilities. They're designed to prompt your thinking. To make the most of the information, read the lists for the signs on your sixth- and tenth-house (Midheaven) cusps and for any planets in those houses. Then read the sign(s) in which the rulers of your sixth- and tenth-house cusps are placed.

For example, if you have an Aries Midheaven, then Mars is the ruling planet. Some Aries careers are metalworking, surgery, firefighting, and the military. If Mars is in Pisces, you might pursue a career in surgery anesthesia (Pisces rules drugs) or as a pharmacist in the military to combine the two influences.

Aries/Mars

Diamond industry
Audiology
Optometry/ophthalmology
Firefighting
Hardware
Iron or metalworking

Manufacturing

Military

Surgery

Physical therapy

Tool design

Carpentry

Dentistry

Sports

Police work

Taurus/Venus

Music

Architecture

Acting

Massage therapy

Art

Banking/lending

Jewelry

Cattle industry

Beauty industry

Numismatics/money

Confectionary

Carpeting

Dancing

Gemini/Mercury

Advertising

Writing

Journalism

Respiratory therapy

Driving

Clerical

Media

Teaching

Customer service

Engineering

Merchandising/buyer

Graphology

Mechanics

Library science

Transportation

Postal/delivery

Neurology

Printing

Cancer/Moon

Food industry

Agriculture

Plumbing

Fishing industry

Childcare

Obstetrics

Real estate

Hotel industry

Parenting

Boating

Nutrition

Oceanography

Silversmith

Leo/Sun

Jewelry

Stocks and bonds

Childcare

Cardiology

Sports

Entertainment

Gambling

Actor

Pediatrics

Government

Politics

Recreation

Military officer

Virgo/Mercury

Accounting
Library science
Chemistry
Mechanics
Retail
Environment
Editorial
Human resources
Medicine
Clothing manufacturing
Sanitation
Engineer
Pharmacy
Volunteer
Veterinary medicine
Event planner

Libra/Venus

Beauty industry
Art
Interior design
Jewelry
Flower industry
Legal industry
Wedding planner
Event planner
Real estate
Sales
Mediation

Scorpio/Pluto

Butcher
Tax agent
Dentistry
Funeral industry
Investigation
Police work

Research
Recycling
Surgery

Sagittarius/Jupiter

Advertising
Publishing
Teaching
College/university
Clergy/religion
Equine industry
Writing
Travel industry
Foreign trade and affairs
Legal industry

Capricorn/Saturn

Masonry
Dermatology
Chiropractic
Real estate
Leather industry
Mining/geology
Orthopaedics
Construction
Engineering
Economics
Government
Gerontology
Project management

Aquarius/Uranus

Aeronautics/aviation
Heating/air conditioning
Astrology
Meteorology
Psychology
Nonprofit sector

Inventions
Electrical
Electronic media
Computer industry

Pisces / Neptune

Medicine
Photography / film
Sales
Beverage industry

Footwear
Chemistry
Oceanography
Podiatry
Fishing
Aquatics
Large institutions
Energy
Environmental work
Pharmaceuticals

CHIRON, ASTEROIDS, FIXED STARS, MOON'S NODES, VERTEX, PART OF FORTUNE

Some astrologers use Chiron, asteroids, fixed stars, the Moon's nodes, the Vertex, and the Part of Fortune (see figure 36). All of these factors have their supporters and detractors. Some astrologers never use them, while others believe it's impossible to read a chart without them. The best techniques are the ones that work for you, so experiment with each of these and reach your own conclusions. Nothing, however, can replace a solid knowledge of the basics—signs, planets, houses, and aspects—and this is what you should do before delving into more. After all, for thousands of years astrologers read charts using only the seven visible planets—Sun, Moon, Mercury, Venus, Mars, Jupiter, and Saturn.

Chiron

Chiron ($\bar{5}$), discovered in 1977, is a comet whose use as an astrological indicator continues to grow, although much about it is still unknown. Astrologers have developed numerous theories on its meaning, the most widespread being its definition as the "wounded healer."

In that role, Chiron represents the areas of life and the experiences as reflected in the birth chart that can lead to self-discovery and self-healing. These areas and experiences, often called "issues," must be resolved in order to achieve personal growth, and are reflected in Chiron's sign, house, and aspects to planets and angles.

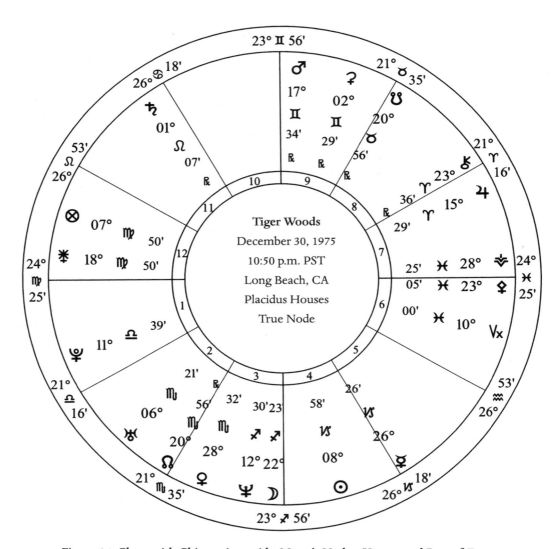

Figure 36. Chart with Chiron, Asteroids, Moon's Nodes, Vertex, and Part of Fortune

Many books have been written about Chiron (see the suggested reading list at the end of the book). Consult them if you're curious about this comet's influence in your birth chart and life.

Asteroids

There are a *lot* of asteroids, and estimates go as high as 200,000. If you used them all, the chart would be so packed with glyphs that you wouldn't be able to see the planets or much of anything else. There are astrologers who use many of them. Most who use asteroids, however, limit their use to the four major ones—*Ceres, Pallas Athena, Juno,* and *Vesta.* Just like the planets, the asteroids are in a sign and house and aspect planets and angles.

The largest of the four asteroids is Ceres (♀), the goddess of the harvest. This asteroid represents domestic life, nurturing, healing, and growth. Pallas Athena (♀), the goddess of wisdom, represents intelligence, intuition, peacemaking, equality, and valor. Pallas is often influential in the career choice, especially for women. Juno (♣), the goddess of marriage and maternity, reflects what the individual expects from a partner. It also can indicate obligations and responsibilities. Vesta (♣), the goddess of the hearth, was associated with keeping the fire burning in the home. Its placement in the birth chart shows where sacrifices are made for the greater good.

Moon's Nodes

Many astrologers use the North Node (☊) and South Node (☋) of the Moon, so you'll often see them in charts. The nodes are points calculated using the Moon's position in reference to the ecliptic; they are not actual bodies. They are always directly opposite each other (just like an opposition aspect), such as Aries North Node / Libra South Node or Cancer North Node / Capricorn South Node.

The basic meaning of the nodes is that the North Node's energy is like Jupiter and the South Node is like Saturn. The North Node thus shows where you can overcome challenges and expand your horizons, and the South Node is where you can expect limitations. Like the opposition aspect, the nodes are associated with relationships and how you relate to other people.

Fixed Stars

The fixed stars are the stars we view in the heavens that make up the constellations. The stars used are mostly those catalogued by Ptolemy and included in his *Tetrabiblos,* along with descriptions of their influence in the birth chart. The fixed stars move very slowly, about one degree every seventy-five years, and each is in a sign and house in your chart. The square, trine, opposition, and conjunction from a fixed star to planets and angles in the chart are used, with the conjunction being the strongest. The orb is thirty minutes to one degree.

Several of the fixed stars and their meanings are as follows:

Algol, at 25° Taurus, was called the "evil" star by ancient astrologers, and represents revenge, anger, and difficulties.

Aldebaran, at 9° Gemini, symbolizes ambition and success through ethical actions.

Formalhaut, at 3° Pisces, represents ideals and ethics.

Regulus, at 29° Leo, signifies luck, ambition, and success .

Rigel, at 16° Gemini, represents quick but fleeting success.

Spica, at 23° Libra, signifies a brilliant mind.

The Vertex

Like the angles (Ascendant, Midheaven, IC, Descendant), the Vertex is not a planet but a point that's calculated and specific to the birth date, time, and place. Some astrologers consider the Vertex to be another angle.

The Vertex has a fateful connotation, and its sign, house placement, and aspects to planets and angles indicate a person's destiny in life. It thus is thought to be karmic in nature and to represent what needs to be learned by the individual to refine the personality. The Vertex also usually involves relationship issues because its opposite point is the Anti-Vertex, which indicates the action or response needed to resolve the issues.

Part of Fortune

The Part of Fortune is one of dozens of Arabic parts, or lots, as they were called by ancient astrologers. The Part of Fortune is the only one in common use today, and many astrologers find its influence to be significant in the birth chart. It is an indicator of financial success. It often is used in horary astrology (see appendix II).

All of the Arabic parts are calculated by adding or subtracting the degrees of distance between two planets and the Ascendant. The Ascendant is a constant; the planets used are those appropriate to the specific part. To calculate the Part of Fortune, add the sign, degrees, and minutes of the Sun, Moon, and Ascendant: Sun + Moon + ASC = Part of Fortune. Here's an example:

Sun at 10° Gemini (Gemini is the third sign in the zodiac, so add 30° for Aries, 30° for Taurus, and 10° for Gemini: 30° + 30° + 10° = 70°).

Moon at 3° Leo (Leo is the fifth sign in the zodiac, so add 30° for each of the first four signs and 3° for Leo: 30° + 30° + 30° + 30° + 3° = 123°).

Ascendant at 18° Libra (Libra is the seventh sign, so add 30° for each of the first six signs and 18° for Libra: 30° x 6 = 180° + 18° = 198°).

Sun 70° + Moon 123° + ASC 198° = 391°

391° is greater than the 360° total of all signs, so subtract 360° from 391°, which equals 31°, or 1 sign and 1 degree:

1° Taurus is the Part of Fortune.

APPENDIX II

THE BRANCHES OF ASTROLOGY

There are a number of specialty areas, or branches, of astrology. Each uses the same principles used in natal astrology: signs, planets, houses, and aspects. Some of the branches use additional rulerships associated with the signs, planets, and houses, such as Aquarius for cold weather and Scorpio and the Moon and Cancer for the kitchen. There are many books available that explain the techniques (see the suggested reading list at the end of the book).

Electional Astrology

This branch of astrology is based on the theory that some dates and times are preferable to others for initiating an activity. It often is used by people in the know to schedule a wedding, business opening, or job interview or acceptance, as well as to list a home for sale, buy a home, sign a contract, or make a major purchase such as a vehicle.

There is no perfect time for anything, so the electional astrologer selects the best possible date and time to maximize the planetary positions in favor of the election. Rulerships and houses are extremely important.

For example, when selecting a wedding chart, it's advantageous to have certain signs on the Ascendant and Descendant (representing the couple) and to have the planetary rulers of these signs in easy aspect to one another.

Mundane Astrology

Mundane astrology is the study of countries, cities, provinces, and states. Each has a birth chart that is used to forecast trends and major events affecting that entity. Mundane astrologers would use a city's chart, for example, to forecast a natural disaster, or a country's chart to forecast the general welfare of the people for a certain time period.

This branch also includes the study of wars, peace agreements, and presidential inaugurations and other government-initiated events. From the birth chart erected for the start of the event, the astrologer can predict the outcome.

Weather forecasting, or astrometeorology, is another area included in mundane astrology. It's possible to forecast the weather for any date, time, and place using specific techniques.

Cardinal ingress charts (charts calculated for when the Sun is at 0° Aries, Cancer, Libra, or Capricorn) and charts for the four Moon phases (New Moon, First Quarter Moon, Full Moon, and Third Quarter Moon) are used extensively in mundane astrology.

Horary Astrology

Horary astrology is used to determine the answer to a question posed by a querent (the person asking the question). It can be used to answer yes or no questions (or almost any question) and to find missing objects. A horary astrologer calculates a chart for the moment the querent asks the question and then interprets the chart to glean the answer.

Horary astrology has a strict and lengthy set of rules handed down from the ancient astrologers. Aspects and the Moon are especially important in horary astrology.

Relocation Astrology

Relocation astrology is used to determine the optimum locations in the world for life activities such as relationship happiness, career success, travel, or retirement. The astrologer relocates the individual's birth chart to a new location as if the person had been born there. The planets are the same, but the birth chart angles (Ascendant, Descendant, Midheaven, and IC) change to reflect the new location; the planets thus make different aspects to the angles. By examining the aspects to the angles, the astrologer can determine what areas of life the new location favors for the individual.

If you want to try this, calculate your chart for another location using the exact time and time zone of your birth. If the distance is far enough (1,000–2,000 miles), then your chart will have different signs on the angles and most of the planets will change house positions. Then read the aspect and house interpretations for your chart in the new location.

Predictive Astrology

Predictive astrology is used to forecast trends and events in an individual's life. There are many predictive techniques, the most popular being the progressed and transiting planets aspecting planets and angles in the birth chart. Solar returns also are used by many astrologers; this technique involves calculating a chart for the exact moment when the individual's Sun returns to the exact sign, degree, and minute of its birth placement.

Predictive astrology is a valuable tool in that it provides advance information an individual can use in decision making. It's helpful to know what's on the horizon, when to pursue career goals, when to conserve and when to spend, when relationships will be upbeat or strained, and when to expect developments in an ongoing matter.

Financial Astrology

A growing number of people are using financial astrology techniques to determine general economic trends and as a tool for investing. This branch involves the use of ingress and lunar phase charts for trends, and incorporation and first-trade charts for investing. There are many books available that explain the theories, as well as highly specialized astrological software to assist the investor.

Cosmobiology

Most Western astrologers use the traditional astrological techniques developed centuries ago, which then were refined in the ensuing years. A small group of astrologers use a system called *cosmobiology*, which was developed in Germany in the 1920s. Cosmobiologists do not use houses or traditional aspects. Instead, they read charts with *midpoints*. The midpoint is the halfway point between any two planets, and the theory is that the midpoint is the place where the energies of both planets unite. The midpoint also is considered a sensitive point in predictive astrology. Cosmobiologists use a midpoint "tree," which is a listing of the midpoints for an individual chart, and note the contacts made to the midpoints by other planets, which result in what they call *planetary pictures*.

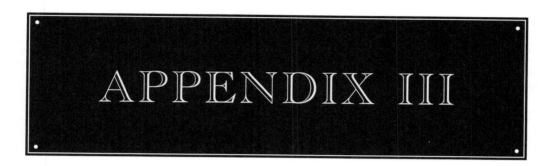

APPENDIX III

ASTROLOGICAL ORGANIZATIONS AND WEBSITES

Astrological Organizations

There are many local astrology groups in addition to the national and international ones listed here, some of which have chapters or affiliate groups in the United States and other countries.

American Federation of Astrologers (AFA)

6535 S. Rural Road, Tempe, AZ 85283

480-838-1751

http://www.astrologers.com

Offers certification testing and a correspondence course.

Association for Astrological Networking (AFAN)

http://www.afan.org

Faculty of Astrological Studies

http://www.astrology.org.uk

Offers classes and certification testing.

National Council for Geocosmic Research (NCGR)

http://www.geocosmic.org

Offers certification testing.

International Society for Astrological Research (ISAR)
http://www.isarastrology.com

Free Online Chart Calculation
You can get free charts at the following websites. For help obtaining an official U.S. birth certificate, visit this web page of the National Center for Health Statistics: http://www.cdc.gov/nchs/howto/w2w/w2welcom.htm.

AIR Software
http://www.alphee.com

Astrodienst
http://www.astro.com

Astrolabe
http://www.alabe.com

Matrix Software
http://www.thenewage.com

SUGGESTED READING

Thousands of astrology books have been written over the centuries, and new books are published every year. Included in this suggested reading list are books on nearly every astrological topic and for every level of astrological knowledge. Some are out of print, but you might find them at used bookstores and on the Internet.

Asteroids

Donath, Emma Belle. *Asteroids in the Birth Chart*. Tempe, AZ: AFA, 1987.

George, Demetra. *Asteroid Goddesses*. Berwick, ME: Ibis Press, 2003.

Guttman, Ariel, and Kenneth Johnson. *Mythic Astrology*. St. Paul, MN: Llewellyn Publications, 1993.

————. *Mythic Astrology Applied*. St. Paul, MN: Llewellyn Publications, 2004.

Biography

Brahy, Gustave-Lambert. *Confidential Recollections Revealed*. Tempe, AZ: AFA, 2006. (Autobiography of Belgian astrologer Gustave-Lambert Brahy, 1930s and 1940s)

Christino, Karen. *Foreseeing the Future: Evangeline Adams and Astrology in America*. Amherst, MA: One Reed Publications, 2002.

Calendars and Annuals

Llewellyn's Astrological Calendar. St. Paul, MN: Llewellyn Publications.

Llewellyn's Daily Planetary Guide. St. Paul, MN: Llewellyn Publications.

Llewellyn's Moon Sign Book. St. Paul, MN: Llewellyn Publications.

Llewellyn's Sun Sign Book. St. Paul, MN: Llewellyn Publications.

Maynard, Jim. *Jim Maynard's Astrologer's Datebook*. Ashland, OR: Quicksilver Productions.

Chiron

Clow, Barbara Hand. *Chiron: Rainbow Bridge Between the Inner and Outer Planets*. St. Paul, MN: Llewellyn Publications, 2004.

Lass, Martin. *Chiron*. St. Paul, MN: Llewellyn Publications, 2005.

Classical Astrology

Cornell, H. L. *The Encyclopaedia of Medical Astrology*. Los Angeles, CA: Cornell Publishing Co., 1933; Bel Air, MD: Astrology Classics, 2004.

Lilly, William. *The Astrologer's Guide*. Tempe, AZ: AFA, 2005. (Originally published in 1647.)

———. *Christian Astrology, Books 1 and 2*. Bel Air, MD: Astrology Classics, 2004. (Originally published in 1647.)

———. *Christian Astrology, Book 3*. Bel Air, MD: Astrology Classics, 2005. (Originally published in 1647.)

Morin, Jean-Baptiste. *Astrologia Gallica, Books 13, 14, 15, 19*. Tempe, AZ: AFA, 2006.

———. *Astrologia Gallica, Book 18: Strengths of the Planets*. Tempe, AZ: AFA, .

———. *Astrologia Gallica, Book 22: Directions*. Tempe, AZ: AFA, 1994.

———. *Astrologia Gallica, Book 23: Revolutions*. Tempe, AZ: AFA, 2004.

———. *Astrologia Gallica, Book 24: Progressions and Transits*. Tempe, AZ: AFA, 2005.

Noonan, George. *Classical Scientific Astrology*. Tempe, AZ: AFA, 1984, 2005.

Pearce, A. J. *The Text-Book of Astrology*. Tempe, AZ: AFA, 2006. (Originally published in 1911.)

Ptolemy. *Tetrabiblos*. Bel Air, MD: Astrology Classics, 2002. (Written in the third century BC.)

Cosmobiology

Ebertin, Reinhold. *The Combination of Stellar Influences*. Aalen, Germany: Ebertin-Verlag, 1940; Tempe, AZ: AFA, 1994, 2004.

———. *Transits*. Aalen, Germany: Ebertin-Verlag, 1928; Tempe, AZ: AFA, 2001.

Kimmel, Eleonora. *Altered and Unfinished Lives*. Tempe, AZ: AFA, 2006.

———. *Cosmobiology for the 21st Century*. Tempe, AZ: AFA, 1979.

———. *Fundamentals of Cosmobiology*. Tempe, AZ: AFA, 1979.

Simms, Maria Kay. *Dial Detective*. Kensington, NH: Cosmic Muse Publications, 2001.

Eclipses

Lineman, Rose. *Eclipses: Astrological Guideposts*. Tempe, AZ: AFA, 1984, 2004.

———. *Eclipse Interpretation Manual*. Tempe, AZ: AFA, 1986, 2004.

———. *Your Prenatal Eclipse*. Tempe, AZ: AFA, 1992, 2003.

Electional Astrology

Hampar, Joann. *Electional Astrology*. St. Paul, MN: Llewellyn Publications, 2005.

Ephemerides

The American Heliocentric Ephemeris, 2001–2050. San Diego, CA: ACS, 1996.

The American Sidereal Ephemeris, 2001–2050. San Diego, CA: ACS.

Astro America's Daily Ephemeris, 2000–2010. Bel Air, MD: Astrology Classics, 2006.

Astro America's Daily Ephemeris, 2010–2020. Bel Air, MD: Astrology Classics, 2006.

Astro America's Daily Ephemeris, 2000–2020. Bel Air, MD: Astrology Classics, 2006.

Astrolabe World Ephemeris, 2001–2050. Atglen, PA: Whitford Press.

The New American Ephemeris, 2007–2020, with Longitude, Latitude and Declinations. San Diego, CA: ACS.

The New American Ephemeris for the 21st Century, 2000–2100 at Midnight. Exeter, NH: Starcrafts Publishing, 2006.

The New American Midpoint Ephemeris, 2001–2020. San Diego, CA: ACS.

Raphael's Ephemeris. (Single year.) Slough, England: W. Foulsham & Co.

Rosicrucian Ephemeris. (Single year, decade, century.) Oceanside, CA: Rosicrucian Fellowship.

Tables of Planetary Phenomena. Second edition. San Diego, CA: ACS, 1995.

Financial Astrology

Meridian, Bill. *Planetary Economic Forecasting.* New York: Cycles Research, 2002. (Out of print.)

———. *Planetary Stock Trading.* New York: Cycles Research, 2002.

Williams, David. *Financial Astrology.* Tempe, AZ: AFA, 1984, 2003.

Fixed Stars

Brady, Bernadette. *Brady's Book of Fixed Stars.* York Beach, ME: Red Wheel/Weiser, 1998.

Ebertin, Reinhold. *Fixed Stars and Their Interpretation.* Aalen, Germany: Ebertin-Verlag, 1971; Tempe, AZ: AFA, 2001.

Robson, Vivian. *The Fixed Stars and Constellations in Astrology.* New York: Samuel Weiser, 1969; Bel Air, MD: Astrology Classics, 2004.

History of Astrology

Holden, James Herschel. *History of Horoscopic Astrology.* Second edition. Tempe, AZ: AFA, 2006.

Horary Astrology

Barclay, Olivia. *Horary Astrology Rediscovered.* Atglen, PA: Whitford Press, 1990.

Jones, Marc Edmund. *Horary Astrology.* Santa Fe, NM: Aurora Press, 1993.

Lavoie, Alphee. *Horary at Its Best.* West Hartford, CT: AIR, 2002.

Louis, Anthony. *Horary Astrology: Plain and Simple.* St. Paul, MN: Llewellyn Publications, 2005.

Locational Astrology

Cozzi, Steve. *Planets in Locality.* St. Paul, MN: Llewellyn Publications, 1988; Tempe, AZ: AFA, 1997.

Penfield, Marc. *Bon Voyage.* Tempe, AZ: AFA, 1992.

Pottenger, Maritha, and Kris Brandt Riske, M.A. *Mapping Your Travels & Relocation.* Tempe, AZ: AFA, 2005.

Medical Astrology

Cramer, Diane. *Dictionary of Medical Astrology.* Tempe, AZ: AFA, 2003.

———. *How to Give an Astrological Health Reading.* Tempe, AZ: AFA, 1996, 2005.

———. *Managing Your Health & Wellness.* St. Paul, MN: Llewellyn Publications, 2006.

Darling, Harry F., M.D. *Essentials of Medical Astrology.* Tempe, AZ: AFA, 1981, 2004.

Faugno, Emily. *Your Fertile Hours.* Tempe, AZ: AFA, 1986.

Hill, Judith A. *Medical Astrology.* Portland, OR: Stellium Press, 2004.

Mundane Astrology

Brown, Philip. *Cosmic Trends.* St. Paul, MN: Llewellyn Publications, 2006.

Campion, Nicholas. *The Book of World Horoscopes.* Revised edition. Bournemouth, England: Wessex Astrologer, Ltd., 2004.

Clement, Stephanie, ed. *Civilization Under Attack.* St. Paul, MN: Llewellyn Publications, 2001.

Dodson, Carolyn. *Horoscopes of U.S. States and Cities.* Tempe, AZ: AFA, 1999.

Green, H. S., C.E.O. Carter, and Raphael. *Mundane Astrology.* Bel Air, MD: Astrology Classics, 2004.

Jones, Marc Edmund. *Mundane Perspectives in Astrology.* Stanwood, WA: Sabian Publishing Society, 1975.

McRae, I. I. Chris. *The Geodetic World Map.* Tempe, AZ: AFA, 1988.

Meadows, David. *Where in the World with Astro*Carto*Graphy.* Tempe, AZ: AFA, 1998.

Penfield, Marc. *Horoscopes of Asia, Australia and the Pacific.* Tempe, AZ: AFA, 2006.

———. *Horoscopes of Latin America.* Tempe, AZ: AFA, 2006.

———. *Horoscopes of the USA and Canada.* Second edition. Tempe, AZ: AFA, 2005.

———. *Stars Over England.* Tempe, AZ: AFA, 2005.

Riske, Kris Brandt. *Astrometeorology: Planetary Power in Weather Forecasting.* Tempe, AZ: AFA, 1997.

Weber, Lind. *Astro-Geology of Earthquakes and Volcanoes.* Tempe, AZ: AFA, 1995.

Natal Astrology

Adams, Helen J. *Understanding Retrogrades.* Tempe, AZ: AFA, 1982, 1996.

Arroyo, Stephen. *Astrology, Karma and Transformation.* Sebastopol, CA: CRCS, 1992.

———. *Astrology, Psychology and the Four Elements.* Sebastopol, CA: CRCS, 1975.

Avery, Jeanne. *Astrological Aspects.* Garden City, NY: Doubleday & Co., 1985; Tempe, AZ: AFA, 2005.

———. *The Rising Sign.* Garden City, NY: Doubleday, 1982.

Burk, Kevin. *The Complete Node Book.* St. Paul, MN: Llewellyn Publications, 2006.

Busteed, Marilyn, and Dorothy Wergin. *Phases of the Moon.* Tempe, AZ: AFA, 1982.

Carelli, Adriano. *The 360 Degrees of the Zodiac.* Tempe, AZ: AFA, 1977, 2004.

Carter, C.E.O. *The Astrological Aspects.* London: L. N. Fowler, 1930; Tempe, AZ: AFA, 2003.

———. *An Encyclopaedia of Psychological Astrology.* London: W. Foulsham & Co., 1924; Bel Air, MD: Astrology Classics, 2003.

———. *Foundations of Astrology.* London: L. N. Fowler, 1947. (Out of print.)

———. *Some Principles of Horoscopic Delineation.* London: L. N. Fowler, 1934. (Out of print.)

———. *The Zodiac and the Soul.* London: Theosophical Publishing House, Ltd., 1928. (Out of print.)

Christino, Karen. *What Evangeline Adams Knew: A Book of Astrological Charts and Techniques.* Brooklyn Heights, NY: Stella Mira Books, 2004.

Cunningham, Donna. *Astrology and Vibrational Healing.* San Rafael, CA: Cassandra Press, 1988.

———. *Being a Lunar Type in a Solar World.* York Beach, ME: Samuel Weiser, 1990. (Out of print.)

———. *Healing Pluto Problems.* York Beach, ME: Red Wheel/Weiser, 1986.

———. *Moon Signs.* New York: Ballantine Books, 1988.

Devlin, Mary. *Astrology and Past Lives.* West Chester, PA: Para Research, 1987.

Falconer, Kim. *Astrology and Aptitude.* Tempe, AZ: AFA, 2005.

Forrest, Steven. *The Inner Sky.* San Diego, CA: ACS, 2001.

George, Llewellyn. *Llewellyn's New A to Z Horoscope Maker and Interpreter.* Fourteenth edition. St. Paul, MN: Llewellyn Publications, 2003.

Goldsmith, Martin. *Moon Phases: A Symbolic Key.* Atglen, PA: Whitford Press, 1988.

———. *Zodiac by Degrees.* York Beach, ME: Red Wheel/Weiser, 2004.

Grebner, Bernice Prill. *Lunar Nodes.* Tempe, AZ: AFA, 1980, 2006.

Guttman, Ariel, and Kenneth Johnson. *Mythic Astrology.* St. Paul, MN: Llewellyn Publications, 1993.

———. *Mythic Astrology Applied.* St. Paul, MN: Llewellyn Publications, 2004.

Hand, Robert. *Horoscope Symbols.* Atglen, PA: Whitford Press, 1981.

———. *Planets in Youth.* Atglen, PA: Whitford Press, 1977.

Henson, Donna. *The Vertex: The Third Angle.* Tempe, AZ: AFA, 2003.

Hickey, Isabel M. *Astrology: A Cosmic Science.* Watertown, MA: Fellowship House Bookshop, 1974; Sebastopol, CA: CRCS, 1992.

Hill, Judith A. *Vocational Astrology.* Tempe, AZ: AFA, 2000.

Jones, Marc Edmund. *Guide to Horoscope Interpretation.* Stanwood, WA: Sabian Publishing Society, 1972.

Kellogg, Joan. *The Yod: Its Esoteric Meaning.* Tempe, AZ: AFA, 1989, 2003.

Leo, Alan. *The Art of Synthesis*. London: L. N. Fowler, 1912, 1971. (Out of print.)

———. *How to Judge a Nativity*. London: L. N. Fowler, 1909. (Out of print.)

Lewi, Grant. *Astrology for the Millions*. St. Paul, MN: Llewellyn Publications, 1990.

———. *Heaven Knows What*. St. Paul, MN: Llewellyn Publications, 1995.

Mason, Sophia. *You and Your Ascendant*. Tempe, AZ: AFA, 1998.

McRae, I. I. Chris. *Understanding Interceptions*. Tempe, AZ: AFA, 2000.

Oken, Alan. *Alan Oken's Complete Astrology*. New York: Bantam Books, 1988.

———. *Houses of the Horoscope*. Freedom, CA: Crossing Press, 1999.

———. *Rulers of the Horoscope*. Freedom, CA: Crossing Press, 2000.

Parker, Julia and Derek. *Parker's Astrology*. London: DK Publishing, 2003.

Pelletier, Robert. *Planets in Aspect*. Atglen, PA: Whitford Press, 1974.

———. *Planets in Houses*. Atglen, PA: Whitford Press, 1978.

Riske, Kris Brandt, M.A. *Mapping Your Money*. St. Paul, MN: Llewellyn Publications, 2005.

Robson, Vivian. *Astrology and Sex*. Philadelphia: W. Foulsham Co., 1941; Bel Air, MD: Astrology Classics, 2004.

Rodden, Lois. *Money: How to Find It with Astrology*. Yucaipa, CA: Data News, 1994; Tempe, AZ: AFA, 2006.

Rogers-Gallagher, Kim. *Astrology for the Light Side of the Brain*. San Diego, CA: ACS, 1995.

Ruiz, Ana. *Interpreting Empty Houses*. Tempe, AZ: AFA, 2006.

Silveira de Mello, Joseph. *Declinations*. Tempe, AZ: AFA, 2003.

———. *Decumbitures and Diurnals*. Tempe, AZ: AFA, 2003.

Simms, Maria Kay. *Moon Tides, Soul Passages*. Kensington, NH: Starcrafts Publishing, 2004.

———. *Your Magical Child*. San Diego, CA: ACS, 1994.

Smith, Debbi Kempton. *Secrets from a Stargazer's Notebook*. New York: Topquark Press, 1999.

Spiller, Jan. *Astrology for the Soul*. New York: Bantam Books, 1997.

Tierney, Bil. *Alive and Well with Neptune*. St. Paul, MN: Llewellyn Publications, 1999. (Out of print.)

———. *Alive and Well with Pluto*. St. Paul, MN: Llewellyn Publications, 1999. (Out of print.)

———. *Alive and Well with Uranus*. St. Paul, MN: Llewellyn Publications, 1999. (Out of print.)

———. *All Around the Zodiac*. St. Paul, MN: Llewellyn Publications, 2001.

———. *Dynamics of Aspects Analysis*. Sebastopol, CA: CRCS, 1983.

———. *The Twelve Faces of Saturn*. St. Paul, MN: Llewellyn Publications, 2002. (Out of print.)

Tyl, Noel. *Synthesis & Counseling in Astrology*. St. Paul, MN: Llewellyn Publications, 1994.

Watters, Barbara. *Sex and the Outer Planets*. Washington DC: Valhalla, 1971.

White, George. *The Moon's Nodes*. Tempe, AZ: AFA, 2004.

Wickenburg, Joanne. *In Search of a Fulfilling Career*. Tempe, AZ: AFA, 1992.

Predictive Astrology

Brady, Bernadette. *The Eagle and the Lark*. York Beach, ME: Samuel Weiser, 1992.

Cope, Lloyd. *Astrologer's Forecasting Workbook*. Tempe, AZ: AFA, 1995.

Forrest, Steven. *The Changing Sky*. Second edition. San Diego, CA: ACS, 2002.

Hand, Robert. *Planets in Transit*. Revised edition. Atglen, PA: Whitford Press, 2001.

Leo, Alan. *The Progressed Horoscope*. London: L. N. Fowler, 1936; Bel Air, MD: Astrology Classics: 2007.

Mason, Sophia. *Delineation of Progressions*. Tempe, AZ: AFA, 1998.

Milburn, Leigh H. *The Progressed Horoscope Simplified*. Tempe, AZ: AFA, 1928, 1989.

Penfield, Marc. *Solar Returns in Your Face*. Tempe, AZ: AFA, 1996.

Riske, Kris Brandt, M.A. *Mapping Your Future*. St. Paul, MN: Llewellyn Publications, 2004.

Rogers-Gallagher, Kim. *Astrology for the Light Side of the Future*. San Diego, CA: ACS Publications, 1998.

Ruperti, Alexander. *Cycles of Becoming*. Sebastopol, CA: CRCS, 1978; Santa Monica, CA: Earthwalk, 2005.

Rushman, Carol. *The Art of Predictive Astrology*. St. Paul, MN: Llewellyn Publications, 2002.

Simms, Maria Kay. *Future Signs*. San Diego, CA: ACS Publications, 1996.

Teal, Celeste. *Eclipses*. St. Paul, MN: Llewellyn Publications, 2006.

———. *Identifying Planetary Triggers*. St. Paul, MN: Llewellyn Publications, 2000.

Townley, John. *Astrological Cycles*. York Beach, ME: Red Wheel/Weiser, 1977. (Out of print.)

———. *Lunar Returns*. St. Paul, MN: Llewellyn Publications, 2003.

Tyl, Noel. *Solar Arcs*. St. Paul, MN: Llewellyn Publications, 2001.

Reference

Aldrich, Elizabeth. *Daily Use of the Ephemeris*. Tempe, AZ: AFA, 1971.

Bills, Rex. *The Rulership Book*. Tempe, AZ: AFA, 1971, 2007.

deVore, Nicholas. *Encyclopedia of Astrology*. New York: Philosophical Library, 1947; Bel Air, MD: Astrology Classics, 2005.

Doane, Doris C. *30 Years Research*. Los Angeles, CA: Church of Light, 1956; Tempe, AZ: AFA, 1985.

Donath, Emma Belle. *Houses: Which & When*. Tempe, AZ: AFA, 1989.

Koch, Beth. *Equal Houses*. Tempe, AZ: AFA, 1992.

Murphy, Peter, and Beth Rosato. *The Math of Astrology*. Tempe, AZ: AFA, 1998.

Rodden, Lois. *Astro Data II*. Revised edition. Tempe, AZ: AFA, 1997.

———. *Astro Data III*. Tempe, AZ: AFA, 1986. (Out of print.)

———. *Astro Data IV*. Tempe, AZ: AFA, 1997.

———. *Astro Data V: Profiles in Crime*. Yucaipa, CA: Data News, 1992.

———. *Profiles of Women*. Yucaipa, CA: Data News, 1996.

Wilson, James. *Dictionary of Astrology*. Bel Air, MD: Astrology Classics, 2006. (Originally published in 1819.)

Relationships

Ebertin, Reinhold. *Cosmic Marriage*. Tempe, AZ: AFA, 1974, 2004.

Forrest, Jodie and Steven. *Skymates*. Revised edition. Chapel Hill, NC: Seven Paws Press, 2005.

Forrest, Steven and Jodie. *Skymates II: The Composite Chart*. Chapel Hill, NC: Seven Paws Press, 2005.

Goodman, Linda. *Linda Goodman's Relationship Signs*. New York: Bantam Books, 1998.

Hand, Robert. *Planets in Composite*. Atglen, PA: Whitford Press, 1975.

Ruiz, Ana. *Prediction Techniques Regarding Romance*. Tempe, AZ: AFA, 2006.

Sargent, Lois. *How to Handle Your Human Relationships*. Tempe, AZ: AFA, 2006.

Townley, John. *Composite Charts*. St. Paul, MN: Llewellyn Publications, 2004.

———. *Planets in Love*. Atglen, PA: Whitford Press, 1978.

GLOSSARY

angles: The Ascendant, Descendant, Midheaven, and IC.

angular house cusp: The cusps of the first, fourth, seventh, and tenth houses.

approaching aspect: A faster-moving planet that is approaching an exact aspect with a slower-moving planet.

Ascendant: The first-house cusp and one of the angles. It represents the individual and his or her outward expression of personality.

aspect: A geometric angle that connects the energy of two or more planets.

aspectarian: A grid that shows the aspects between the planets in a chart.

asteroids: The four major asteroids used in astrology are Juno, Vesta, Ceres, and Pallas Athena.

Chiron: A comet that is most commonly defined as the "wounded healer."

conjunction: A major aspect where two or more planets are within 0°–8° of each other. Its keyword is *intensity*. A conjunction can be an easy or hard aspect, depending on the planets involved.

contraparallel: An aspect that indicates two planets are at opposite degrees north and south of the celestial equator. The contraparallel functions like an opposition.

decanate: One-third of a sign. Each sign has three decanates—0°–10°, 11°–20°, and 21°–30°—and each has its own ruling sign and planet.

declination: The degrees a planet is north or south of the celestial equator.

degree: The zodiac has 360°, and each sign has 30°. Degrees identify the position of a planet within a sign.

Descendant: The seventh-house cusp and one of the angles. It represents marriage and other close relationships.

detriment: A planet in the sign opposite its ruling sign, such as the Sun in Aquarius.

dignity: A planet in its ruling sign, such as Uranus in Aquarius.

easy aspect: The trine, sextile, and conjunction (depending on the planets in the conjunction) are easy aspects that represent a smooth flow of energy.

eclipse: Approximately four to six eclipses occur every year. A solar eclipse is also a New Moon, when the Sun and Moon are at the same degree and sign of the zodiac. A lunar eclipse is also a Full Moon, when the Sun and Moon are opposite each other.

element: Each of the twelve signs is classified according to one of the four elements—fire, earth, air, or water. The elements are also called quadruplicities.

ephemeris: A book or computer printout of the positions of the planets.

exaltation: A planet in the sign other than its ruling sign in which it functions well, such as Jupiter in Cancer.

fall: A planet in the sign opposite its sign of exaltation, such as Saturn in Aries.

fixed stars: The stars that make up the constellations.

Full Moon: A Full Moon occurs approximately every four weeks, two weeks after the New Moon. At the Full Moon, the Sun and Moon are opposite each other—180° apart.

glyph: The symbol used for a planet, sign, or aspect.

grand square (grand cross): An aspect configuration formed by two oppositions at right angles to each other, forming a cross.

grand trine: An aspect configuration involving three (or more) planets, each 120° apart and forming a triangle.

hard aspect: The square, opposition, semisquare, sesquisquare, and conjunction (depending on the planets in the conjunction) are hard aspects that represent challenges and obstacles.

hemisphere: The four major sections of the horoscope—southern (top half of the chart), northern (bottom half of the chart), eastern (left side of the chart), and western (right side of the chart).

house: One of the twelve pie-shaped sections (houses) of the horoscope. Each house governs specific areas of life.

house cusp: The sign and degree of the zodiac at which a house begins.

IC (Imum Coeli): The fourth-house cusp and one of the angles. It represents home, family, and parents.

inconjunct: A minor aspect (also known as a *quincunx*) where two or more planets are 150° apart. It indicates separation, strain, and uneasiness, because it is difficult to mix the energies of the planets involved.

intercepted sign: A zodiac sign that is contained wholly within a house and thus is not on a house cusp.

intermediate house cusp: The cusps of the second, third, fifth, sixth, eighth, ninth, eleventh, and twelfth houses.

latitude: The distance in degrees north or south of the equator, which is 0° latitude. Used along with longitude to define a geographic location.

longitude: The distance in degrees east or west of Greenwich, England, which is 0° longitude. Used along with latitude to define a geographic location.

luminaries: The Sun and Moon, which are also called the Lights.

Midheaven: The tenth-house cusp and one of the angles. It represents career and status.

mode: See *quality.*

Moon's nodes: The North and South nodes of the Moon are not actual bodies, but points. The North Node is similar to Jupiter, and the South Node is similar to Saturn.

mutual reception: Two planets in any aspect that are also in each other's ruling sign, such as the Moon in Aries and Mars in Cancer.

natural chart: A chart that shows the natural order of the zodiac from Aries through Pisces, beginning with Aries in the first house.

New Moon: A New Moon occurs approximately every four weeks, when the Sun and Moon are at the same degree and sign of the zodiac.

opposition: A major aspect where two or more planets are 180° apart, or opposite each other, in the zodiac. Its keyword is *separation.*

orb: The allowable distance between two or more planets that puts them in aspect to one another. The closer the aspect, the stronger its influence.

out-of-sign aspect: An aspect between two planets that are in orb but not in the same mode or element.

parallel: An aspect that indicates two planets are at the same number of degrees north or south of the celestial equator. The parallel functions like a conjunction.

Part of Fortune: Also called the Lot of Fortune, this indicates luck, especially when in aspect to a planet or angle.

polarities: The opposite signs of the zodiac, such as Aries/Libra and Gemini/Sagittarius.

quadrants: The four sections of the horoscope that blend the influence of the four hemispheres—first quadrant (houses one, two, and three), second quadrant (houses four, five, and six), third quadrant (houses seven, eight, and nine), and fourth quadrant (houses ten, eleven, and twelve).

quality (mode): Each of the twelve signs is identified with one of the three qualities, or modes of expression—cardinal, fixed, or mutable.

retrograde: The period of time during which planets appear to move backward.

rulership: Each planet has rulership over, or is associated with, one (or two) signs. A planet that rules the sign on a house cusp rules that house. The planets ruling other signs in a house are called *co-rulers.* Planets and signs also have natural rulership over specific areas of life, such as career, health, family, and money.

semisextile: A 60° angle between two planets. This aspect is mildly beneficial.

semisquare: A minor aspect where two or more planets are 45° apart. It represents action and conflict.

separating aspect: This indicates that a planet is moving away from another planet after having formed an exact aspect with the second planet.

sesquisquare: A minor aspect where two or more planets are 135° apart. It represents action and conflict.

sextile: A major aspect where two or more planets are 60° apart. Its keyword is *opportunity*.

solar chart: A chart erected without a specific birth time, usually set for noon or sunrise, and with the Sun as the Ascendant.

square: A major aspect where two or more planets are 90° apart. It represents action and conflict.

stationary planet: A planet that appears to stop before changing to direct or retrograde motion.

stellium: A group of three or more planets, all of which are conjunct.

synastry: A chart comparison method used to judge compatibility between two individuals.

T-square: An aspect configuration where two (or more) planets are in opposition and square a third planet.

trine: A major aspect where two or more planets are 120° apart. It represents ease and luck.

trinities: The three houses associated with each of the elements—fire, trinity of life; earth; trinity of wealth; air, trinity of association; and water, trinity of endings.

unaspected planet: A planet that makes no aspects to other planets or angles.

Vertex: A calculated point that has a fateful connotation, indicating a person's destiny in life.

void-of-course Moon: The Moon's position from the time it makes its last major aspect in one sign until it enters the next sign.

yod: An aspect configuration in which a planet (the apex planet) is inconjunct two other planets that are sextile each other.